AI Innovations for Travel and Tourism

Ricardo Correia
Instituto Politécnico de Bragança, Portugal & CiTUR, Portugal

Márcio Martins
Instituto Politécnico de Bragança, Portugal & CiTUR, Portugal

Ruta Fontes
Aveiro University, Portugal & GOVCOPP, Portugal

A volume in the Advances in Hospitality, Tourism, and the Services Industry (AHTSI) Book Series

IGI Global
PUBLISHER of TIMELY KNOWLEDGE

Published in the United States of America by
IGI Global
Business Science Reference (an imprint of IGI Global)
701 E. Chocolate Avenue
Hershey PA, USA 17033
Tel: 717-533-8845
Fax: 717-533-8661
E-mail: cust@igi-global.com
Web site: http://www.igi-global.com

Library of Congress Cataloging-in-Publication Data

Names: Correia, Ricardo Fontes, 1978- editor. | Martins, Márcio Ribeiro, 1979- editor. | Fontes, Ruta, 1985- editor.
Title: AI innovations for travel and tourism / Edited by Ricardo Correia, Márcio Martins, Ruta Fontes.
Other titles: Artificial intelligence innovations for travel and tourism
Description: Hershey, PA : Business Science Reference, [2024] | Includes bibliographical references and index. | Summary: "This book explores the dynamic intersection of AI and tourism, shedding light on the ways in which AI is reshaping the entire travel ecosystem"-- Provided by publisher.
Identifiers: LCCN 2024010152 (print) | LCCN 2024010153 (ebook) | ISBN 9798369321379 (hardcover) | ISBN 9798369344767 (paperback) | ISBN 9798369321386 (ebook)
Subjects: LCSH: Tourism--Technological innovations. | Artificial intelligence--Marketing applications.
Classification: LCC G156.5.I5 A78 2024 (print) | LCC G156.5.I5 (ebook) | DDC 910.285/63--dc23/eng/20240323
LC record available at https://lccn.loc.gov/2024010152
LC ebook record available at https://lccn.loc.gov/2024010153

This book is published in the IGI Global book series Advances in Hospitality, Tourism, and the Services Industry (AHTSI) (ISSN: 2475-6547; eISSN: 2475-6555)

British Cataloguing in Publication Data
A Cataloguing in Publication record for this book is available from the British Library.

Advances in Hospitality, Tourism, and the Services Industry (AHTSI) Book Series

ISSN:2475-6547
EISSN:2475-6555

Editor-in-Chief: Maximiliano Korstanje, University of Palermo, Argentina

MISSION

Globally, the hospitality, travel, tourism, and services industries generate a significant percentage of revenue and represent a large portion of the business world. Even in tough economic times, these industries thrive as individuals continue to spend on leisure and recreation activities as well as services.

The Advances in Hospitality, Tourism, and the Services Industry (AHTSI) book series offers diverse publications relating to the management, promotion, and profitability of the leisure, recreation, and services industries. Highlighting current research pertaining to various topics within the realm of hospitality, travel, tourism, and services management, the titles found within the AHTSI book series are pertinent to the research and professional needs of managers, business practitioners, researchers, and upper-level students studying in the field.

COVERAGE

- Customer Service Issues
- Health and Wellness Tourism
- Travel Agency Management
- Casino Management
- Service Management
- Hotel Management
- Leisure & Business Travel
- Service Training
- Cruise Marketing and Sales
- Service Design

IGI Global is currently accepting manuscripts for publication within this series. To submit a proposal for a volume in this series, please contact our Acquisition Editors at Acquisitions@igi-global.com or visit: http://www.igi-global.com/publish/.

The Advances in Hospitality, Tourism, and the Services Industry (AHTSI) Book Series (ISSN 2475-6547) is published by IGI Global, 701 E. Chocolate Avenue, Hershey, PA 17033-1240, USA, www.igi-global.com. This series is composed of titles available for purchase individually; each title is edited to be contextually exclusive from any other title within the series. For pricing and ordering information please visit http://www.igi-global.com/book-series/advances-hospitality-tourism-services-industry/121014. Postmaster: Send all address changes to above address.

Titles in this Series

For a list of additional titles in this series, please visit:
http://www.igi-global.com/book-series/advances-hospitality-tourism-services-industry/121014

Social Media Strategies for Tourism Interactivity
Célia M.Q. Ramos (University of Algarve, Portugal) Teresa Costa (Instituto Politécnico de Setúbal, Portugal) Filipe Segurado Severino (Estoril Higher Institute for Tourism and Hotel Studies, Portugal) and Maria de Lurdes Calisto (Estoril Higher Institute for Tourism and Hotel Studies, Portugal)
Business Science Reference • copyright 2024 • 345pp • H/C (ISBN: 9798369309605) • US $285.00 (our price)

Gastronomic Sustainability Solutions for Community and Tourism Resilience
Shivam Bhartiya (Jain University, India) Vaibhav Bhatt (Central University of Tamil Nadu, India) and Andrea Edurne Jimenez Ruiz (Universidad Autonoma del Estado de Mexico, Mexico)
Business Science Reference • copyright 2024 • 315pp • H/C (ISBN: 9798369341353) • US $295.00 (our price)

Shifts in Knowledge Sharing and Creativity for Business Tourism
Muhammad Waseem Bari (Government College University, Faisalabad, Pakistan) Mohammad Soliman (Research and Consultation Department, University of Technology and Applied Sciences, Salalah, Oman) and Emilia Alaverdov (Georgian Technical University, Georgia)
Business Science Reference • copyright 2024 • 336pp • H/C (ISBN: 9798369326190) • US $295.00 (our price)

Mountain Tourism and Ecological Impacts Himalayan Region and Beyond
Soumendra Nath Biswas (Assam University, Silchar, India) and Pradip Kumar (Assam University, Silchar, India)
Business Science Reference • copyright 2024 • 280pp • H/C (ISBN: 9798369308233) • US $250.00 (our price)

Promoting Sustainable Gastronomy Tourism and Community Development

For an entire list of titles in this series, please visit:
http://www.igi-global.com/book-series/advances-hospitality-tourism-services-industry/121014

IGI Global
PUBLISHER of TIMELY KNOWLEDGE

701 East Chocolate Avenue, Hershey, PA 17033, USA
Tel: 717-533-8845 x100 • Fax: 717-533-8661
E-Mail: cust@igi-global.com • www.igi-global.com

Table of Contents

Preface xiv

Introduction xviii

Chapter 1
Artificial Intelligence and Visitors' Spatiotemporal Behaviour: A Critical Literature Review and Directions for Future Research 1
Márcio Ribeiro Martins, Politécnico de Bragança, Portugal & CiTUR, Portugal
Ricardo Correia, Instituto Politécnico de Bragança, Portugal & CiTUR, Portugal
Ruta Fontes, Universidade de Aveiro, Portugal & GOVCOPP, Portugal

Chapter 2
Using Artificial Intelligence in Tourism Sustainability Research 21
Isabel Sofia Loureiro, Polytechnic Institute of Cávado and Ave, Portugal
Vânia Costa, Polytechnic Instittute of Cávado and Ave, Portugal
Alexandra Malheiro, Polytechnic Instittute of Cávado and Ave, Portugal

Chapter 3
Artificial Intelligence and the Tourism Film: Challenges and Possibilities......... 40
Tiago Fernandes, Instituto Politécnico de Bragança, Portugal & LabCom -Communication and Arts, Portugal
Rogério Tavares, Instituto Politécnico de Bragança, Portugal
João Paulo Sousa, Instituto Politécnico de Bragança, Portugal
Ricardo Correia, Instituto Politécnico de Bragança, Portugal & CiTUR, Portugal

Chapter 4
Impact of AI on the Flower of Service Model in the Hospitality Industry..........58
Nurhafihz Noor, James Cook University, Singapore
Karen Sim, James Cook University, Singapore

Chapter 5
Can Serious Games and AI Rejuvenate Museums?...82
Michel Plaisent, Université du Québec à Montreal, Canada
Jean-Marie Lafortune, Université du Québec à Montreal, Canada
Lili Zheng, EXCELIA Business School, France
Pascal Ndinga, Université du Québec à Montreal, Canada
Daniel Tomiuk, Université du Québec à Montreal, Canada
Sylvester Cortes, Cebu Technological University, Philippines
Agnès Czubinski, Independent Researcher, Canada
Prosper Bernard, Université du Québec à Montréal, Canada

Chapter 6
Literature Review on the XR Technologies in Tourism: One Decade of Virtual Continuum in Tourism..104
Rogerio Tavares, Instituto Politécnico de Bragança, Portugal
João Paulo Sousa, Instituto Politécnico de Bragança, Portugal
Ricardo Correia, Instituto Politécnico de Bragança, Portugal & CiTUR, Portugal
Tiago Fernandes, Instituto Politécnico de Bragança, Portugal & LabCom - Communication and Arts, Portugal

Chapter 7
Transforming Hospitality Experiences: An Exploratory Study of Service Robots in the Hospitality Industry 121
Seema Jaipuriar, Amity University, Jaipur, India
Sanjeeb Pal, Amity University, Jaipur, India
Yashwant Singh Rawal, Parul University, Gujarat, India

Chapter 8
Travel Redefined: Future Trends in AI-Enhanced Tourism Experiences 135
Jeganathan Gomathi Sankar, BSSS Institute of Advanced Studies, Bhopal, India

Chapter 9
Prospect of Smart Tourism Destination in Bangladesh 163
Mohammad Badruddoza Talukder, International University of Business Agriculture and Technology, Bangladesh
Kamarun Muhsina, Daffodil Institute of IT, Bangladesh

Chapter 10
Digital Marketing, Artificial Intelligence, and Online Social Networks in Tourism: Case of the Municipality of Amares (Portugal) 180
Marta Beatriz Silva, Polytechnic Institute of Cávado and Ave, Portugal
Jorge Lima Pacheco, Polytechnic Institute of Cávado and Ave, Portugal & ISCAP, Polytechnic of Porto, Portugal
Bruno Barbosa Sousa, Polytechnic Institute of Cávado and Ave, Portugal & CiTUR, Portugal & UNIAG, Portugal

Conclusion 198

Compilation of References 200

Related References 231

About the Contributors 259

Index 265

Detailed Table of Contents

Preface xiv

Introduction xviii

Chapter 1
Artificial Intelligence and Visitors' Spatiotemporal Behaviour: A Critical Literature Review and Directions for Future Research 1
Márcio Ribeiro Martins, Politécnico de Bragança, Portugal & CiTUR, Portugal
Ricardo Correia, Instituto Politécnico de Bragança, Portugal & CiTUR, Portugal
Ruta Fontes, Universidade de Aveiro, Portugal & GOVCOPP, Portugal

The main purpose of this chapter is to understand how artificial intelligence (AI) has evolved in the academic literature on visitors' spatiotemporal behaviour (STB), identifying the key thematic areas that have drawn most research interest to help academics and professionals to gain a better understanding of AI usage on this topic. The literature review was based on a search of scientific documents available on the Scopus platform concerning the use of AI on visitors' STB studies. On a first stage the number of documents published per year and the identification of the most representative journals and authors are presented and discussed. On second stage, a content analysis was conducted, and bibliometric method such as, co-occurrence analysis, was used. The most productive and cited authors were identified and although the number of articles published is not very high, reveal some interest of researchers on this issue, particularly during 2023. The most important key thematic areas and some implications for future research were also identified and discussed.

Chapter 2
Using Artificial Intelligence in Tourism Sustainability Research 21
Isabel Sofia Loureiro, Polytechnic Institute of Cávado and Ave, Portugal
Vânia Costa, Polytechnic Instittute of Cávado and Ave, Portugal
Alexandra Malheiro, Polytechnic Instittute of Cávado and Ave, Portugal

Artificial intelligence has become one of the strongest tools used in a variety of sectors, including academic research. AI has the potential to revolutionize communication and research, facilitating the collection of data and providing more efficiency in the research process. This chapter aims to highlight the importance of AI research by using ChatGPT, a generative pre-trained transformer. ChatGPT was used to structure an interview directed to tourism agents in order to understand their vision of sustainability models in monitoring tourism companies' activity in the sector. The tool was also interviewed to understand the possible input it would give to assist tourism agents in becoming more sustainable. It is concluded that AI can be a useful tool in research and in developing sustainability practices, projections, and the interpretation of data. However, it is essential to consider the ethical challenges and ensure a proper understanding of the limitations of these tools.

Chapter 3
Artificial Intelligence and the Tourism Film: Challenges and Possibilities.........40
Tiago Fernandes, Instituto Politécnico de Bragança, Portugal & LabCom -Communication and Arts, Portugal
Rogério Tavares, Instituto Politécnico de Bragança, Portugal
João Paulo Sousa, Instituto Politécnico de Bragança, Portugal
Ricardo Correia, Instituto Politécnico de Bragança, Portugal & CiTUR, Portugal

Today, the importance of audiovisual production in the tourism industry is undeniable. Whether it's through products designed specifically to promote a particular territory, such as tourism films, or the recent phenomenon known as "film tourism," in which tourists travel to places they know from the movies, this reality ends up being valued and celebrated at festivals dedicated specifically to this area, such as the Portuguese festival "Art&Tur - International Tourism Film Festival," the German festival "The Golden City Gate," part of "ITB Berlin," or the "World Tourism Film Awards," organized by the CIFFT - International Committee of Tourism Film Festivals. With the recent massification of artificial intelligence, which even though it's not a recent technology has become the order of the day due to the recent events involving the company Open AI and, more specifically, its online chatbot Chat GPT, the population in general and the scientific community in particular have begun to take a closer look at AI. In the specific case of audiovisual production, while there were a number of tools that already made use of technology in the past and were mainly used in the post-production process (special effects, sound manipulation, etc.), the truth is that AI currently presents some challenges and, on the other hand, some potential, precisely in the first phase of designing an audiovisual work, more specifically, in pre-production. The aim of this chapter is to focus an analysis on the specific case of audiovisual productions conceived in the context of the tourism industry and, from there, try to understand how AI can be an important tool in the creative phase of script design for these works. In the absence of a specific bibliography on the case under analysis, some possibilities for using artificial intelligence to enhance the reach and effectiveness of an audiovisual product designed, above all, to highlight a particular territory or tourist experience will be raised.

Chapter 4
Impact of AI on the Flower of Service Model in the Hospitality Industry..........58
Nurhafihz Noor, James Cook University, Singapore
Karen Sim, James Cook University, Singapore

With increasing opportunities for the hospitality industry to interact with customers using artificial intelligence (AI), hospitality managers need to decide on the services that are most suited to integrate AI. This requires an understanding of how AI affects different service activities. To address this, this study discusses the impact of AI on various service components using the Flower of Service Model. This chapter contributes to the study of AI innovation in services marketing by showing the relevance of seminal services marketing frameworks in the emerging AI landscape and providing strategic insights for hospitality managers to effectively implement AI in hospitality services.

Chapter 5
Can Serious Games and AI Rejuvenate Museums?...82
Michel Plaisent, Université du Québec à Montreal, Canada
Jean-Marie Lafortune, Université du Québec à Montreal, Canada
Lili Zheng, EXCELIA Business School, France
Pascal Ndinga, Université du Québec à Montreal, Canada
Daniel Tomiuk, Université du Québec à Montreal, Canada
Sylvester Cortes, Cebu Technological University, Philippines
Agnès Czubinski, Independent Researcher, Canada
Prosper Bernard, Université du Québec à Montréal, Canada

Museums are an important player in the "heritage industry" because they hold a huge potential for the development of tourism, especially in regions far from large cities. Serious games and artificial intelligence are responsible for their new success. This research explores the issues and challenges posed by their introduction. It used a questionnaire distributed to museum directors. Among the benefits of serious games, directors agree on public diversification, improving visitors experience, rejuvenating the museums image, and increase in-site and distant visits. AI is recognized to permit interactive exhibits and personalization of visit experience. Financial and technical issues slow their introduction among the strategies used to increase digital services; cooperation with other museums and other actors are more cited than increasing resources. But a lack of knowledge (not of interest) characterized respondents to this study. The question is no more "Yes or No" to implementation, but "When and How."

Chapter 6
Literature Review on the XR Technologies in Tourism: One Decade of Virtual Continuum in Tourism..104
Rogerio Tavares, Instituto Politécnico de Bragança, Portugal
João Paulo Sousa, Instituto Politécnico de Bragança, Portugal
Ricardo Correia, Instituto Politécnico de Bragança, Portugal & CiTUR, Portugal
Tiago Fernandes, Instituto Politécnico de Bragança, Portugal & LabCom - Communication and Arts, Portugal

This chapter begins with a concise overview of recent studies and reports on how the tourism industry is embracing digital transformation. This initial section aims to provide context for the current significance of technology adoption in tourism and an insight into the prevailing strategies and challenges faced by the industry. In light of this context, it becomes essential to delve into the scientific literature to comprehend how it reflects the evolution of technology adoption within tourism, including themes under investigation and potential trends. Hence, the following section delves into a bibliometric analysis of scientific production related to the use of technologies in tourism over the past decade. This study enables us to gain a comprehensive understanding of the evolving scientific literature on technology adoption in tourism and it sets forth an agenda for future research, paving the way for advancements in the realm of new digital technologies in the tourism sector.

Chapter 7
Transforming Hospitality Experiences: An Exploratory Study of Service Robots in the Hospitality Industry 121
Seema Jaipuriar, Amity University, Jaipur, India
Sanjeeb Pal, Amity University, Jaipur, India
Yashwant Singh Rawal, Parul University, Gujarat, India

Artificial intelligence applications and robotic technologies, which are rapidly spreading and widely used throughout the world, are discussed by different disciplines in literature including tourism. In this context, robots come to the fore in the application areas of the tourism sector. However, there are many artificial intelligence applications that are becoming widespread in the tourism sector. From this point of view, this conceptual study, firstly artificial intelligence applications and robotic technologies were evaluated, traits of service robots were revealed, then the current technologies and a brief comparison of service robots over human employees were examined, and as a result, the future of these technologies in the hospitality industry was discussed. In this context, it can be said that this study, in which the current situation is revealed, and sector-experienced writers make inferences for the future, is an important study that can contribute to the literature and industry practitioners.

Chapter 8

Travel Redefined: Future Trends in AI-Enhanced Tourism Experiences 135

Jeganathan Gomathi Sankar, BSSS Institute of Advanced Studies, Bhopal, India

In the vision of future travel, advanced technology emerges as the linchpin, orchestrating a paradigm shift in planning, experiencing, and securing journeys. Central to this evolution is the concept of personalized itineraries, where algorithms craft unique travel experiences tailored to individual preferences, breaking away from conventional one-size-fits-all packages. Proactive addressing of travel challenges becomes paramount, with predictive analytics identifying and mitigating hurdles in real-time for a stress-free experience. Guided tours transform into dynamic experiences as AI-powered guides adapt narratives, enriching exploration with personalized insights. Virtual reality reconstructions transport travelers to historical landmarks, transcending temporal boundaries for accessible cultural exploration. Streamlined city navigation via mobile apps or wearables provides real-time information. Advanced security, driven by technology and AI, ensures a safe travel environment.

Chapter 9

Prospect of Smart Tourism Destination in Bangladesh 163

Mohammad Badruddoza Talukder, International University of Business Agriculture and Technology, Bangladesh

Kamarun Muhsina, Daffodil Institute of IT, Bangladesh

The ongoing expansion of the tourism sector in Bangladesh has created opportunities for future development through the adoption of smart tourism destinations. The notion of smart tourism destinations encompasses incorporating every facet of a tourist's experience, including planning activities. By adopting this particular strategy, Bangladesh can cultivate a tourism industry characterized by enhanced cohesion and effectiveness, thereby augmenting the overall experience for both local and international tourists. This article emphasizes several vital aspects of smart destinations, such as heightened financial gains, enhanced tourism infrastructure, and bolstered sustainability efforts. Furthermore, this paper also addresses the difficulties associated with implementing the proposed approach. It explores potential strategies to overcome these challenges. The concept of smart tourism destinations in Bangladesh offers significant potential for growth and development in the tourism industry.

Chapter 10
Digital Marketing, Artificial Intelligence, and Online Social Networks in Tourism: Case of the Municipality of Amares (Portugal) 180
Marta Beatriz Silva, Polytechnic Institute of Cávado and Ave, Portugal
Jorge Lima Pacheco, Polytechnic Institute of Cávado and Ave, Portugal & ISCAP, Polytechnic of Porto, Portugal
Bruno Barbosa Sousa, Polytechnic Institute of Cávado and Ave, Portugal & CiTUR, Portugal & UNIAG, Portugal

The present chapter involved a thorough investigation into the tourist destination in question, Amares, where the research results suggest that the Municipality of Amares can improve its digital marketing and online social networks strategy to attract more tourists. Thus, the research adds value to the tourist destination of Amares (Portugal), as it allows understanding in which direction the municipality should focus its efforts in tourism promotion. The conclusions drawn from benchmarking and questionnaire results showed that digital marketing and online social networks are important tools in promoting tourism in the Municipality of Amares. Additionally, some more effective practices were presented, such as the creation of strategic content tailored to different market segments, the use of attractive images and videos inspiring people to visit the tourist destination, and the development of influencer marketing campaigns.

Conclusion 198

Compilation of References 200

Related References 231

About the Contributors 259

Index 265

Preface

As editors of *AI Innovations for Travel and Tourism*, we are delighted to present this comprehensive exploration of the transformative power of artificial intelligence (AI) in the tourism industry. In recent years, the integration of AI technologies has posed both challenges and opportunities for the travel sector. Our aim with this edited reference book is to address the critical need for a deeper understanding of AI's impact on travel and tourism, elucidating its role in reshaping the landscape of the industry.

In today's fast-paced world, where travelers seek personalized experiences and businesses strive for operational efficiency, AI emerges as a catalyst for innovation. However, alongside its potential benefits, ethical considerations loom large. It is imperative to navigate the ethical dimensions of AI implementation in tourism responsibly, ensuring that technology serves as a tool for positive transformation rather than a source of concern.

This book begins by laying the groundwork with an insightful introduction to AI's influence on tourism. From there, it delves into the nuances of personalized travel planning, exploring how AI-powered destination recommendations redefine the travel experience. We navigate through smart booking systems and travel experiences, showcasing how AI optimizes operations and elevates customer satisfaction.

Moreover, *AI Innovations for Travel and Tourism* extends its exploration to AI's role in travel marketing, emphasizing targeted campaigns and enhanced customer engagement. Through in-depth discussions on AI, big data, and user-generated content, we uncover the intricate connections that drive innovation within the industry. Additionally, our analysis of visitors' spatiotemporal behavior offers invaluable insights for destination managers and marketers, facilitating informed decision-making.

The chapters in AI Innovations for Travel and Tourism offer a comprehensive journey through the transformative impact of artificial intelligence on the tourism industry. Beginning with an insightful introduction to AI's influence on travel, we delve into personalized travel planning, exploring how AI reshapes destination recommendations and travel experiences. Our exploration extends to the optimization of operational efficiency through smart booking systems and the enhancement of customer satisfaction. Furthermore, we uncover the role of AI in revolutionizing travel marketing, emphasizing targeted campaigns and advanced customer engagement strategies. Delving deeper, we analyze visitors' spatiotemporal behavior to provide valuable insights for destination managers and marketers. Throughout, ethical considerations remain paramount, guiding our discussions on responsible AI implementation in tourism. Each chapter offers valuable insights and practical applications, making this book essential reading for scholars, educators, students, researchers, and industry professionals navigating the intersection of AI and tourism.

Chapter 1 provides a meticulous exploration into the evolution of Artificial Intelligence (AI) in academic literature concerning visitors' spatiotemporal behavior (STB). By scrutinizing research trends and thematic areas, this chapter serves as a compass for academics and professionals seeking deeper insights into AI's utilization in STB studies. Through a comprehensive literature review conducted via the Scopus platform, key publications, authors, and journals are identified, shedding light on the landscape of AI research in this domain. Utilizing bibliometric methods like co-occurrence analysis, the chapter unveils productive authors and significant thematic areas, offering implications for future research endeavors.

Chapter 2 underscores the pivotal role of AI in academic research, particularly in advancing sustainability models within the tourism sector. By employing ChatGPT, a Generative Pre-Trained Transformer, the chapter demonstrates AI's potential in structuring interviews and generating insights from tourism agents. Highlighting AI's efficacy in data interpretation and sustainability practices, the chapter advocates for ethical considerations amidst AI integration, emphasizing the importance of understanding the tools' limitations.

Chapter 3 delves into the realm of tourism marketing through the lens of "tourism film" production, contemplating AI's role in streamlining the creative process. Focusing on the hypothetical creation of a tourist film using AI for the Terra Fria Transmontana, the chapter explores AI's application in the pre-production phase, assessing its potential benefits and creative implications. While acknowledging AI's efficiency in expediting tasks, the chapter raises questions regarding its impact on creativity and artistic expression.

Chapter 4 examines the transformative impact of AI on service activities within the hospitality industry, employing the Flower of Service Model as a framework for analysis. By elucidating how AI influences various service components, the chapter offers strategic insights for hospitality managers aiming to integrate AI effectively. Through a comprehensive exploration of AI innovation in services marketing, this chapter illuminates the intersection of seminal frameworks and emerging technologies, paving the way for enhanced service delivery in hospitality.

Chapter 5 delves into the intersection of serious games, artificial intelligence, and museum management, elucidating the challenges and benefits of their integration. Drawing insights from a questionnaire distributed to museum directors, the chapter unveils the potential of AI and serious games in diversifying visitor experiences and rejuvenating museum engagement. Despite financial and technical challenges, the chapter advocates for collaborative strategies to harness the transformative potential of AI in museum settings.

Chapter 6 embarks on a journey through the evolving landscape of technology adoption in the tourism industry, offering a bibliometric analysis of scientific production over the past decade. By synthesizing recent studies and reports, the chapter provides context for technological advancements in tourism and sets forth an agenda for future research endeavors. Through a meticulous examination of emerging trends and challenges, this chapter lays the foundation for advancements in digital technologies within the tourism sector.

Chapter 7 explores the burgeoning applications of artificial intelligence and robotic technologies in the tourism sector, offering insights into their current utilization and future prospects. By evaluating the traits of service robots and comparing them to human employees, the chapter navigates the evolving landscape of AI in hospitality. Through sector-experienced insights and inferences, this conceptual study contributes to both academic literature and industry practices, shedding light on the transformative potential of AI in hospitality.

Chapter 8 envisions the future of travel through the lens of advanced technology, highlighting the role of AI in crafting personalized travel experiences. From predictive analytics to dynamic guided tours, the chapter paints a picture of seamless and enriched travel experiences enabled by AI. By addressing travel challenges and enhancing security measures, AI emerges as a linchpin in reshaping the travel landscape, offering unparalleled convenience and safety to travelers.

Chapter 9 delves into the burgeoning concept of smart tourism destinations in Bangladesh, advocating for their adoption to foster sustainable growth in the tourism industry. By accentuating the multifaceted benefits of smart destinations, the chapter outlines strategies for heightened financial gains, enhanced infrastructure, and bolstered sustainability efforts. Despite challenges, the chapter underscores the potential of smart tourism destinations to elevate Bangladesh's tourism sector, offering a roadmap for future development endeavors.

Chapter 10 This chapter delves into an examination of Amares, a tourist destination in Portugal, suggesting that the Municipality of Amares could enhance its tourism appeal through improvements in digital marketing and online social networking strategies. By analyzing benchmarking data and survey results, the research identifies avenues for the municipality to concentrate its tourism promotion efforts. Key findings highlight the significance of digital marketing and social media in attracting tourists to Amares. Moreover, the study recommends specific practices like crafting targeted content for diverse market segments, leveraging compelling visuals to entice visitors, and implementing influencer marketing initiatives for more effective promotion.

Ethical considerations remain at the forefront of our discussions throughout the book. We delve into the responsible use of AI in tourism, underscoring the importance of ethical guidelines in harnessing technology for the betterment of industry and society at large.

We believe that this book will serve as a valuable resource for tourism scholars, educators, students, researchers, and industry professionals alike. It is our sincere hope that *AI Innovations for Travel and Tourism* contributes to a deeper understanding of AI's potential to revolutionize the travel ecosystem while promoting ethical and responsible technology use.

Ricardo Correia
Instituto Politécnico de Bragança, Portugal & CiTUR, Portugal

Márcio Martins
Instituto Politécnico de Bragança, Portugal & CiTUR, Portugal

Ruta Fontes
Universidade de Aveiro, Portugal & GOVCOPP, Portugal

Introduction

In the dawn of a new digital era, the union of artificial intelligence (AI) with the travel and tourism industry ushers in a thrilling future. This future is not just about the destination, but equally about the journey, which is now reshaped by technology. Our book, "AI Innovations for Travel and Tourism", takes a unique approach to this uncharted territory. It highlights the profound transformation being experienced across the travel ecosystem, offering a mosaic of insights into the influence of AI in crafting a more intuitive, efficient, and responsive tourism landscape.

As the gears of innovation turn, AI stands at the forefront, revolutionizing how we interact with the world, plan our journeys, and experience diverse cultures and places. Personalized travel planning, with AI-driven recommendation systems, changes the travel narrative from a universal story to a personal odyssey. AI's ability to refine operational aspects, such as smart booking systems, enhances customer satisfaction and redefines the meaning of hospitality in the digital age.

Beyond operational genius, AI also amplifies the voice of the tourism industry, transforming marketing strategies through targeted campaigns and advanced customer engagement tactics. By sifting through big data and user-generated content, AI helps businesses understand and cater to travellers' nuanced preferences. This understanding extends to careful analysis of visitors' spatiotemporal behaviour, allowing for unparalleled service personalization and efficient resource management.

The exploration of AI's transformative impact is meticulously navigated chapter by chapter, offering a tapestry of case studies, theories, and practical applications. Whether it's the evolution of AI in academic literature or its role in enhancing sustainability models, each section delves deep, providing clarity and guidance to scholars, educators, and industry professionals. The intersection of AI with serious games and museum management unfolds new horizons for engaging cultural experiences, while the rise of service robots in hospitality sketches the contours of the future workforce.

At every turn, *AI Innovations for Travel and Tourism* upholds the importance of ethical considerations. It advocates for a future where AI enhances rather than overshadows the human touch. Our book strives to ensure that technology serves as a beacon for positive transformation, illuminating the path to a travel experience that is as responsible as it is revolutionary.

With great anticipation and hope, we present this book as a compass for navigating the dynamic confluence of AI and tourism. For those poised to embrace digital transformation, this text will illuminate the path forward, offering an informed, innovative, and inclusive vision of the travel and tourism industry.

Chapter 1
Artificial Intelligence and Visitors' Spatiotemporal Behaviour:
A Critical Literature Review and Directions for Future Research

Márcio Ribeiro Martins
https://orcid.org/0000-0003-3343-3155
Politécnico de Bragança, Portugal & CiTUR, Portugal

Ricardo Correia
https://orcid.org/0000-0002-0132-4002
Instituto Politécnico de Bragança, Portugal & CiTUR, Portugal

Ruta Fontes
https://orcid.org/0000-0001-8697-1323
Universidade de Aveiro, Portugal & GOVCOPP, Portugal

ABSTRACT

The main purpose of this chapter is to understand how artificial intelligence (AI) has evolved in the academic literature on visitors' spatiotemporal behaviour (STB), identifying the key thematic areas that have drawn most research interest to help academics and professionals to gain a better understanding of AI usage on this topic. The literature review was based on a search of scientific documents available on the Scopus platform concerning the use of AI on visitors' STB studies. On a first stage the number of documents published per year and the identification of the most representative journals and authors are presented and discussed. On second stage, a content analysis was conducted, and bibliometric method such as, co-occurrence

DOI: 10.4018/979-8-3693-2137-9.ch001

analysis, was used. The most productive and cited authors were identified and although the number of articles published is not very high, reveal some interest of researchers on this issue, particularly during 2023. The most important key thematic areas and some implications for future research were also identified and discussed.

INTRODUCTION

The significant increase in the number of documents on the spatiotemporal behaviour of tourists (SBT) available on the Scopus platform leads us to conclude that the interest of tourism researchers in this topic has been growing over the last few decades (Shoval & Ahas, 2016), with new technologies being used to accurately track movements, such as Global Position System (GPS) devices (Shoval et al., 2020), smartphone GPS applications (M. R. Martins et al., 2022), Bluetooth (Versichele et al., 2012), Passive mobile positioning data (Ahas et al., 2008) or the user-generated content (UGC) of some social networks (Chua et al., 2016; Hausmann et al., 2018; Kádár & Gede, 2022) where users share geotagged photographs or georeferenced walking trails in natural and/or urban environments. All these modern methods and techniques used to collect information on the movements made by tourists are more efficient and accurate and reduce the responsibility of the individuals, as they are not reliant on their enthusiasm and memory. GPS technology is also mature and easy to use (Xia, 2007), particularly through the Geographic Information Systems (GIS) software.

However, the large amount of data collected results in terabytes of information available for knowledge extraction and decision-making (Jayawardena et al., 2013) and "require the development of more algorithms to enable automatic scripts to analyze the data in a fast and practical way" (Shoval & Ahas, 2016, p.16), as well as researchers, specialised in different areas of knowledge such as computer science, programming, geography, among others. Therefore, it will be necessary to use advanced data analysis methods and techniques and develop machine learning technologies and deep learning algorithms to interpret the data accurately and efficiently apply the outcomes (West et al., 2018).

Generally speaking, AI can be defined as the science of making machines that can think like humans, processing large amounts of data in order to recognize patterns, make decisions, and judge like humans (Pattam, 2021), i.e., is a technology that simulates human intelligence and problem-solving capabilities (IBM, 2024a). In the age of Big Data, AI plays a crucial role, particularly through the use of machine learning and deep learning. The first is widely recognized as a branch of artificial intelligence emphasizing the use of data and algorithms to imitate how humans learn (IBM, 2024c). The latter is a subset of machine learning that uses multi-layered neural networks - deep neural networks - to simulate the complex decision-making power of the human brain (IBM, 2024b). These disciplines involve the development of AI algorithms, modeled after the decision-making processes of the human brain, that can 'learn' from available data and make increasingly more accurate classifications or predictions over time (IBM, 2024a).

The spatiotemporal behaviour term "can be defined as the sequence of attractions visited by tourists within a geographic space and the respective movements between an attraction and another in that geographic space (…) [and] it is described by spatial and temporal references and by attributive components, such as the nature of the place visited, time of arrival at attractions or the respective length of stay" (Caldeira & Kastenholz, 2022, p.196). Based on these definitions, the practical applications of AI in studies on tourists' STB seem very obvious. AI can be very useful, not only from the perspective of the tourist, i.e., supporting the visit, but also from the perspective of the researcher, since it can play a relevant role in the way georeferenced information on visitor movements is collected and in the way this information is processed and analysed to recognize movement patterns, to understand the tourists' decision-making process, among others.

To our knowledge, no literature review analyses AI and visitors' STB in destinations. Such a study has great value, enabling academics to understand how AI has evolved over time in research on visitors' spatiotemporal behaviour and how it has been employed in this field of research. The scientific database Scopus, was selected to analyze trends and predict future research paths in this field. Our research objectives are:

RO1. To analyze the body of research in terms of principal authors and volume of publication.

RO2. To identify the key thematic areas that have drawn most research interest in AI on visitors' spatiotemporal behaviour.

RO3. To help academics and professionals better understand how AI is used in research on visitors' spatiotemporal behaviour.

RESEARCH DESIGN AND DATA COLLECTION

The literature review was based on a search of scientific documents available on the Scopus platform concerning the use of Artificial Intelligence (AI) in visitors' spatiotemporal behaviour studies. Its purpose was to answer the following research question: How has AI evolved in the academic literature on visitors' spatiotemporal behaviour?

The search and code scheme used was tourism AND "artificial intelligence" OR ai AND "tourist behavio*" OR "spatiotemporal behavio*" OR "space-time behavio*" in the title, abstract and keywords. Data collection was carried out on 8th November 2023, and all documents published up to the search date were considered. During the first phase, all indexed documents were taken into consideration (n=34), and a quantitative and descriptive analysis was carried out regarding the number of documents published per year and the identification of the most representative journals and authors. All documents that were not written in English (n=1) were excluded, as it was considered that the articles that have been published are representative of the knowledge produced on how AI has evolved in the academic literature on visitors' spatiotemporal behaviour.

On a first stage the number of documents published per year and the identification of the most representative journals and authors are presented and discussed. On second stage, a content analysis was conducted, and bibliometric method such as, co-occurrence analysis, was used, allowing a systematic, transparent, and reproducible review process (Zupic & Čater, 2015). Bibliometric networks were also combined with manual analysis of documents, as done by (Agapito, 2020). The creation of a keyword co-occurrence map – "the number of times one keyword appears in close relation with another within the publications in the dataset" (Agapito, 2020, p.6) allows to scrutinize the "themes and their relations that represent the conceptual space of a field" (Koseoglu et al., 2016, p.183).

The research was carried out using the Scopus database because, apart from being recognised as the largest abstract and citation database of peer-reviewed literature, "[offering] a more comprehensive view of scientific production worldwide in the areas of science, technology, medicine, social sciences, Arts and Humanities" (Elsevier, 2014, p.1), it has greater coverage of tourism journals.

RESULTS AND DISCUSSION

First Stage of Analysis

Although the number of published articles on the use of Artificial Intelligence (AI) on visitors' STB studies (n=33) is not very high, it shows some interest of researchers in this issue, particularly during 2023, the year in which the most articles were published (n=9).

The documents retrieved from Scopus are divided into the following categories: Articles (n=20), Conference Papers (n=9), Review Articles (n=2), Book Chapter (n=1) and Research Letter (n=1). The scientific journals that have published more articles on this topic are the Asia Pacific Journal of Tourism Research and the Tourism Management with 3 articles each, followed by the Annals of Tourism Research, Journal of Travel Research, Sustainability Switzerland,

Figure 1. Evolution of the number of documents found in Scopus, 2007-2023

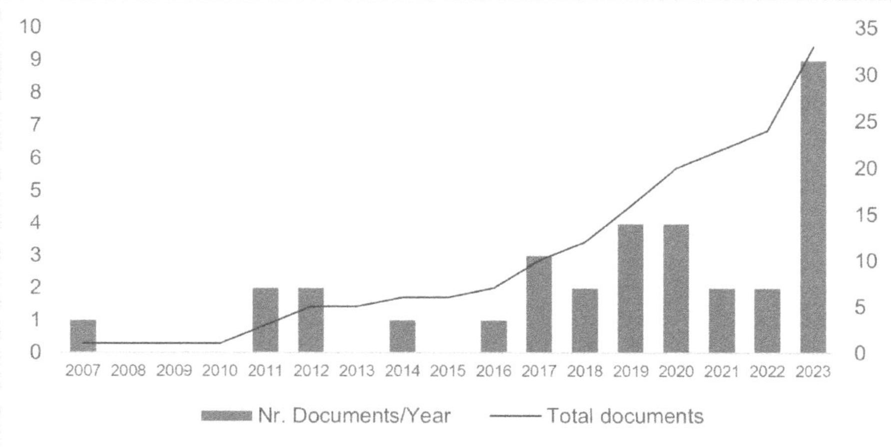

and Tourism Review with 2 articles each (table 1). These journals account for 53.8% of all articles published. The remaining journals published just 1 article each. The majority of works (53,8%) are dispersed by 6 distinct journals (Table 1), identified in Scopus as belonging to three main scientific areas: Business, Management and Accounting (n=21), Social Sciences (n=20) and Computer Science (13). With less incidence, there are the Environmental Science (n=5), Mathematics (n=4), among others.

The most productive authors are Hall, C.M., and Kim, M.J., with 3 documents each, followed by Chen, Y., Kwon, O., Sohn, K., and Zhang, K., with 2 documents each. The most cited documents are represented in table 2. With the exception of the work developed by Hadavandi et al., (2011), the rest are articles published in recent years.

Second Stage: Qualitative Analysis

Bibliometric Analysis

In this stage, the database of selected articles was analysed using the VOSViewer software, a program developed by van Eck and Waltman (van Eck & Waltman, 2010) used for constructing and viewing bibliometric maps that have been employed by several disciplinary areas, including for some tourism research (Herrera-Franco et al., 2020; M. Martins & Costa, 2022).

The bibliometric analysis was carried out using the co-occurrence maps, selecting all keywords, and the minimum number of occurrences of a keyword

Table 1. Number of articles published in scientific journals on AI and visitors' STB, 2007-2023

SOURCE TITLE	No. Articles	%	Freq. Accumul. (%)
Asia Pacific Journal of Tourism Research	3	11,5	11,5
Tourism Management	3	11,5	23,1
Annals of Tourism Research	2	7,7	30,8
Journal of Travel Research	2	7,7	38,5
Sustainability Switzerland	2	7,7	46,2
Tourism Review	2	7,7	53,8
ACM International Conference Proceeding Series	1	3,8	
Advances in Information Sciences and Service Sciences	1	3,8	
Current Issues in Tourism	1	3,8	
International Archives of The Photogrammetry Remote Sensing and Spatial Information Sciences ISPRS Archives	1	3,8	
International Journal of Sustainable Development and World Ecology	1	3,8	
International Journal of Technology Management	1	3,8	46,2
International Journal of Tourism Cities	1	3,8	
Lecture Notes in Computer Science Including Subseries Lecture Notes in Artificial Intelligence and Lecture Notes In Bioinformatics	1	3,8	
Spanish Journal of Marketing Esic	1	3,8	
Technological Forecasting and Social Change	1	3,8	
Tourist Studies	1	3,8	
Worldwide Hospitality and Tourism Themes	1	3,8	
	26	**100**	

was 2. Of the 317 keywords, 39 meet the threshold. In a co-occurrence network (Fig.2) "the more a cluster is in the centre of the map, the stronger the relationship between the keywords that form it" (Serrano et al., 2019, p.13). However, this is not observed. As this is a relatively recent research topic, there are still few studies on the spatiotemporal behaviour of tourists in which AI has been applied. Therefore, the relationship between the keywords that form it reveals that AI is not a very important concept within tourists' spatiotemporal behaviour area of knowledge, i.e., is not an intertwined and widespread topic among the analysed publications. The most significative cluster is the RED, marked by the keyword's "tourism", "virtual reality" and "behavioral research"; and the GREEN cluster, where "tourist behavior", "tourism management" and "tourism development" keywords are highlighted.

Table 2. Most cited documents (top five)

Author(s)	Documents	Year	No. Citations
Zhang, K., Chen, Y., Li, C	Discovering the tourists' behaviors and perceptions in a tourism destination by analyzing photos' visual content with a computer deep learning model: The case of Beijing	2019	164
Kim, K., Park, O.-J., Yun, S., Yun, H.	What makes tourists feel negatively about tourism destinations? Application of hybrid text mining methodology to smart destination management	2017	114
Hadavandi, E., Ghanbari, A., Shahanaghi, K., Abbasian-Naghneh, S.	Tourist arrival forecasting by evolutionary fuzzy systems	2011	71
Chi, O.H., Gursoy, D., Chi, C.G.	Tourists' Attitudes toward the Use of Artificially Intelligent (AI) Devices in Tourism Service Delivery: Moderating Role of Service Value Seeking	2022	54
López-Sánchez, Y., Pulido-Fernández, J.I.	Factors influencing the willingness to pay for sustainable tourism: a case of mass tourism destinations	2017	43

In the BLUE cluster, the most important keywords are "big data", "data mining" and "internet of things"; and the YELLOW cluster is marked by the "tourist destination" and "social media" keywords where we can find the tourists' spatiotemporal behaviour researches that have used user-generated content (UGC) such as geotagged photos (Zhang et al., 2019, 2020). The keyword with more links and more total link strength is "artificial intelligence" in the PURPLE cluster. We also find the words "deep learning" and "sustainability" in this cluster. The LIGHT BLUE cluster only comprises one word: "tourist satisfaction".

Regarding the number of occurrences of each keyword and their lexical relation, the existence of 2 large groups of published studies can be considered:

i) a majority group consisting of a set of keywords related to big data and deep learning, where the large amounts of information used in research require the use of data collection and processing techniques and technologies, such as data mining and intelligent systems (B. S. Li et al., 2020).

ii) A group of researches focuses on tourist behaviour where AI is employed in studies related to tourist destinations with focus on marketing, virtual reality and decision support systems. For instance, using user-generated photos and adopting an artificial intelligence computer vision technologies, Zhang et al., (2020) identified the differences in the perceived destination image and behavioral patterns between Hong Kong residents and tourists.

Figure 2. Co-occurrences network map (2007-2023)

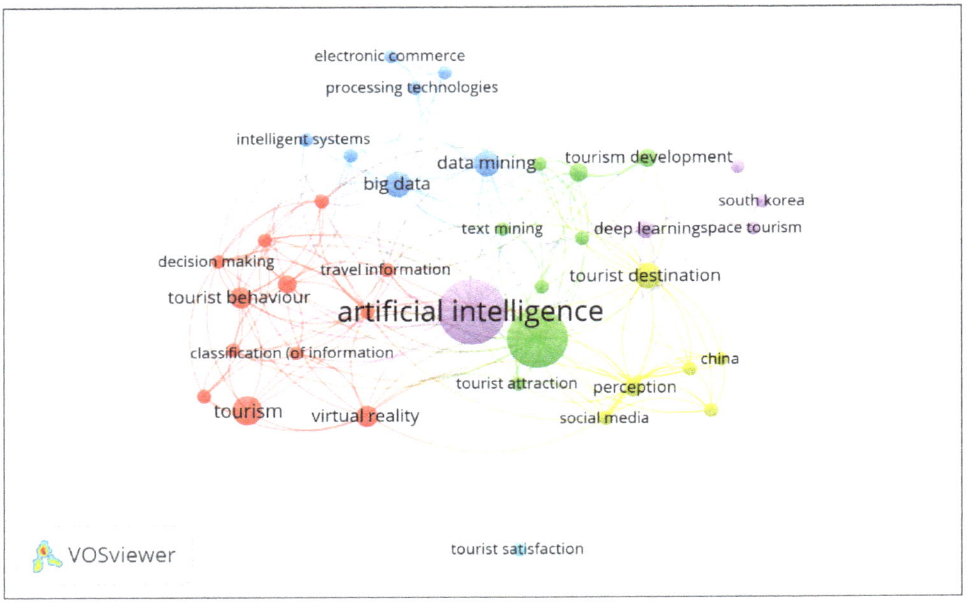

The analysis of the temporal network citation allows us to conclude that there has been a growing interest in the use of AI on tourists' spatiotemporal behaviour research, namely in South Korea and China, with focus on tourist attractions, hospitality industry and space tourism (Fig.3). Social media and tourism marketing are still hot topics in this field of research.

Content Analysis

In the second stage, a content analysis was carried out based on a full reading of the more relevant selected documents (n=19). The data was divided into research methods, analytical tools, study aim, and geographic area used in empirical studies (Table 3). From a methodological point of view, most of the documents analysed correspond to quantitative investigations (n=12) in which questionnaires were applied. Only three studies adopted a qualitative methodology by analysing the content of interviews (Pricope Vancia et al., 2023), online reviews (K. Kim et al., 2017) or Twitter posts (Nozawa et al., 2017). Two documents are literature reviews on user-generated photos (H. Li et al., 2023) and on tourism demand forecasting (Moro & Rita, 2016), and other three documents are conceptual/theoretical studies on the impact of text-to-image AI tools on tourism experiences (Miao & Yang, 2023), on the methodological potential that digital technology, such as AI, has for tourism

Figure 3. Temporal co-occurrences network map (2007-2023)

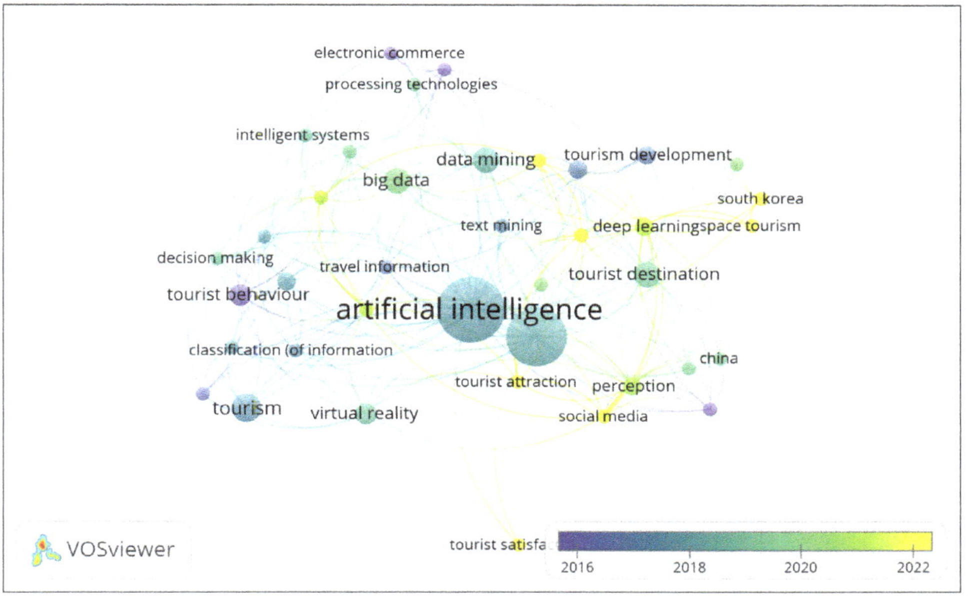

studies (van Nuenen & Scarles, 2021) and, on the description and construction of the extensive data analysis and intelligent service platform of urban scenic spot location service (B. S. Li et al., 2020). Most of the studies were also conducted in Asian countries (Table 3).

At this point it is possible to analyse how AI has evolved in the academic literature on visitors' spatiotemporal behaviour. In Hadavandi et al., (2011) research they used a hybrid artificial intelligence (AI) model, a genetic algorithm and a fuzzy system (Genetic Fuzzy Systems) to forecast tourist arrivals with high accuracy. However, this study does not deal with predicting the behaviour of tourists in destinations but is limited to the forecasting accuracy of GFS.

More recently, Nozawa et al., (2017) employed a method to classify a tourism tweet into the four classes of "sightseeing", "business", "eat", and "buy". They used a Support Vector Machine (SVM) and Multi-label SVM to classify Twitter users into tourist behaviour and tourism purposes, extracting related information from Twitter posts in Tokyo, Japan. A Support Vector Machine algorithm (SVM) and a Genetic search algorithm were used by Sriporn & Tsai (2018) to create a model to predict tourists' behaviour in a virtual museum. Although these two works focus on visitor behaviour, they don't address any spatiotemporal perspective.

After a detailed reading of all the documents listed in Table 3, only two studies, specifically related to spatiotemporal behaviour of tourists in which AI was used

Table 3. Methodologies and geographical area of empirical studies

	Author(s)	Instruments/techniques	Aim/Targets/Sample	Geographical Area
Reviews and theoretical research	(B. S. Li et al., 2020)	Theoretical (AI deep learning algorithm is described)	Describe and constructs the big data analysis and intelligent service platform of urban scenic spot location service using several big data analysis methods to extract valuable information.	Guilin City, Guangxi, China
	(H. Li et al., 2023)	Literature review on user generated photos		
	(Miao & Yang, 2023)	Research note on the impact of text-to-image AI tools on tourism experiences.		
	(Moro & Rita, 2016)	Literature review on tourism demand forecasting		
	(van Nuenen & Scarles, 2021)	n.a. (Conceptual/Theoretical)	To explore the use of AI in tourism, and the methodological potential that digital technology has for tourism studies.	n.a.
	(K. Kim et al., 2017)	Sentiment analysis method: Stanford sentiment analysis tool based on JAVA1.7.0_65	To analyse travellers' online reviews (n= 19835) collected from www.virtualtourist.com	Paris
	(Nozawa et al., 2017)	Support Vector Machine (SVM) Multi-label SVM	To propose a method to classify Twitter user into tourist behavior and tourism purposes, extracting related information from Twitter posts	Tokyo, Japan
	(Pricope Vancia et al., 2023)	Content analysis method	To identify their current travel behavior in the digital age and Generation Z tourists' perception of the future of travel in the context of recent technological developments, namely AI, and virtual reality. (Semi-structured interviews, n=20 Generation Z tourists)	n.a.
Quantitative research	(Chen et al., 2020)	AI cognitive analysis and Microsoft computer vision algorithm methods (Programming language C#); SentiWordNet	To interpret the information of images (n=3705) from the Skypixel (https://www.skypixel.com/) (2199 textual captions and 1869 geographic coordinates)	World
	(Chi et al., 2022)	AIDUA model; Confirmatory factor analysis (CFA); Covariance-based structural equation modeling (CB-SEM) analysis.	To examine tourists' attitudes toward the use of AI devices in either relatively more utilitarian or hedonic tourism services. (Survey n=423 Amazon Mechanical Turk)	n.a.
	(Hadavandi et al., 2011)	Hybrid artificial intelligence (AI) model; Genetic algorithm for learning rule base; Tuning data base of fuzzy system (Genetic Fuzzy Systems)	To develop a Mamdani-type fuzzy rule-based system to forecast tourist arrivals with high accuracy	Taiwan
	(M. J. Kim, Hall, Chung, et al., 2023)	Multi-analyses methods of partial least squares – structural equation modeling (PLS-SEM); Multi-group analysis (MGA); Fuzzy-set qualitative comparative analysis (fsQCA)	To better understand domestic tourist behavioral intention on public transport use. Questionnaire (n=498)	South Korea
	(M. J. Kim, Hall, Kwon, Hwang, et al., 2023)	Partial least squares; Structural equation modelling; Fuzzy-set qualitative comparative analysis; Multi-group analysis; Deep learning	To examine what factors make consumers participate in orbital and/or suborbital space tourism Questionnaire (n=664)	South Korea
	(M. J. Kim, Hall, Kwon, & Sohn, 2023)	Symmetrical (PLS-SEM and MGA); Asymmetrical (fsQCA); Deep learning methods.	To create and assess an extended value-belief-norm model including ESG as well as trust in and benefits of AI relevant to space tourism, along with comparisons between three types of space tourism to examine potential sustainable space tourist behavior. (Survey n=1000)	South Korea

continued on following page

Table 3. Continued

	Author(s)	Instruments/techniques	Aim/Targets/Sample	Geographical Area
Quantitative research	(Oh & Lee, 2021)	Game theory-based framework [SHapley Additive exPlanations (SHAP)]	To understand the prediction results and to obtain insight into how tourist satisfaction with local festivals can be improved. (Surveys n=476)	South Korea
	(Sriporn & Tsai, 2018)	Combination of the feature selection method and the wrapper method; Support Vector Machine algorithm (SVM); Genetic search algorithm; Greedystepwise algorithm.	To create a model to predict tourists' behavior on virtual museum.	Thailand
	(van Esch et al., 2022)	ANOVA; t-test; Mediation analysis using PROCESS macro in SPSS.	Examine how tourists respond to AI in hotel service settings during a pandemic. 4 studies were conducted with surveys (n= 154; n=145; n=598; and n=260 Amazon Mechanical Turkers)	USA
	(Zhang et al., 2020)	Convolutional Neural Networks (CNN); ResNet; Deep learning structure for scene recognition; ArcGIS.	To adopt one of the latest AI computer vision technologies to perform big data analysis on user-generated geotagged photos (Flickr) to uncover the perceptional and behavioral differences between residents and tourists.	Hong Kong
	(Zhang et al., 2019)	Visual content analysis by computer deep learning model; ResNet; ANOVA; Hierarchy cluster; Kernel density analysis	"How to effectively apply computer vision technology into tourists' behaviors and perception analysis in the field of tourism destination study?". Data from Flickr.	Beijing, China

Source: Authors' construction.

were identified (Zhang et al., 2019; Zhang et al., 2020). In 2019, Zhang et al., (2019) used AI to discover the tourists' behaviors and perceptions in Beijing by analyzing photos' visual content. The authors employed a visual content analysis of big pictorial data by computer deep learning model to examine data from the Flickr social network, providing a new way of understanding tourists' preferences. They found some intercontinental differences with a focus on the spatial perspective. For instance, Asian tourists are more interested in the mall courtyard and aircraft, European tourists prefer to overlook at night, and North American tourists are more interested in flowers. To identify differences in the perceived image of the destination (Hong Kong) and behaviour patterns between residents and tourists, Zhang et al., (2020) also employed user-generated photographs from the Flickr social network. This modern tracking technique is very popular in this kind of studies (M. Martins & Costa, 2022). Subsequently, they adopted one of the latest AI computer vision technologies to analyze a large amount of data to uncover the perceptional and behavioral differences between residents and tourists. The authors analyse the distribution of tourists' and residents' footprint, the density distribution of residents' and tourists' trajectory, and the density distribution of tourists' and residents' behavioral activities. They found specific hot spots for both groups, such as their primary experience of cultural and recreational activities. However, in these two studies, the spatial perspective continues to dominate the analysis methodology, and a temporal approach is still lacking to analyse differences between visitor preferences over time.

A similar research framework was used by Campo Chen et al.Chen et al., (2020). These authors employed AI cognitive analysis and Microsoft computer vision algorithm methods to interpret the information in massive image data and the image content into multiple keywords to profile Unmanned Aerial Vehicles (UAV) photography tourists. They found that UAVs are predominantly used to photograph natural scenery, and the sentiment analysis indicates that tourists' opinions of photography are typically positive.

The most recent researches are those conducted by M. J. Kim, Hall, Chung, et al., (2023), M. J. Kim, Hall, Kwon, & Sohn (2023) and M. J. Kim, Hall, Kwon, Hwang, et al., (2023). Although they relate to tourist behaviour, they do not address the spatiotemporal perspective. Instead, they focus on understanding domestic tourist behavioural intention on public transport use, finding that High and low AI knowledge groups have distinctive public transport use characteristics (M. J. Kim, Hall, Chung, et al., 2023). The other works focus on the factors that make consumers participate in orbital and/or suborbital space tourism and on the potential sustainable space tourist behaviour.

There are two critical stages where AI can be used when researching the spatiotemporal behaviour of tourists: data collection and data analysis. The documents presented in Table 3 reveal that AI has been used by researchers as a tool to support data analysis (post-visit), ignoring that some technologies supported by AI can be used in the data collection period (during consumption), namely through the use of smartphone applications where all together, GPS tracking, suggestions on attractions to visit and activities to do, and gamification can dramatically improve the visit experience with significant benefits for Destination Management Organizations (DMOs). van Nuenen & Scarles (2021, p.121) mention that itineraries can be planned with platforms such as Google StreetView "that enable us to access acurate, high-resolution digital images of locations around the globe, while AI technology present in mapping services uses GPS to provide information on the shortest or most convenient routes to take".

Using new technologies also allows the process of co-creating experiences in tourism. The process of co-creation can begin when individuals start preparing for their travel, i.e., when they start researching and selecting the places to visit and the activities to do in the destinations (Fig. 4). The AI combined with deep learning and virtual reality could provide short simulations of experiences, personalized to each user's profile. The use of mobile technologies such as smartphones connected to the internet allows access to information and data that drives decision-making in real-time purchasing and engagement, as highlighted by Campo Lamsfus et al.Lamsfus

Figure 4. The visit experience (pre-visit, onsite, and post-visit)
Source: Godovykh & Tasci (2020). Adapted.

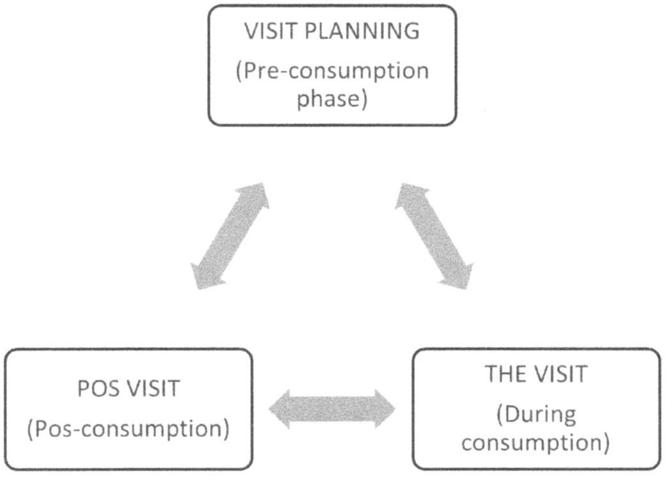

et al., (2015). It will, therefore, be very pertinent to examine how the incorporation of AI could influence the spatiotemporal behaviour of visitors.

To date, AI has proved very useful in studies that use social networks as a source of information. The large amount of metadata available in photographs posted on Flickr, Panoramio, and Skypixel, among others, requires robust tools to read the massive picture data and to visual content recognition, providing a new way of understanding tourists' preferences (Zhang et al., 2019).

According to Li et al., (2023, p.8) geotagged photos have been used to analyse tourists' spatiotemporal behavior through two main topics: i) exploratory and descriptive research (discovering tourists' favorite locations and describing tourists' trajectories and travel patterns); ii) and demand forecasting (actual visitor arrivals and spatiotemporal behavior). So far, tourists STB and AI have focused on discovering tourists' favorite locations and activities and forecasting visitor arrivals.

No studies have yet been carried out on the spatiotemporal behaviour of tourists using GPS devices where AI has been used. However, the "algorithmic culture" as mentioned by van Nuenen & Scarles (2021), referring to the computational processes such as the sorting, classifying and hierarchising of people, places, objects and ideas, certainly has a promising field of application in the future. Machine learning estimation models can include both predictive and explainable models, as done by Oh & Lee (2021, p.15) to identify the critical success factors for each local Korean festival, but also explain what factors should be improved to capture more tourists' attention.

To finalise, all researches presented in Table 3 appear data-dominated without solid theoretical bases" (Li et al., 2023, p.9). Understandably, studies applying new data collection and processing techniques are centred on the design of new methodological frameworks. Still, it is essential that the use of new technologies also contributes to the emergence of new theories.

CONCLUSION

Since the emergence of GPT chat, the concept of artificial intelligence has been widely used in various areas of knowledge. Tourism is no exception, and given the importance that studies into the spatiotemporal behaviour of visitors can bring to the sustainable management of destinations, it seems pertinent to examine how AI has evolved in the academic literature on visitors' spatiotemporal behaviour, identifying the key thematic areas that have drawn most research interest to help academics and professionals to gain a better understanding of AI usage on this topic.

Answering the first research objective (RO1), the most productive authors were identified: Hall, C.M., and Kim, M.J., Chen, Y., Kwon, O., Sohn, K., and Zhang, K. The most cited authors on this topic are Zhang, K., Chen, Y., Li, C. (2019); Kim, K., Park, O.-J., Yun, S., Yun, H. (2017) and Hadavandi, E., Ghanbari, A., Shahanaghi, K., Abbasian-Naghneh, S. (2011). The number of published articles is not very high. However, it shows some interest of researchers on this issue, particularly during 2023.

A bibliometric analysis was conducted to identify the key thematic areas that have drawn most research interest in AI on visitors' spatiotemporal behaviour (RO2). It was found that AI is not an intertwined and widespread topic among the analysed publications. The most significative cluster is RED, marked by the keywords "tourism," "virtual reality," and "behavioral research,"; and the GREEN cluster, where "tourist behavior," "tourism management," and "tourism development" keywords are highlighted. Regarding the number of occurrences of each keyword and their lexical relation, the existence of 2 large groups of published studies can be considered: i) a majority group consisting of a set of keywords related to big data and deep learning, where the large amounts of information used in researches require the use of data collection and processing techniques and technologies, such as data mining and intelligent systems (B. S. Li et al., 2020); and ii) a group of studies with a focus on tourist behaviour where AI is employed in studies related with tourist destinations with a focus on marketing, virtual reality, and decision support systems.

To help academics and professionals better understand AI usage in research on visitors' spatiotemporal behaviour (RO3), a content analysis was carried out based on a full reading of the more relevant selected documents. The research methods, the analytical tools, the study aim, and the geographic area used in empirical studies were identified. From a methodological point of view, most of the documents analysed correspond to quantitative investigations in which questionnaires were applied. Only three studies adopted a qualitative methodology by analysing the content of interviews (Pricope Vancia et al., 2023), online reviews (K. Kim et al., 2017) or Twitter posts (Nozawa et al., 2017). Two documents are literature reviews on user generated photos (H. Li et al., 2023) and on tourism demand forecasting (Moro & Rita, 2016), and other three documents are conceptual/theoretical studies on the impact of text-to-image AI tools on tourism experiences.

The main benefits/implications of using AI on STB of tourists are:

1. In the planning stage
    - AI and virtual reality can simplify the travel planning process (Pricope Vancia et al., 2023);
    - To organize visits according to a specific time budget, motivations, and group of visits, among others.
2. During the visit
    - To predict tourist flows/movements;
    - To manage tourism flows through destinations;
    - To estimate tourist sentiments, (Kim et al., 2017).
3. Post visit
    - To analyze unstructured data (e.g., photos) in an automatic and scalable way (Li et al., 2023, p.5), i.e., the perceptional and spatial behavior pattern of tourists;
    - To identify and analyze tourist flows;
    - to improve the planning and promotion of tourism destinations (Chen et al., 2020);
    - to predict and classify tasks, including image recognition and language modelling (van Nuenen & Scarles, 2021);
    - To analyze image content (Hao et al., 2020) and tourist sentiments (Kim et al., 2017).

AI has the potential to impact human behavior and decision-making (M. J. Kim, Hall, Kwon, Hwang, et al., 2023) and according to van Esch et al., (2022), the pandemic has accelerated the intrusion of AI in our lives. However, tourists continue to seek "human touch" in services as it enhances their subjective happiness. That means that tourists still prefer services provided by humans (vs. AI), but as advances in AI allow the penetration rate of these technologies to increase, we will also see a growth in the acceptance of interactions between machines and visitors. At first, you find it strange, then you get used to it!

There are some limitations to the research that has been carried out. It would be appropriate to use more than one social media platform. Combining data from different social networks will make it possible to solve some problems regarding the representativeness of their users. The supporting requirements for AI technology in tourism studies are also minimal. So, developing more specific and precise tourism research methods is essential.

Future research could use data mining technology to collect data in different platforms (Zhang et al., 2020) and should focus on how DMOs can use AI as a viable and necessary part of the operations of Campo (Zhang et al., 2019) on tourist STB.

REFERENCES

Agapito, D. (2020). The senses in tourism design: A bibliometric review. *Annals of Tourism Research*, *83*(August), 102934. doi:10.1016/j.annals.2020.102934

Ahas, R., Aasa, A., Roose, A., Mark, Ü., & Silm, S. (2008). Evaluating passive mobile positioning data for tourism surveys: An Estonian case study. *Tourism Management*, *29*(3), 469–486. doi:10.1016/j.tourman.2007.05.014

Caldeira, A. M., & Kastenholz, E. (2022). Spatiotemporal Tourist Behaviour. Encyclopedia of Tourism Management and Marketing, 196–199. doi:10.4337/9781800377486.spatiotemporal.tourist.behaviour

Chen, X., Li, G., Yang, L., Nie, Q., Ye, X., Liang, Y., & Xu, T. (2020). Profiling unmanned aerial vehicle photography tourists. *Current Issues in Tourism*, *23*(14), 1705–1710. doi:10.1080/13683500.2019.1653832

Chi, O. H., Gursoy, D., & Chi, C. G. (2022). Tourists' Attitudes toward the Use of Artificially Intelligent (AI) Devices in Tourism Service Delivery: Moderating Role of Service Value Seeking. *Journal of Travel Research*, *61*(1), 170–185. doi:10.1177/0047287520971054

Chua, A., Servillo, L., Marcheggiani, E., & Vande Moere, A. (2016). Mapping Cilento: Using geotagged social media data to characterize tourist flows in southern Italy. *Tourism Management*, *57*, 295–310. doi:10.1016/j.tourman.2016.06.013

Elsevier. (2014). *Scopus* (Issue August). Elsevier. https://z3.hs-offenburg.de/uploads/media/Scopus-Facts-and-Figures-LO.pdf

Godovykh, M., & Tasci, A. D. A. (2020). Customer experience in tourism: A review of definitions, components, and measurements. *Tourism Management Perspectives*, *35*(May 2019), 100694. doi:10.1016/j.tmp.2020.100694

Hadavandi, E., Ghanbari, A., Shahanaghi, K., & Abbasian-Naghneh, S. (2011). Tourist arrival forecasting by evolutionary fuzzy systems. *Tourism Management*, *32*(5), 1196–1203. doi:10.1016/j.tourman.2010.09.015

Hao, J., Liu, H., Chen, J., Sun, F., & Yang, J. (2020). Study on City-Level Optimization of Tourism Industry Spatial Organization Nodes and Organization Mode for Tourist Destinations. *Complexity*, *2020*, 1–13. doi:10.1155/2020/2807817

Hausmann, A., Toivonen, T., Slotow, R., Tenkanen, H., Moilanen, A., Heikinheimo, V., & Di Minin, E. (2018). Social Media Data Can Be Used to Understand Tourists' Preferences for Nature-Based Experiences in Protected Areas. *Conservation Letters*, *11*(1), 1–10. doi:10.1111/conl.12343

Herrera-Franco, G., Montalván-Burbano, N., Carrión-Mero, P., Apolo-Masache, B., & Jaya-Montalvo, M. (2020). Research trends in geotourism: A bibliometric analysis using the scopus database. *Geosciences*, *10*(10), 1–29. doi:10.3390/geosciences10100379

IBM. (2024a). *What is AI?* IBM. https://www.ibm.com/topics/artificial-intelligence

IBM. (2024b). *What is deep learning?* IBM. https://www.ibm.com/topics/deep-learning

IBM. (2024c). *What is machine learning?* IBM. https://www.ibm.com/topics/machine-learning

Jayawardena, C., McMillan, D., Pantin, D., Taller, M., & Willie, P. (2013). Trends in the international hotel industry. *Worldwide Hospitality and Tourism Themes*, *5*(2), 151–163. doi:10.1108/17554211311314100

Kádár, B., & Gede, M. (2022). The Measurable Predominance of Weekend Trips in Established Tourism Regions—The Case of Visitors from Budapest at Waterside Destinations. *Sustainability (Basel)*, *14*(6), 3293. doi:10.3390/su14063293

Kim, K., Park, O., Yun, S., & Yun, H. (2017). What makes tourists feel negatively about tourism destinations? Application of hybrid text mining methodology to smart destination management. *Technological Forecasting and Social Change*, *123*, 362–369. doi:10.1016/j.techfore.2017.01.001

Kim, M. J., Hall, C. M., Chung, N., Kim, M., & Sohn, K. (2023). Why do tourists use public transport in Korea? The roles of artificial intelligence knowledge, environmental, social, and governance, and sustainability. *Asia Pacific Journal of Tourism Research*, *28*(5), 467–484. doi:10.1080/10941665.2023.2247099

Kim, M. J., Hall, C. M., Kwon, O., Hwang, K., & Kim, J. S. (2023). Orbital and sub-orbital space tourism: Motivation, constraint and artificial intelligence. *Tourism Review*. doi:10.1108/TR-01-2023-0017

Kim, M. J., Hall, C. M., Kwon, O., & Sohn, K. (2023). Effects of Value-Belief-Norm Theory, ESG, and AI on Space Tourist Behavior for Sustainability With Three Types of Space Tourism. *Journal of Travel Research*, 00472875231191514. doi:10.1177/00472875231191514

Koseoglu, M. A., Rahimi, R., Okumus, F., & Liu, J. (2016). Bibliometric studies in tourism. *Annals of Tourism Research*, *61*, 180–198. doi:10.1016/j.annals.2016.10.006

Lamsfus, C., Wang, D., Alzua-Sorzabal, A., & Xiang, Z. (2015). Going Mobile: Defining Context for On-the-Go Travelers. *Journal of Travel Research*, *54*(6), 691–701. doi:10.1177/0047287514538839

LiB. S.LiaoM. Z.HuangL. L. (2020). RESEARCH on BIG DATA ANALYSIS of LOCATION SERVICE and INTELLIGENT SERVICE PLATFORM of URBAN SCENIC SPOTS: A CASE STUDY of GUILIN CITY, Guangxi, China. *International Archives of the Photogrammetry, Remote Sensing and Spatial Information Sciences - ISPRS Archives*, *42*(3/W10), 1135–1138. doi:10.5194/isprs-archives-XLII-3-W10-1135-2020

Li, H., Zhang, L., & Hsu, C. H. C. (2023). Research on user-generated photos in tourism and hospitality: A systematic review and way forward. *Tourism Management*, *96*(August 2022), 104714. doi:10.1016/j.tourman.2022.104714

Martins, M., & Costa, R. (2022). Tracking Technologies in Tourism: A Bibliometric and Content Review. In J. V. de Carvalho, P. Liberato, & A. Peña (Eds.), *Advances in Tourism, Technology and Systems* (pp. 215–230). Springer Nature Singapore. doi:10.1007/978-981-16-9701-2_18

Martins, M. R., da Costa, R. A., & Moreira, A. C. (2022). Backpackers' space–time behavior in an urban destination: The impact of travel information sources. *International Journal of Tourism Research*, *24*(3), 456–471. doi:10.1002/jtr.2514

Miao, L., & Yang, F. X. (2023). Text-to-image AI tools and tourism experiences. *Annals of Tourism Research*, *102*, 103642. doi:10.1016/j.annals.2023.103642

Moro, S., & Rita, P. (2016). Forecasting tomorrow's tourist. *Worldwide Hospitality and Tourism Themes*, *8*(6), 643–653. doi:10.1108/WHATT-09-2016-0046

Nozawa, Y., Endo, M., Ehara, Y., Hirota, M., Yokoyama, S., & Ishikawa, H. (2017). Inferring tourist behavior and purposes of a twitter user. Lecture Notes in Computer Science (Including Subseries Lecture Notes in Artificial Intelligence and Lecture Notes in Bioinformatics), 10004 LNAI. Springer. doi:10.1007/978-3-319-60675-0_9

Oh, H., & Lee, S. (2021). Evaluation and interpretation of tourist satisfaction for local korean festivals using explainable ai. *Sustainability (Basel)*, *13*(19), 10901. doi:10.3390/su131910901

Pattam, A. (2021). *Artificial Intelligence, defined in simple terms*. HCLTech. https://www.hcltech.com/blogs/artificial-intelligence-defined-simple-terms

Pricope Vancia, A. P., Băltescu, C. A., Brătucu, G., Tecău, A. S., Chițu, I. B., & Duguleană, L. (2023). Examining the Disruptive Potential of Generation Z Tourists on the Travel Industry in the Digital Age. *Sustainability (Basel)*, *15*(11), 8756. doi:10.3390/su15118756

Serrano, L., Sianes, A., & Ariza-Montes, A. (2019). Using bibliometric methods to shed light on the concept of sustainable tourism. *Sustainability (Basel)*, *11*(24), 6964. doi:10.3390/su11246964

Shoval, N., & Ahas, R. (2016). The Use of Tracking Technologies in Tourism Research : A Review of the First Decade. *Tourism Geographies*, *18*(5), 587–606. doi:10.1080/14616688.2016.1214977

Shoval, N., Kahani, A., De Cantis, S., & Ferrante, M. (2020). Impact of incentives on tourist activity in space-time. *Annals of Tourism Research*, *80*(September 2019), 102846. doi:10.1016/j.annals.2019.102846

Sriporn, K., & Tsai, C. F. (2018). Predicting Tourists' Behavior of Virtual Museum Using Support Vector Machine with Feature Selection Technique. *Proceedings - International Conference on Machine Learning and Cybernetics*, *2*, 433–438. doi:10.1109/ICMLC.2018.8526959

van Eck, N. J., & Waltman, L. (2010). Software survey: VOSviewer, a computer program for bibliometric mapping. *Scientometrics*, *84*(2), 523–538. doi:10.1007/s11192-009-0146-3 PMID:20585380

van Esch, P., Cui, Y., Das, G., Jain, S. P., & Wirtz, J. (2022). Tourists and AI: A political ideology perspective. *Annals of Tourism Research*, *97*, 103471. doi:10.1016/j.annals.2022.103471

van Nuenen, T., & Scarles, C. (2021). Advancements in technology and digital media in tourism. *Tourist Studies*, *21*(1), 119–132. doi:10.1177/1468797621990410

Versichele, M., Neutens, T., Delafontaine, M., & Van de Weghe, N. (2012). The use of Bluetooth for analysing spatiotemporal dynamics of human movement at mass events: A case study of the Ghent Festivities. *Applied Geography (Sevenoaks, England)*, *32*(2), 208–220. doi:10.1016/j.apgeog.2011.05.011

West, A., Clifford, J., & Atkinson, D. (2018). "Alexa, Build Me a Brand" — An Investigation into the Impact of Artificial Intelligence on Branding. *Journal of Business Economics*, *9*(10), 877–887. doi:10.15341/jbe(2155-7950)/10.09.2018/005

Xia, C. (2007). *Modelling The Spatial-Temporal Movement Of Tourists* (S. O. M. A. G. Sciences (ed.). Rmit University. https://researchbank.rmit.edu.au/view/rmit:6320

Zhang, K., Chen, Y., & Li, C. (2019). Discovering the tourists' behaviors and perceptions in a tourism destination by analyzing photos' visual content with a computer deep learning model: The case of Beijing. *Tourism Management*, *75*, 595–608. doi:10.1016/j.tourman.2019.07.002

Zhang, K., Chen, Y., & Lin, Z. (2020). Mapping destination images and behavioral patterns from user-generated photos: A computer vision approach. *Asia Pacific Journal of Tourism Research*, *25*(11), 1199–1214. doi:10.1080/10941665.2020.1838586

Zupic, I., & Čater, T. (2015). Bibliometric Methods in Management and Organization. *Organizational Research Methods*, *18*(3), 429–472. doi:10.1177/1094428114562629

Chapter 2
Using Artificial Intelligence in Tourism Sustainability Research

Isabel Sofia Loureiro
https://orcid.org/0000-0003-1291-569X
Polytechnic Institute of Cávado and Ave, Portugal

Vânia Costa
https://orcid.org/0000-0002-4202-8779
Polytechnic Instittute of Cávado and Ave, Portugal

Alexandra Malheiro
Polytechnic Instittute of Cávado and Ave, Portugal

ABSTRACT

Artificial intelligence has become one of the strongest tools used in a variety of sectors, including academic research. AI has the potential to revolutionize communication and research, facilitating the collection of data and providing more efficiency in the research process. This chapter aims to highlight the importance of AI research by using ChatGPT, a generative pre-trained transformer. ChatGPT was used to structure an interview directed to tourism agents in order to understand their vision of sustainability models in monitoring tourism companies' activity in the sector. The tool was also interviewed to understand the possible input it would give to assist tourism agents in becoming more sustainable. It is concluded that AI can be a useful tool in research and in developing sustainability practices, projections, and the interpretation of data. However, it is essential to consider the ethical challenges and ensure a proper understanding of the limitations of these tools.

DOI: 10.4018/979-8-3693-2137-9.ch002

INTRODUCTION

Artificial intelligence is mobilizing the world in various sectors of activity. According to Khedkar (2023), artificial intelligence will also be used in academic research, supporting research processes. Esplugas (2023) states that artificial intelligence has the power to revolutionize communication and research. Despite concerns about the misuse of artificial intelligence tools, their advantages should not be ignored (Khedkar, 2023). The last author points out that not only can it facilitate data analysis, but it can also support the literature of scientific articles, enabling the researcher to reduce the number of hours invested in reading articles in full. With artificial intelligence tools, it is also possible to understand and identify the content of articles in mere seconds. These tools also make it possible to correct the language used when producing articles, planning and structuring methods, reducing the possibility of error and making the study more effective. However, the results obtained from these tools should not be taken as "the truth". Despite the advantages presented by the author, artificial intelligence cannot replace people.

The study by Pisica, Edu, Zaharia, & Zaharia (2023) reports on the factors for and against the implementation of artificial intelligence in higher education in Romania. The authors conclude that the use of this tool is seen by academics as a future process rather than a current reality. The academics interviewed show interest in its use but downplay its use in the academic sphere. However, this is a country that the authors classify as less digitalized, which in their view explains the lack of value given to artificial intelligence tools. In terms of the positive factors identified, these include, for example, better functioning of the teaching-learning process in higher education institutions, generating more skills, allowing personalized teaching - which contributes to greater inclusion - and greater efficiency in teaching. Concerning the negative aspects, the following are highlighted, for example: the replacement of human beings by these tools, the increase in compulsive disorders - in which the user becomes obsessed with using these tools and cannot live without them - and the violation of data protection.

This article presents a set of general and specific objectives. The main objective of this study is to present a proposal for a tool to support interviews in the context of the study of existing sustainability indicator models in tourism. The aim is to understand the use of artificial intelligence in the context of academic research. The main research question of this study is based on the following question: "Can artificial intelligence help to build methodological tools for academic research?". The article is divided into four parts. The first part presents ChatGPT, then the method used is presented and it's followed by showcasing the results and the respective discussion. Lastly, conclusions are presented.

ChatGPT

Esplugas (2023) explains that ChatGPT corresponds to a chatbot launched as a prototype in November 2022. The free version is ChatGPT 3.5 and corresponds to a tool that generates conversational responses in various areas. However, it is limited to providing content information until 2021, which means that if you are asked about events that occurred after that year, the tool will not have an answer. The term GPT, according to the author, refers to "Generative Pre-trained Transformer", which explains why it doesn't have information on events after 2021. The tool is only trained with information prior to that year. It is a computer system based on a biological brain, made up of several "neurons" and built on human information processing. With a small prompt it is possible to generate a significant number of texts. Esplugas adds that ChatGPT 3 and 3.5 correspond to the largest neural networks that have ever been produced and that, for this reason, they surpass any other model previously produced by transmitting convincing information that can be mistaken for human language.

Concerning the risks of using ChatGPT for the researcher, the author Esplugas highlights some that are in line with those presented above, namely the fact that the tool can collect personal data, affecting our privacy and security. The fact that the researcher doesn't understand the limitations of the tool and the possibility of wrong answers can be a risk and generate misinformation. According to the author, references given by ChatGPT may not exist, which requires the researcher to confirm the information and search for the truth. As it is an artificial intelligence tool, ChatGPT does not display emotions and it is therefore impossible to interpret the sentimental response given, which would only occur in the context of a human-to-human conversation. Finally, the ease of access to this type of tool makes us dependent on that content, hindering our ability to form thoughts and solve problems.

In the view of Ferreira, Garcia, & Brasil (2023), the opening up of these tools to the general public in the academic context has brought new opportunities that could be positive or negative. It depends solely on the ability of institutions to understand how they work and at the same time requires a reformulation of assessment methods. The authors fear that these new artificial intelligence tools could be replacing human beings. However, the harmful consequences of these tools depend on how they are used, thus highlighting the risks highlighted by Esplugas. Despite the risks involved, ChatGPT, like other artificial intelligence tools, could make a positive contribution to the development of academic studies. ChatGPT could be a useful tool for creating action plans for sustainability in tourism, identifying indicators, monitoring tourism activity, developing business, identifying trends and providing customer support. Chat bots, such as ChatGPT, can be a means of conversing with customers and facilitating decision-making. Biswas (2023) highlights the role that

ChatGPT could play in advancing our knowledge of climate change and improving the accuracy of climate projections. According to the author, ChatGPT can help with model parameterization, data interpretation, scenario development and model evaluation. The author also recognizes that the results provided by the tool must be interpreted with care as it depends on the information that has been entered into the system.

METHODOLOGY

This study uses the ChatGPT tool to structure and define an interview script according to the objectives defined for the study. The interview script aims to understand the vision of sustainability stakeholders on the construction of sustainability assessment indicator models in tourism companies. The aim is to find out which practices are applied in the businesses where they operate, how they evaluate the application of these practices, to find out the needs of these businesses and how a tool made up of indicators would be useful to them. The semi-structured interview designed to accompany this study was aimed specifically at this group. The main research questions to answer with this interview script were:

1. "How do you see sustainability in tourism?"
2. "How can sustainability indicator models in tourism be useful in your professional context?"
3. "How can technological tools help make tourism businesses more sustainable?"
4. "How important is sustainability certification in tourism?"

The prompt to be used in ChatGPT should follow the logic of a conversation between humans. However, it was necessary to understand the interview context. According to Lousã, Santos & Cabral (2018) there are a variety of techniques available for data collection. The semi-structured interview consists of following a script with general questions, which only serves as a starting point for the interview. According to the authors, this type of interview is ideal for interviewers with little experience. ChatGPT was assigned several prompts.

The use of multiple prompts makes it possible to get several questions on a specific topic, allowing for a more comprehensive set of questions. The prompts were used according to the research questions defined for this study, namely those of the third research question:

Prompt 1: "Hi. Could you create an interview script aimed at tourism professionals that addresses sustainable tourism?"

Prompt 2: "Hi. Could you create an interview script aimed at tourism professionals that addresses the importance of monitoring sustainability in tourism activity?"

Prompt 3: "Hi. Could you create an interview script aimed at tourism professionals that addresses the use of indicators in tourism businesses?

Prompt 4: "Hi. Could you create an interview script aimed at tourism professionals that addresses the use of technology to promote sustainability?

Prompt 5: "Hi. Could you create an interview script aimed at tourism professionals that addresses the certification of businesses as sustainable?"

For each of these prompts, different results were obtained. Some questions ended up being off-topic and were excluded. Other questions were also excluded because they were repeated or asked about the same subject in different ways. After collecting each of the questions, ChatGPT was asked to organize the questions presented to draw up an interview script.

The resulting interview script was then directly applied to tourism professionals to understand if the questions included were giving the desired result and the overall satisfaction of the respondents with the interview. For an even more interesting use of ChatGPT, the same interview script was also applied to the tool itself contributing with information of a man versus machine context.

RESULTS

For each prompt, it was obtained multiple questions that followed the desired theme of the prompts. After analyzing ChatGPT responses, 11 questions were selected that followed the main goal of the intended research. Table 1 provides these questions.

Interviews to Individuals Interested in Tourism Sustainability

The respondents were selected at random and contacted beforehand to present the study and request their participation. A total of 15 people were interviewed by telephone between October 29th, 2023, and November 18th, 2023.

The 15 respondents are mostly women and come from different areas within and outside the sector. Respondents ranged from municipal employees to students and workers in the sector, to researchers and entrepreneurs. Table 2 shows the profile of the respondents.

The respondents indicated that the interview is adequate, easy to follow and feasible. All questions were answered properly and the desired results of the interview were obtained. The use of ChatGPT, an artificial intelligence tool, showed that it can support researchers in developing investigation tools. For a better understanding

Table 1. Interview script with ChatGPT questions

Questions	Theme
How do you define sustainable tourism and what are its main principles?	The concept of sustainable tourism.
What are the best practices to ensure that sustainable tourism is successfully implemented?	Sustainable tourism practices.
What are the main challenges that sustainable tourism is facing?	Challenges of sustainable tourism.
How do you see the future of sustainable tourism?	The future of sustainable tourism.
How do you measure sustainability in tourism and what indicators do you use?	Measuring sustainability in tourism.
What are the main sustainability indicators used in the tourism industry?	Sustainability indicators in tourism.
What is the importance of monitoring sustainability in tourism businesses and how can this help improve existing business practices?	Importance of monitoring sustainability in tourism.
What are the best tools and technologies currently available to monitor and improve sustainability in tourism businesses?	Tools and technologies for sustainability in tourism.
How important is sustainability certification in the tourism sector?	Sustainability certification in tourism.
What are the next strategic steps you believe the tourism industry should take to meet the Sustainable Development Goals and the 2030 Agenda?	Sustainability strategies in tourism.
How important is the collaboration between companies, governments and non-governmental organizations in promoting sustainable tourism?	Promoting sustainable tourism.

Source: Own elaboration adapted from ChatGPT collection.

of the obtained results from this interview script the main results obtained will be presented.

In the view of the respondents, sustainable tourism is based on a form of tourism that considers its limits above any benefit. For them, it is the development of tourism that considers the future of the activity. It means considering the impacts resulting from tourism while promoting the advantages of tourism. In terms of the principles governing sustainable tourism, the respondents highlighted respect for the environment, consideration for local communities, resource management and commitment. For them, sustainable tourism requires commitment from people, organizations and companies.

Some examples of practices shared by the respondents that can lead to the successful implementation of sustainable tourism include raising awareness in the community so that everyone is informed. It also involves instilling the concept of sustainability in children and young people in particular. It also involves putting pressure on large entities to be more sustainable. Tourism professionals highlighted the importance of collaborating with municipalities and other companies in the

Table 2. Profile of respondents

Gender	
Man	**33%**
Woman	67%
Age	
18-24	7%
35-44	47%
45-54	33%
55-64	13%
Related to the Tourism area	
Yes	73%
No	27%
Profession	
Student "Nature and Heritage - Interpretive Guide"	7%
Local Accommodation Manager	13%
Local Accommodation Employee	27%
Municipality worker	13%
Trainer	20%
Researcher	7%
Consultant	13%

Source: Own elaboration

sector to educate both residents and tourists about the sustainable practices they can carry out. The researcher mentions that the successful implementation of sustainable tourism depends on a good strategic action plan, not only at the destination level but also in a business context.

Sustainable tourism faces some challenges in terms of implementation. Firstly, it is mentioned that making the activity sustainable requires a change in behaviour at all levels. Some accommodation managers mention that, even though tourists are made aware of the importance of maintaining socially responsible behaviour, the tourists they receive often end up having attitudes that disregard the term sustainability. One example is the misuse of energy by guests who, while not in the hotel, left the air conditioning on for several hours. Others mention the costs involved in switching to sustainable practices, such as the cost of installing solar panels in their buildings. And some point out that what is reported as a sustainable item may not be so sustainable, with other consequences on a social and ethical level. Here they refer to cloth bags, which are increasingly used, but which may originate from production in which human resources are disrespected or the materials that make them up have other consequences, such as the use of dyes and chemicals to dye fabric, which often pollute rivers and important water sources.

The respondents gave different answers regarding the future of sustainable tourism. Some are optimistic and believe that in the future there will be more and more sustainable tourism initiatives and success stories, as a result of the social pressure currently being exerted and the efforts of governments. However, others see it as an illusion. Despite the efforts made, they believe that the future will be occupied by pseudo-greens. The term pseudo-green used by one of the respondents reinforces the idea of greenwashing. In this view, the sustainable tourism of the future will be made up of companies that claim to follow a sustainable approach but don't implement it. It is increasingly clear that climate change is in constant retreat, and so these respondents indicate that even with a radical change in current behavior, serious consequences for the climate will prevail.

The respondents indicated that the way they measure their sustainability actions depends only on compliance with sustainability certification standards. Others say that they check cost figures, particularly in terms of energy, water consumption and waste. Some of the respondents indicated that they have pre-defined objectives in the sustainability plan of the companies they work for and that they check annually whether these objectives are being met. As an example of an objective, the percentage of energy consumption from renewable sources was given. Some of the people interviewed explained that they had only learned about the existence of different types of indicators through training at Turismo de Portugal and that they therefore didn't fully understand the concept of using sustainability measurement models in tourism.

In terms of the sustainability indicators that they consider to be most used in tourism, energy consumption and its sources, water consumption and the carbon footprint are highlighted, similarly to those indicated above.

Individuals recognize the importance of monitoring sustainability in the sector and consider that constantly evaluating the operation of the business makes it possible to take measures in advance and find problem areas based on the indicators defined. Monitoring also helps to ensure that they meet the proposed objectives and demonstrates the company's interest in becoming sustainable.

In terms of tools and technologies that can help monitor sustainability in tourism businesses, the respondents indicated that they use their own systems integrated into their company, which they don't know much about. Others mention that there is software they can use to calculate their carbon footprint and that they even use this in a personal context. And some mention that they don't know of any tools that they use themselves, but that there must certainly be solutions.

For the respondents, sustainability certifications are important because they allow companies to have concrete sustainability measures in their businesses. And it allows them to separate the real apologists for sustainability from the pseudo-greenies. On the managers' side, certification allows them to attract a new audience to their businesses, an audience that will be willing to pay more for a product or service if it means that it will contribute to sustainability. At the same time, for them, certification gives the business some credibility and allows them to see it as something different, making it more attractive. On the other hand, the researcher questions the credibility of certification, particularly in terms of the rigour imposed in certifying compliance with standards. She wonders whether the level of auditing required is sufficient to verify that the company does in fact comply with a set of sustainable indicators. Another raises a similar issue, questioning whether certification is really possible to avoid greenwashing in tourism.

Respondents think that monitoring sustainability in tourism using indicators could be the next strategic step for the sector. For them, monitoring can serve as an ally in achieving the SDGs and the 2030 Agenda. However, the notion of commitment is emphasized. The plans exist, but if they are nothing more than plans, nothing will be done. They point out that the pandemic has been a difficult time, especially for the tourism sector, and that the climate tragedies that have occurred frequently are frightening and impose the need to take serious measures to reverse the situation. A change in behaviour, the re-education of habits and cooperation between everyone is needed to ensure that the current climate situation does not regress. The need for companies to communicate is highlighted by the respondents, who say that the clearer and more concise they are with their social, economic and environmental impact, the better the results and the greater the progress towards sustainability.

Collaboration between companies, governments and non-governmental organizations is identified as one of the main strategies to be adopted. For them, it is only through cooperation that it will be possible to develop a sustainability standard in the sector and comply with the SDGs and the 2030 Agenda. From the managers' point of view, this cooperation will later enable specific sustainability policies to be developed for each business and that talking to other sectors and governments can help to devise concrete solutions for each business sector. One of the participants used the saying "one hand washes the other", referring to the importance of cooperation.

Interview With ChatGPT

The ChatGPT interview followed the same logic as the human conversation. Firstly, they were asked if they would be willing to be interviewed for an academic paper and after confirming this, a conversation was generated similar to the 15 previously interviewed. ChatGPT responses are more informative because they include a greater amount of information. The results are therefore more complex and varied.

ChatGPT defined sustainable tourism as a set of practices and approaches carried out in the tourism sector that seek to reduce environmental, social and cultural impact, promoting economic benefits for local communities and the preservation of resources, namely natural and cultural resources. It indicates that sustainable tourism is an approach that seeks a balance between the development of the activity and long-term conservation, in order to ensure that future generations enjoy the same set of resources that are available today. Six principles governing sustainable tourism have been highlighted. These principles are shown in Table 3.

For ChatGPT, the successful implementation of sustainable tourism depends on the adoption of good practices in different areas. Some of the practices highlighted by the tool, in addition to those previously mentioned, are shown in Table 4.

Some of the main challenges of sustainable tourism are highlighted. Namely, overcrowding and pressure on destinations and the negative environmental impacts that even following sustainable practices can create various environmental problems such as pollution. There are also challenges in terms of resource management, specifically with the use of plastics. This type of tourism can lead to greater social inequalities, marginalizing groups, as well as causing a disconnection between tourism and local communities by not involving them in decision-making. The lack of awareness on

Table 3. Principles governing sustainable tourism

Principle	Explanation
Environmental conservation	This type of tourism aims to minimise the negative impact on the environment, which requires the application of certain measures such as proper waste management, conservation of biodiversity, preservation of natural ecosystems and reduced consumption of resources.
Respect for local culture	Sustainable tourism aims to promote respect for local traditions, customs and cultures. This requires promoting cultural authenticity and minimising the de-characterisation of tourist destinations due to external influence.
Benefits for local communities	This tourism should contribute to the economic, social and cultural development of local communities. This includes creating job opportunities, encouraging local entrepreneurship and community participation in the sector's decisions.
Education and awareness-raising	Awareness is important for sustainable tourism. Awareness-raising involves educating visitors about sustainable practices, and involving local communities in understanding the benefits and challenges associated with tourism.
Sustainable resource management	Responsible use of natural resources such as water and energy to ensure long-term preservation. It includes equitable management of the benefits that tourism brings.
Quality over quantity	This format of tourism allows for a business model that favours the quality of the tourist experience over the quantity of visitors. This can be associated with the existence of capacity limits in tourist destinations to avoid overcrowding.

Source: Own elaboration based on ChatGPT.

Table 4. Practices for the successful implementation of sustainable tourism

Practices	Example
Environmental preservation	Promote practices such as recycling, the efficient use of natural resources and the protection of ecosystems and establish conservation areas.
Sustainability certifications and seals	Seek out sustainable tourism certifications or seals that recognise responsible environmental and social practices. Use these certifications to emphasise your commitment to sustainability.
Sustainable transport	Encourage the use of transport such as public transport, bicycles or electric vehicles and develop infrastructure to facilitate movement within tourist destinations.
Partnerships and collaborations	Collaborate with local stakeholders, non-governmental organisations and companies to promote sustainable practices.
Monitoring and evaluation	Implement monitoring systems to assess the impact of tourism on communities and the environment. Use continuous feedback to adjust policies and practices, ensuring the effectiveness of sustainable initiatives.

Source: Own elaboration based on ChatGPT.

the part of tourists is also highlighted as a challenge, as they are not always aware of the impacts their actions can have. The difficulty in implementing certifications can become a challenge, which ChatGPT points out is particularly focused on less developed destinations. There may also be conflicts of interest between environmental conservation objectives, the tourism sector and the needs of the local community, which makes it difficult to create practical solutions. There is also mention of the initial costs that adopting sustainable practices requires for companies. Finally, one of the main challenges for the tourism sector is climate change.

Climate change can cause extreme events, rising sea levels and other negative impacts that do not provide long-term sustainability. According to ChatGPT, in order to meet these challenges, it is necessary to develop partnerships between governments, the private sector, local communities and tourists.

The future of sustainable tourism for the tool is essential for the preservation of resources and the well-being of communities. The future trends for sustainable tourism are highlighted in Table 5.

For ChatGPT, measuring sustainability in tourism involves the use of various indicators belonging to the social, environmental and economic areas. According to ChatGPT, different evaluation systems and certifications have been developed to measure sustainability in the sector. Among the various models, the EarthCheck, Green Key, Travelife and GSTC certifications are mentioned. The tool emphasises that these indicators vary according to the type of scale used - whether local, regional or global - and the type of tourism company - whether hotel, tour operator or destination. It also emphasises that in addition to quantitative indicators there are other factors such as the quality of management, stakeholder involvement and compliance with

Table 5. The future of sustainable tourism

Trend	Explanation
Growing awareness	As awareness increases globally, it is expected that more tourists will seek out sustainable travel options and support destinations that showcase sustainable practices.
Technological innovations	Emerging technologies such as artificial intelligence, virtual reality and blockchain can be used to monitor and optimise sustainable practices, make operational efficiency better for companies and enable more responsible experiences.
Multi-sector collaborations	Cooperation between governments, the private sector, non-governmental organisations and local communities is expected to increase. This collaboration will be focused on developing and putting into practice sustainable initiatives. Effective partnerships can result in more balanced and comprehensive solutions.
Regulations and incentives	Governments and international institutions can put in place strict regulations and offer incentives to promote more sustainable practices. This can lead to implementing environmental and social standards and offering tax benefits to the most sustainable companies.
Niche tourism and authentic experiences	Tourist demand for authentic experiences can lead to the growth of niche tourism, favouring less explored destinations and authentic cultural practices.
Lifelong learning	Lifelong learning of tourists and local communities will be key to ensuring the implementation of sustainable practices and the understanding of long-term benefits.
Smart destination management	Smart technologies in destination management will make it possible to balance supply and demand, manage the flow of tourists, improve infrastructure and minimise the negative impacts of tourism.
Circular and local economy	This concept can become a key element in sustainable tourism as it helps to distribute the benefits of the activity fairly.
Regenerative tourism	There is also interest in regenerative tourism, which actively seeks to regenerate ecosystems and revitalise communities, contributing to the positive impact of the activity.
Resilience to climate change	Sustainable tourism will have to adapt to climate change by preparing destinations and businesses for extreme events and implementing practices that reduce vulnerability to negative impacts.

Source: Own elaboration based on ChatGPT.

standards and regulations that affect the assessment of sustainability in tourism. The indicators that ChatGPT identifies as being used by the sector are shown in Table 6.

Monitoring sustainability in the sector is recognised as fundamental to ascertaining the impacts caused. Some of the reasons given for monitoring are that it allows an assessment of current performance in relation to sustainability criteria in the sector, leading to the identification of areas that need improvement. By identifying these areas, it is possible to implement, for example, more efficient technologies, optimise processes and introduce innovative initiatives. Knowing the areas to work on allows decisions to be made based on evidence. It also makes it possible to reduce costs, make operational activity more efficient and manage the risks of identified problems. By monitoring the activity, you are also analysing compliance with the certifications and standards to which you are committed and making the tourism

Table 6. Indicators for measuring sustainability in tourism

Theme	Indicator
Environmental management	Efficient use of energy. Effective waste management. Water conservation and consumption. Protection of biodiversity.
Social management	Involvement and benefits for local communities. Fair employment practices and equal opportunities. Respect for human rights. Promotion of ethical practices.
Cultural impact	Respect for local traditions. Preservation of cultural heritage. Promoting cultural authenticity in tourist experiences.
Economic	Equitable distribution of economic benefits to the community. Stimulating entrepreneurship. Creation of employment opportunities.
Awareness and education	Educational programmes for tourism. Environmental and cultural awareness. Community involvement in education initiatives.
Sustainable transport	Use of low-impact transport. Encouraging public transport, cycling and walking.
Financial performance indicators	Follow investments in sustainable practices. Evaluate the financial return on these practices.
Resilience to climate change	Adaptation to climatic events. Slowing down greenhouse gas emissions.
Overall impact assessment	The total carbon footprint of the destination. Global social impact assessment.
Sustainable customer satisfaction index	Measuring customer satisfaction in relation to the sustainable experiences they enjoy, considering factors such as cultural authenticity, environmental practices and social impact.

Source: Own elaboration based on ChatGPT.

activity transparent to tourists, investors, governments and local communities. The commitment to fulfil these certifications leads to the attraction of tourists who are more concerned about sustainable practices, attracting a new tourist segment. At the same time, monitoring sustainability in the tourism sector allows for continuous innovation and improves the brand's reputation, placing it in a stronger market position and making customers loyal to the brand.

ChatGPT identifies the technological tools currently available as solutions for capturing data, managing sustainable practices and communicating transparently with stakeholders. Table 7 provides a set of tools and technologies that ChatGPT identifies as relevant.

Sustainability certification in tourism is important for several reasons. Of these, the tool highlights a factor that contributes to brand recognition and credibility, competitive differentiation, the continuous improvement of tourism companies and their commitment. It also mentions the possibility of attracting new tourists, accessing different markets and meeting tourists' expectations. Certification contributes to the preservation of destinations, the efficient management of resources and the establishment of standards of sustainable practices that can be compared with other

Table 7. Tools and technologies for monitoring sustainability in tourism

Type of tool	Example
Sustainability management systems	Platforms such as EarthCheck and Green Key.
Carbon footprint assessment tools	Tools such as the Carbon Trust and the GHG Protocol.
Energy efficiency software	Platforms such as building management systems.
Waste tracking applications	Applications such as TrashOut and Rubicon.
Water management systems	Software such as WaterHub.
Blockchain technologies for transparency	Blockchain technology to guarantee chain-wide transparency of product origin and associated sustainable practices.
Artificial intelligence solutions	Use artificial intelligence to analyse large-scale data in order to identify patterns and predict impacts.
Sustainable booking platforms	Platforms such as BookDifferent and Kind Traveler.
Tourist awareness applications	Educational applications such as Leave No Trace.
Geographical information systems	Tools such as ArcGIS to monitor areas of environmental importance in destinations.
Internet of Things sensors for environmental monitoring	Sensors connected to the Internet of Things can help monitor air quality, noise pollution and more in real time.
Stakeholder management software	Platforms such as StakeWave support management and communication with stakeholders.

Source: Own elaboration based on ChatGPT.

companies. ChatGPT defines some strategic steps that are consistent with what is presented as the future trends of sustainable tourism, emphasising the integration of the SDGs into business strategies.

In order to fulfil the SDGs and the 2030 agenda, ChatGPT believes that some strategic steps must be taken, starting with the adoption of the SDGs in the business strategy and the foundation of partnerships. The strategic steps also include adopting global certifications and standards such as the GSTC, implementing sustainable destination management plans, and technological innovation and encouraging new types of tourism such as community-based and regenerative tourism. According to ChatGPT, community-based tourism consists of empowering communities, while regenerative tourism is based on exploring models that seek, for example, to restore ecosystems. The strategy should also include raising consumer awareness, crisis management plans, greater transparency and continuous evaluation and monitoring of progress towards the SDGs.

According to ChatGPT, collaboration between companies, governments and non-governmental organisations makes it possible to define a strategy capable of achieving the objectives of sustainability in tourism. It has several advantages, such as integrating the efforts of all those involved, leading to the sharing of resources, obtaining a holistic image of the sector and the common development of sustainable policies involving the whole community. It allows for better destination management and promotes innovation and constant research into new solutions to the sustainability problems encountered. This cooperation makes it possible to strengthen public-private partnerships, contributing to efficient responses to global challenges and to the education and awareness of all those involved. Finally, it contributes to greater transparency in the sector and more effective accountability.

DISCUSSION OF RESULTS

The obtained interview script shows that artificial intelligence can be used to create methodological tools for academic research. The application of ChatGPT in this research took in consideration the risks it has implied. By providing multiple prompts the questions obtained were broader and could be put together more efficiently according to the goal of the research. Excluding questions that do not fit into the theme or that could be overlapping with other questions allowed the responses to be more specific and the respondents to provide better answers for the search. The adaptation of the interview script to the respondent, as being a semi-structured interview, allowed for a better dialogue. By not depending exclusively on the response of the artificial intelligence tool it was possible to use it according to the context. Has a researcher it was possible to critically evaluate and interpret the results, taking into account the ethical implications associated with its use. The combination of human thinking and artificial intelligence permitted to develop a research tool with rapid application, reducing research time and possible costs. It's adaptability and customization make its usage flexible for the researcher. The main research question was answered.

As for the obtained results with the interview script, all research questions were answered. For the respondents' sustainable tourism is to consider the limits above any benefit. It's about developing a tourism that considers the future of the activity. It's considering the impacts while promoting the benefits of tourism. Sustainable tourism means respecting the environment, considering local communities, resource management and commitment. Tourism sustainability correspondents to a set of practices and approaches carried out in the sector that seek to reduce environmental, social and cultural impacts, while promoting economic benefits for local communities and preserving resources. It is an approach that seeks a balance between the development of the activity and long-term conservation, ensuring that future generations enjoy the same set of resources available today. Sustainability in tourism involves conserving the environment, respecting local culture, benefiting the local community, educating and raising awareness, managing resources sustainably and prioritizing quality over quantity. The use of indicators to monitor tourism sustainability makes it possible to constantly evaluate the functioning of tourism businesses, helping to take measures in advance, finding problem areas, ensuring that they meet the proposed objectives and demonstrating that they are interested in sustainability. It helps to identify the impacts caused, compare performance with sustainability criteria in the sector, identify areas in need of improvement, leading to efficient implementation of technologies and optimization of processes. They make it possible to reduce operating costs, make the activity more efficient, manage risks and make the activity more transparent. By demonstrating that they are more concerned about sustainability by using indicators, they are attracting new market segments and investing in continuous improvement. By following sustainability indicator models, they are improving their brand reputation and making customers loyal to the company. Technological tools can help monitor the sustainability of tourism businesses. They make it possible to calculate the carbon footprint, for example. They make it possible to capture data, manage sustainable practices and communicate transparently with stakeholders. Tourism sustainability certification makes it possible to have concrete measures of sustainability in tourism and to separate the real apologists for sustainability from the pseudo-green ones. Certification attracts a new audience to your business, an audience that is willing to pay more for a product or service if it is synonymous with contributing to sustainability. Certification gives the business credibility and makes it more attractive. It helps combat greenwashing. Certification leads to competitive differentiation, continuous improvement and commitment. It allows destinations to be preserved, resources to be managed efficiently and standards to be set for sustainable practices that can be compared.

CONCLUSION

This study has produced a wide range of results on the subject of sustainability in tourism and monitoring and evaluation indicators. It also reveals the importance of using artificial intelligence tools in academic production and in building solutions for tourism companies. Artificial intelligence is positioned as a support for sustainability and research (Biswas, 2023). It has made it possible to develop a research tool, supporting the construction of questions and also contributing relevant information to the topic under study. The chapter ends up including four studies, one in which artificial intelligence was used to support the construction of instruments, another in which unstructured observation was used, one in which sustainability stakeholders were interviewed and, finally, one in which artificial intelligence was used to construct results.

Using ChatGPT to build the interview script made the process of building the instrument easier. The results given always depend on the prompts, so other prompts may give different results. However, the prompts used correspond to what was intended for this study and the answers given by the tool were analyzed to exclude or include questions according to the author's intentions. The interview script was only used to help determine the topics to be covered during the interview. The support of this tool was fundamental, but the questions provided may not be the most appropriate for the context of the study and the concept of the interview. It was therefore necessary to analyze the answers given by ChatGPT individually in order to exclude or include questions. The questions collected that make up the interview script are in line with what was desired for the interviews, but they could have been better structured and applied. Despite the advantages of using this tool, it is important to recognize its limitations.

The interview with those interested in sustainability raised relevant issues. On the one hand, it raised the need for commitment, which was one of the main points of all the interviews, including ChatGPT itself. On the other hand, the existence of various sustainability certifications that guarantee the construction of sustainable measures for companies was emphasised, but it was questioned whether these certifications would allow the concept of greenwashing to be avoided. They emphasised that certification audits should be more rigorous in order to avoid "pseudo-greens". They also emphasise the importance of cooperation in setting a course towards sustainability. The difference in perception about the future of sustainability shows, to a certain extent, the individual's disposition on the subject. On the one hand, they think that there will be more and more sustainability initiatives, while on the other they say that it won't be a sustainable future, but a future of sustainable illusions. This raises the question: What is truly sustainable in tourism? How can I distinguish greenwashing? How can we tackle greenwashing? Through commitment. Companies must make a commitment to sustainability with transparency and due clarity on the subject, thus avoiding the illusion of sustainability.

The respondents recognise the importance of monitoring in tourism, but confess that they don't have much information on the subject and are limited to the standards they undertake to comply with. As indicators, they mention energy consumption, percentage of energy from renewable sources, water consumption, waste management and carbon footprint. They admit to using their own systems to monitor spending and also calculate their carbon footprint. They don't know of any specific tools, but recognise that technological solutions may exist. They see sustainability monitoring in tourism as a strategic step forward.

ChatGPT presents a diverse range of information. This tool emphasises the importance of cooperation in meeting the challenges of implementing sustainability. With a more positive outlook, ChatGPT indicates that sustainable tourism will grow in the future. There will be, among other things, more technological innovations, greater awareness, more cooperation and more regulation. The expected increase in regulation is in line with the need for greater rigour in certification. ChatGPT recognises the monitoring of sustainability in tourism businesses as fundamental, as it makes it possible to assess performance and identify areas in need of improvement. At the same time, this monitoring contributes to the continuous improvement of their businesses. The indicators that ChatGPT recognises as important for monitoring sustainability in tourism cover different areas, namely environmental and social management, cultural impact, economic aspects, awareness and education, sustainable transport, financial performance indicators, resilience to climate change, global impact and the sustainable customer satisfaction index.

In conclusion, monitoring sustainability in tourism is fundamental for tourism companies. Both groups of respondents recognise the importance of monitoring. Sustainability is seen as advantageous for tourism businesses and for the planet. Some problems are recognised, such as the need for collaboration, commitment, transparency and clarity in order to meet sustainable objectives. There is also a need for greater rigour in certification. Despite the lack of awareness of some technological tools that could help make the business more sustainable, ChatGPT provides a varied set that is available for use. Thus, a diverse range of information and support tools is now available for companies to access at the click of a button.

REFERENCES

Biswas, S. (2023). Potential Use of ChatGPT in Global Warming. *Annals of Biomedical Engineering*, *51*(6), 1126–1127. doi:10.1007/s10439-023-03171-8 PMID:36856927

Esplugas, M. (2023). The use of artificial intelligence (AI) to enhance academic communication, education and research: A balanced approach. *The Journal of Hand Surgery*, *48*(8), 819–822. doi:10.1177/17531934231185746 PMID:37417005

Ferreira, R., Garcia, G., & Brasil, D. (2023). The emergence of Chat GPT and insecurity about the future of academic papers. *Cadernos de Dereito Actual*, *21*, 130–143. doi:10.5281/zenodo.8043807

Khedkar, S. (2023). *Using AI-powered tools effectively for academic researcg*. Editage Insights. https://www.editage.com/insights/using-ai-powered-tools-effectively-for-academic-research

Lousã, M., Santos, J., & Cabral, A. (2018). Quais as técnicas de recolha de dados a utilizar em trabalhos académicos? In *Como fazer trabalhos académicos: Guia Prático para elaborar projetos, relatórios, teses, dissertações, artigos e muito mais* (pp. 65–87). Porto Editora.

Pisica, A. I., Edu, T., Zaharia, R. M., & Zaharia, R. (2023). Implementing Artificial Intelligence in Higher Education: Pros and Cons from the Perspectives of Academics. *Societies (Basel, Switzerland)*, *13*(118), 118. doi:10.3390/soc13050118

Chapter 3
Artificial Intelligence and the Tourism Film:
Challenges and Possibilities

Tiago Fernandes
https://orcid.org/0000-0002-1412-291X
Instituto Politécnico de Bragança, Portugal & LabCom -Communication and Arts, Portugal

Rogério Tavares
Instituto Politécnico de Bragança, Portugal

João Paulo Sousa
https://orcid.org/0000-0002-9005-084X
Instituto Politécnico de Bragança, Portugal

Ricardo Correia
https://orcid.org/0000-0002-0132-4002
Instituto Politécnico de Bragança, Portugal & CiTUR, Portugal

ABSTRACT

Today, the importance of audiovisual production in the tourism industry is undeniable. Whether it's through products designed specifically to promote a particular territory, such as tourism films, or the recent phenomenon known as "film tourism," in which tourists travel to places they know from the movies, this reality ends up being valued and celebrated at festivals dedicated specifically to this area, such as the Portuguese festival "Art&Tur - International Tourism Film Festival," the German festival "The Golden City Gate," part of "ITB Berlin," or the "World Tourism Film Awards," organized by the CIFFT - International Committee of Tourism Film Festivals. With the recent massification of artificial intelligence, which even though it's not a recent technology has become the order of the day due to the recent events involving the company OpenAI and, more specifically, its online chatbot Chat GPT, the population in general and the scientific community in particular have begun to take a closer look at AI. In the specific case of audiovisual production, while there were a number

DOI: 10.4018/979-8-3693-2137-9.ch003

of tools that already made use of technology in the past and were mainly used in the post-production process (special effects, sound manipulation, etc.), the truth is that AI currently presents some challenges and, on the other hand, some potential, precisely in the first phase of designing an audiovisual work, more specifically, in pre-production. The aim of this chapter is to focus an analysis on the specific case of audiovisual productions conceived in the context of the tourism industry and, from there, try to understand how AI can be an important tool in the creative phase of script design for these works. In the absence of a specific bibliography on the case under analysis, some possibilities for using artificial intelligence to enhance the reach and effectiveness of an audiovisual product designed, above all, to highlight a particular territory or tourist experience will be raised.

INTRODUCTION

In an era in which audiovisual communication is playing an increasingly important role and new communication platforms make it possible for these stimuli to be disseminated ever more quickly, with all the associated advantages and disadvantages, the tourism industry has opted for differentiated marketing strategies, but which are fundamental to the promotion of a given territory. According to Sousa and Rocha (2019, p. 189) territorial marketing is a vital instrument for place promotion, and local government authorities must incorporate it into their plans to support and encourage the areas' long-term social and economic growth. Regardless of the medium selected, the relationship generated between the media/advertising and tourism is briefly defined by Urry (2002), when he suggests that over time, through media and advertising, pictures created from various tourist perspectives create a system of self-persuasion of illusions that give visitors a foundation for choosing and assessing possible places to visit (Pan, Tsai, & Lee, 2011, p. 596). At the same time, local tourist actors have become increasingly important, with technological promotion tools accessible to companies and individuals (Marinho, Correia and Morais, 2021, p. 2) and in this process of promoting a tourist destination, the audiovisual component, particularly content that uses moving images, finds a wide and effective means of dissemination in the media

Television is the source of the imagery with which we do our imagining of the future, and the holiday imagery now so omnipresent on the screen – in the soaps as well as the ads and in the travel programmes of all sorts – is one of the best places to find our fantasies of the free and fulfilled life (Inglis 2000: 5).

Although the importance of audiovisual production in promoting tourist destinations and experiences is obvious, it is curious that this is an area that has been relatively rarely studied in the academic context, particularly in the field of tourism. If we search for terms such as "audiovisual production tourism" or "tourist film" on one of the main search engines for scientific articles, Google Scholar, we realize that most of the results, sorted by relevance, concern research centered on the phenomenon of film tourism or film-induced tourism, a term that has gained relevance in recent years and which is recognized as a type of tourism that is prompted by the sight of a moving picture and includes film, television, and digital media (Connell, 2012). This phenomenon, which began to gain the attention of researchers in the early 1990s, can be read from the perspective of film studies, namely the social psychology of the viewing experience and the language of cinema from the perspective of semiotics placed on the landscape in the film (Connell, 2012). However, it is not this concept that we intend to analyze in this text, but rather the very materiality of the production of a tourist film like those that are produced daily as part of tourism marketing campaigns all over the world. In this sense, we understand the Tourist Film as a format and term that brings together a series of audiovisual productions with accentuated specificities (promotional videos, documentaries, vlogs, short films, etc.).

With artificial intelligence on the agenda, largely due to the recent controversies involving the company Open AI, which made ChatGPT available to the public and thus put AI in the hands of the ordinary user in a different way to what had happened before, some very relevant hypotheses have emerged about the relationship between this technology and its usefulness in the tourism industry, based on multiple forms of Information and Communication Technologies (ICT). AI has enhanced ICTs by facilitating the integration of physical and online/virtual elements, providing technology-enhanced tourist experiences and personalizing tourist services have been made possible by all these Technologies (Grundner and Neuhofer, 2021). An example of the use of AI in the tourism industry can be seen in online travel and hotel booking sites or enhancing customer engagement in hotels and restaurants with robotics applications (Doborjeh et al., 2021). Based on this relationship and using bibliography related to film production, we intend to understand how IA can contribute to the production of a tourist film, focusing our research specifically on the first stage of audiovisual production, specifically pre-production, using a hypothetical case study based on the pre-production of a tourist film about a particular territory.

THE PRE-PRODUCTION PHASE

According to Cartwright (1996), in his book "Pre-Production Planning for Video, Film, and Multimedia", preparing for every step needed to carry out the production and post-production of a video, film, or multimedia project is known as pre-production planning. Pre-production, as the first stage of the audiovisual production process, is a fundamental stage for understanding the creative possibilities and making strategic decisions for the visual and sound design of a given work, which will have repercussions in the following stages. Production planning entails identifying the issue or communication need and choosing the vehicle that will best address it (Cartwright, 1996, p. 2). Since there is no fixed methodology and this phase is always very dependent on the problem and the author's objective, it is difficult to define a formula that can be used in most audiovisual productions and in a tourist film. However, it is important to note that before the actual pre-production phase begins, we have a previous phase that is of the highest importance: the development phase, and from an idea, the planning process begins (Cartwright, 1996, p. 33).

Script

It is at this stage that the project begins to take shape, starting with the writing of the Script, an essential document from the point of view of narrative structure that also indicates the number of scenes, at what time of day they take place, the specific location, whether it is indoors or outdoors, the characteristics of the spaces, the number of characters and their physical and psychological characteristics, among many other elements. There are currently two different ways of thinking about what to do. One approach is to write the screenplay first, then visualize it. The second is that you compose the script after visualizing the content (Cartwright, 1996, p. 37). Regardless of the method chosen, it is after the script has been written that we can move on to pre-production of the project. Using the publication "Oficios del Cine - Manual para Prácticas Cinematográficas", edited by Pedro Alves and Francisco García García (2017), and based on the contribution of Pedro Alves and his text that specifically addresses the area of production (2017) which is adapted to the reality of production in the Portuguese context, we can organize the pre-production phase as follows:

Script Breakdown/Decoupage

Once the production guide has been decided upon and finalized, production can begin with a fundamental first task that addresses awareness of the true needs of the film: The Script Breakdown. This division consists in the separation of the script into its component sections, or sequences, with an analysis of the production requirements for each section (Gates, 1999: 50). From this survey, we can gather crucial information such as the number of actors, extras, props, décors, among other elements (Simon & Wiese, 2001: 29).

Technical Script

The Technical Script is a document based on the Script, but which adds additional information that is very important for the production phase, especially from a visual and directing point of view, such as the number of shots, scales, camera movements (if any) and angles (Alves, 2017: 114). When it comes to pre-production tasks like budgeting, hiring the crew, scheduling, and determining equipment requirements, the technical script is a crucial document (Merrit, 1998, p. 15).

Storyboard

The Storyboard is a visual document, also based on the script, which presents a sequence of photographs or drawn pictures that visually represents the Project. This is an important document, as it gives you a clear idea of the framing of each shot in the film and, as a result, you can make production decisions based on these choices (Cartwright, 1996, p. 40).

Budget Development

As in the previous cases, Budget Development requires a Script, because without understanding the production needs (number of actors, filming locations, technical requirements) it is impossible to calculate the costs of the project (Cartwright, 14: 1996). The aim of this process is precisely to gather as much information as possible to be able to calculate the foreseeable costs of a given project as accurately as possible (Alves, 2017: 116).

Casting/Hiring the Team

After defining the production needs and forecasting the associated cost, it's time to start hiring the cast and crew (Alves, 2017: 122). In the case of casting, or more specifically hiring actors, this process will be based on the characteristics of the characters identified in the Script (Cartwright, 112: 1996), but also in the weighting of the casting team. As for the technical team, to avoid delays, unforeseen costs, or accidents, it is important to have motivated, responsible staff with the qualities required for production (Gates, 1999: 8).

Répérage

In a very brief way, *répérage* consists of searching for and identifying recording locations that are suitable for the needs of a particular audiovisual production and which can be natural or artificially created (Lopes, 2014: 72). In the specific case of a tourist film, we believe that this phase is of the utmost importance, given the importance of landscapes, just to mention one example, in this type of production.

Once all these documents/phases have been drawn up, there are several other requirements that must be met, such as authorizations for image transfers, copyright, contracts, insurance, filming schedules, among many other things. For the analysis intended in this research, we will summarize the pre-production phase of a tourist film in the seven stages mentioned, since it is important for us, in the light of contemporary times, to understand how artificial intelligence can be used in this crucial phase of audiovisual production, specifically in a concrete typology such as the tourist film, and at the same time, what challenges it may pose in the near future (Thaichon & Quach, 2022).

AI: ARTIFICIAL INTELLIGENCE

AI (hereafter AI) refers to programs, algorithms, and machines that can demonstrate intelligence (Shankar, 2018, p. 6). Defining the concept of Artificial Intelligence is not simple, but its genesis dates back to the 1940s, in the middle of the Second World War, when Alan Turing, a pioneer in computer science and artificial intelligence, began to carry out some experiments based on affordance of human intelligence to machines, which would be summarized in the famous "Turing Test" (Turing, 1950) that summarized the following idea: If a machine can talk to a human being without being detected as a machine, then this is an example of human intelligence (French, 2000). However, the term "Artificial Intelligence" was only officially introduced a few years later, in 1955, during the Dartmouth Summer Research Workshop, and in the final phase of that decade AI research focused mainly on programming computers to solve math and logical reasoning problems. It wasn't until the 1980s that there was a paradigm shift when AI research reached a stage of widespread commercialization, became an exponentially growing industry and the focus of research began to focus on the machine learning method (Dung Le Jenny et al., 4: 2023). The concept of Machine Learning is briefly described as

a computer program said to learn from experience E with respect to some class of tasks T and performance measure P, if its performance at tasks in T, as measured by P, improves with experience E (Mitchell, 1997)

We can understand that this sub-field of AI focuses on the development of algorithms and models that allow patterns to be learned so that the computer can make decisions autonomously, without the need to program the machine to carry out specific tasks. From then on, Machine Learning became a rapidly developing field that used different methods to accomplish different tasks (Ma & Sun, 2020) and today we can find sophisticated algorithms on online platforms such as *Amazon* or *Netflix* (Dung Le Jenny et al., 4: 2023). After the turn of the millennium, AI moved to a new level with the concept of Deep Learning, which is basically a subset of machine learning that involves algorithms that can learn networks of deep and direct beliefs, individually, as long as these two upper layers form an indirect associative memory, these networks being called "artificial neural networks" (ANN) or "deep neural networks" (DNN) (Hinton et al., 2006). This subfield of artificial intelligence has developed over the last few decades and there are countless examples of everyday applications that use the basic principles of this concept, such as movie and music streaming platforms when they make recommendations based on the user's history; virtual assistants such as Apple's Siri or Amazon's Alexa; Google Translate, when it uses language models to translate; among many other examples. This new approach has substantially improved the performance of AI to assist in commercial decisions and those related to marketing campaigns (Dung Le Jenny et al., 5: 2023). With this brief contextualization, we come to the present day, at a time when AI is permanently present in our daily lives, although sometimes we don't immediately realize it. Without ignoring the widespread discussion about the potential and dangers of this technology, which has become the order of the day, in this research we will try to understand what its contribution could be to the pre-production phase of a tourist film, based on applications that we use every day or that have been designed specifically for the tasks described, but which have in common the use of AI algorithms.

PRE-PRODUCTION USING ARTIFICIAL INTELLIGENCE

Our case study will focus on a hypothetical possibility rather than a real case, something we intend to do in future research. For this purpose, we will consider the need to produce a tourist film for a specific area in the north-east of Portugal, in the region of Trás-os-Montes, known as the "Terra Fria Transmontana", which covers five of the twelve municipalities in the district of Bragança, specifically: Bragança, Miranda do Douro, Mogadouro, Vimioso and Vinhais. To the north and east, this territory borders the Autonomous Regions of Galicia and Castilla y León, in neighboring Spain, either by the longitudinal dry streak or by the alternating latitudinal courses of the Douro and Maçãs rivers. To the south it borders the municipalities of Mirandela, Macedo de Cavaleiros, Alfândega da Fé, Torre de Moncorco and Freixo de Espada à Cinta. To the west it borders the municipalities of Chaves and Valpaços (Fonseca & Associados, Cunha 2014, 10). For this case study, we will consider that this tourist film was commissioned with the aim of attracting more visitors to this specific territory, namely national and international citizens who are unfamiliar with Terra Fria Transmontana. The film should be no more than 4 minutes long, depict local sites and the territory's added value (gastronomy, handicrafts, etc.) and will be broadcast on the internet, specifically on the YouTube channel of a fictitious territorial organization. To this end, the aim of this research is to put into perspective the use of artificial intelligence tools that could be useful specifically for the pre-production phase of the project. First of all, we would like to point out that several of the tools listed below may be part of our daily lives, such as applications that we use on a daily basis, or others that are more unknown, but always taking availability as a selection criterion - most of the solutions have free access; the user interface - intuitive use; and the use of functionalities that can be considered artificial intelligence.

Research/Treatment

Regardless of the subject matter, the first stage in the production of a tourism film consists of in-depth research into the territory and the elements that might be of interest. Traditionally, this research work is carried out by the director and/or screenwriter themselves, who at this stage are looking for raw material to start devising a script (Cartwright, 1996). Since the creative process is highly dependent on the subjectivity of the author, how can we introduce artificial intelligence tools at this stage that can speed up and optimize the creative process? The following table shows some possibilities:

As we can see in table 1, in the search/processing phase we can use two Google applications, specifically Google Maps (https://www.google.com/maps) and Google Photos (www.google.com/photos), as both use AI to offer a series of resources that can be useful in the research/treatment phase. In the case of the first, the possibility of indicating intelligent routes using algorithms based on Machine Learning makes it possible to identify distances between locations within the region of Trás-os-Montes and to calculate journey times and the best routes, considering variables such as traffic, weather conditions and other information. Satellite images and the possibility of using Google Street View could be useful features for analyzing the relief of the territory, watercourses, vegetation and, from photographs uploaded by users of the platform itself, suggesting possible places of tourist interest and obtaining a visual reference of these places.

Table 1. Software that can be used in the research/treatment phase

Research/Treatment		
Software:	**AI Resources:**	**Results:**
Google Maps[1]	Traffic forecasting; Automatic route calculation; Location suggestions; Photographs and Street View;	Prediction of distances and expected travel times; Indication of places of interest; Visual reference of places;
Google Fotos[2]	Facial recognition; Intelligent photo grouping; Automatic tagging; Visual search based on terms;	Identification of people; Organization of visual content; Automatic cataloguing; Visual identification of relevant places and spaces based on search terms;
Microsoft Azure[3]	Sentiment analysis	Analyzing texts and determining the polarity of feelings
Brandwatch[4]	Social network analysis	Understand the trends and interests of social media users

After this research exercise based mainly on the morphology of the territory, the second tool, Google Photos, has a series of features that can be useful in cataloguing and organizing visual content related to the territory, such as the facial recognition option, intelligent grouping of photos and automatic tagging, which make it possible to quickly identify and organize objects and scenes. In addition, the visual search option based on terms also allows you to search from textual elements, something that can be very useful at this stage of the search. It is expected that at the end of this phase, the following elements will be identified: the most relevant tourist sites, according to the preferences of the platform users, such as cultural events and events that may deserve a mention in the film - a good example of possible results is the Transmontana winter festivals themselves, the caretos and the utensils used (masks, costumes, among others). As mentioned, Google's two tools, combined with the company's search engine, could be important tools for this research and processing phase, as they have AI algorithms to assist the user in various processes. With regard to Microsoft Azure (www.azure.microsoft.com), although it is a tool that requires more advanced computer skills in order to be used, we highlight text-based sentiment analysis as a resource that could be relevant at this stage.

After Amazon, Microsoft is the second-largest cloud provider. It provides both PaaS (Platform as a Service) and IaaS (Infrastructure as a Service). Sentiment analysis is the computational examination of people's beliefs, attitudes, and behaviors about a product, event, or organization (Qaisi, Aljarah, 2016). Using text analysis, it may be possible to identify the polarity of feelings by classifying them as positive, negative or neutral and, as a result, determine details that are relevant to the plot of a tourist movie. Regarding Brandwatch (www.brandwatch.com), we highlight the possibility of it being an AI that allows for the analysis of social networks. Using automated methods that are more economical than manual media analysis, social media analytics collects and analyzes data from social media platforms to assist researchers and decision makers in addressing certain issues (Lee 2018). Along with sentiment analysis, social network analysis can be very relevant to this phase of research/processing in that it allows you to gather data related to the target audience and direct the tourist film accordingly. A hypothetical example would be the perception of the gastronomic and cultural interests of tourists who have already visited Terra Fria Transmontana and, from there, being able to design a new storyline based on the absence or relevance of these interests.

Script

Once the research and processing phase is over, it's time to start writing the script, by the scriptwriter and/or director, with the possibility of contributions from other members of the team. As this is a writing process based mainly on subjectivity, we believe that AI tools can contribute, but obviously they are no substitute for human creativity - as is the case with the other examples in this text. In this sense, we can start by mentioning the possibility of using OpenAI's ChatGPT or GPT-4 (www.openai.com/chatgpt), as an AI-generated language model, which can help with text writing and narrative development, among other possibilities presented in the following table:

Regarding ChatGPT, a conversational model developed by the OpenAI company, it could be useful in writing the script because it can generate text in a coherent way and from a wealth of information available online. This feature allows ChatGPT to generate text in a creative way, which means it can be used as an interesting tool to find inspiration for the script of a tourist movie, to develop characters and to explore narrative options.

Table 2. Software that can be used to write the script

Script		
Software:	**AI Resources:**	**Results:**
ChatGPT[5]	Text generation; Natural Language Processing (NLP); Question answering; Adapting to writing style and tone; Grammar correction;	Experiences using text writing; Checking natural language; General information; Adapting the text to the objectives; Proofreading texts;
Google Cloud Speech-to-Text[6]	Audio to text transcription;	Transcribing interviews and other audio sources;
ScriptBook[7]	Script analysis	Script revision and optimization
IBM Watson Tone Analyzer[8]	Detect emotional and language tones in written text	Script revision and optimization
Turnitin[9]	Detecting plagiarism	Ensure the originality of the script
Celtx[10]	Formatting; Data analysis;	Script writing and formatting; Script overview;

The Google Cloud Speech-to-Text application (www.cloud.google.com/speech-to-text) can be interesting when there are sound recordings that need to be transcribed. An example is the transcription of interviews with local inhabitants about the potential of Terra Fria Transmontana, which must then be converted into text to be analyzed and worked on properly.

ScriptBook (www.scriptbook.io) is an application that has been developed specifically for analyzing scripts and has been used in the film industry. From this application and after uploading the script, it is possible to obtain the following information: examines the characters to identify the protagonists and antagonists and evaluates each character's emotional state; predicts the target demographic considering factors like gender and color; among other important information.

The IBM Watson Tone Analyzer (https://cloud.ibm.com) can be an important tool for detecting emotional and linguistic tones in written texts and is an important aid for analyzing the text at an intermediate stage and for perfecting dialogues. Turnitin (www.turnitin.pt), being a plagiarism detection tool, could be interesting for validating the script's originality, despite the limitations related to the fact that there are few scripts published on the internet, which can make this analysis difficult.

Celtx (www.celtx.com) is software developed specifically for scriptwriting and allows you to format a script quickly and automatically obtain a range of information that may be relevant to the pre-production of a tourist movie.

Script Breakdown/Découpage

To carry out the Script Breakdown, Studiobinder (www.studiobinder.com) automatically divides the script, identifying scenes, characters, locations, costumes and other relevant information. Based on this systematization, the software allows you to create various production documents in an automated way, which is extremely useful at this stage.

Table 3. Software that can be used for the script Breakdown/Découpage

Script breakdown/Découpage		
Software:	**AI Resources:**	**Results:**
StudioBinder[11]	Script Breakdown; Automatic document generation;	Automatic script division; Automated generation of production documents;
ShotPro[12]	Creation of 2D and 3D models based on Script;	Planning sequences and camera movements; Adding characters and objects; Creating scene diagrams;
Unreal Engine[13]	Simulate lighting and climate conditions in 3D scenarios	Simulate production scenarios/options

Shotpro (www.shotprofessional.com) was developed specifically for the film industry, just like Script Breakdown, and allows 2D and 3D models to be created from the script, making it very useful for visualizing shots virtually and testing directing options.

Unreal Engine (www.unrealengine.com) is a collaborative 3D software that allows you to take 3D scenarios and simulate lighting and weather conditions, something useful for thinking about the photography of the tourist movie and, as mentioned, for the directing department to be able to make their creative choices.

We can consider Studio Binder to be extremely useful for the Script Breakdown process and the other two pieces of software, ShotPro and Unreal Engine, to be useful for testing visual solutions in a way that is very close to what we might find. If we imagine a shot that must be filmed in a dimly lit location, of a group of characters tasting traditional dishes from Trás-os-Montes, this software can be useful for understanding the needs of audiovisual production equipment, and specifically lighting, and thus anticipating specific expenses and needs.

Storyboard

The Storyboard That application (www.storyboardthat.com) allows storyboards to be created quickly and intuitively from visual elements previously uploaded to the platform, such as scenarios, characters, items and more. This type of option allows you to speed up this phase considerably and create interactive storyboards that can be changed at any time, helping you to visualize your plans consistently.

In cases where it is advantageous to have a more detailed storyboard, Storyboard Pro (www.toonboom.com/products/storyboard-pro) is an advanced storyboard creation tool that combines drawing with animation, generating impactful visual results. There are currently several tools developed in the context of the storytelling industry and the film industry itself that can be useful for creating and optimizing dynamic and visually appealing storyboards. These two solutions could be used, together or separately, to generate the storyboard for the entire audiovisual project.

Table 4. Software that can be used to create a storyboard

Storyboard		
Software:	**AI Resources:**	**Results:**
Storyboard That[14]	Creating interactive storyboards from models	Create storyboards intuitively and quickly
Storyboard Pro[15]	Creating animated storyboards	Creating dynamic and visually appealing storyboards

Table 5. Software that can be used for budget development

Budget Development		
Software:	**AI Resources:**	**Results:**
Movie Magic Budgeting[16]	Automated calculations; Creation of reports;	Calculation of financial requirements; Production documents;

Budget Development

Movie Magic Budgeting (www.ep.com/movie-magic-budgeting) is an application developed specifically for the film industry that allows you to generate detailed budgets divided into categories such as: technical crew, cast, equipment, post-production, among others. With an intuitive interface, the software allows you to create detailed budgets and enter financial data that is relevant to optimizing the budget. Unlike other solutions that are more complex to program, this software allows you to evaluate incentives, compare budgets from different locations and perform complex cost analyses. For these reasons, we believe it is a very important piece of software to consider during the Budget Development phase, since it allows you to take into account the specificities of the territory (cost of accommodation, meals, etc.) and generate production documents based on these specificities.

Casting/Hiring the Team

As for Imotion's Facial Expression Analysis software (www.imotions.com), as the name suggests it uses AI algorithms to analyze facial expressions. This option can be useful for analyzing the performance of actors during auditions - if the recording of images is authorized. By analyzing facial expressions in real time, valuable inputs can be generated for evaluating candidates.

Textio (www.textio.com), as AI software developed for the human resources area with a series of features optimized for this type of work, uses AI to analyse

Table 6. Software that can be used for casting/hiring the technical team

Casting/Hiring the team		
Software:	**AI Resources:**	**Results:**
Imotions – Facial Expression Analysis[17]	Real-time analysis of facial expressions	Evaluation of the actors' performance during auditions
Textio[18]	Analysis of job advertisements; Adaptation for specific audiences;	Optimization of advertisements; Optimized ranking of candidates;

and suggest improvements to vacancy advertisements for a particular role - squad or technical team - and additionally offers useful features such as adapting advertisements for specific audiences in order to guarantee the greatest possible efficiency in the process of hiring a team. These two possibilities could be useful for casting actors for the tourist film and for hiring the technical team. As filming is expected to take place in the territory of Terra Fria Transmontana, and as it is a sparsely populated region, we believe that both solutions could be useful for this pre-production phase.

To conclude this list of options, we could also mention others that could be used in the scheduling or project management phase. However, due to the number of options available and the fact that these are applications that can be used in countless situations and only in this context of pre-production of an audiovisual project, we have limited our search to the results mentioned above.

CONCLUSION

From this research it was possible to see that there is a lot of accessible software that uses AI and that could be used in the pre-production of a tourist film or any other type of promotional film or cinematographic work, insofar as none of the solutions presented are limited to the context portrayed in this research. Our aim was to gather some evidence to support the usefulness of AI algorithms and respective software for the pre-production phase of a film about the territory of Terra Fria Transmontana and we can draw some conclusions. Firstly, most of the software presented is free and has a simple user interface, with a few exceptions such as Microsoft Azure, BranWatch, IBM Watson Tone Analyzer, Unreal Engine and Storyboard Pro. The fact that these softwares are more complex for the user and involve other types of computer skills doesn't mean that they shouldn't be considered, but rather that their use should be carefully considered according to the intended objectives. The premise of using AI for the pre-production of a tourist film has the implicit advantage of making the process faster and simpler, and this condition should always be considered when selecting working tools. However, we believe that the software received could be useful above all in the production logic of an audiovisual production company that could waste time acquiring the skills to use the software in question, but it would be less interesting for a small production company where this type of advantage does not benefit from a scale of production that justifies the investment of time and money. With a few exceptions, the rest of the software is very intuitive and, in many cases, is already used in most people's daily lives - as is the case with Google Maps, to name but one example. With short adaptation times, we recognize that using this software can be very beneficial for many tasks, such as creating a script or storyboard. The territory of Terra Fria Transmontana is very particular in terms of its architectural and historical heritage and, as such, software for mapping the territory and providing visual aids could also be very useful for planning a tourist film about the territory. The main obstacle in this case is the fact that this is a low-density area that may have less online content than other areas where there is mass tourism, which naturally generates more results on social networks and online search engines. While further research is needed into the potential of software in a real production context, we believe that these tools can make a very valuable contribution to the pre-production of a tourism film, as they facilitate and optimize the process and, in addition, ensure that the final objective can have more visibility and impact with consumers. If AI tools are used in a way that complements the work carried out by the production team, we believe that originality and ethical commitment will not be compromised, generating added value in production that can boost results.

REFERENCES

Alves, P. (2017). "If you fail to prepare, prepare to fail": a produção fílmica. In P. Alves, F. García (Eds.), Oficios del cine: manual para prácticas cinematográficas. ICONO14/CITCEM.

Alves, P., & García, F. (2017). Oficios del cine: manual para prácticas cinematográficas. ICONO14/CITCEM.

Cartwright, S. R. (1996). *Pre-production planning for video, film, and multimedia*. Focal Press. doi:10.1016/B978-0-240-80271-8.50010-9

Connell, J. (2012). Film tourism: evolution, progress and prospects. *Tourism Management*, *33*(5), 1007-1029. Elsevier.

Doborjeh, Z., Hemmington, N., Doborjeh, M., & Kasabov, N. (2022). Artificial intelligence: A systematic review of methods and applications in hospitality and tourism. *International Journal of Contemporary Hospitality Management*, *34*(3), 1154–1176. doi:10.1108/IJCHM-06-2021-0767

Fonseca & Associados. (2014). *Matos, Cunha, Rui*. Guia Terra Fria Transmontana. Associação de Municípios da Terra Fria do Nordeste Transmontano.

French, R. M. (2000). The Turing Test: The first 50 years. *Trends in Cognitive Sciences*, *4*(3), 115–122. doi:10.1016/S1364-6613(00)01453-4 PMID:10689346

Gates, R. (1999). *Production Management for Film and Video*. Routledge. doi:10.4324/9780080515007

Grundner, L., & Neuhofer, B. (2020). The Bright and Dark Sides of Artificial Intelligence: A Futures Perspective on Tourist Destination Experiences. *Journal of Destination Marketing & Management*, *19*, 100511. doi:10.1016/j.jdmm.2020.100511

Hinton, G. E., Osindero, S., & Teh, Y. W. (2006). A fast learning algorithm for deep belief nets. *Neural Computation*, *18*(7), 1527–1554. doi:10.1162/neco.2006.18.7.1527 PMID:16764513

Inglis, F. (2000). *The Delicious History of the Holiday*. Routledge.

Jenny, D. L., Kyunghwa, C., Quach, S., & Thaichon, P. (2023). Introduction to artificial intelligence (AI): Definition and scope of AI. In P. Thaichon & S. Quach (Eds.), *Artificial Intelligence for Marketing Management* (pp. 3–51). Routledge.

Lee, I. (2018). Social media analytics for enterprises: Typology, methods, and processes. *Business Horizons*, *61*(2), 199–210. doi:10.1016/j.bushor.2017.11.002

Lopes, S. (2014). *Manual prático de produção*. Chiado Editora.

Ma, L., & Sun, B. (2020). Machine learning and AI in marketing – Connecting computing power to human insights. *International Journal of Research in Marketing*, *37*(3), 481–504. doi:10.1016/j.ijresmar.2020.04.005

Marinho, M., Correia, R., & Morais, E. P. (2021). Understanding the role of local tourist actors as online destination promoters: the "Terras de Trás-os-Montes" case. *Journal of Marketing Research and Case Studies*.

Merrit, G. (1998). *Film production: the complete uncensored guide to independent filmmaking*. Lone Eagle Publishing.

Mitchell, T. M. (1997). *Machine Learning*. McGraw-Hill.

Pan, S., Tsai, H., & Lee, J. (2011). *Framing New Zealand: Understanding tourism TV commercials. Tourism Management*. Taylor & Francis.

Qaisi, L. M., & Aljarah, I. (2016). A twitter sentiment analysis for cloud providers: A case study of Azure vs. *AWS. Proceedings of the 7th International Conference on Computer Science and Information Technology (CSIT)*, Amman, Jordan. 10.1109/CSIT.2016.7549473

Shankar, V. (2018). How artificial intelligence (AI) is reshaping retailing. *Journal of Retailing*, *94*(4), vi–xi. doi:10.1016/S0022-4359(18)30076-9

Simon, D., & Wiese, M. (2001). *Film & video budgets*. Michael Wiese Productions.

Sousa, B., & Rocha, A. (2019). The role of attachment in public management and place marketing contexts: A case study applied to Vila de Montalegre (Portugal). *International Journal of Public Sector Performance Management*, *5*(2), 189–205. doi:10.1504/IJPSPM.2019.099094

Thaichon, P., & Quach, S. (2022). *Artificial Intelligence for Marketing Management*. Routledge. doi:10.4324/9781003280392

Turing, A. M. (1950). Computing machinery and intelligence. *Mind*, *59*(236), 433–460. doi:10.1093/mind/LIX.236.433

Urry, J. (2002). *The Tourist Gaze*. SAGE Publications Ltd.

ENDNOTES

1 Information gathered from the official Google Maps website, 2024 (https://blog.google/products/maps/)

2 Information gathered from the official Google Photos website, 2024 (https://www.google.com/intl/pt-PT/photos/about/)

3 Information gathered from the official Microsoft Azure website, 2024 (https://azure.microsoft.com/pt-pt/products/ai-services/ai-language#features)

4 Information gathered from the official Brandwatch website, 2024 (https://www.brandwatch.com/)

5 Information gathered from the official Open AI website, 2024 (https://openai.com/blog/chatgpt)

6 Information gathered from the official Google Cloud website, 2024 (https://cloud.google.com/speech-to-text)

7 Information gathered from the official ScriptBook website, 2024 (https://www.scriptbook.io/#!/scriptbook)

8 Information gathered from the official IBM Cloud website, 2024 (https://cloud.ibm.com/docs/openwhisk?topic=openwhisk-pkg_tone_analyzer)

9 Information gathered from the official Turnitin website, 2024 (https://www.turnitin.pt/)

10 Information gathered from the official Celtx website, 2024 (https://www.celtx.com/company/about/)

11 Information gathered from the official Studio Binder website, 2024 (https://www.studiobinder.com/)

12 Information gathered from the official Shot Professional website, 2024 (https://www.shotprofessional.com/)

13 Information gathered from the official Unreal Engine website, 2024 (https://www.unrealengine.com/pt-BR)

14 Information gathered from the official Storyboard That website, 2024 (https://www.storyboardthat.com/pt/artigos/educa%c3%a7%c3%a3o/recursos-para-professores)

15 Information gathered from the official Storyboard Pro website, 2024 (https://www.toonboom.com/products/storyboard-pro)

16 Information gathered from the official Movie Magic Budgeting website, 2024 (https://www.ep.com/movie-magic-budgeting/)

17 Information gathered from the official Imotions website, 2024 (https://imotions.com/products/imotions-lab)

18 Information gathered from the official Textio website, 2024 (https://textio.com/)

Chapter 4
Impact of AI on the Flower of Service Model in the Hospitality Industry

Nurhafihz Noor
https://orcid.org/0000-0001-8502-5722
James Cook University, Singapore

Karen Sim
James Cook University, Singapore

ABSTRACT

With increasing opportunities for the hospitality industry to interact with customers using artificial intelligence (AI), hospitality managers need to decide on the services that are most suited to integrate AI. This requires an understanding of how AI affects different service activities. To address this, this study discusses the impact of AI on various service components using the Flower of Service Model. This chapter contributes to the study of AI innovation in services marketing by showing the relevance of seminal services marketing frameworks in the emerging AI landscape and providing strategic insights for hospitality managers to effectively implement AI in hospitality services.

INTRODUCTION

Artificial Intelligence (AI) devices such as chatbots and robots are becoming a common sight in the business landscape (Pelau et al., 2021), affecting how service firms interact with consumers for the provision of service (Schulze, 2019). This

DOI: 10.4018/979-8-3693-2137-9.ch004

development is especially prevalent in the lucrative hospitality sector (Tussyadiah, 2020), with an expectation that the global hospitality AI market will grow at a Compound Annual Growth Rate (CAGR) of 10% from 2021 to 2026 (GME, 2023).

Emerging research has responded to this phenomenon by illuminating the impact of AI on various aspects of services such as consumer acceptance (Ladeira et al., 2023) and engagement (Fang et al., 2023). Other studies have also looked at the changes AI will bring to service in terms of their capabilities ranging from mechanical, thinking and feeling intelligences (Huang & Rust, 2020). While these studies advance our understanding of the impact of AI in these different service perspectives, greater clarity is required on how AI affects the different components of services. This holistic understanding is useful for crafting appropriate strategies across services. To address this gap in the literature, the objective of this chapter is to update and discuss one such foundational services model in the age of AI: the Flower of Service Model by Christopher Lovelock (Lovelock, 1995).

FLOWER OF SERVICE

According to the Flower of Service Model (Lovelock, 1995; Wirtz & Lovelock, 2022), services consist of two common components: a core service which delivers the fundamental benefit to consumers and eight supplementary services or petals which support the core service and can help differentiate and add value to the overall service experienced by the customer. Supplementary services such as information exchange, order-taking, billing and payment processing are required to facilitate the core service, whereas other supplementary services such as consultation, hospitality, safekeeping and exceptions (for example, special requests) enhance the core service. For instance, while hotels in general provide the core service of providing accommodation to guests facilitated through convenient booking and payment methods, the hotel experience can be enhanced with guest personalization through consultation which the hotel focuses on due to its positioning strategy. Additional value for the guest can be unlocked if the hotel operator collaborates with a third-party shuttle bus service to offer an enhanced supplementary service of providing convenient transport for guests to nearby attractions.

Since its introduction, the decoupling lens provided by Flower of Service has been useful in systematically considering the components that constitute any service. The role of technology, particularly in supplementary services which are more information-dependent to the role of virtual teams, has also been acknowledged since the model's conceptualization (Lovelock, 1995). Accordingly, the changing service environment and the prevalence of digital technologies in service have resulted in scholars revisiting the relevance of foundational service models in marketing thought including the Flower of Service (Ahmad et al., 2022; Bitner et al., 2010).

This chapter continues this research tradition by explaining how key AI technologies have impacted the core service and the eight petals in the Flower of Service Model. Before this discussion, it is useful to provide an overview of the state of AI and services in Hospitality.

AI AND SERVICES IN HOSPITALITY

The global hospitality industry is undoubtedly one of the world's largest and fastest-growing industries. Worldwide, it brings in USD 7.6 billion and creates 292 million jobs, and these contribute to nearly 10% of the global gross domestic product (GDP) (World Travel & Tourism Council, 2017; Statista Research Department, 2018; OECD, 2018). According to Ruel and Njoku (2021), the success of the hospitality industry is attributed to the service quality and customer satisfaction delivered by the hospitality businesses.

However, hospitality continues to face an exceedingly competitive environment industry (Zhao & Kerdpitak, 2023), saturated with customers who expect superior service, demand for speed and quick turnaround time for service requests and challenges of rising costs (Limna, 2023). The survival of these businesses is frequently determined by their overall financial performance, ability to adapt to changing environments and how they transform and expand their services to meet the demanding needs and expectations of their hotel guests (Van Niekerk, 2016; Wikhamn, 2019).

To stay afloat with the competition and to continue its businesses in this fast-moving industry, the hospitality industry has shown a keen interest in cutting-edge AI technologies such as robots, facial recognition, and chatbots to provide excellent customer service and improve their stay experience in their hotel (Goel et al., 2022). AI adds intelligence to the hospitality industry through AI-enabled hotel operations and management systems, thus redefining the hospitality sector into a technologically intelligent industry (Lai and Hung, 2018). For example, chatbots are now increasingly used for travel planning, customer booking, customer support and providing recommendations and suggestions to the customer regarding travel issues. These chatbots provide 24/7 customer support, more revenue opportunities, automatic lead capturing, reduced costs, competitive advantage and time-saving (Bowen and Morosan, 2018). Consequentially, a survey done by Aspect Research Software shows that 44% of consumers are excited to use AI-based chatbots over human customer care executives (Sweezey, 2018).

Indeed, within the hospitality industry, there continues to be a rising adoption of service robots (Liu et al., 2023; Yu et al., 2023). Because of their advantages in labour cost reduction and service efficiency improvement (Ruiz-Alba and Martin-Pena, 2020; Zhou et al., 2020), intelligent technologies have been infused into various hospitality services. Overall, the impact of these underlying technologies such as the Internet of Things (IoT), virtual reality (VR), augmented reality (AR) and service robots cannot be ignored in the hospitality industry (Chi et al., 2020; Ivanov and Webster, 2019).

IMPACT OF AI ON THE FLOWER OF SERVICE IN HOSPITALITY

While traditionally the delivery of the core and supplementary services was done by different service departments and employees, increasingly these services are now performed by AI. Figure 1 represents a summary of how AI would impact the Flower of Service. The arrangement of the supplementary services in Figure 1 follows the order from the original model (Lovelock, 1995; Wirtz & Lovelock, 2022).

In the following sections, we will elaborate on how AI has affected the core service before proceeding to further discuss its effects on facilitating supplementary services and thereafter enhancing supplementary services in the Flower of Service.

Impact of AI on Core Services

On the surface, it seems ironic that the hospitality industry, being people-caring centric, is adopting AI which is often thought of as short-changing hotel guests from the advantages associated with the human touch (Jarrahi, 2018). However, the use of technology and AI has the potential to transform the hospitality industry beyond its traditional core service of providing accommodation.

One central way in which AI can impact the core service of hospitality is by truly redefining the hospitality industry as a sector in which its value propositions are designed around the guest to improve their well-being. In line with the transformative service research agenda (Anderson & Ostrom, 2015), hospitality brands can now reposition themselves with a focus on well-being by using AI to access customers and provide new personalized solutions. This extends beyond health tracking and monitoring capabilities. For instance, in one innovation which will be further discussed in the hospitality subsection, guests may no longer need to worry about hotel locations and can experience their hotel accommodation with greater flexibility by using mobile hotel complexes (Lazarus, 2018). The ability of hotels to offer excellent tour-guiding services with novel recommendations beyond traditional human guides will also be explored in this chapter.

Figure 1. Impact of AI technologies on the Flower of Service

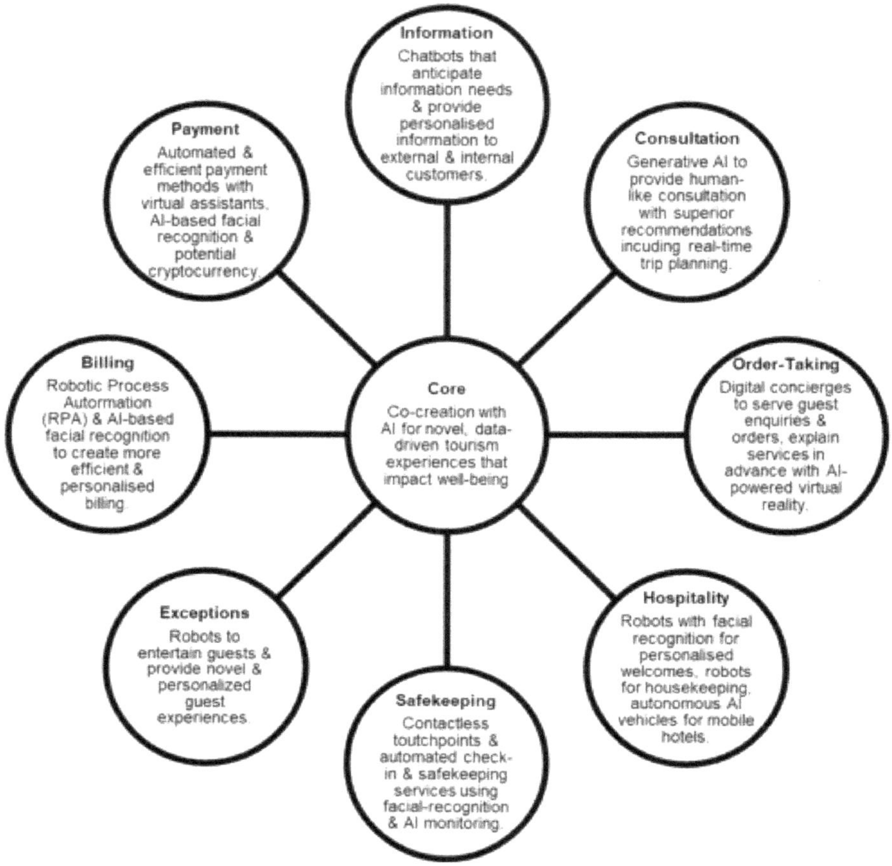

The above transformations of the traditional core functions of the hospitality industry can be realized by enabling the customer to play a deeper role in the co-creation of the hospitality service value (Daniela et. al., 2022). Using a service-dominant-logic (Vargo & Lusch, 2016), the combination of customer data and new AI capabilities can unravel new customer benefits based on the various hospitality contexts in which the customer will use AI.

There need not be a trade-off in customer well-being due to the lack of human touch (Noor et al., 2022a). Ultimately, the industry will continue to evolve; there will be greater collaboration between human service staff and AI based on an understanding of the unique benefits they can bring to the service experience (Noble et al., 2022).

Impact of AI on Information

To obtain the full value from the service, customers need relevant information especially if they are first-time users (Wirtz & Lovelock, 2022). This information includes how to get to the place, the opening hours, prices of products and services, usage instructions, ticket confirmation, reservation status and information on receipts and invoices. Indeed, the information-intensive nature of the hospitality industry requires regular communication between hotels and customers (Ukpabi, D. et al., 2019). There is a high expectation for the human service employee to be knowledgeable.

To continue to deliver reliable information to guests sustainably, hotels have begun to use chatbots. Chatbots can quickly identify languages used by website visitors based on their location. They can also manage simultaneous guest inquiries from all over the world (Cvent, 2020). Guests may even view chatbots as travel assistants rather than obstacles between them and a live representative.

An example of a hotel which uses chatbots is Marina Bay Sands in Singapore. The use of AiChat (2023) allows the hotel to increase the efficacy of its engagement on Facebook Messenger in addressing users' queries, driving awareness of its shopping and dining offers, responding to general requests and providing recommendations. This need is particularly widespread during the festive and peak seasons when there is scarce manpower. As a result, the chatbot leverages a mix of rich media to offer an immersive experience in chats. AI is also designed to anticipate further questions by offering information relevant to the customers' queries. For instance, while hotel rooms in the past were based on historical data and current reservations, the use of AI enables hotels to factor in additional information that may affect demand such as local event schedules, global news events and consumer sentiments from hotel reviews (Klint, 2020) to give the best hotel yield.

Beyond providing guests with useful information, AI can help generate valuable insights for hospitality management. For instance, AI can be used for monitoring capabilities to help hotels save the environment and improve their revenue through suitable energy, water and waste management recommendations. One example of a hotel playing its role in environmental sustainability with the reduction of carbon emissions facilitated by AI is the Hilton (Cvent, 2020). Other hotels such as the luxury hotel brand Dorchester Collections use AI to provide information that enables service managers to personalise guest experiences from reservations to improved breakfast menus (Cvent, 2020). Finally, hotels such as IHG Europe use information derived by AI on the personality profiles of existing team members to improve recruitment by recommending suitable positions based on employee profiles (Cvent, 2020).

Overall, AI will improve information management in hotels and allow hotel managers to add more information value to both frontend as well as backend service operations.

Impact of AI on Order-Taking

Order-taking involves onsite or online order entries, making reservations and completing applications in programs offered by the service provider (Wirtz & Lovelock, 2022). Developments in AI and its usage by service industries impacted customer demand and behaviours including how they make orders and bookings with hospitality services (Wu et al., 2017; Filieri et al., 2021). With more than 80% of travel today being booked online, the booking process is going to be one of the best use cases of AI in hospitality today (MacKenzie, n.d.).

During the pandemic, restaurants had to cut down labour costs while pivoting to customer ordering experiences using AI systems (Luna, 2023). As for hotels, digital concierges emerged which allowed chatbots to answer guest inquiries, make bookings and take room service orders (CNBC, 2020). Chatbots can support customers with their bookings and answer questions about availability, pricing and amenities. They are also capable of providing suggestions based on customer favourites such as room type and location. Furthermore, chatbots in touch screen check-ins can simplify the upselling and cross-selling processes of giving the guest options to order breakfast, upgrade to a deluxe room or scan a quick-response code to order food, potentially leading to more orders as compared to service by a traditional human employee (JLL, 2023).

The use of AI in order-taking has truly flourished in hotels. AI-driven virtual assistants can now help travellers make reservations conversationally, assisting with personal requests beyond the standard reservation, for example, booking adjoining rooms, reserving restaurant slots, checking in and other arrangements that often require human intervention (Fisher Philips, 2023). AI-powered augmented virtual reality can also enhance the customer experience, helping customers visualise the event or experience before booking it. Repetitive booking and check-in processes can also be automated by AI (Hollander, 2023), freeing up staff to focus on providing personalised service to guests.

Some examples of hotels implementing AI booking systems include the Yotel group of hotels which offers a "pocket-size virtual concierge" app which guests can use for bookings, order food-to-go and even request amenities (Futr, 2020). The Cosmopolitan Las Vegas deploys Rose, a chatbot that guests can use 24/7 to book various amenities as well as concert and tour tickets (MGM, 2023). Finally, at Caesars Entertainment Las Vegas, guests are treated to the AI-enabled system Ivy which can help with order-taking of services required (Caesars, 2018) while

Softbank Robotics' Pepper can facilitate order-taking similar to a human being (Tuomi et al., 2021).

AI in order-taking saves hotel staff time and resources as the chatbots can undertake many enquiries concurrently without the need for human intervention. As a result, staff can focus on more strategic activities such as building relationships with their customers.

Impact of AI on Billing

Billing involves informing the customer of the amount that is due for the service including methods of billing and improving the billing process (Wirtz & Lovelock, 2022). For instance, a traveller planning their trip via an online travel agency may be able to view the total amount on the website or mobile app. A billing statement could also be sent to the customer's email reminding them of the payments due.

With digital technologies, billing has become more automated with guests undergoing the billing process without much human intervention. For instance, the traveller who is considering a bigger room at the hotel can instantaneously view the price difference which is displayed on screen during the selection process. Accordingly, due to the transparent nature of online pricing and the ability of customers to easily compare prices, hotels are also under pressure to design promotions such as early-bird discounts and group packages to communicate more value-added services to guests. Customers thus have greater control and clarity of the billing process.

One of the immediate ways AI has impacted billing is in its ability to automate the process using robotic process automation (RPA) processes. With RPA, services have a relatively cost-effective and easy way to extract information from multiple document types and formats to prepare and follow up on billing (Davenport & Ronanki, 2018). With AI, processes in managing the accounts payable can be more automated and result in cost efficiencies (Yaramada, 2021). In terms of the amount to be billed for customers in hotels and restaurants, AI-based facial recognition can also be used to trigger an automatic discount based on facial expressions and probability of satisfaction (Gupta et al., 2023). The amount to be billed can be displayed on the digital screen of the robot with an automated email sent to the customer.

While the discussion on billing seems to mimic its brief and seemingly simple steps in the service process, the contribution of AI to this vital service petal should not be discounted. The billing process is the moment in which the customer accesses if the amount to be paid is justified based on the expected service rendered. The efficiency, accuracy and automation advantages brought about by AI in billing will significantly reduce manual errors and delays and is a welcomed change for the hospitality manager and all service staff involved in the billing process.

Impact of AI on Payment

The payments cluster in the Flower of Service involves matters associated with payment methods, parties as well and issues surrounding security and control (Wirtz & Lovelock, 2022). With payments being one of the services in which information processing is key, technology plays a key role in better facilitating this service petal (Lovelock, 1995).

Digital technologies have certainly unleashed the age of self-service payments, with customers being able to make payments conveniently using their credit cards via the service firm's website, intermediaries such as online travel agency websites or even at the firm's premise via self-service technologies such as kiosks. Payments can also be facilitated using mobile applications such as e-wallets which are already integrated with the customer's existing payment sources. Often, the payment process is smooth and automated. For instance, if guests in the hotel were to consume additional services during their stay, these would be charged to the credit card automatically without additional steps required during the check-out process. Accordingly, one of the immediate benefits of AI is its ability to further automate these routine payment activities (Huang & Rust, 2021). As the mechanical and automation capabilities of AI are established, this makes the utilization of AI such as service robots on payment facilitation – a relatively standardized task – manageable and appropriate (Meyer-Waarden et al., 2020). Hotel guests will find robots particularly useful and easy to use when performing such routine tasks (Alma Çallı et al., 2023).

The AI revolution has also brought about new ways of making payments. With AI, customers can make payments conveniently by interacting with the virtual assistants on their smartphones and smartwatches which are more accessible as opposed to dedicated payment terminals (Shankar, 2018). Perhaps a more exciting development is facial recognition; with AI-based facial recognition technology being capable of detecting the unique geometries of faces, payment can also be more seamless, allowing customers to check out without needing to interact with staff (Gupta et al., 2023). However, this requires that service providers take the time to explain to customers how their personal information is being captured and used by the payment facility to mitigate privacy concerns (Cheng et al., 2022). Indeed, despite the security advantages such as fraud detection that AI offers to the service provider (Wahid & Hassini, 2024), often customers are more cautious when it comes to technologies and have different degrees of acceptance and resistance (Parasuraman & Colby, 2015). Thus, the need to educate customers remains an inherent feature in services even in the age of AI technologies, and customers need to understand the value that AI can bring in terms of faster and more secure payments (Grewal et al., 2021).

The discussion of AI and payments will be incomplete without a mention of blockchain and its application in the field of cryptocurrencies such as Bitcoin. While it is beyond the scope of this chapter to discuss how blockchain and cryptocurrencies work in detail, the allowance of cryptocurrencies by regulators will usher in a truly unified and seamless cashless system that will benefit international travellers (Önder & Gunter, 2022). AI can help to accelerate this realization of a more fluid payment currency as AI can assist the development of cryptocurrency in various aspects including data processing, analysing, making price predictions and improving the underlying blockchain infrastructure supporting cryptocurrencies (Choithani et al., 2022).

Overall, the use of AI in payment will lead to a further reduction in manpower for the facilitation of payment processes and result in more efficient cost-effective service excellence (Wirtz & Zeithaml, 2018). However, to truly reap these benefits and enable customers to use AI for payments, systems need to be integrated and secured, and customers must be educated on the high-level security advantages associated with using AI for payment (Kasilingam, 2020).

Impact of AI on Consultation

Consultations involve dialogues between the customer and the service provider to better understand the customer's needs and can result in a direct suggestion from the service provider or solutions from the customers themselves through subtle counselling with the service provider (Wirtz & Lovelock, 2022). In hotels, traditionally consultations would be done with staff the customer encounters at the service touchpoint. This includes the hotel receptionist, concierge, room service staff and even the restaurant personnel. Such consultations may be done before, during or after the service delivery, depending on the matter that is being enquired. For instance, guests may make early enquiries as to whether certain hotel and room amenities could be catered to their needs. Upon arriving and looking at the restaurant menus, guests may ask if certain meals could be customized due to their dietary preferences. They may also ask if transportation could be catered to them to visit nearby attractions more conveniently. A more complex request may come in the form of asking the hotel to suggest a suitable itinerary. After the service is rendered, guests could give feedback which may result in better personalization in the future.

With traditional self-service technologies not powered by AI, guests could make such enquiries with a non-human service provider. However, in such instances, there is no true dialogue and personalization, as the interaction is rigid and responses are fairly limited (Wirtz et al., 2018). For instance, self-service check-in kiosks in hotels may allow guests to indicate room preferences based on the preloaded script and options programmed in the kiosk. However, these kiosks may struggle when it comes to offering more complex personalization such as taking into account guest preferences due to cultural influences (Noor, 2022) which requires more uncovering through dialogue. Indeed, while traditional self-service technologies may be more readily available to customers as opposed to their human counterparts, these technologies are not capable of activities which require complex thinking and feeling intelligence such as service interactions in consultation (Huang & Rust, 2020).

Advancements in AI have removed this technological limitation significantly. Today, guests can have a full conversation with an AI agent and similarly receive their solution as if they had consulted with a human service staff. Emerging research also suggests that guests find hotel robots useful for tasks which are interactional, social and relational (Alma Çallı et al., 2023). One key development enhancing customer consultations is Generative AI, specifically ChatGPT. The ability of ChatGPT to search and combine different data sources before interacting with guests via text and voice in multiple languages opens up a variety of possibilities including AI concierge services for hotel queries and AI travel guides for booking and reservations during their trip (Dwivedi et al., 2023). These interactions could also be analysed to improve the customer service rendered by the AI. One of the intriguing aspects of this is that ChatGPT – with its ability to access and analyse volumes of data including information from the internet – is mimicking what the human service provider would have done when approached with a question from a guest. The advantages of using ChatGPT over human service staff are that the AI can access and scan more information, is more responsive and could even offer more novel solutions to customers (Dwivedi et al., 2023). For instance, the AI could instantly plan a trip itinerary by recommending the best times to visit a particular attraction based on real-time data and forecasts of crowd, traffic and weather conditions.

Some of the ChatGPT software that is being proposed to hotels to improve consultation services such as guest communications and analysis include DuveAI for direct interaction between guests and hoteliers and Easyway Genie which will assist human hotel receptionists in providing more personalized solutions (Hollander, 2023). Others such as AiChat (2023) allow for more personalised targeting of customers. For hotel and hospitality managers in general, this results in a more empowered service staff who are capable of more meaningful consultations with guests. With AI, guests can experience human-like consultation that is more available and efficient, resulting in improved service quality and greater customer satisfaction and loyalty (Noor et al., 2022b).

Impact of AI on Hospitality

Hospitality involves caring for new and returning customers and is associated with activities which include greeting, food and beverages, waiting facilities and transport (Wirtz & Lovelock, 2022). The traditional approach of attending to the guests from the hotel front desk and answering their calls physically is slowly disappearing. The days of businesses training staff to authenticate documents of guests during the check-in process and answer their queries are also declining due to the inability to serve with consistent hospitality when guest traffic surges (HospitalityNet, 2022). The constraint of attending to one person at a time limits hotel businesses from achieving efficiency, thus decreasing hospitality and service to hotel guests.

As hotels look for ways to boost their operations and deliver an exclusive guest experience, more and more are turning to robots. One of the most common types of robot hotels use today is those for welcoming guests (Low, 2023). These robots are usually situated in the lobby and can provide hospitality service by greeting guests and having conversations with them. Some are even equipped with facial recognition capabilities that allow them to recognise guests and make them feel warm.

In addition, another area where robots are deployed to provide hospitality service is in housekeeping where the robots are used to clean, organise and maintain hotel rooms. Major hotel chains have deployed housekeeping robots to clean lobbies, corridors and other public spaces. According to Merle Ayers, Director of Banquet at Garden City Hotel on Long Island, amid ongoing staffing shortages, the two robots that the hotel adopted are proving their work many times over by filling in manpower gaps in various departments (Hsu, 2022).

Robots are not merely providing hospitality by greeting guests and making beds; they are transforming the concept of mobile hospitality. With improved agility from shared autonomous AI vehicles, hotel locations will become less important than it is today (Bainbridge, 2022). This is because hotels can use autonomous vehicles to extend the brand experience into the city. One example of this mobility innovation is the self-driving hotel room, also known as the Autonomous Travel Suite (ATS) (Lazarus, 2018). The ATS vehicle is a cross between a hotel room and a self-driving vehicle, comes fully furnished and in a range of sizes to accommodate solo travellers, couples or families.

In restaurants, robots have a particular two-fold advantage in hospitality. Robots with cameras and laser sensors can be used to carry plates of food from the kitchen to tables in the dining room, directly contributing to a unique hospitality experience. The efficiency provided by robots would also result in indirect benefits to hospitality, as this allows human servers more time to chat with customers and attend to more tables which may require greater interaction and hospitality.

The implementation of robots enhances the service tasks involving hospitality by ensuring that service standards in hospitality are met consistently. Indeed, the role of robots in providing hospitality is crucial for business sustainability (Ivanov et al., 2018). Therefore, the adoption of robots has indeed been supporting the labour-intensive hospitality industry with the much-needed hospitality in many areas, particularly since current hospitality robots have been developed with a higher level of intelligence to make customer engagement with front-line robots more hospitable and no longer a trade-off when compared to human service staff (Choi, 2021).

Impact of AI on Safekeeping

Safekeeping involves assuring customers in caring for them as well as their possessions (Wirtz & Lovelock, 2022). In a regular hotel experience, from the check-in process, there are numerous touchpoints for guests to get into their room; during the pandemic, this was particularly stark with at least ten public touchpoints that could carry the virus (Brostoff, 2022). Accordingly, safety and no-contact experiences were paramount from the moment guests pulled into the front door until they entered their hotel rooms.

One measure implemented involving AI was in the use of facial recognition and consequentially, removing the need for physical touchpoints while still sustaining safety for hotel guests (Brostoff, 2022). By creating a digital profile for each guest upon booking the room, all transactions and exchanges are already enabled before the guest arrives. Entering their room has now become automated as intelligent elevators can use the same facial profile to let guests onto the appropriate floors and a camera-enabled lock can verify identities to open the right doors automatically, thus keeping the guests and their belongings safe. Another illustration of safekeeping through facial recognition in the hospitality industry is in the replacement of room keycards. Room keycards can be easily lost or stolen, thus decreasing the safekeeping of guests' belongings in their rooms. Facial recognition ensures that any guest can only enter predetermined elevator levels and doors, further strengthening the level of safety and safekeeping of the guests and their belongings (FaceMe, 2023).

In the industry, Yotel, a capsule-type hotel chain based in London, indulgences guests with a fully automated check-in service featuring Yobot, a theatrically-lit robotic baggage drop-off machine that can load and safe-keep their belongings (Borgobello, 2011). Other baggage robots can also deliver guest luggage to rooms all by themselves (DeMuro, 2018). Once outside the guest room, the robot automatically dials the in-room phone and informs the guest that they can unlock the code that will open the robot doors to release the luggage accordingly. At the airport, AI is also being used to ensure the safekeeping of passengers' possessions through autonomous robot valet parking (Krok, 2019). Drivers just need to drive their car to the pre-determined drop-off site and send for the robot through a touchscreen. The car will be scanned to determine its size and the robot will load the car onto its built-in ramp before safely ferrying the car to the parking spot. In terms of safekeeping for hotel properties, advanced physical security technologies using AI are also deployed in hotels, casinos and resorts which allow the monitoring of the operations and a continuous security presence (Oitzman, 2022).

Enhanced safekeeping provided by AI will lead to better more assured and satisfied customers and improve service quality.

Impact of AI on Exceptions

Exceptions refer to special requirements by the customer to which the service provider can accede (Wirtz & Lovelock, 2022). These include service provisions based on particular or unexpected circumstances and compensations after service failures. For instance, hotel guests may be offered complimentary umbrellas during a sudden heavy downpour. On birthdays, restaurants may surprise guests with a birthday cake, and the hotel may even offer a complimentary room upgrade to delight guests. Guests could also be offered a discount for a future stay if they encountered service failures during their current visit. Often, offering timely and personalized exceptions requires that frontline staff be empowered to make decisions. Among the supplementary services, offering exceptions that are relevant to the customer can further differentiate the service provider.

When it comes to offering entertainment as a form of service exception, research by Alma Çallı et al. (2023) indicates that guests will find robots useful for providing entertainment in hotels. Indeed, the very presence of AI in the hospitality setting, such as a robot server in a restaurant, might be still relatively new for most customers, causing them to feel surprised and entertained (Bagozzi et al., 2022). For instance, during the COVID-19 pandemic, a burger shop in South Korea capitalized on the need for contactless human service by differentiating itself with robot servers which proved to be useful functionally as well as amazed customers (Kim, 2020).

One of the main strengths of AI in providing exceptions is that the AI can impress the guest with service surprises that are also relevant and tailored to their needs. For instance, hotel room environments can be adjusted based on information gathered from guest profiles, while restaurant menus can be tweaked based on the guest's previous orders and dietary information (Maharaj, 2023). These will delight guests and can increase repeat patronage. While human service employees may struggle with providing exceptional service and customization, especially during peak periods, the AI robot can continue to perform consistently while offering exceptionally personalized recommendations when required (Bagozzi et al., 2022).

In the area of service recovery, unlike traditional self-service technologies, there is potential for the AI service to offer alternative solutions similar to a human service employee when required (Wirtz et al., 2018). However, on the flip side, one area worth noting is the relationship between AI and service recovery in situations where service failures are caused by the AI services themselves. This can especially occur when the AI is being used for more complex tasks as opposed to simple, routine tasks. Indeed, the consequences of service failures by AI can be pronounced, as emerging research indicates that voice AI service failures can lead to negative customer emotions, and both service failure and negative emotions will result in customer complaints (Li et al., 2023).

For hotel operators attempting to maximize the use of AI for traditional as well as novel tasks, this means that they need to work closely with AI designers and programmers during the design stage as well as early implementation phases to minimize service failures and address them with ready service recovery strategies when necessary. Closer attention should also be paid to the interaction itself, with the AI service adjusting its conversation should it detect negative emotions from the customer's responses, to reduce the possibility of customer complaints (Li et al., 2023). Overall, this petal will continue to remain fresh with advances in AI.

CONCLUSION

The objective of this chapter was to illustrate how the Flower of Service continues to be a relevant foundational services marketing framework that can be used as a suitable guide to assess the overall impact of AI on services, particularly in the hospitality industry. Through synthesizing research that touches on the impact of AI on various components of service as classified in the Flower of Service, the framework provides clarity on how the changing environment can affect the performance of the different service components which are commonly present across all services. This gives service managers across hospitality sectors a useful strategic perspective in their decision to implement AI based on the types of service activity rendered.

While this chapter has attempted to highlight the key AI technologies driving each service cluster, benefits found in one petal can certainly be relevant to other petals and even reinforce the other, showing the interconnectedness of central AI technologies in blooming the entire Flower of Service. Accordingly, our chapter has shown the extent to which AI has truly permeated the components of services commonly found across the hospitality industry, and how the effective implementation of AI technologies can continue to facilitate and enhance services for customers. A summary of the technical advantages of AI as discussed in this chapter as well as the challenges and research opportunities of AI and the Flower of Service is shown in Table 1.

Table 1. Technical advantages, challenges and research opportunities on AI and the Flower of Service

Component	Technical advantages	Challenges and research questions
Core service	Deeper co-creation of services with customer data.	With the rapid innovation of AI, more research is required to theorize and assess how AI will continue to disrupt the hospitality industry and service roles once monopolized by human service personnel.
Information	Real-time, personalized information.	Access to accurate data is key to providing reliable information. How can service providers and developers continue to ensure that personal guest data remains secure and that external data sources are unbiased?
Order-taking	Superior and efficient explanations to guests.	Human staff will be required to undertake more strategic relationship-building roles with guests. What are these roles and how can staff better accept and prepare for these new roles?
Billing	Automated and personalized billing.	With a significant reduction in manual errors and delays in billing, how can more value with the customer be captured by the hospitality provider?
Payment	Automated & more convenient payment methods.	Personal information and data privacy will remain pressing issues as customers enjoy more convenient payment facilities. How can customers continue to remain empowered in the management of their personal data? To this, what is the role of blockchain?
Consultation	Human-like consultation with superior recommendations.	The need for service staff to provide consultation with guests will continue to evolve. With AI, what are the guests' expectations in terms of meaningful consultation and interactions with human staff?
Hospitality	Robots which are cost-effective and provide high service quality consistently.	Labor-intensive hospitality will be supported by AI. In what hospitality contexts would guests prefer AI hospitality over human hospitality?
Safekeeping	Contactless and automated with robust monitoring systems.	A continuous security presence requires buy-in from stakeholders including guests. What are the factors that can affect guest acceptance of increased monitoring and surveillance in the hospitality industry?
Exceptions	Highly personalized novel entertainment.	As robots become more mainstream, the novelty associated with robotic interaction may wear off. How can entertainment provided by AI continue to remain effective and safe?

REFERENCES

Ahmad, A., Kakeesh, D., & Abuhashesh, M. (2022). The role of the online flower of service in enhancing guest loyalty via the mediating role of guest experience: A structural equation modelling approach. *International Journal of Electronic Marketing and Retailing*, *13*(1), 1–24. doi:10.1504/IJEMR.2022.119243

AiChat. (2023). Marina Bay Sands: Increasing resort brand awareness with a messenger bot. AI Chat. https://aichat.com/marina-bay-sands-chatbot

Alma Çallı, B., Çallı, L., Sarı Çallı, D., & Çallı, F. (2023). The impact of different types of service robots usage in hotels on guests' intention to stay. *Journal of Hospitality and Tourism Technology*, *14*(1), 53–68. doi:10.1108/JHTT-09-2021-0266

Bagozzi, R., Brady, M., & Huang, H. (2022). AI service and emotion. *Journal of Service Research*, *25*(4), 499–504. doi:10.1177/10946705221118579

Bainbridge, A. (2022). *12 reasons travel should care about autonomous vehicles*. PhocusWire. https://www.phocuswire.com/12-reasons-travel-suppliers-resellers-should-care-autonomous-vehicles

Bitner, M., Zeithaml, V., & Gremler, D. (2010). Technology's impact on the gaps model of service quality. Handbook of Service Science, 197-218. doi:10.1007/978-1-4419-1628-0_10

Borgobello, B. (2011). *Yotel New York features the world's first hotel robotic luggage handler*. News Atlas. https://newatlas.com/yotel-worlds-first-hotel-robotic-porter/19576

Bowen, J., & Morosan, C. (2018). Beware hospitality industry: The robots are coming. *Worldwide Hospitality and Tourism Themes*, *10*(6), 726–733. doi:10.1108/WHATT-07-2018-0045

Brostoff, G. (2020). Using facial recognition to renew trust in hospitality. *Today's Hotelier*. https://www.todayshotelier.com/2020/07/15/using-facial-recognition-to-renew-trust-in-hospitality

Caesars. (2018). *Caesars Entertainment Las Vegas Resorts elevates customer service with Ivy, a personalized virtual concierge service*. Investor. https://investor.caesars.com/news-releases/news-release-details/caesars-entertainment-las-vegas-resorts-elevates-customer

Cheng, X., Lin, X., Shen, X.-L., Zarifis, A., & Mou, J. (2022). The dark sides of AI. *Electronic Markets*, *32*(1), 11–15. doi:10.1007/s12525-022-00531-5 PMID:35600917

Chi, O., Denton, G., & Gursoy, D. (2020). Artificially intelligent device use in service delivery: A systematic review, synthesis, and research agenda. *Journal of Hospitality Marketing & Management*, *29*(7), 757–786. doi:10.1080/19368623.2020.1721394

Choi, S., & Wan, L. (2021). The rise of service robots in the hospitality industry: some actionable insights. *Boston Hospitality Review*. https://www.bu.edu/bhr/2021/10/04/the-rise-of-service-robots-in-the-hospitality-industry-some-actionable-insights

Choithani, T., Chowdhury, A., Patel, S., Patel, P., Patel, D., & Shah, M. (2022). A comprehensive study of artificial intelligence and cybersecurity on Bitcoin, crypto currency and banking system. *Annals of Data Science*, 1-33. doi:10.1007/s40745-022-00433-5

CNBC. (2020). Singapore hopes artificial intelligence will help boost its tourism industry. CNBC. https://www.cnbc.com/2020/09/24/singapore-looks-to-artificial-intelligence-ai-to-boost-tourism.html

Corsaro, D., Vargo, S. L., Hofacker, C., & Massara, F. (2022). Artificial intelligence and the shaping of the business context. *Journal of Business Research*, *145*, 210–214. doi:10.1016/j.jbusres.2022.02.072

Cvent (2020). Artificial intelligence for hotels: 9 trends to know. *Cvent*. Cvent. https://www.cvent.com/en/blog/hospitality/artificial-intelligence-for-hotels

Davenport, H., & Ronanki, R. (2018). Artificial intelligence for the real world. *Harvard Business Review*, *96*(1), 108–116.

Demuro, R. (2018). *Robots take over luggage duties in New Hotel*. KTLA5. https://ktla.com/news/technology/luggage-robots-sheraton-hotel-san-gabriel

Dwivedi, Y. K., Kshetri, N., Hughes, L., Slade, E. L., Jeyaraj, A., Kar, A. K., Baabdullah, A. M., Koohang, A., Raghavan, V., Ahuja, M., Albanna, H., Albashrawi, M. A., Al-Busaidi, A. S., Balakrishnan, J., Barlette, Y., Basu, S., Bose, I., Brooks, L., Buhalis, D., & Wright, R. (2023). "So what if ChatGPT wrote it?" Multidisciplinary perspectives on opportunities, challenges and implications of generative conversational AI for research, practice and policy. *International Journal of Information Management*, *71*, 102642. doi:10.1016/j.ijinfomgt.2023.102642

FaceMe. (2023). *How to build unique customer experiences for hospitality with facial recognition technology*. FaceMe website. https://www.cyberlink.com/faceme/insights/articles/480/facial-recognition-in-hospitality-travel-industry

Fang, S., Han, X., & Chen, S. (2023). The impact of tourist–robot interaction on tourist engagement in the hospitality industry: A mixed-method study. *Cornell Hospitality Quarterly*, *64*(2), 246–266. doi:10.1177/19389655221102383

Filieri, R., D'Amico, E., Destefanis, A., Paolucci, E., & Raguseo, E. (2021). Artificial intelligence (AI) for tourism: An European-based study on successful AI tourism start-ups. *International Journal of Contemporary Hospitality Management*, *33*(11), 4099–4125. doi:10.1108/IJCHM-02-2021-0220

Fisher Phillips. (2023). *The new hospitality balance act: Leveraging artificial intelligence while showing care for your guests*. Fisher Phillips. https://www.fisherphillips.com/en/news-insights/hospitality-leveraging-artificial-intelligence.html

Futr. (2020). *AI in hotels: How tech is transforming the guest experience*. FutrAI. https://futr.ai/ai-in-hotels-how-tech-is-transforming-the-guest-experience

GME. (2023). *AI in Hospitality Market. Global Market Estimates*. Global Market Estimates. https://www.globalmarketestimates.com/market-report/ai-in-hospitality-market-3546

Goel, P., Kaushik, N., Sivathanu, B., Pillai, R., & Vikas, J. (2022). Consumers' adoption of artificial intelligence and robotics in hospitality and tourism sector: Literature review and future research agenda. *Tourism Review*, *77*(4), 1–16. doi:10.1108/TR-03-2021-0138

Grewal, D., Guha, A., Satornino, C. B., & Schweiger, E. B. (2021). Artificial intelligence: The light and the darkness. *Journal of Business Research*, *136*, 229–236. doi:10.1016/j.jbusres.2021.07.043

Gupta, S., Modgil, S., Lee, C.-K., & Sivarajah, U. (2023). The future is yesterday: Use of AI-driven facial recognition to enhance value in the travel and tourism industry. *Information Systems Frontiers*, *25*(3), 1179–1195. doi:10.1007/s10796-022-10271-8 PMID:35529102

Hollander, J. (2022). What is hospitality? An in-depth look for professionals. HotelTechReport. Retrieved Jan 26, 2022 from https://hoteltechreport.com/news/what-is-hospitality

Hollander, J. (2023). ChatGPT for hotels: Whar's apps are actually live right now? *Hotel Tech Report*. https://hoteltechreport.com/news/chatgpt-for-hotels

HospitalityNet. (2022). *What's the impact of artificial intelligence in the hotel industry*. Hospitality Net. https://www.hospitalitynet.org/news/4110360.html

Hsu, A. (2022). Hotels say goodbye to daily room cleanings and hello to robots as workers stay scarce. *NRP*. https://www.npr.org/2022/12/21/1143475374/hotels-labor-worker-shortage-robots-automation

Huang, M., & Rust, T. (2020). Engaged to a robot? The role of AI in service. *Journal of Service Research*, *24*(1), 30–41. doi:10.1177/1094670520902266

Huang, M., & Rust, T. (2021). A strategic framework for artificial intelligence in marketing. *Journal of the Academy of Marketing Science*, *49*(1), 30–50. doi:10.1007/s11747-020-00749-9

Ivanov, S., & Webster, C. (Eds.). (2019). *Robots, artificial intelligence, and service automation in travel, tourism and hospitality*. Emerald Publishing Limited. doi:10.1108/9781787566873

Ivanov, S., Webster, C., & Garenko, A. (2018). Young Russian adults' attitudes towards the potential use of robots in hotels. *Technology in Society*, *2018*(55), 24–32. doi:10.1016/j.techsoc.2018.06.004

Jarrahi, M. (2018). Artificial intelligence and the future of work: Human-AI symbiosis in organizational decision making. *Business Horizons*, *61*(4). 2018. doi:10.1016/j.bushor.2018.03.007

JLL. (2023). *How hotels are turning to AI*. JLL website. https://www.jll.com.sg/en/trends-and-insights/investor/how-hotels-are-turning-to-ai

Kasilingam, D. L. (2020). Understanding the attitude and intention to use smartphone chatbots for shopping. *Technology in Society*, *101280*, 101280. doi:10.1016/j.techsoc.2020.101280

Kim, J. Y. (2020). *AI Robots serve restaurant customers in South Korea*. The Associated Press. https://apnews.com/article/south-korea-virus-outbreak-restaurants-a1d11fe838b631e3ab744abda15c9789

Klint, M. (Jan 30, 2020). Airlines + hotels embrace "hyperdynamic" pricing model. *Live and Let's Fly*. https://liveandletsfly.com/hyperdynamic-pricing/

Krok, A. (2019). Gatwick Airport will test robot valet for parking cars. CNET. Retrieved Jan 25, 2019 from https://www.cnet.com/roadshow/news/gatwick-airport-robot-valet-car-park/

Ladeira, W., Perin, M. G., & Santini, F. (2023). Acceptance of service robots: A meta-analysis in the hospitality and tourism industry. *Journal of Hospitality Marketing & Management*, *32*(6), 694–716. doi:10.1080/19368623.2023.2202168

Lai, W. C., & Hung, W. H. (2018). A framework of cloud and AI based intelligent hotel. *Proceedings of the 18th International Conference on Electronic Business*. ICEB, Guilin.

Lazarus, S. (2018). *This self-driving hotel room could revolutionise travel*. CNNTravel. https://edition.cnn.com/travel/article/autonomous-travel-suites/index.html

Li, B., Liu, L., Mao, W., Qu, Y., & Chen, Y. (2023). Voice artificial intelligence service failure and customer complaint behavior: The mediation effect of customer emotion. *Electronic Commerce Research and Applications*, *59*, 101261. doi:10.1016/j.elerap.2023.101261

Limna, P. (2023). Artificial Intelligence (AI) in the hospitality industry: A review article. *International Journal of Computing Sciences Research*, *7*, 1306–1317. doi:10.25147/ijcsr.2017.001.1.103

Liu, Y., Wang, X., Du, Y., & Wang, S. (2023). Service robots vs. human staff: The effect of service agents and service exclusion on unethical consumer behavior. *Journal of Hospitality and Tourism Management*, *55*, 401–415. doi:10.1016/j.jhtm.2023.05.015

Lovelock, C. (1995). Competing on service: Technology and teamwork in supplementary services. *Planning Review*, *23*(4), 32–47. doi:10.1108/eb054517

Low, B. (2023). Hotel robots: An overview of different robots used in hotels. *365Robot*. https://www.365robot.sg/hotel-robots

Luna, N. (2023). From taking orders to cutting avocados, AI is solving the labour shortage problem for fast-food chains. *Insider*. https://www.businessinsider.com/how-restaurants-use-ai-robots-chatbots-voice-assistants-drive-thru-2023-9

MacKenzie, J. (n.d.). AI for hotels: A guide to artificial intelligence for hospitality leaders. *Hotel Operations*. Hotel Operations. https://hoteloperations.com/ai-hotels-hospitality/#AI_use_case_Hotel_bookings

Maharaj, S. (2023). Next-gen guest experience: How AI is shaping hospitality. *Medium*. https://medium.com/@sahirmaharaj/next-gen-guest-experience-how-ai-is-shaping-hospitality-4a8d08bb870a

Meyer-Waarden, L., Pavone, G., Poocharoentou, T., Prayatsup, P., Ratinaud, M., Tison, A., & Torné, S. (2020). How service quality influences customer acceptance and usage of chatbots? *SMR - Journal of Service Management Research, 4*(1), 35-51. doi:10.15358/2511-8676-2020-1-35

MGM. (2023). *Meet Rose, your ultimate insider*. MGM. https://www.cosmopolitanlasvegas.com/rose

Noble, S. M., Mende, M., Grewal, D., & Parasuraman, A. (2022). The fifth industrial revolution: How harmonious human–machine collaboration is triggering a retail and service [r]evolution. *Journal of Retailing*, *98*(2), 199–208. doi:10.1016/j.jretai.2022.04.003

Noor, N. (2022). Halal Service Marketing: A Strategic Perspective. In Strategic Islamic Marketing: A Roadmap for Engaging Muslim Consumers (pp. 11-29). Springer. doi:10.1007/978-3-030-98160-0_3

Noor, N., Rao Hill, S., & Troshani, I. (2022a). Artificial intelligence service agents: Role of parasocial relationship. *Journal of Computer Information Systems*, *62*(5), 1009–1023. doi:10.1080/08874417.2021.1962213

Noor, N., Rao Hill, S., & Troshani, I. (2022b). Developing a service quality scale for artificial intelligence service agents. *European Journal of Marketing*, *56*(5), 1301–1336. doi:10.1108/EJM-09-2020-0672

OECD. (2018). *OECD tourism trends and policies 2018*. OECD publishing. doi:10.1787/tour-2018-

Oitzman, M. (2022). *Knightscope robots to patrol Fortune 1000 hotel properties. Mobile Robot Guide*. Mobile Robot Guide. https://mobilerobotguide.com/2022/02/08/knightscope-robots-to-patrol-fortune-1000-hotel-properties

Önder, I., & Gunter, U. (2022). Blockchain: Is it the future for the tourism and hospitality industry? *Tourism Economics*, *28*(2), 291–299. doi:10.1177/1354816620961707

Parasuraman, A., & Colby, C. L. (2015). An updated and streamlined technology readiness index: TRI 2.0. *Journal of Service Research*, *18*(1), 59–74. doi:10.1177/1094670514539730

Pelau, C., Dabija, D.-C., & Ene, I. (2021). What makes an AI device human-like? The role of interaction quality, empathy and perceived psychological anthropomorphic characteristics in the acceptance of artificial intelligence in the service industry. *Computers in Human Behavior*, *122*, 106855. doi:10.1016/j.chb.2021.106855

Ruel, H., & Njoku, E. (2021). AI redefining the hospitality industry. *Journal of Tourism Futures*, *7*(1), 53–66. doi:10.1108/JTF-03-2020-0032

Ruiz-Alba, L., & Martín-Peña, L. (2020). Guest editorial. *Journal of Business and Industrial Marketing*, *35*(3), 385–389. doi:10.1108/JBIM-03-2020-419

Schulze, E. (2019). Everything you need to know about the Fourth Industrial Revolution. CNBC. Retrieved 11 Jul, 2023 from https://www.cnbc.com/2019/01/16/fourth-industrial-revolution-explained-davos-2019.html

Shankar, V. (2018). How artificial intelligence (AI) is reshaping retailing. *Journal of Retailing*, *94*(4), vi–xi. doi:10.1016/S0022-4359(18)30076-9

Statista Research Department. (2018). *Global travel and tourism industry: statistics & facts*. Statista. https://statista.com/topics/962/global-tourism

Sweezey, M. (2018). The value of chatbots for today's consumers. *Forbes*. https://forbes.com/sites/forbescommunicationscouncil/2018/02/13/the-value-of-chatbots-for-todaysconsumers/#5c0669cd2918

Tuomi, A., Tussyadiah, I., & Hanna, P. (2021). Spicing up hospitality service encounters: The case of Pepper. *International Journal of Contemporary Hospitality Management*, *33*(11), 3906–3925. doi:10.1108/IJCHM-07-2020-0739

Tussyadiah, I. (2020). A review of research into automation in tourism: Launching the Annals of Tourism Research Curated Collection on Artificial Intelligence and Robotics in Tourism. *Annals of Tourism Research*, *81*, 102883. doi:10.1016/j.annals.2020.102883

Ukpabi, D., Aslam, B., & Karjaluoto, H. (2019). Chatbot adoption in tourism services: A conceptual exploration. Ivanov, S. and Webster, C. (Ed.) Robots, Artificial Intelligence, and Service Automation in Travel, Tourism and Hospitality. Emerald Publishing Limited. doi:10.1108/978-1-78756-687-320191006

Van Niekerk, M. (2016). Business, technology, and marketing trends influencing the financial performance of the hotel industry. *The Journal of Hospitality Financial Management*, *24*(2), 153–157. doi:10.1080/10913211.2016.1236582

Wahid, D., & Hassini, E. (2024). An augmented AI-based hybrid fraud detection framework for invoicing platforms. *Applied Intelligence*, *54*(2), 1297–1310. doi:10.1007/s10489-023-05223-x

Wikhamn, W. (2019). Innovation, sustainable HRM, and customer satisfaction. *International Journal of Hospitality Management*, *76*, 102–110. doi:10.1016/j.ijhm.2018.04.009

Wirtz, J., & Lovelock, C. (2022). *Services marketing: People, technology, strategy* (9th ed.). World Scientific.

Wirtz, J., Patterson, P. G., Kunz, W. H., Gruber, T., Lu, V. N., Paluch, S., & Martins, A. (2018). Brave new world: Service robots in the frontline. *Journal of Service Management*, *29*(5), 907–931. doi:10.1108/JOSM-04-2018-0119

Wirtz, J., & Zeithaml, V. (2018). Cost-effective service excellence. *Journal of the Academy of Marketing Science*, *46*(1), 59–80. doi:10.1007/s11747-017-0560-7

World Travel & Tourism Council. (2017). *Travel & tourism economic impact 2017*. WTC. https://wtc.org/about/media-centre/press-releases/press-releases/2017/tourism-supports-1-in-10-jobs-outpacingglobal-economy-for-6th-conservative-year-wttc

Wu, D., Song, H., & Shen, S. (2017). New developments in tourism and hotel demand modeling and forecasting. *International Journal of Contemporary Hospitality Management*, *29*(1), 507–529. doi:10.1108/IJCHM-05-2015-0249

Yaramada, K. (2021). How to upgrade your accounts payable function with AI. *Forbes*. https://www.forbes.com/sites/forbesbusinesscouncil/2021/08/05/how-to-upgrade-your-accounts-payable-function-with-ai/?sh=304304ee21c6

Yu, R., Tong, Z., & Xiao, H. (2023). Close or distant? The impacts of robot services and spatial distance on service satisfaction. *Journal of Hospitality and Tourism Management*, *54*, 447–456. doi:10.1016/j.jhtm.2023.01.011

Zhao, J., & Kerdpitak, C. (2023). *A study of consumer innovativeness and service convenience on the intention to use robot services in hotels. International Academic Multidisciplinary Research Conference*, Zurich.

Zhou, G., Chu, G. L. L., & Meng, L. (2020). The effect of artificial intelligence on China's labor market. *China Economic Journal*, *13*(1), 24–41. doi:10.1080/17538963.2019.1681201

Chapter 5
Can Serious Games and AI Rejuvenate Museums?

Michel Plaisent
Université du Québec à Montreal, Canada

Daniel Tomiuk
Université du Québec à Montreal, Canada

Jean-Marie Lafortune
Université du Québec à Montreal, Canada

Sylvester Cortes
Cebu Technological University, Philippines

Lili Zheng
https://orcid.org/0000-0002-4824-5803
EXCELIA Business School, France

Agnès Czubinski
https://orcid.org/0009-0005-3677-6913
Independent Researcher, Canada

Pascal Ndinga
https://orcid.org/0009-0001-1533-7525
Université du Québec à Montreal, Canada

Prosper Bernard
Université du Québec à Montréal, Canada

ABSTRACT

Museums are an important player in the "heritage industry" because they hold a huge potential for the development of tourism, especially in regions far from large cities. Serious games and artificial intelligence are responsible for their new success. This research explores the issues and challenges posed by their introduction. It used a questionnaire distributed to museum directors. Among the benefits of serious games, directors agree on public diversification, improving visitors experience, rejuvenating the museums image, and increase in-site and distant visits. AI is recognized to permit interactive exhibits and personalization of visit experience. Financial and technical issues slow their introduction among

DOI: 10.4018/979-8-3693-2137-9.ch005

the strategies used to increase digital services; cooperation with other museums and other actors are more cited than increasing resources. But a lack of knowledge (not of interest) characterized respondents to this study. The question is no more "Yes or No" to implementation, but "When and How."

INTRODUCTION

Museums are important as they allow sharing a rich cultural heritage both tangible (painting, costumes, jewels, arms and intangible) and intangible (expressive art forms and rituals, living folklore, oral performative acts, distinctive practices, knowledge and skills of people). Not only are the cultural aspects important in the cultural heritage field, but also the economic and social dimensions. Cultural heritage holds enormous potential for the development of large cities, but especially of small and medium-sized cities (Turek, 2019).

The question of introducing AI in museums is no more Yes or No but When and How. According to many authors, AI is a disruptive technology at the eve of transforming radically how museums operate and how visitors are served (Păvăloaia & Necula, 2023; Rani et al., 2023; Simone et al., 2021; Hugues-Noehrer, 2022).

This chapter aims to provide to the reader an illustration in the case of museums of the need to rejuvenate the practices in order to continue to attract visitors. It also seeks to demonstrate to the reader how AI can be disruptive in a changing world where the consumer claims for change to feed its appetite of culture.

This research borrows its conceptual frame of Task-technology-fit theory initially describe by Goodhue and Thonpson (1995) which states that the output of a system depends on the fit of the technology with the requirements of the task. Since its introduction it has been used in many environments and many technologies to describe and explain success and failures as it appears from the systematic review of Spies et. al. (2020)

AI is present in Art museums as a mediation tool, especially in terms of accessibility, as the centerpiece of interactivity and even immersion in the room, even as an artist (think of the fake Beatle music produced by AI) and as a critic evaluating, classifying and linking objects automatically (Dehan, 2022).

Since the introduction of digital technologies in museums to improve back-office operations and customer services, their use has increased in scope and quality. Indeed, the decline of public funding, the need to incorporate volunteers into the staff, and the need to keep pace with technological development induce high pressure and increased complexity in the management of museums (Taormina & Baraldi, 2022).

According to a Museum Barometer 2021 survey of 39 countries and 200 museums, 70% estimate that new technologies are either very or extremely important for their success (Tykhonova & Widmann, 2021) to attract more visitors (90%), diversify the audience (83%), and improve relevance in content creation and mediation (85%). If museums are gaining opportunities, they also face challenges since each new revolution comes with a lot of promises and deceptions.

A systematic examination of 94 articles on organizational issues related to the digitalization of museums concluded that besides getting clear advantages of the introduction of technology, the museum must also face serious challenges, namely defining a strategy and increasing in-house technical capacity while integrating traditional and digital operations (Taormina & Baraldi, 2022).

According to Endsley (2023), AI is still subject to skepticism, namely that AI systems are not that intelligent (ex. ChatGPT and Siri are only natural language processing that relay information to the retrieving system, not a creative or critical system; the smarter the system the less its understandability by its user). Another problem is linked to the flaws of AI deep learning algorithms that can convey a colonialist continuum and bias on race, class, sex, age, etc. (Moreschi et al., 2022).

Whatever the level of use of AI in museums, Ozmen Garibay et al. (2023) argue that human-centered principles must apply, namely being centered on human well-being, respecting privacy, designed responsibly. But as for many new technology vendors persuasively introduce first their enthusiastic product to managers, more than happy to improve their customer experience.

Many practices permitted by AI pose a concern for privacy or another ethical issue. As an example, the data capture of visitors' behavior and its processing to enhance corporate decision support, called datafication, is rarely questioned by visitors although it conveys ethical concern, namely the impossibility for visitors to opt-out (Pruulmann-Vengerfeldt, 2022).

Vorobeva (2023) study on the introduction of AI as a complement (instead of substitution) shows that it can increase the satisfaction of users when technology is easy to use. AI can re-engage with visitors and connect with younger by providing more interesting artworks with a more dynamic interaction (Hettmann et al., 2022). As an example, the case of mini-games linked to items that increase the entertainment level for the visitor is cited. Indeed, most users of museum online provisions visit to learn and be intellectually stimulated, followed by seeking entertainment (Hugues-Noehrer, 2022).

Summarizing 271 studies, Pisoni et al. (2021, propose that to improve human-centered accessibility, novel approaches should be used from many disciplines (ex. robotics for arts), and incorporate pedagogical and instructional approaches, human-computer interactions, and participatory design with users. According to Aristova et al. (2020), museums enriched by AI shall focus on the democratization of their role and extend it to outside the museum for a lasting effect on its users.

There is a need to perform an investigation to explore how museums adopt or intend to adopt AI in their development strategy.

BACKGROUND

Evolution of Museums From Traditional Onsite to Social Onlife

According to Mas & Monfort (2021), museums have evolved from a traditional to a social organism. They are no longer for experts only but for everybody. Exhibitions are no longer chosen only by the curator but based on visitors' interests. The focus is no more only on knowledge, but also on visitor involvement. They now need to evolve to a digital social nature, which implies interaction between the exhibits and the visitors, personalized, with a virtual community perspective. Simone et al. (2021) summarize the evolution of museums on two axes scales (Y axis for the growth involvement of visitors and the X axis with three categories: onsite, online, and onlife, where early museums occupy the lower quadrant while the upper right welcome the augmented museums.

A Porter chain analysis by Simone et al. (2021) and Recuero Virgo & Lopez (2019) suggests that value chain creation is supported by technology, and organized around the following processes qualified with the Mas and Monfort (2021) typology:

a) A back-office approach dedicated to the preservation (low involvement from users).
b) An onsite with some IT to improve the quality of the museum experience (low involvement onsite model).
c) An online approach to offer services outside the museums, like serious games and virtual museums (medium involvement online model).
d) An "onlife" approach based on multisensory and interactive technologies, LOD, and IoT aimed at maximizing personalized visitor experience (online with IoT and high involvement of visitors).

This paper focuses on the later phase of the evolution of museums and on the "onlife" approach permitted by AI, namely the use of interactive technologies and personalized experience, to provide an immersive experience to visitors, favored by Rani et al. (2023) who advocate for improving the visitor using AI for immersion offering an automated personalization and real-time access to data.

Automated personalization: facial recognition techniques can be used to catch user reactions in an interaction with an artifact and provide the user with more information on what is the focus of the visitor. A study by Cuennet & Schegg

(2022) mentions that the main advantages of AI are to present a clearer message (helping visitors to understand), provide more information, and allow for greater interactivity because technology permits personalization through a diversity of forms in the visitor experience.

Real-time access to relevant information: being connected to a database or the internet any piece in the museum can provide the visitor with much more information and more specific data than any planned information to be delivered; this process is ideally directly done from the phone of the visitor (Ioannakis et al., 2019).

Immersion

Immersion is defined as a sensory and cognitive human experience creating an enjoyable atmosphere to capture and keep the audience's attention and generate an enjoyable visitor experience, surpassing the traditional mode of presentation of artifacts (Yu & Yao, 2023). Technologies like front-projected holographic displays, virtual reality, and augmented reality can create those types of immersive experiences in museums, significantly impacting the visitor experience and interest (Hijazi et al., 2022). Other technologies used to increase immersion are multimedia touch screens, intelligent display devices, holographic projection, and virtual reality scenes (Jiang et al., 2022; Tu, 2019).

Immersion is based namely on the conversational capacities of the objects. This is achieved by technology in conjunction with natural language capacity which is to be appreciated according to three competencies: cognitive, relational, and emotional (Chandra et al., 2022). It may be realized by new interaction modes: visitor control of the special location of an exhibit, modification of its shape or size, and experimenting with the object (Baloian et al., 2021).

One of the most spectacular improvements in the visitor experience in museums is due to the immersive art exhibition that modifies or rather revolutionizes the sensorial extending perception beyond the vision with touch and hear (Yu & Yao, 2023).

According to a systematic review of 39 scientific papers about virtual humans in museums, Sylaiou & Fidas (2022) conclude that investments in Mixed reality and virtual reality increased since 2016, an indication of the belief in their capacity to enrich visitors' experience.

In China, the Museum of Central China Normal University is even depicted as a model of an advanced modality of the intelligent museum, relying heavily on virtual reality, the Internet of things, virtual and holographic display, and application of AI in audience guide through knowledge mapping techniques (Li, 2021).

It can also be used to explore and highlight the richness of its collections. As an example, a museum dedicated to Salvador Dali in St. Petersburg allows visitors to live various experiences with the painter who talks about his life and interprets his works himself, by creating a "deepfake" (Georges, 2019).

Chatbots: Live chat service quality has an impact on behavioral intentions and relationship quality, according to a systematic review of 29 topical studies (Kilani & Rajaobelina, 2022). To adopt chatbot technology, trust perceived usefulness and attitude are the most important factors (Li, 2023). A meta-analysis of 12 recent investigations on systematic study of user satisfaction with AI-powered chatbots relates it to four types of gratification: utilitarian, technological, hedonic, and social (Xie et al., 2022) and proved to be engaging when combined with gamification with teenagers of the Case Museo di Milano (Gaia et al., 2019). Chatbots can answer 80% of the questions according to Chen (2020). Because they are repetitive, which can reduce human resources who can focus on more complex topics.

Robots guide: Used initially in manufacturing, they are invading public life as servers in restaurants, floor cleaners, prescription, medication, and file carriers in hospitals and museums as guides. To play their role effectively as guides, they should integrate several features according to Hallou et al. (2022):

- Navigation capacities (to avoid obstacles and visitors who change their path upon orders by visitors).
- Perception (identifying and tracking their user, ideally recognizing facial emotions).
- Speech capacity allows them to present exhibits and answer questions.
- Recognizing and generating gestures.

Such capacities have been implemented in an RFID context by Pliasa et al. (2021) in the Greece Museum. Three of the Washington-based museums of the Smithsonian have been equipped with such robots since 2018 (Levere, 2018). Many other museums followed the lead.

Empowering Curators With AI Capacities

Rani et al. (2023) suggest that AI be used to improve museum management, namely face recognition permits to follow visitors in the many rooms of museums and better understand the interests of the visitors to adapt their planning to users' needs, keeping trace of most popular artifacts, and questions asked, which can be analyzed by a machine learning system to define patterns and give sense to individual behaviors.

Among the role of IT in museums, Cai et al. (2023) mention the power of a database management system coupled with interactive devices to permit better control to management in terms of data integration with historical facts, voice-control interactions, data analysis of visitor behaviors and recommendations to improve exhibitions.

Many AI technologies can be used to improve the conservation mission of museums and authentication concerns, namely machines to predict patterns and create replica infrared spectroscopy radiometric dating, gas chromatography techniques, and nanotechnologies for restoration (Ricuero Virto & Lopes, 2019).

METHODOLOGY

The instrument is composed of four sections:

a) Information about the museum location, size, main customers (ex. family, adults, students, etc.), and the main focus (multidisciplinary archeology, sciences, environment, arts, etc.). The categories chosen are indebted to Tykhonova & Widmann (2021) and Luther et al. (2023).
b) Reasons to introduce new technologies in museums are adapted from Perroud (2016) and Ogle & Lamb (2019), and the relevance of main AI applications for their museum is based on Rani et al (2023) and French & Villaespesa (2019) typology of relevance vs. effort and cost of AI applications.
c) Issues and challenges to the adoption of AI, namely financial. The choices were decided following Rani et al. (2023).
d) Knowledge and perception of AI among museum directors (Cuennet and Schegg, 2022).

As one of the major Canadian provinces, Quebec hosts 306 museums. Each of them received a solicitation letter ending with a link to a SurveyMonkey (specialized website), where the questionnaire was adapted to fit, phones, tablets, and computer formats. This sample is judged sufficient to deepen our understanding of museum concerns especially as it will be completed by in-depth interviews later. Data collection was unfortunately made during the busiest period of the year, which reduced the response rate expectancy. Nevertheless, the number of answers over the first week was sufficient to compute the main statistics to highlight AI perceptions among several types of museums.

DATA ANALYSIS

Respondents

Our sample comprises 38 respondents. It is composed of various types of museums, but mainly with history vocation, as is shown in Figure 1 below:

Their target public belongs almost equally to all ages and profiles as seen in Table 1 below.

Almost half of them are located in regions far from urban centers as shown in Figure 2 below:

Actual Involvement With New Technologies

When asked about their resources regarding the implementation of digital tools, as a percentage of their budget, it is clear from Figure 3 that the needs exceed the capacities.

Most of them are offering a mobile service to their users, and other museums are in the process of doing so as seen in Figure 4 below:

To increase their digital offer of services they apply various strategies among which the most popular are presented in Figure 5 below:

Figure 1. Museum categories

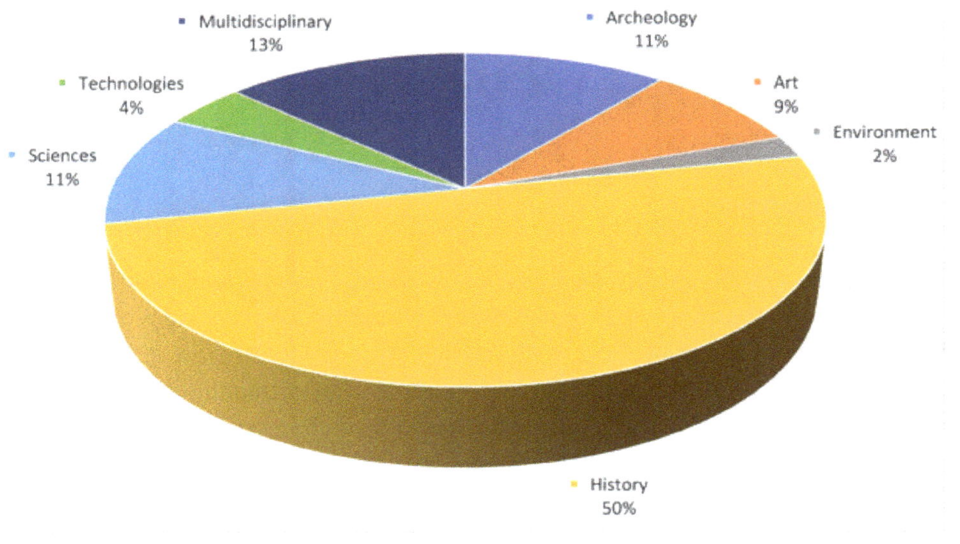

Table 1. Target public of sample

Category	Mean	Std. dev.	Median	Mode
Kids	3.7	1.11	4.00	4.0
Teens	3.6	1.04	4.00	4.0
Young adults (18-35)	3.9	0.78	4.00	4.0
Adults (36-65)	4.4	0.53	4.00	4.0
Seniors (66 &+)	4.3	0.66	4.00	4.0
Families	4.2	0.73	4.00	4.0
School groups	4.2	0.82	4.00	5.0
Tourists	4.3	0.82	4.00	5.0
Other public	3.2	1.05	3.00	3.0

Figure 2. Museum localization

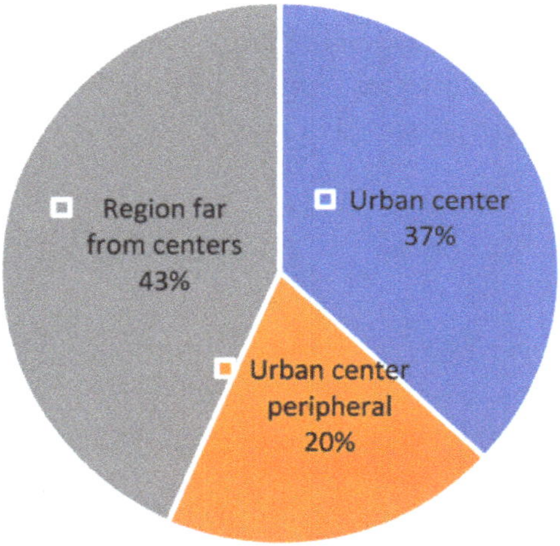

Serious Games

Serious games are becoming more and more popular among museums to increase their audience, especially the young public. Museum directors were asked about their knowledge of serious games. The results are presented below in Figure 6

Asked where they get their information, most of them mentioned a conference or their research. The distribution of answers is given below in Figure 7

Museum directors were asked to enumerate the advantages of serious games. Their perception is detailed in Figure 8 below:

Figure 3. Resource for implementing new technologies

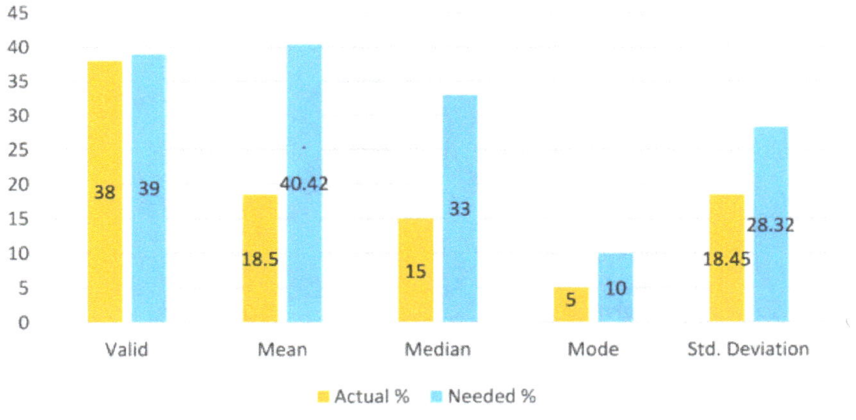

Figure 4. Actual mobile numeric experience offered

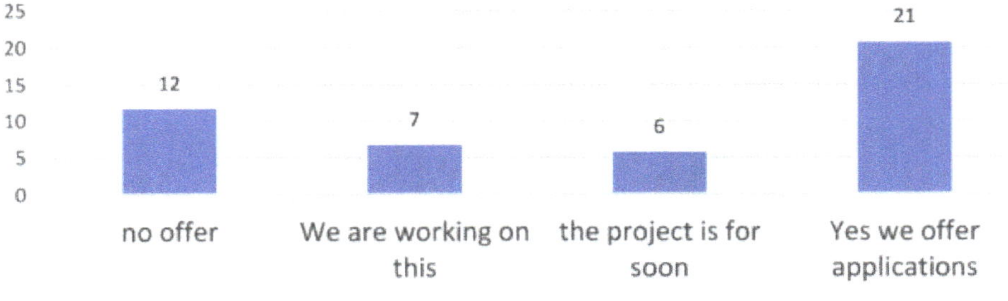

Figure 5. Strategy to increase digital services

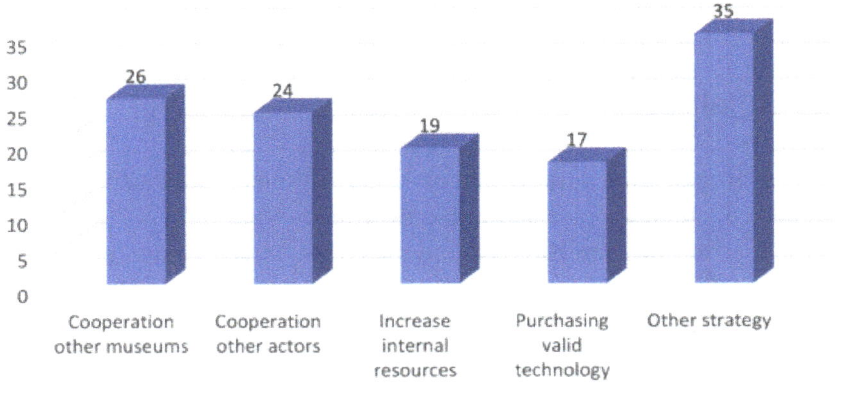

Figure 6. Director's knowledge of serious games

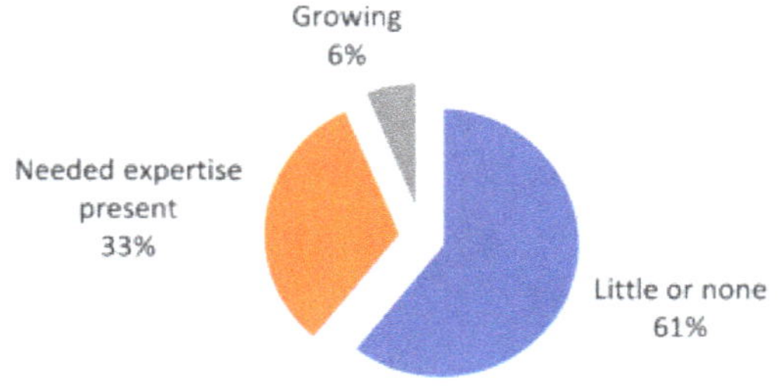

Figure 7. Source of information

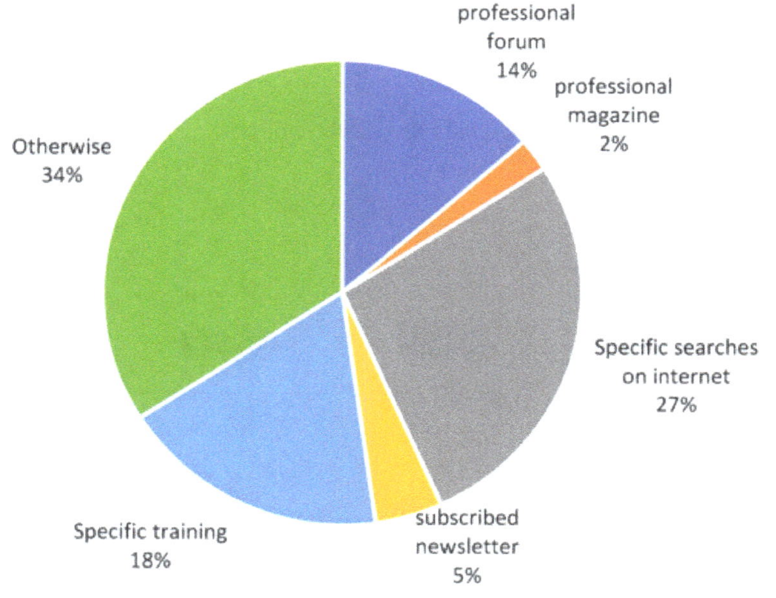

Artificial Intelligence

Another new avenue is the introduction of AI in museums. Here too their knowledge was prospected, and it is presented in Figure 9 below:

Despite it seems that few directors are ready, they perceive the relevance of AI applications for their museum, as can be seen from Table 2 below (where 1 = useless and 5 = greatest importance):

According to our respondents, adopting AI is challenged by the motives presented in Table 3 below:

As the reader will note, the financial and technical issues are predominant.

Figure 8. Serious games advantages

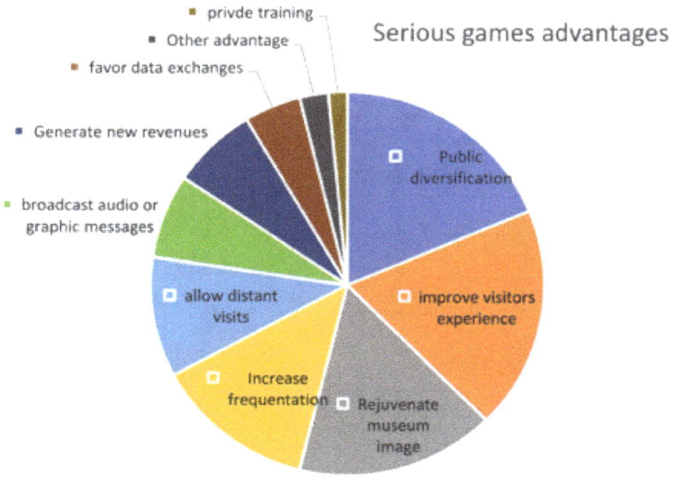

Figure 9. Knowledge bout AI for museum

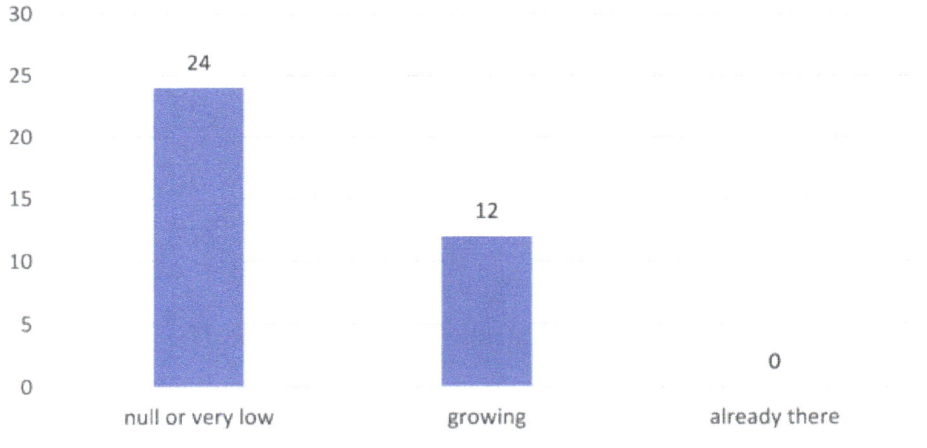

Other Analysis

To see how the personal attitude of directors could influence their perceptions, they were asked to indicate on a 0-100% scale their perception from totally opposed to totally favorable. The mean attitude is 60 favorable with an important std. deviation of 26. The mode is 50 and the median is 62.5 which indicates a slight positive attitude. They also indicate a slight preference (6.5%) for serious games over AI

Table 2. Potential applications

Potential AI application	mean	std dev	Median	Mode
Personalization of visitor experience	3.69	0.97	4.0	4
Interactive exhibits	3.64	0.76	4.0	4
Predictive analysis of customers preferences	3.24	1.05	3.0	3
Discovering available exhibits unavailable to public	3.11	1.26	3.0	4
Classification of artefacts	2.86	1.15	3.0	4
Help in organizing an exhibition	2.83	0.97	3.0	3
Authentification of pieces	2.66	1.04	3.0	2
Preservation of pieces (restauration)	2.63	1.10	2.0	2
Chatbot to answer questions	2.47	1.14	2.0	2
Searching pieces around the world for a thematic	2.24	0.83	2.0	2
Facial recognition of visitors	2.04	1.08	2.0	1
Using robots as guide	1.86	0.88	2.0	2

Table 3. Issues and challenges

	Mean	Median	Mode	Std. Dev.
Financial resources	4.18	5.00	5.00	1.193
Technical resources	4.09	4.00	5.00	1.164
Confidentiality and security concerns	3.59	4.00	5.00	1.284
Lack of maturity of applications	3.36	3.00	3.00	1.282
Ethic considerations	3.41	3.00	3.00	1.264

introduction. Finally, they express interest in the topic but maybe not enough to participate, as seen in Figure 10.

CONCLUSION: KEY FINDINGS, RECOMMENDATIONS, AND FUTURE RESEARCH

This research findings are congruent with recent research about the impact of new technologies on museums namely that AI is the disruptive technology at the eve of transforming radically how museums operate and how visitors are served (Pavaloiai & Necula, 2023; Rani et al., 2023; Simone et al., 2021; Hugues-Noehrer, 2022; Hettmann et al., 2023) cited in the beginning of he text . More specifically it confirms Tykhonova & Widmann (2021) who estimate that new technologies are

Figure 10. Interest in participating in university study

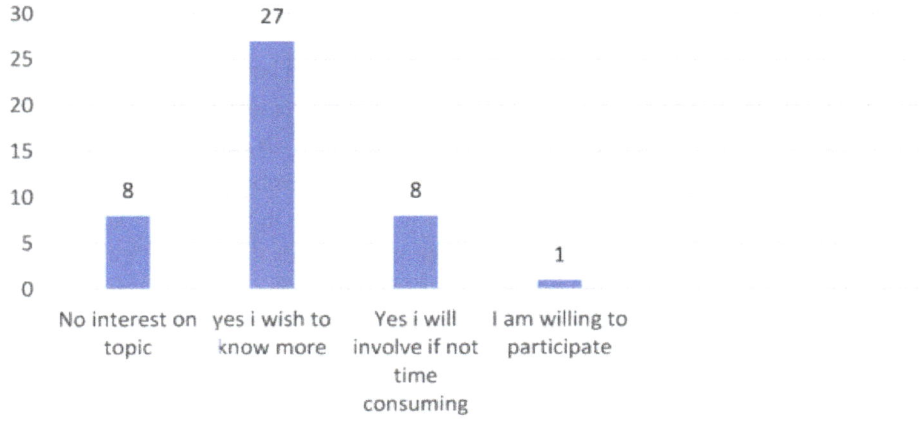

responsible of museums success in terms of profit, new and growing audience and relevance of content.

The actual findings of this research also reinforces those who mention the contraints linked to their introduction, namely Taormina & Baraldi, 2022), Endsley (2023) and Moreschi et al. (2022), also cited in the beginning of the text.

This research nevertheless suffers from acute limits namely the sample taken from a single geographical scope, the low number of respondents, and the results are appreciated from a closed-question survey.

Key Findings

The study reveals that museums managers have a growing awareness of the potential of new technologies such as serious games and Artificial intelligence to five a second breath to museums and bring new customers to their tourism offer. It also shows that the move toward rejuvenation is started in the industry and that main constraints to their implementation are linked to the lack of funding and of technical expertise.

This paper has presented the main issues and challenges of the museum mediatized by AI and the results of a survey among museum directors. Museum directors began to be aware of new technologies since they perceived that they could bring advantages to their museum. They are slowed by a lack of knowledge about these new technologies, and a lack of budget and technical expertise. Nevertheless, they have a positive attitude and will engage resolutely in this direction when those issues are overcome.

Recommendations

In order to increase their visitors' satisfaction and the scope of their market, museum must change their old strategy of passive wait of the visitors and develop new approaches in attracting them, since they are in a tourism market. It is important to satisfy their needs and improve their visit experience with new technologies like immersion to generate new revenues and increase the number of visitors.

Government should provide funding to museums since they are pivotal in the tourism market because museum are often the main factor that will decide tourists to choose a destination. To keep the relative advantage from a regional and national point of view, it is important to fund adequately museums in order to help them overcome their transition toward the new modernity.

Academics should pay more attention to the problematic of lack of awareness of the museum directors and provide more information on the potential benefits of new technologies, and mosty on how to implement them in their environment. The theory of the diffusion of new technology can certainly constitutes a beginning to favor the transition.

Future Research

This chapters open the door to the need of a deeper study of the relevance of introducing new technologies in museums and how to proceed given the level of awareness of the management.

An examination of the methodology deployed by successful museums and of those who suffered from a failure would help to produce normative approach to implementing new technologies in museums.

Further research is also needed in order to better understand the need of museum visitors and how to satisfy them. Most of people are now using a smart phone and I could be interesting to find how to use this powerful tool to link more visitors to their museum in a permanent manner.

More research is needed to understand the new expectations of visitors in terms of interactivity before, during and after the visit. The question of the use of AI for expanding the link with visitors poses ethics questions since the use of AI and serious games in museums touches very intimate aspects of the personalization, the privacy and the confidentiality of gained information on visitors. Ethical guidelines need more researches to be defined and adapted o the specific situation encountered in museums.

REFERENCES

Aristova, U. V., Rolich, A. Y., Staruseva-Persheeva, A. D., & Rolich, A. O. (2020). Digital museum transformation: From a collection of exhibits to a gamut of emotions. In *International Conference on Digital Transformation and Global Society* (June 2020), 419-435. Springer International Publishing, Cham. 10.1007/978-3-030-65218-0_31

Baloian, N., Biella, D., Luther, W., Pino, J. A., & Sacher, D. (2021). Designing, Realizing, Running, and Evaluating Virtual Museum—A Survey on Innovative Concepts and Technologies. *JUCS. Journal of Universal Computer Science*, *27*(12), 1275–1299. doi:10.3897/jucs.77153

Cai, P., Zhang, K. and Pan, Y. (2023). *Application of AI Interactive Device Based on Database Management System in Multidimensional Design of Museum Exhibition Content.*

Chandra, S., Shirish, A., & Srivastava, S. C. (2022). To be or not to be… human? Theorizing the role of human-like competencies in conversational artificial intelligence agents. *Journal of Management Information Systems*, *39*(4), 969–1005. doi:10.1080/07421222.2022.2127441

Chen, T. T. (2020). Chatbots for Smart Customer Services on Official Museum Websites. In *Frontier Computing: Theory, Technologies and Applications (FC 2019), 8, 292-297.* Springer. doi:10.1007/978-981-15-3250-4_34

Cuennet, M. (2022). *New Technologies at the Service of Swiss Museums: Analysis of Their Potential to Improve the Visitor Experience.* [Master's Thesis, School of Management, University HES-SO Valais-Wallis].

Dehan, Sasha (2022). *Les 4 rôles de l'intelligence artificielle dans les musées. 2022.* Decodagecom.

Doroz-Turek, M. (2019, February). Revitalization of small towns and the adaptive reuse of its cultural heritage. [IOP Publishing.]. *IOP Conference Series. Materials Science and Engineering*, *471*(5), 052006. doi:10.1088/1757-899X/471/5/052006

Endsley, M.R. (2023). Ironies of Artificial Intelligence. *Ergonomics*, 1-18.

French, A., & Villaespesa, E. (2019). AI, visitor experience, and museum operations: a closer look at the possible. In Humanizing the Digital: Unproceedings from the MCN 2018 Conference, (pp. 101-113). IEEE.

Gaia, G., Boiano, S., & Borda, A. (2019). Engaging museum visitors with AI: The case of chatbots. In *Museums and Digital Culture* (pp. 309–329). New Perspectives and Research. doi:10.1007/978-3-319-97457-6_15

Georges, B. (2019). L'intelligence artificielle entre au musée. *Les Echos*. https://www.lesechos.fr/idees-debats/sciences-prospective/lintelligence-artificielle-entre-au-musee-1134249

Goodhue, D. L., & Thompson, R. L. (1995). Task-technology fit and individual performance. *Management Information Systems Quarterly*, *19*(2), 213–233. doi:10.2307/249689

Hellou, M., Lim, J., Gasteiger, N., Jang, M., & Ahn, H. S. (2022). Technical Methods for Social Robots in Museum Settings: An Overview of the Literature. *International Journal of Social Robotics*, *14*(8), 1767–1786. doi:10.1007/s12369-022-00904-y

Hettmann, W., Wölfel, M., Butz, M., Torner, K., & Finken, J. (2022). Engaging Museum Visitors with AI-Generated Narration and Gameplay. In *Proceedings of the International Conference on ArtsIT, Interactivity and Game Creation*. Springer Nature, Cham, Switzerland.

Hijazi, A. N., & Baharin, H. (2022). The Effectiveness of Digital Technologies Used for the Visitor's Experience in Digital Museums: A Systematic Literature Review from the Last Two Decades. *International Journal of Interactive Mobile Technologies*, *16*(16).

Hughes-Noehrer, L. (2022). *Artificial Intelligence, museum environments, and their constituents: a cross-disciplinary study using recommender systems to explore digital collections*. [Ph.D. Dissertation. University of Manchester].

Ioannakis, G., Bampis, L., & Koutsoudis, A. (2019). Artificial intelligence as a low-cost solution for museum visit digital content enrichment: The case of the folklore museum of Xanthi. *The International Archives of the Photogrammetry, Remote Sensing and Spatial Information Sciences*, *42*(W15), 585–590. doi:10.5194/isprs-archives-XLII-2-W15-585-2019

Jiang, A. N., Gan, X. E., Liang, Z., & Luo, G. (2022). AIDM: Artificial intelligent for digital museum autonomous system with mixed reality and software-driven data collection and analysis. *Automated Software Engineering*, *29*(1), 22. doi:10.1007/s10515-021-00315-9

Kilani, N., & Rajaobelina, L. (2022). Impact of live chat service quality on behavioral intentions and relationship quality: A meta-analysis. *International Journal of Human-Computer Interaction*, 1–28.

Levere, J. L. (2018). Artificial intelligence, like a robot, enhances museum experiences. *The New York Times*, 25.

Li, B., Chen, Y., Liu, L., & Zheng, B. (2023). Users' intention to adopt artificial intelligence-based chatbot: a meta-analysis 智能聊天机器人的用户采纳意愿研究: 一项元分析. *Service Industries Journal*, 1–23.

Li, H., & Luo, S. (2021). The Present Situation and Development Direction of Wisdom Museum from the Perspective of New Technology. In *Proceedings of the 2021 3rd International Conference on Artificial Intelligence and Advanced Manufacture*. ACM. 10.1145/3495018.3495330

Luther, W., Baloian, N., Biella, D., & Sacher, D. (2023). Digital Twins and Enabling Technologies in Museums and Cultural Heritage: An Overview. *Sensors (Basel)*, *23*(3), 1583. doi:10.3390/s23031583 PMID:36772623

Mas, J. M., & Monfort, A. (2021). From the social museum to the digital social museum. *ADResearch: Revista Internacional de Investigación En Comunicación*, *24*(24), 8–25. doi:10.7263/adresic-024-01

Moreschi, B., Jurno, A., & Beiguelman, G. (2022). Historical continuum and norms in art collections and datasets–Experiments with Artificial Intelligence at Paulista Museum. *Journal of Art History*, *6*(2).

Ogle, A., & Lamb, D. (2019). The role of robots, artificial intelligence, and service automation in events. In *Robots, artificial intelligence, and service automation in travel, tourism and hospitality* (pp. 255–269). Emerald Publishing Limited. doi:10.1108/978-1-78756-687-320191012

Ozmen Garibay, O., Winslow, B., Andolina, S., Antona, M., Bodenschatz, A., Coursaris, C., Falco, G., Fiore, S. M., Garibay, I., Grieman, K., Havens, J. C., Jirotka, M., Kacorri, H., Karwowski, W., Kider, J., Konstan, J., Koon, S., Lopez-Gonzalez, M., Maifeld-Carucci, I., & Xu, W. (2023). Six human-centered artificial intelligence grand challenges. *International Journal of Human-Computer Interaction*, *39*(3), 391–437. doi:10.1080/10447318.2022.2153320

Păvăloaia, V. D., & Necula, S. C. (2023). Artificial intelligence as a disruptive technology—A systematic literature review. *Electronics (Basel)*, *12*(5), 1102. doi:10.3390/electronics12051102

Perroud, A. (2016). *Quelle place occupent les Nouvelles Technologies de l'Information et de la Communication et notamment les applications mobiles dans les musées?* [Master's Thesis. Haute école spécialisée de Suisse occidentale, University of Applied Sciences Western Switzerland].

Pisoni, G., Díaz-Rodríguez, N., Gijlers, H., & Tonolli, L. (2021). Human-centered artificial intelligence for designing accessible cultural heritage. *Applied Sciences (Basel, Switzerland)*, *11*(2), 870. doi:10.3390/app11020870

Pliasa, S., Velentza, A. M., Dimitriou, A. G., & Fachantidis, N. (2021). Interaction of a Social Robot with Visitors inside a Museum through RFID Technology. In *Proceedings of the 2021 6th International Conference on Smart and Sustainable Technologies (SpliTech)* (September), (pp. 1-6). IEEE. 10.23919/SpliTech52315.2021.9566435

Pruulmann-Vengerfeldt, P. (2022). Datafying museum visitors: A research agenda. *Information & Culture*, *57*(1), 63–81. doi:10.7560/IC57105

Rani, S., Jining, D., Shah, D., Xaba, S., & Singh, P. R. (2023). Exploring the Potential of Artificial Intelligence and Computing Technologies in Art Museums. In *Proceedings of the ITM Web of Conferences,* Vol. 53. EDP Sciences. 10.1051/itmconf/20235301004

Recuero Virto, N., & López, M. F. B. (2019). Robots, artificial intelligence, and service automation to the core: remastering experiences at museums. In *Robots, artificial intelligence, and service automation in travel, tourism and hospitality* (pp. 239–253). Emerald Publishing Limited. doi:10.1108/978-1-78756-687-320191018

Simone, C., Cerquetti, M., & La Sala, A. (2021). Museums in the Infosphere: Reshaping value creation. *Museum Management and Curatorship*, *36*(4), 322–341. doi:10.1080/09647775.2021.1914140

Spies, R., Grobbelaar, S., & Botha, A. (2020, April). A scoping review of the application of the task-technology fit theory. In *Conference on e-Business, e-Services and e-Society* (pp. 397-408). Cham: Springer International Publishing. 10.1007/978-3-030-44999-5_33

Sylaiou, S., & Fidas, C. (2022). Virtual Humans in Museums and Cultural Heritage Sites. *Applied Sciences (Basel, Switzerland)*, *12*(19), 9913. doi:10.3390/app12199913

Taormina, F., & Baraldi, S. B. (2022). Museums and digital technology: A literature review on organizational issues. *European Planning Studies*, *30*(9), 1676–1694. doi:10.1080/09654313.2021.2023110

Tu, S. (2019). Analysis on the development trend and application technology of digital museum. In *Proceedings of the 1st International Symposium on Innovation and Education, Law and Social Sciences (IELSS 2019)* (August 2019), 138-141. Atlantis Press. 10.2991/ielss-19.2019.26

Tykhonova, O., & Widmann, S. (2021). Museum innovation barometer. Culture Action Europe. https://cultureactioneurope.org/knowledge/museum-innovation-barometer-2021/

Vorobeva, D., Costa Pinto, D., António, N., & Mattila, A. S. (2023). The augmentation effect of artificial intelligence: Can AI framing shape customer acceptance of AI-based services? *Current Issues in Tourism*, 1–21.

Xie, C., Wang, Y., & Cheng, Y. (2022). Does artificial intelligence satisfy you? A meta-analysis of user gratification and user satisfaction with AI-powered chatbots. *International Journal of Human-Computer Interaction*, 1–11.

Yu, D., & Yao, W. (2023, February). Research on holographic display and technology application of art museum based on immersive design. [IOP Publishing.]. *Journal of Physics: Conference Series, 2425*(1), 012048. doi:10.1088/1742-6596/2425/1/012048

ADDITIONAL READINGS

Azmi, E., Che Rose, R. A., Awang, A., & Abas, A. (2023). Innovative and competitive: A systematic literature review on new tourism destinations and products for tourism supply. *Sustainability (Basel), 15*(2), 1187. doi:10.3390/su15021187

Bauer, J. E., Sohn, A. P. L., & Oliveira, B. S. D. (2019). Cultural Tourism: A study on museums and the Internet. *Turismo: Visão e Ação, 21*, 291–308.

Campa, J. L., Pagliara, F., López-Lambas, M. E., Arce, R., & Guirao, B. (2019). Impact of high-speed rail on cultural tourism development: The experience of the Spanish museums and monuments. *Sustainability (Basel), 11*(20), 5845. doi:10.3390/su11205845

Capstick, B. (1985). Museums and tourism. *International Journal of Museum Management and Curatorship, 4*(4), 365–372. doi:10.1016/0260-4779(85)90018-4

Izzo, F., Camminatiello, I., Sasso, P., Solima, L., & Lombardo, R. (2023). Creating customer, museum and social value through digital technologies: Evidence from the MANN Assiri project. *Socio-Economic Planning Sciences, 85*, 101502. doi:10.1016/j.seps.2022.101502

Kasemsarn, K., Harrison, D., & Nickpour, F. (2023). Applying inclusive design and digital storytelling to facilitate cultural tourism: A review and initial framework. *Heritage, 6*(2), 1411–1428. doi:10.3390/heritage6020077

Khalil, S., Kallmuenzer, A., & Kraus, S. (2023). Visiting museums via augmented reality: An experience fast-tracking the digital transformation of the tourism industry. *European Journal of Innovation Management*. Advance online publication. doi:10.1108/EJIM-09-2022-0479

Lee, H. M., & Smith, S. L. (2015). A visitor experience scale: Historic sites and museums. *Journal of China Tourism Research*, *11*(3), 255–277. doi:10.1080/19388160.2015.1083499

Lord, B. (2002). Cultural tourism and museums. *LORD Cultural Resources Planning and Management Inc*, *1*, 12.

Merciu, F. C., Merciu, G. L., & Cercleux, A. L. (2018, May). The role of museums in the development of cultural tourism. Case study: Bucharest Municipality. In *International Economic Conference of Sibiu* (pp. 173-186). Cham: Springer International Publishing.

Mura, P., & Wijesinghe, S. N. (2023). Critical theories in tourism–a systematic literature review. *Tourism Geographies*, *25*(2-3), 487–507. doi:10.1080/14616688.2021.1925733

Navarrete, T. (2019). Digital heritage tourism: Innovations in museums. *World Leisure Journal*, *61*(3), 200–214. doi:10.1080/16078055.2019.1639920

Piekkola, H., Suojanen, O., & Vainio, A. (2014). *Economic impact of museums*. Vaasan yliopisto.

Prentice, R. (2001). Experiential cultural tourism: Museums & the marketing of the new romanticism of evoked authenticity. *Museum Management and Curatorship*, *19*(1), 5–26. doi:10.1080/09647770100201901

Prideaux, B. R., & Kininmont, L. J. (1999). Tourism and heritage are not strangers: A study of opportunities for rural heritage museums to maximize tourism visitation. *Journal of Travel Research*, *37*(3), 299–303. doi:10.1177/004728759903700312

Qizi, M. K. I. (2021). The role of museums in the development of tourism. *Academicia: An International Multidisciplinary Research Journal*, *11*(2), 121–124. doi:10.5958/2249-7137.2021.00309.8

Reyes-García, M. E., Criado-García, F., Camúñez-Ruíz, J. A., & Casado-Pérez, M. (2021). Accessibility to cultural tourism: The case of the major museums in the city of Seville. *Sustainability (Basel)*, *13*(6), 3432. doi:10.3390/su13063432

Richards, G. (2013). Cultural tourism. In *Routledge handbook of leisure studies* (pp. 483–492). Routledge.

Silberberg, T. (1995). Cultural tourism and business opportunities for museums and heritage sites. *Tourism Management*, *16*(5), 361–365. doi:10.1016/0261-5177(95)00039-Q

Stylianou-Lambert, T. (2011). Gazing from home: Cultural tourism and art museums. *Annals of Tourism Research*, *38*(2), 403–421. doi:10.1016/j.annals.2010.09.001

Chapter 6
Literature Review on the XR Technologies in Tourism:
One Decade of Virtual Continuum in Tourism

Rogerio Tavares
https://orcid.org/0000-0001-9366-2617
Instituto Politécnico de Bragança, Portugal

João Paulo Sousa
Instituto Politécnico de Bragança, Portugal

Ricardo Correia
https://orcid.org/0000-0002-0132-4002
Instituto Politécnico de Bragança, Portugal & CiTUR, Portugal

Tiago Fernandes
https://orcid.org/0000-0002-1412-291X
Instituto Politécnico de Bragança, Portugal & LabCom - Communication and Arts, Portugal

ABSTRACT

This chapter begins with a concise overview of recent studies and reports on how the tourism industry is embracing digital transformation. This initial section aims to provide context for the current significance of technology adoption in tourism and an insight into the prevailing strategies and challenges faced by the industry. In light of this context, it becomes essential to delve into the scientific literature to comprehend how it reflects the evolution of technology adoption within tourism, including themes under investigation and potential trends. Hence, the following section delves into a bibliometric analysis of scientific production related to the

DOI: 10.4018/979-8-3693-2137-9.ch006

use of technologies in tourism over the past decade. This study enables us to gain a comprehensive understanding of the evolving scientific literature on technology adoption in tourism and it sets forth an agenda for future research, paving the way for advancements in the realm of new digital technologies in the tourism sector.

INTRODUCTION

Technology has become a crucial part of the tourism industry, with its integration growing significantly in recent years. As we continue to move towards a digitized society, the demand for advanced tech applications from tech-savvy generations has soared. Cutting-edge digital tools, such as touch-screen devices, audio guides, augmented and Virtual Reality, and beacon technology, have emerged as essential elements in enhancing visitors' tourism experience. These innovations offer immersive, personalized, and captivating content, elevating the visitor's journey.

Art resources are a significant aspect of tourism, representing cultural heritage and unique artistic value. Traditional presentation methods often lack the vividness and sharpness to make these resources feel charmless. Immersive technologies like VR, AR, and MR have the potential to create unforgettable tourist experiences, especially in heritage tourism (Alexandra Bec et al. 2019). Moreover, emerging digital technologies are critical to the sustainable preservation and communication of cultural heritage to the general public (Nikonova and Biryukova 2017).

The opening section of this paper explores recent studies and reports on how the tourism industry is embracing digital transformation. These studies highlight various factors propelling the tourism sector forward, including the increasing demand from tech-savvy younger generations, the potential for enhancing visitor experiences, and the unprecedented access and availability facilitated by the internet. Additionally, the section also delves into the challenges that come with technology adoption in tourism, such as maintenance requirements, digital literacy considerations, and resource limitations.

The visual support provided by software-generated tables and graphs enhances result interpretation, enabling us to comprehend the evolving scientific literature on technology adoption in the tourism industry. Through this visual aid, we address pertinent questions, such as:

- What are the prevailing XR technologies currently propelling the tourism sector towards digital transformation?
- Which published articles hold the greatest influence and explore which themes?
- Who are the most prolific authors and what technologies do they focus on?

- How do countries collaborate in advancing technology adoption within tourism?
- What are the most frequently used keywords in articles, revealing insights into the trending technology usage in the tourism sector?
- In what ways does XR technology play a role in the tourism industry?
- Which groundbreaking articles have the greatest influence on tourism?

BACKGROUND

The concept of a "virtuality continuum" was introduced in 1994 (Paul Milgram and Kishino 1994) and it refers to a spectrum ranging from complete virtuality to complete realism (Fig. 1). Essentially, it encompasses all possible variations and compositions of real and virtual components. The term is commonly used in the context of Virtual Reality and Augmented Reality technologies. A "virtual continuum" is described as a way to identify the various levels of immersion and interaction that can be experienced in virtual environments, ranging from fully immersive virtual worlds to Mixed Reality experiences that blend virtual and real elements.

Virtual Reality (VR) is a technology that generates simulated three-dimensional surroundings, allowing users to interact with them in a way that feels real and physical (Zheng, Chan, and Gibson 1998; Machover and Tice 1994). Augmented Reality is a technology that allows the superimposing of digital information (text, video, images, 3D objects, and others) onto our view of the real world in real-time (Azuma et al. 2001; Cipresso et al. 2018). In contrast to Virtual Reality (VR), which generates a completely artificial environment, Augmented Reality (AR) allows users to interact with the real world while having computer-generated information overlaid on top of it. The Mixed Reality concept combines elements of the real and virtual worlds to allow physical and digital objects to coexist and interact in real-time. Mixed Reality blends the real and the virtual world seamlessly in contrast to Virtual Reality, which is entirely virtual, and Augmented Reality, which adds virtual elements to the real world (Paul Milgram and Kishino 1994). The term Extended Reality (XR) refers to Augmented Reality (AR), Virtual Reality (VR), and Mixed Reality (MR) (Mann et al. 2023).

Extended Reality (XR) serves as an all-embracing term that contains the entire range of realities that are assisted by immersive technology, such as Augmented Reality (AR), Augmented Virtuality (AV), Mixed Realities (MR), Virtual Reality (VR), as well as potential future realities (Kwok and Koh 2021; P. Milgram and Kishino 1994). XR facilitates users' engagement within a reality formed through the convergence of humans and machines, achieved through the integration of a cyber and physical environment utilizing computers and wearables (Mann et al.

Figure 1. Reality-Virtuality continuum adapted from P. Milgram and Kishino 1994

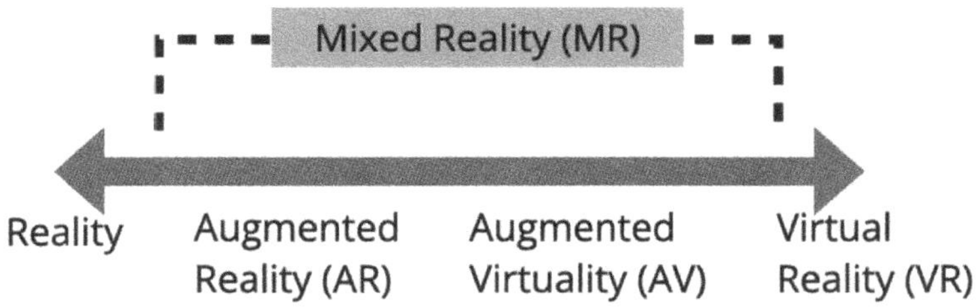

2023). As a result, XR enhances the user's perception of the simulation from an external standpoint and provides a distinctive sense of presence by extending their reality as they become situated within the simulation itself. This integration blurs the boundaries between the real and simulated environments to the point where they become indistinguishable (Suh and Prophet 2018).

XR has emerged as a valuable tool in the tourism industry. It has been utilized in various aspects of tourism, such as planning, management, promotion, education, and enhancing tourist experiences. It offers the opportunity for researchers to study multisensory phenomena and analyze tourist behavior by immersing participants in virtual situations. Additionally, it provides new possibilities for social scientists in psychology and sociology to study the tourism context, as multiple individuals can interact and share tasks in virtual environments. The number of papers on XR in tourism has been increasing over the years, indicating the growing interest in these technologies for the industry (Loureiro, Guerreiro, and Ali 2020).

MATERIALS AND METHODS

Bibliometric citation analysis stands as a well-established form of meta-analytical research (Garfield, E. 1983; Donohue 1972; Magyar 1974), which utilizes statistical methods to quantitatively assess scientific articles and other published works, revealing valuable publication patterns, including productivity, collaboration, impact, and trends. While its origins lie in the realms of sciences and humanities (Windsor 1976), this analytical approach quickly found its footing in diverse sectors like economics and management (Leeebvre and Fetterman 1985, 1977–1983). Nowadays, its versatility extends across an array of research areas (Sousa et al. 2022; Morais, Cunha, and Sousa 2021), offering profound insights into current trends, future directions, and author collaborations within the dynamic world of tourism.

Given our study's focus on illuminating the research landscape of technology adoption in the tourism industry, bibliometric citation analysis proves to be an astute meta-analytic approach. By harnessing this methodology, we aim to unravel the intricate web of scholarly contributions within the tourism domain, providing a comprehensive understanding of how technology has evolved within this thriving sector.

For this tourism-focused study, we collected data from one of the most renowned academic databases in the field, Web of Science (WoS), which includes the Social Sciences Citation Index (SSCI). Being multidisciplinary, the WoS database offers a broad perspective on publications across various science areas, providing valuable insights into technology adoption within tourism. To conduct the bibliometric analysis, we utilized the powerful Bibliometrix 3.1 in R 4.1.1 software, and the results were visually presented through the user-friendly Bibliophily application, which will be showcased in the upcoming sections. Leveraging the Bibliometrix package, we harnessed a plethora of routines to import bibliographic data from numerous scientific databases, conduct comprehensive bibliometric analysis, and construct data matrices for co-citation, coupling, scientific collaboration analysis, and co-word analysis (Aria and Cuccurullo 2017).

In our investigation, we focused on publications from the past ten years, spanning January 2013 to September 2023. This interval allowed us to capture recent advancements and trends, providing a comprehensive outlook on the role of technology within the tourism industry. Data was meticulously collected from the Scopus database, employing the advanced search interface. Our search encompassed the terms "virtual reality", "augmented reality", "mixed reality", "extended reality", "tourism" and "heritage" within the title or abstract of the publication, yielding a total of 262 relevant publications. To ensure precision and focus on scholarly works, we applied a filter, refining the search to include only: journal articles (127), proceedings papers (75), and book series (51) and books (9). By narrowing our scope to English language publications and focusing on diverse types of scholarly contributions, we aim to offer a comprehensive understanding of VR, AR, ER technology adoption within the thriving tourism sector. This rigorous approach allows us to extract valuable insights and meaningful trends that illuminate the role of technology in shaping the tourism landscape.

Table 1. Query and number of papers retrieved

Database	Query	Results
Scopus	TITLE-ABS-KEY (virtual AND reality OR augmented AND reality OR mixed AND reality OR extended AND reality AND tourism AND heritage) AND PUBYEAR > 2012 AND (LIMIT-TO (DOCTYPE, "ar") OR LIMIT-TO (DOCTYPE, "cp") OR LIMIT-TO (DOCTYPE, "ch") OR LIMIT-TO (DOCTYPE, "cr") OR LIMIT-TO (DOCTYPE, "re")) AND (LIMIT-TO (LANGUAGE, "English"))	262

FINDINGS

Documents

The chart in Fig. 1(a), shows the growth of the number of publications published annually, the highest annual growth was between 2018 and 2021 with a growth of 300%, and the maximum number of articles published in a year occurs in 2022, with 138 publications. In addition, the number of article citations per year Fig. 1(b), shows that the number of citations has slightly increased, where the publications from 2020 are the most cited.

Table 2 presents the top 10 publications by number of citations. The first paper (Alexandra Bec et al. 2019) proposes a four-stage conceptual model for heritage preservation aimed at heritage management in digital tourism experiences, including the presentation of historical facts, contested heritage, integration of historical facts and contested heritage, and/or an alternative scenario. Demonstrating that the integration of history with technology to create immersive environments has the potential to preserve and manage heritage and enrich the visitor's experience. In (El-Said and Aziz 2022) Technology Acceptance Model (TAM) and Protective Action Decision Model (PADM) are integrated to determine factors affecting people's decision to adopt virtual tours (VTs) during crises. Data from 401 respondents who experienced VTs simulating Egyptian heritage sites showed that TAM and PADM antecedents effectively predict users' intention to adopt VTs, with adoption intention positively impacting actual site visitation. In (A. Bec et al. 2021) the authors explore the effectiveness of creating tourism experiences in destinations affected by over-tourism, deterioration, and destruction. The proposed framework aims to provide data on-site preservation and impact mitigation, offering a second chance to reduce pressure on inherently fragile destinations. (Lin, Huang, and Ho

Figure 2. (a) Annual scientific production, and (b) total citations per year

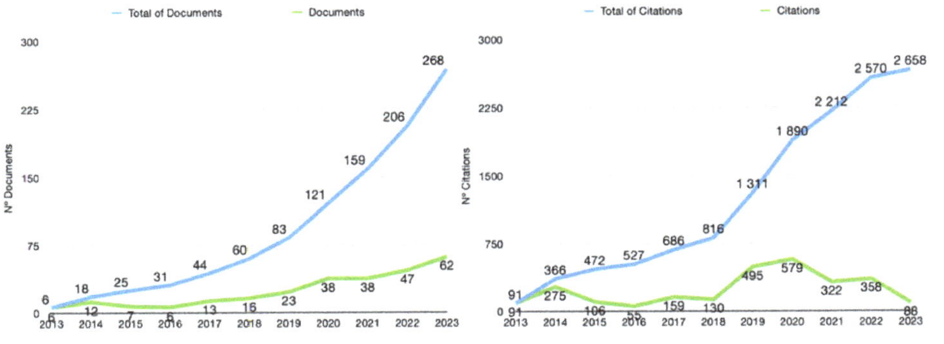

2020) profiles museum visitors based on their perceptions and attitudes towards VR applications, investigating whether they differ significantly in terms of socio-demographic characteristics and emotional responses to the VR-mediated experience at cultural attractions. Three clusters were identified with significant differences in attitudes, perceptions, and emotional feelings. The study (Lin, Huang, and Ho 2020) examines the effect of VR use in the tourism industry, intending to understand the associations for potential tourists among VR use, destination marketing, and travel intention, particularly when the object city is relatively unknown. In (Alexandra Bec et al. 2019) The effect of the use of technologies, particularly augmented reality, on the understanding and perception of authenticity and its effects on heritage is studied. The conceptual definition of heritage authenticity can be quite complex, so the authors suggest that the levels and standards of authenticity between groups of actors are fundamental to the discussion on authenticity and its role in tourism contexts. (Martínez-Graña, Goy, and Cimarra 2013) studies the use of Augmented Reality and QR Codes in the creation of virtual tours to show geological heritage to tourists. This article (Han, Tom Dieck, and Jung 2019) makes a specific study of the adoption of a class of augmented reality devices, augmented reality smart glasses (ARSG), to improve the experience of cultural tourism visitors. To this end, factors such as the social impact, benefits, innovation, and resistance of ARSG adoption in cultural tourism are studied. The (Garau 2014) article makes a specific study of the possibilities and challenges of using virtual reality in the context of Smart Cities, to promote cultural tourism. (Koeva, Luleva, and Maldjanski 2017) studies the use of VR, other technologies, and media, such as the integration of spherical panoramas, maps, GPS, sound, and textual information, to improve the viewing experience of different types of cultural heritage objects.

Table 2 is the result of analyzing the content of the 10 most cited papers returned in the initial query. The purpose of using XR technologies is diverse, but there has been a greater focus on the user experience. From Table 2 it is also possible to see that VR is used more off-site, while AR is used more in on-site experiences.

Sources

A total of 262 publications were found from 2013 to 2023, which present a wide range of scientific topics. Figure 2a shows the top 10 sources, which had 25 publications, thus comprising 10% of all publications. The top 3 sources with more publications were: Lecture Notes and Computer Science (LNCS), followed by the Springer Series on Cultural Computing and the Springer Proceedings in Business and Economics. Figure 2b shows the most locally cited sources, the most cited source was the journal Current Issues in Tourism 24% of the total citations of the top 10 most cited sources. The following two were the Computers in Human Behaviour Journal and the Journal

Table 2. Top ten publications by the number of citations (right)

Paper	Total Citations
Management of immersive heritage tourism experiences: A conceptual model (Alexandra Bec et al. 2019)	127
Virtual Tours a Means to an End: An Analysis of Virtual Tours' Role in Tourism Recovery Post COVID-19 (El-Said and Aziz 2022)	125
Virtual reality and mixed reality for second chance tourism (A. Bec et al. 2021)	109
Exploring the implications of wearable virtual reality technology for museum visitors' experience: A cluster analysis (Errichiello et al. 2019)	109
Could virtual reality effectively market slow travel in a heritage destination? (Lin, Huang, and Ho 2020)	93
Heritage authenticities – A case study of authenticity perceptions at a Danish heritage site (Dueholm and Smed 2014)	71
A virtual tour of geological heritage: Valourising geodiversity using Google Earth and QR code (Martínez-Graña, Goy, and Cimarra 2013)	68
Augmented Reality Smart Glasses (ARSG) visitor adoption in cultural tourism (Han, Tom Dieck, and Jung 2019)	65
From Territory to Smartphone: Smart Fruition of Cultural Heritage for Dynamic Tourism Development (Garau 2014)	60
Integrating spherical panoramas and maps for visualization of cultural heritage objects using virtual reality technology (Koeva, Luleva, and Maldjanski 2017)	57

Table 3. A summary of technology, local and purpose of the ten most cited papers

Paper	Technology	Place	Purpose
(Alexandra Bec et al. 2019)	VR and AR	on-site/off-site	Heritage preservation
(El-Said and Aziz 2022)	VR	off-site	Virtual tour
(A. Bec et al. 2021)	VR and MR	off-site	Destination preservation
(Errichiello et al. 2019)	VR	on-site	Visitor experience
(Lin, Huang, and Ho 2020)	VR	off-site	Marketing destination
(Dueholm and Smed 2014)	Any	on-site/off-site	Heritage authenticity
(Martínez-Graña, Goy, and Cimarra 2013)	AR and QR Code	on-site	Visitor experience
(Han, Tom Dieck, and Jung 2019)	AR	on-site	Visitor experience
(Garau 2014)	AR	on-site	Visitor experience
(Koeva, Luleva, and Maldjanski 2017)	VR and Web	off-site	Marketing destination

of Heritage Tourism. Figure 2c shows the most local impact coming firstly from the Sustainability, followed by the Applied Sciences journal, and, third, by the Current Issues in Tourism journal.

Figure 3. Analysis of sources: (top) Most relevant sources; (middle) Most local cited sources; Most h-index impact sources

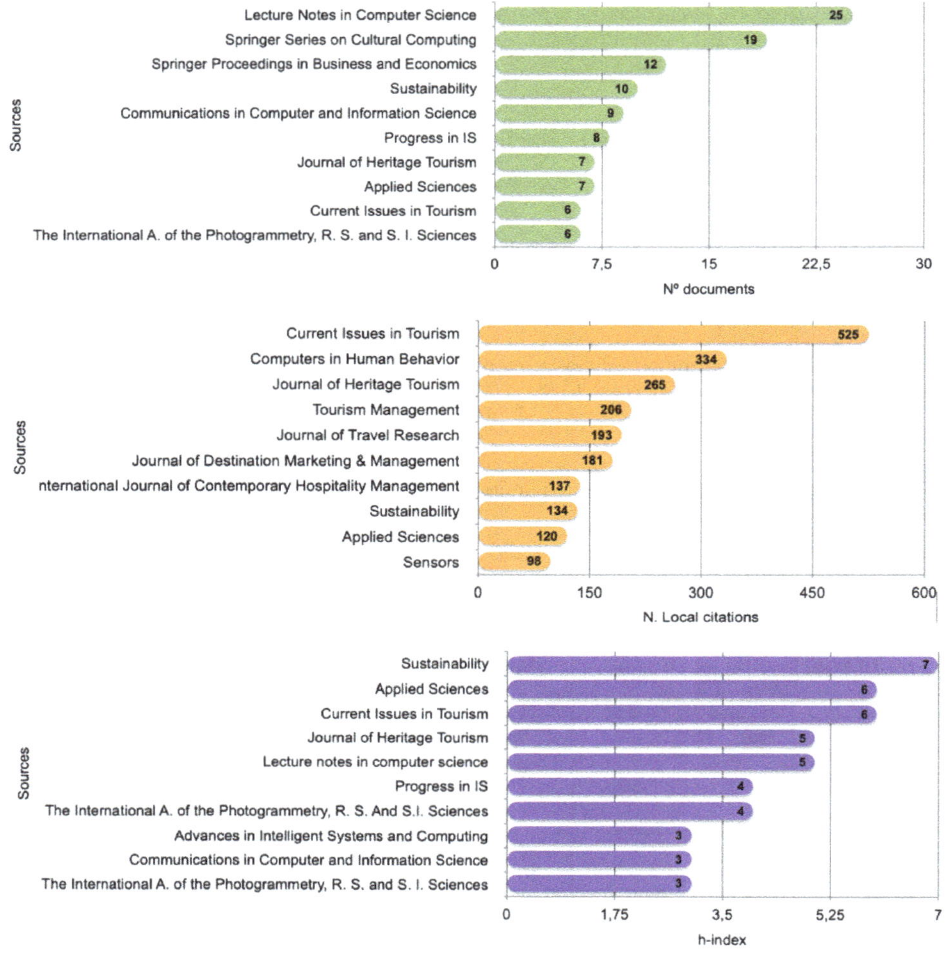

Authors

In Figure 3a, the ten most relevant authors are listed based on the number of articles they have published. Timothy H. Jung was the most productive author with 14 publications, followed by Mandy C. T. Dieck with 7 publications. In terms of the most cited authors, the same authors, Timothy H. Jung and Mandy C. T. Dieck hold the first two places. Timothy H. Jung was the most cited author, followed by Mandy C. T. Dieck, with Nam-Ho Chung in third place. These two graphics provide insight into the productivity and impact of these authors within the context of the articles being analyzed.

Figure 4, shows the author's network collaboration, and our findings suggest that collaboration networks between authors are mostly between authors from the same country.

Countries

The search returned a total of 67 countries. Italy was the most productive country, with a total of 117 publications, followed by China (89) and Spain (64).

Figure 6 illustrates the collaborative connections between these nations. The thickness of the lines reflects the intensity of the relationships. China, Spain, and

Figure 4. Author analysis: (a) Most relevant authors; (b) Most local cited authors

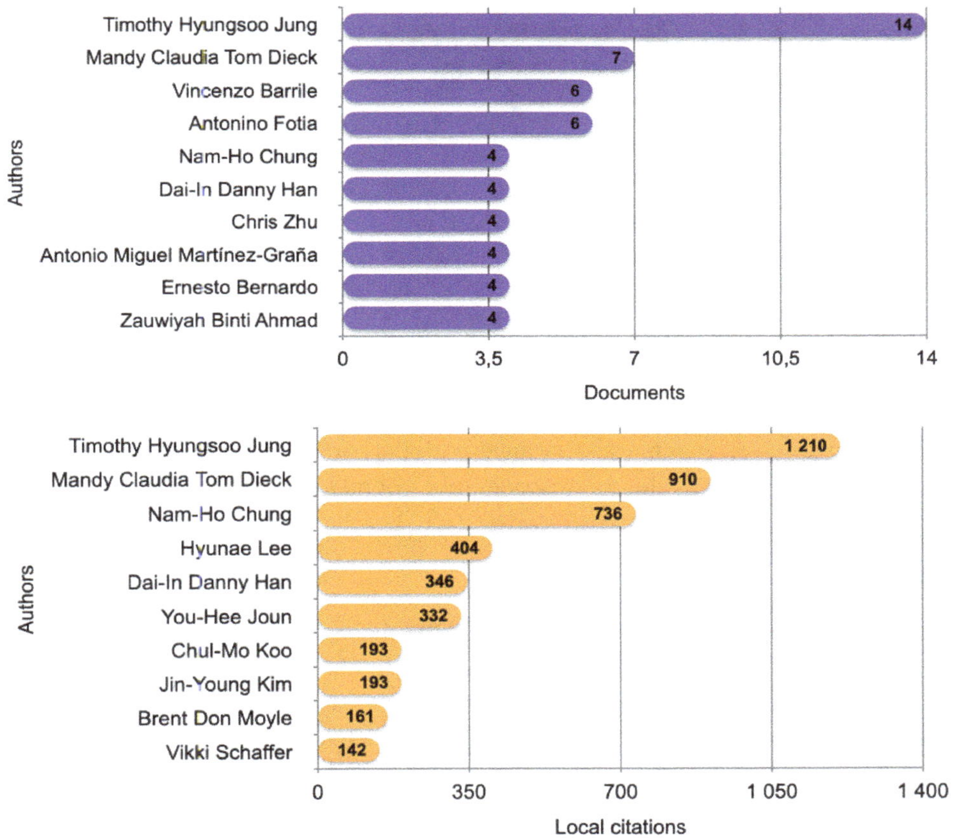

Figure 5. Author collaboration network

Figure 6. Country collaboration network

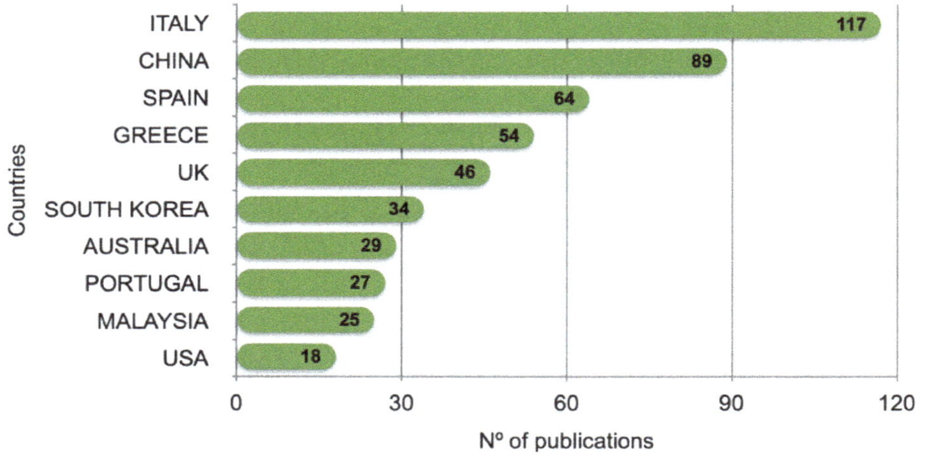

Portugal exhibit comparable significance in global cooperation. Additionally, Spain and the UK stand out as the most cooperative countries.

Words Co-Occurrence

The treemap depicted in Figure 7 displays the distribution of keywords from the conducted searches. Not surprisingly, "Virtual Reality" emerged as the most frequently searched term, making an appearance in 18% of the searches. "Cultural Heritages" and "Augmented Reality" shared the second spot, each with 13%, whereas "Tourism" settled for a fourth-place finish with 7%. These four keywords alone garnered half of the searches, accounting for 51%. The remaining 26 tags, sampled from the searches,

Figure 7. Country collaboration network

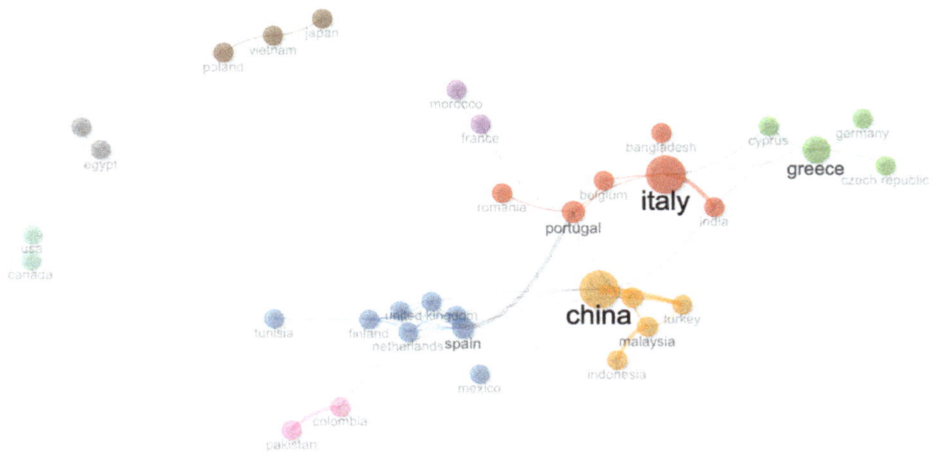

occupy the other half, with a distribution ranging from 4% to 1%. Of these, 22 tags fall in the range of 1% to 2%.

Figure 8 shows the current trend topics and future directions in the use of technologies for tourism. The popular topics between 2018 and 2022 were "Virtual Reality", "Cultural Heritages", and "Augmented Reality", but they have now been replaced by emerging topics such as "3D Modeling", "Image Reconstruction" and "Heritage Tourism". On the other hand, "Visualization" and "Human-Computer Interaction" were popular from 2014 to 2020 but are no longer relevant.

CONCLUSION

In this study, we have created scientific maps of various aspects related to XR Technologies in Tourism, such as documents, sources, authors, countries, and keyword co-occurrence. Our findings reveal a consistent increase in publications on technology in tourism over the past decade, with Italy and China being the major contributors to research in this field. The largest and most impactful source is the Lecture Notes in Computer Science (LNCS) journal, and Kuflik T is the researcher with the greatest impact. The research trends in terms of technology are "mixed reality", "artificial intelligence", "data linked", "3D scanning", and "3D printing". Additionally, we have identified significant research trends in "accessibility", "immersion", and "visitor experience". The integration of technology in the tourism industry has grown rapidly over the past decade, fundamentally transforming the tourist experience. Digital tools have become central to every aspect of tourism exploration, from touch devices and

Figure 8. Treemap of 50 most frequently used words

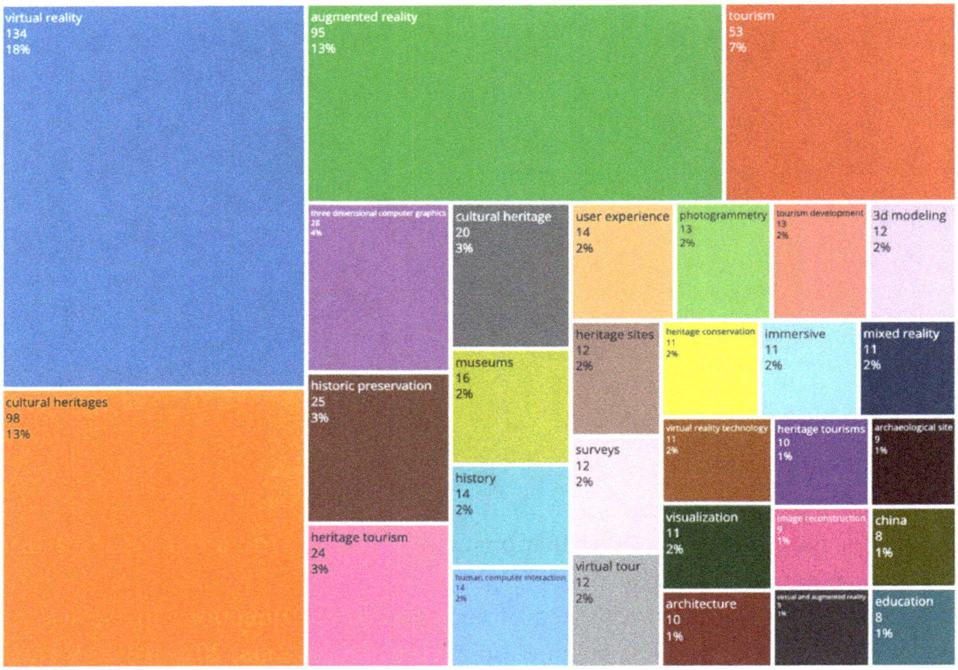

Figure 9. Top trend topics during the period

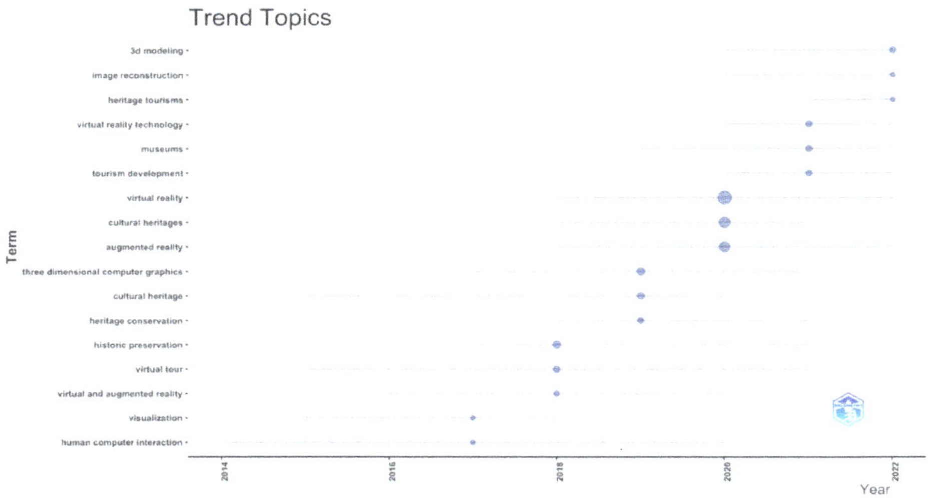

audio guides to augmented and virtual reality and beacon technology. The range of innovations available enhances the visitor's journey, offering unparalleled levels of immersion, personalization, and content richness.

From our analysis, it is also possible to see that VR is used more off-site experiences to provide immersive and attractive experiences for tourists. As can be seen in section 4.1, some examples of its use are the possibility of virtually exploring tourist destinations before their visit, supporting the decision-making process (El-Said and Aziz 2022); the creation of virtual museums and exhibitions, allowing visitors to explore works of art and artifacts without being physically present (Errichiello et al. 2019), or even training employees as tour guides (Tseng et al. 2015). In turn, AR has been used more during the visit, with the main aim of improving the experience of that visit. Some of the use cases identified were: the use of AR Apps mainly on mobile devices to obtain real-time information on sights and attractions (Han, Tom Dieck, and Jung 2019); the creation of immersive and interactive experiences during their visits (Alexandra Bec et al. 2019); the promotion of tourist destinations (Rahimi, Hassan, and Tekin 2020).

By embracing a tech-savvy approach to tourism, we can enhance visitor experiences and revolutionize the entire industry. In today's digitized society, the seamless integration of technology is necessary to cater to the ever-evolving demands of modern travelers. When wanderlust meets innovation, technology and tourism come together to create unforgettable journeys where immersive experiences and personalized adventures intertwine seamlessly. As we make progress towards a more interconnected world, the dynamic fusion of technology and tourism holds the potential to unlock a new era of exploration and entice curious souls from around the globe.

The blend of technology and tourism offers boundless opportunities for exploration, ignites curiosity, and fosters a deeper connection with the destinations we encounter. As we continue to embrace these digital advancements, the tourism industry is poised for a future filled with endless possibilities and unforgettable experiences.

ACKNOWLEDGMENTS

The authors are grateful to the Foundation for Science and Technology (FCT, Portugal) for financial support through national funds FCT/MCTES (PIDDAC) to CeDRI (UIDB/05757/2020 and UIDP/05757/2020) and SusTEC (LA/P/0007/2021).

REFERENCES

Aria, M., & Cuccurullo, C. (2017). Bibliometrix: An R-Tool for Comprehensive Science Mapping Analysis. *Journal of Informetrics*, *11*(4), 959–975. doi:10.1016/j.joi.2017.08.007

Azuma, R., Baillot, Y., Behringer, R., Feiner, S., Julier, S., & MacIntyre, B. (2001). Recent Advances in Augmented Reality. *IEEE Computer Graphics and Applications*, *21*(6), 34–47. doi:10.1109/38.963459

Bec, A., Moyle, B., Schaffer, V., & Timms, K. (2021). Virtual Reality and Mixed Reality for Second Chance Tourism. *Tourism Management*, *83*, 104256. doi:10.1016/j.tourman.2020.104256

Bec, A., Moyle, B., Timms, K., Schaffer, V., Skavronskaya, L., & Little, C. (2019). Management of Immersive Heritage Tourism Experiences: A Conceptual Model. *Tourism Management*, *72*(June), 117–120. doi:10.1016/j.tourman.2018.10.033

Cipresso, P., Irene, A. C. G., Raya, M. A., & Riva, G. (2018). The Past, Present, and Future of Virtual and Augmented Reality Research: A Network and Cluster Analysis of the Literature. *Frontiers in Psychology*, *9*, 2086. https://www.frontiersin.org/articles/10.3389/fpsyg.2018.02086. doi:10.3389/fpsyg.2018.02086 PMID:30459681

Donohue, J. C. (1972). A Bibliometric Analysis of Certain Information Science Literature. *Journal of the American Society for Information Science*, *23*(5), 313–317. doi:10.1002/asi.4630230506

Dueholm, J., & Smed, K. M. (2014). Heritage Authenticities – A Case Study of Authenticity Perceptions at a Danish Heritage Site. *Journal of Heritage Tourism*, *9*(4), 285–298. doi:10.1080/1743873X.2014.905582

El-Said, O., & Aziz, H. (2022). Virtual Tours a Means to an End: An Analysis of Virtual Tours' Role in Tourism Recovery Post COVID-19. *Journal of Travel Research*, *61*(3), 528–548. doi:10.1177/0047287521997567

Errichiello, L., Micera, R., Atzeni, M., & Del Chiappa, G. (2019). Exploring the Implications of Wearable Virtual Reality Technology for Museum Visitors' Experience: A Cluster Analysis. *International Journal of Tourism Research*, *21*(5), 590–605. doi:10.1002/jtr.2283

Garau, C. (2014). From Territory to Smartphone: Smart Fruition of Cultural Heritage for Dynamic Tourism Development. *Planning Practice and Research*, *29*(3), 238–255. doi:10.1080/02697459.2014.929837

Garfield, E. (1983). *How to Use Citation Analysis for Faculty Evaluations, and When Is It Relevant? Part 1*.

Han, D.-I. D., Tom Dieck, M. C., & Jung, T. (2019). Augmented Reality Smart Glasses (ARSG) Visitor Adoption in Cultural Tourism. *Leisure Studies*, *38*(5), 618–633. doi:10.1080/02614367.2019.1604790

Koeva, M., Luleva, M., & Maldjanski, P. (2017). Integrating Spherical Panoramas and Maps for Visualization of Cultural Heritage Objects Using Virtual Reality Technology. *Sensors (Basel)*, *17*(4), 829. doi:10.3390/s17040829 PMID:28398230

Kwok, A. O. J., & Koh, S. G. M. (2021). COVID-19 and Extended Reality (XR). *Current Issues in Tourism*, *24*(14), 1935–1940. doi:10.1080/13683500.2020.1798896

Leeebvre, V. M., & Fetterman, N. I. (1985). Bibliometric Analysis of the Journal of Consumer Studies and Home Economics, 1977–1983. *Journal of Consumer Studies & Home Economics*, *9*(1), 11–22. doi:10.1111/j.1470-6431.1985.tb00437.x

Lin, L.-P. L., Huang, S.-C. L., & Ho, Y.-C. (2020). Could Virtual Reality Effectively Market Slow Travel in a Heritage Destination? *Tourism Management*, *78*, 104027. doi:10.1016/j.tourman.2019.104027

Loureiro, S. M. C., Guerreiro, J., & Ali, F. (2020). 20 Years of Research on Virtual Reality and Augmented Reality in Tourism Context: A Text-Mining Approach. *Tourism Management*, *77*(April), 104028. doi:10.1016/j.tourman.2019.104028

Machover, C., & Tice, S. E. (1994). Virtual Reality. *IEEE Computer Graphics and Applications*, *14*(1), 15–16. doi:10.1109/38.250913

Magyar, G. (1974). Bibliometric Analysis of a New Research Sub-Field. *The Journal of Documentation*, *30*(1), 32–40. doi:10.1108/eb026568

Mann, S., Yuan, Y., Lamberti, F., El Saddik, A., Thawonmas, R., & Prattico, F. G. (2023). eXtended Meta-Uni-Omni-Verse (XV): Introduction, Taxonomy, and State-of-the-Art. *IEEE Consumer Electronics Magazine*, 1–9. doi:10.1109/MCE.2023.3283728

Martínez-Graña, A. M., Goy, J. L., & Cimarra, C. A. (2013). A Virtual Tour of Geological Heritage: Valourising Geodiversity Using Google Earth and QR Code. *Computers & Geosciences*, *61*, 83–93. doi:10.1016/j.cageo.2013.07.020

Milgram, P., & Kishino, F. (1994). A Taxonomy of Mixed Reality Visual Displays. *IEICE Transactions on Information and Systems*. Semantic Scholar. https://www.semanticscholar.org/paper/A-Taxonomy-of-Mixed-Reality-Visual-Displays-Milgram-Kishino/f78a31be8874eda176a5244c645289be9f1d4317

Milgram, P., & Kishino, F. (1994, December). A Taxonomy of Mixed Reality Visual Displays. *IEICE Transactions on Information and Systems*, *E77-D*(12), 1321–1329.

Morais, E.P. (2021). *Digital Marketing and Big Data: A bibliometric analysis of scientific production from the Scopus database.* . doi:10.23919/CISTI52073.2021.9476515

Nikonova, A., & Biryukova, M. (2017). The Role of Digital Technologies in the Preservation of Cultural Heritage. *Muzeologia a Kulturne Dedicstvo*, *5*(February), 169–173.

Rahimi, R., Hassan, A., & Tekin, O. (2020). Augmented Reality Apps for Tourism Destination Promotion. In Destination Management and Marketing: Breakthroughs in Research and Practice. doi:10.4018/978-1-7998-2469-5.ch059

Sousa, J. P., Tavares, R., Gomes, J. P., & Mendonça, V. (2022). Review and Analysis of Research on Video Games and Artificial Intelligence: A Look Back and a Step Forward. doi:10.1016/j.procs.2022.08.038

Suh, A., & Prophet, J. (2018). The State of Immersive Technology Research: A Literature Analysis. *Computers in Human Behavior*, *86*(September), 77–90. doi:10.1016/j.chb.2018.04.019

Tseng, S.-P., Huang, M.-W., Liu, H.-J., Chung, C.-C., & Chiu, C.-M. (2015). A Virtual Reality Based Training System for Cultural Tourism. Lecture Notes in Computer Science (Including Subseries Lecture Notes in Artificial Intelligence and Lecture Notes in Bioinformatics). doi:10.1007/978-3-662-46315-4_29

Windsor, D. A. (1976). Could Bibliometric Data Be Used to Predict the Clinical Success of Drugs? *The Journal of Documentation*, *32*(3), 174–181. doi:10.1108/eb026623

Zheng, J. M., Chan, K. W., & Gibson, I. (1998). Virtual Reality. *IEEE Potentials*, *17*(2), 20–23. doi:10.1109/45.666641

Chapter 7
Transforming Hospitality Experiences:
An Exploratory Study of Service Robots in the Hospitality Industry

Seema Jaipuriar
https://orcid.org/0009-0002-4009-0664
Amity University, Jaipur, India

Sanjeeb Pal
https://orcid.org/0000-0003-0567-9086
Amity University, Jaipur, India

Yashwant Singh Rawal
https://orcid.org/0000-0001-5367-7443
Parul University, Gujarat, India

ABSTRACT

Artificial intelligence applications and robotic technologies, which are rapidly spreading and widely used throughout the world, are discussed by different disciplines in literature including tourism. In this context, robots come to the fore in the application areas of the tourism sector. However, there are many artificial intelligence applications that are becoming widespread in the tourism sector. From this point of view, this conceptual study; firstly artificial intelligence applications and robotic technologies were evaluated, traits of service robots were revealed, then the current technologies and a brief comparison of service robots over human employees were examined, and as a result, the future of these technologies in the hospitality industry was discussed. In this context, it can be said that this study, in which the current situation is revealed, and sector-experienced writers make inferences for the future, is an important study that can contribute to the literature and industry practitioners.
DOI: 10.4018/979-8-3693-2137-9.ch007

INTRODUCTION

Researchers' interests have been piqued by AI in every industry globally. Automated dissemination, robotic concierges, chatbots, conveyor belt restaurants, and other advancements in the hospitality sector are examples of how the sector is starting to use robotics and artificial intelligence. Service robots are defined as independent, flexible system-based interfaces that interact, communicate, and provide services to the customers of its organization.

Most people think of robots as machines that can do intricate series of tasks (Singer, 2009). On the basis of information that they retrieve from various sources, they are capable of making their independent decisions and also, they do transform to the situation and learn from the past experiences (Pagallo, 2013; Allen et al., 2000). They can be thought of as social robots because they serve as the customer's interaction counterpart in front-line service environments.

Earlier robots were used in factories or manufacturing houses for performing repeated or complex tasks. But nowadays, robots have entered into service sectors too and are contributing in several areas.

LITERATURE REVIEW

In order to have a better understanding of the study, the literature review has been portrayed in the form of Table 1 as follows:

Traits of Service Robots

According to Jochen Wirtz et al (2018) there are majorly three traits of service robots as- Representation, anthropomorphism, and task- orientation as shown in Figure 1. Service robots may be physically present like *Pepper* or may be only virtually present like *Alexa*. Service robots either be like human in appearance i.e., humanoid like *Sophia* or be like non- humanoid like *Roomba cleaning robot*. As per task- orientation, service robots may perform cognitive- analytical tasks like *medical analysis's image analyzing assistant* or social-emotional tasks like *Reception robots*.

In the coming decades it is presumed that robots will be a maestro in performing cognitive and analytical tasks of unrivalled intricacy (Manyika et al., 2013, 2017). Huang and Rust (2018) have distinguished four levels of analytical intelligence of robots which are as follows: -

Table 1. Literature review

Sl. No.	Author/ Publication/ Year	Paper Title	Methodology	Discussion
1	Ivanov and Webster Social Science Research Network (SSRN)	Adoption Of Robots, Artificial Intelligence And Service Automation By Travel, Tourism And Hospitality Companies – A Cost-Benefit Analysis	Review Paper	Robots are not so much employees' replacements as they are technical tools and "extensions" of human workers. The use of robotics, AI, and service automation with their potential advantages and disadvantages are discussed.
2	Wirtz, et.al.	Brave new world: service robots in the frontline	Review Paper	Complex cognitive tasks involving strong emotional demands are likely to be performed by humans with assistance from robots. However, for high-frequency activities, it is expected that robots will be developed and used to do them; service personnel will operate in teams, with robots handling the heavy lifting or other tasks that humans find unpleasant, challenging, or even dangerous. Perhaps these service robots should be seen as intelligent, self-sufficient machines that collaborate with staff members.
3.	Bowen and Morosan, 2018	Beware hospitality industry: the robots are coming	Review Paper	The majority of robotics and artificial intelligence solutions have been created for business application (Meike and Ribickis, 2011). However, in the last ten to fifteen years, a number of robotics- and AI-based systems have been developed that customers may use to make more informed financial decisions and enjoy a smoother stay (e.g., chatbots, shopping assistants, etc.) (Kolodny, 2016).
4.	Lin, Shi, and Gursoy, 2020	Antecedents of customers' acceptance of artificially intelligent robotic device use in hospitality services	Survey- 5-point Likert scale	There were two surveys administered: one was meant to gauge the adoption of AI robotic service devices in full-service hotels, while the other was meant to be used in limited-service hotels. Customers of full-service hotels are unlikely to accept robotic AI gadgets for service delivery to the fullest extent. Customers at limited-service hotels are more inclined to accept the usage of robotic AI devices for service delivery.
5.	Ana Rosete, et.al.	Service Robots in the Hospitality Industry: An Exploratory Literature Review	Review paper	Since the integration of service robots has not yet reached the necessary level of service delivery, frontline services are thought to be directly tied to empathetic intelligence. employing AI and service robots; when done correctly, these technologies can enhance future customer experiences.
6.	Ai-Hsuan Chiang and Silvana Trimi	Impact of service robots on service quality	Survey- 7-point Likert scale	Robots fall short of clients' expectations in terms of timeliness, assurance, and dependability of quality.

continued on following page

Table 1. Continued

Sl. No.	Author/ Publication/ Year	Paper Title	Methodology	Discussion
7.	KichanNam, et.al. Springer 2020	The adoption of artificial intelligence and robotics in the hotel industry: prospects and challenges	Exploratory- Personal interview	Hotels will employ artificial intelligence (AI) and robotics more in areas where the benefits are felt quickly. Analytics and cost reduction have a great deal of potential to boost sales and improve customer satisfaction. The intricacy of AI per se does not deter hotels from using this technology, as long as outside IT vendors supply a dependable system. Participants believed that staff resistance to the new technology wouldn't prevent it from being adopted to the fullest degree possible.
8.	Belanche, Casalo and Flavian Springer 2020	Frontline robots in tourism and hospitality: service enhancement or cost reduction?	Survey- 7-point scale	In order to improve consumers' impressions of affinity (as a sense of familiarity and tighter connection) with the service robot, human likeness should be viewed as an instrumental variable.
9.	Cain and Berezina Springer 2021	Robo-Tipping: Are Customers Game?	Survey- multiple-choice and open-ended questions	Efficiency and upkeep were mentioned by respondents as justifications for tipping; in order to increase client satisfaction, practitioners must make sure the equipment functions well and is regularly updated. The server's expression of gratitude is an essential element.
10.	Minglong Li, et.al. Springer 2021	A systematic review of AI technology-based service encounters: Implications for hospitality and tourism operations	Review Paper	In public health situations, service contact is crucial to service management, and AI tools may be able to help.

Source- Author's Own

a) <u>Mechanical Intelligence</u>- These are related to those tasks which are repeated ones and routinely followed. *For example*- Vacuum cleaning of public areas in hotels.

b) <u>Analytical intelligence</u>- These are related to tasks like problem solving, machine learning, information processing and performing composite but systemized and anticipated tasks. *For example*- Forecasting the demand and optimizing the price.

c) <u>Intuitive intelligence</u>- This means the capability to comprehend intricate data, think comprehensively and creatively, and function well in unfamiliar circumstances that need understanding. *For example*- Legal advice in case of robbery, theft, or any other crime.

d) <u>Empathetic intelligence</u>- This means the capability to recognize, comprehend, and react to the emotions of others. *For example*- Understanding the guest needs and personalizing the product or package.

Figure 1. Three traits of service robots
Source- Author's Own

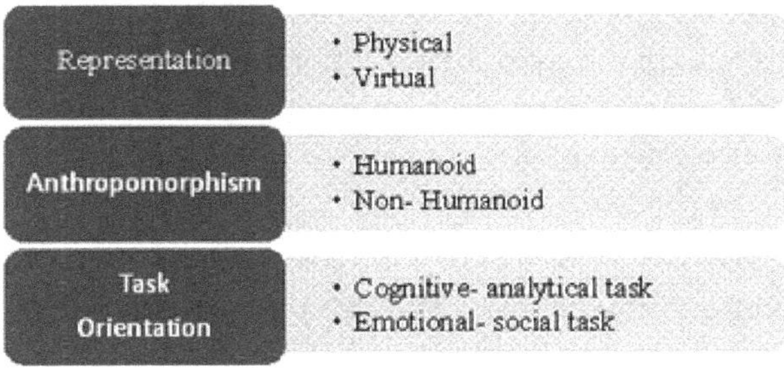

In the literature there is a consensus that the first three levels of AI will reach an advanced stage soon and that robots will take over as the primary method of delivering services that require these levels. However, the fourth level is a topic of much discussion that whether the robots will be capable of delivering social and emotional services at a level comparable to what humans can.

Advantages of Robots Over Humans

According to Wirtz et. al. (2018) following Table 2 provides certain differentiation and advantages of services robots over service employees.

Table 2. Differentiation and advantages of service robots over service employees

Service Employees	Service Robots
They have limited memory.	They have virtually endless memory.
They need training.	They need upgradation.
It is an individual learning.	It is a system learning.
They need deep understanding of their customers.	They follow pattern recognition, codified knowledge.
The output provided is heterogenous.	The output provided is homogenous,
Employee's skills and efforts define customization and personalization.	Personalization and customization can be delivered at consistent quality and performance.
They are unintended biased.	They are potentially unbiased.
They incur high incremental cost.	They incur low incremental cost.
They bear low economies of scale and scope.	They bear high economies of scale and scope.
The important services delivered by service employees are expensive and scarce.	Services delivered by service robots are lower in prices due to cost-savings made by them.

Source- Author's Own

Types of Robots

Robotic services are an important application of artificial intelligence in the hospitality industry. They are among the most efficient hotel technologies, and their use will assist in guaranteeing higher levels of customer satisfaction. Following are some of the examples of robotic technologies to be used in hospitality-

i. ***Robot Receptionist***- Henn-na hotel in Japan which is the world's first robotic hotel has employed humanoid robot receptionist for check-in ((Tung & Au, 2018), check-out, greeting the guests, furnish reception services (Lewis-Kraus, 2016).
ii. ***Robotic Bellboy***- 'Sacarino' is a robot which performs bellboy services in Hotel Novotel (Valladolid, Spain) (Zalama et al., 2014). It performs various activities like calling the taxi, video conferencing, providing information about the hotel facilities to the guests, etc. Another example of robotic bellboy is Yobot used by Yotel New York (2020).
iii. ***Robotic Concierge***- 'Connie' is a humanoid robotic concierge used by hotel Hilton (Davis, 2016; Hilton Worldwide, 2016; Park, 2020, p. 3). Connie interacts with the guests to provide information regarding the various facilities and services offered by the hotel. It also provides information about the local site seeing to the guests. Connie learns new information provided with the guest and experiences and hence improves itself to provide better answers to the queries that might arise in the future (Ivanov et al., 2017, p. 1506). 'Robby Pepper' is the first robotic concierge in Italy which is capable of serving Italian, English, and German languages (Barry, Pele, 2018).
iv. ***Robotic Bartender***- Royal Caribbean's Quantum of the Seas has two robotic bartenders at Bionic Bar taking the orders from the customers, mixing, stirring, shaking, and preparing the orders while the customers enjoy watching their drinks being prepared.

The robot gets the precise quantity of the ingredients needed for the mixture and serves the guests' beverages with lemon and ice as it is pre-programmed with the mixture amounts (Sloan, 2014). A robotic bartender may have the look of a humanoid or may only appear in the shape of an arm (Tussyadiah et al., 2020).

v. ***Robotic Butler***- 'Botlr' is a robotic butler employed in hotel Aloft- one of the brands of Starwood hotels, for delivering orders to the rooms (Crook, 2014; Markoff, 2014; Park, 2020, p. 3). If there is any guest request for toothbrush, soap, extra tea bags, towels, etc. then the service employees can load these items on the service robots and these robots can deliver them to the guests

(Crook, 2014). These robots are capable of using the elevators, roaming around the hotel, delivering the orders to the guests (Ivanov et al., 2017, p. 1506).

vi. ***Robotic Chef***- 'Ausca' is a robotic chef employed by hotel M Social Singapore in 2017. It is said that it can make omlettes and sunny-side up egg dishes and can become better by gaining knowledge about more advanced egg-cooking methods (Lin, 2017).

vii. ***Robotic Waiter***- 'Lucy' and 'Mary' are two robots employed by a restaurant named Rong Heng, Singapore which serves orders to the guests (Ang, 2016). Robotic waiters or bussers can help the service employees when there is a rush in the restaurants or during peak hours (Ivanov & Webster, 2020, p. 1073). It has been noted that restaurant proprietors search for robotic waiters for helping in serving customers during the rush hours or peak hours (Cheong et al., 2016, p. 681).

viii. ***Robotic Housekeeper***- 'Robie' is a robotic housekeeper employed by hotel Park Avenue Rochester, Singapore. It assists housekeeping staff in moving bulky items such as garbage, large volumes of items, and linens between the floors. Its performance throughout the day allows it to perform the duties of 3.5 full-time staff members by itself, saving the company cost (Lin, 2017).

ix. ***Robotic Hostess/Host***- 'Ruby' a robotic host has been employed by a restaurant named Tanuki in Dubai to captivate the guests to the restaurant. The robotic host can interact with the customers, provide them with coupons & discounts, and encourage them to come to the eatery (Ivanov & Webster, 2020, p. 1073). For tech-savvy consumers interacting with these robots can be a fascinating experience, also they enable these consumers to enjoy themselves while they are at the eatery (Berezina et al., 2019, p. 198).

x. ***Drone***- A drone is said to be a flying robot. As per Oxford Learner's Dictionaries (2020), a drone can be defined as "an aircraft without a pilot, controlled from the ground, used for taking photographs, dropping bombs, delivering goods, etc." In hospitality industry drones can be used for delivering orders (Hwang, Lee, & Kim, 2019; Hwang, Cho, & Kim, 2019; Hwang, Kim, & Kim, 2019; Hwang, Kim, & Kim, 2020). Drones can also be used for shooting video for destination marketing (Stankov et al., 2019) or doing photography at archeological sites for monitoring visitors (Donaire, Galí & Gulisova, 2020). In food and beverage industry, a customer in Auckland, New Zealand received the first commercial drone pizza delivery from Domino's Pizza (Lui, 2016).

Analysis of Robotic Bartender

A study was conducted by Lisa Cain and Katerina Berezina (2021) to look at customer opinions regarding tipping robot staff in bars by showing them a video about a robot bartender and responding to the questions. The respondents were from United States and had frequently visited to bars. An online survey was conducted using Amazon's Mechanical Turk (MTurk) platform. The result shows that out of **102** usable responses only 15 respondents had experienced robotic bartender at any casino or cruise line bars. Table 3 depicts certain other data: -

The result showed that out of 102 respondents 63 (61.76) of them agreed to tip robotic bartender and rest of them disagreed.

Table 4 provides the current and potential uses of robotics:

FINDINGS AND DISCUSSION

As depicted in Table 3, the customers were willing to offer tip to the robotic bartenders moreover the customers having experienced the robotic bartenders had influence on their intention of tipping them. This depicts that the bar operators can expect an extra revenue through this tipping from the customers which might also increase with repeat customers and the customers already having experience of robotic bartenders in the past.

Customer's interaction with the robots also plays significant role in the process of evaluation. Customers comes in less contact with the hotel employees but service robots are frequently remarked about in the comments (Cheong and Law, 2023). Robots increase productivity and reduce costs for restaurants, hotels, and various other hospitality enterprises in the service sector. When used in conjunction with

Table 3. Analysis of study conducted by Cain and Berezina (2021)

	Number	Percentage	Reason
Respondents who had experienced robotic bartender and who would tip a robot staff.	10	9.8	It hardly spills, it is quick and easy. Tip is for bar and robot maintenance
Respondents who had not experienced robotic bartender and who would tip a robot staff.	1	0.98	To see if there is a positive reaction to the tip.
Inexperienced respondents who initially had refused but eventually agreed to tip a robot staff.	52	50.98	If the collected fund goes to human employees. If the collected fund is used as learning experience for robot to understand the likes and dislikes of the customer.
Inexperienced respondents who refused to tip a robotic bartender.	39	38.24	Many reasons like robots do not have soul, they do not need income to survive, etc.

Source- Author's Own

Table 4. Current and potential uses of robotics

Current Use	Potential Use
In hotels robots are used at front desk, concierge, delivering, porter services.	Robots can be used for housekeeping services like cleaning, doing laundry, etc.
Robotic chefs, waiters, bartenders are being used.	Dishwashing robots, food and beverage ordering robots can also be used.
In banquet and meeting services, robot attendants and servers are used.	An interactive booth attendant robot can be used in such areas.
Robots are not a part of sales and marketing.	Instead, robots can be used as sales agent and can be featured in marketing campaigns.

Source- Author's Own

current branding initiatives, service robots can give the marketing division an interesting point of uniqueness (Mukherjee S., 2023).

CONCLUSION AND FUTURE IMPLICATIONS

Robots are heavily utilizing Artificial Intelligence technology in the hospitality and tourist sectors. It is one of the most revolutionary technological effects in the hospitality sector. Service robots enable hospitality companies' efficient ways to boost productivity and save costs. Service robots provide managers with alluring points of product differentiation if they sink properly with the current branding approaches. Service robots could alter current methods of human resource management. Like for frontline services the service employees may notice a change from traditional waiting duties for order taking or payment processing to more specialized tasks like room consultants, product ambassadors, etc. Similarly, for back-end services the employees may experience a change from repetitive vegetable chopping or omelette tossing to more innovative tasks like food platting, developing new recepies, etc. Even though a significant number of companies are trying to embrace service robots in the hotels, only few have succeeded. As such, business leaders should therefore carefully assess where and how to apply developing technology. This study makes a contribution to hospitality management by highlighting contemporary frontline service practices, such as the use of service robots. In particular, at the frontline, where the use of these service technologies necessitates significant cognitive and emotional activities, more study is required to provide effective, manageable, and replicable solutions.

Although there are ample number of AI tools and techniques which can be used by used by hospitality industry, but the main point of concern is the safety and security attached to it along with best possible outcomes, which in return can be effectively efficient. For this, AI neural network, Synthetic Minority Oversampling Technique (SMOTE), Decision Tree, Random Forest, etc. can be used for appropriate output. In the future implications we can use any abovementioned technique to get effective and efficient result. Secondly, as machines and humans run parallelly in today's era hence areas of other disciplines can be like psychology, environment, communication, sustainability, etc. can be reviewed and studied combinedly with AI and robotics.

REFERENCES

Allen, C., Varner, G., & Zinser, J. (2000). Prolegomena to any future artificial moral agent. *Journal of Experimental & Theoretical Artificial Intelligence*, *12*(3), 251–261. doi:10.1080/09528130050111428

Ang, B. (2016). *Robot Lucy at your service at newly opened Rong Heng Seafood.* The Strait Times Lifestyle.

Barry, C., & Pele, C. (2018). *Italy's robot concierge a novelty on the way to better AI.*

Belanche, D., Casaló, L. V., & Flavián, C. (2021). Frontline robots in tourism and hospitality: Service enhancement or cost reduction? *Electronic Markets*, *31*(3), 477–492. doi:10.1007/s12525-020-00432-5

Berezina, K., Ciftci, O., & Cobanoglu, C. (2019). Robots, artificial intelligence, and service automation in restaurants. In *Robots, artificial intelligence, and service automation in travel, tourism and hospitality* (pp. 185–219). Emerald Publishing Limited. doi:10.1108/978-1-78756-687-320191010

Bowen, J., & Morosan, C. (2018). Beware hospitality industry: The robots are coming. *Worldwide Hospitality and Tourism Themes*, *10*(6), 726–733. doi:10.1108/WHATT-07-2018-0045

Cain, L., & Berezina, K. (2021). Robo-tipping: are customers game? In *Information and Communication Technologies in Tourism 2021: Proceedings of the ENTER 2021 eTourism Conference, January 19–22, 2021* (pp. 222-227). Springer International Publishing.

Cheong, A., Lau, M. W. S., Foo, E., Hedley, J., & Bo, J. W. (2016). Development of a robotic waiter system. *IFAC-PapersOnLine*, *49*(21), 681–686. doi:10.1016/j.ifacol.2016.10.679

Cheong, F., & Law, R. (2023). Human employees versus robotic employees: Customers and hotel managers' perceived experience at unmanned smart hotels. *Cogent Social Sciences*, *9*(1), 2202937. doi:10.1080/23311886.2023.2202937

Crook, J. (2014). Starwood introduces robotic butlers at Aloft hotel in Cupertino. *Techcrunch. com.*

Davis, L. K. (2016). Hilton and IBM pilot "Connie," The world's first Watson-enabled hotel concierge robot. *Retrieved May, 22*, 2023.

Donaire, J. A., Galí, N., & Gulisova, B. (2020). Tracking visitors in crowded spaces using zenith images: Drones and time-lapse. *Tourism Management Perspectives*, *35*, 100680. doi:10.1016/j.tmp.2020.100680

Huang, M. H., & Rust, R. T. (2018). Artificial intelligence in service. *Journal of Service Research*, *21*(2), 155–172. doi:10.1177/1094670517752459

Hwang, J., Cho, S. B., & Kim, W. (2021). Consequences of psychological benefits of using eco-friendly services in the context of drone food delivery services. In *Future of tourism marketing* (pp. 67–78). Routledge. doi:10.4324/9781003176039-7

Hwang, J., Kim, H., & Kim, W. (2019). Investigating motivated consumer innovativeness in the context of drone food delivery services. *Journal of Hospitality and Tourism Management*, *38*, 102–110. doi:10.1016/j.jhtm.2019.01.004

Hwang, J., Kim, W., & Kim, J. J. (2020). Application of the value-belief-norm model to environmentally friendly drone food delivery services: The moderating role of product involvement. *International Journal of Contemporary Hospitality Management*, *32*(5), 1775–1794. doi:10.1108/IJCHM-08-2019-0710

Hwang, J., Lee, J. S., & Kim, H. (2019). Perceived innovativeness of drone food delivery services and its impacts on attitude and behavioral intentions: The moderating role of gender and age. *International Journal of Hospitality Management*, *81*, 94–103. doi:10.1016/j.ijhm.2019.03.002

Ivanov, S., & Webster, C. (2020). Robots in tourism: A research agenda for tourism economics. *Tourism Economics*, *26*(7), 1065–1085. doi:10.1177/1354816619879583

Ivanov, S. H., Webster, C., & Berezina, K. (2017). Adoption of robots and service automation by tourism and hospitality companies. *Revista Turismo & Desenvolvimento (Aveiro)*, *27*(28), 1501–1517.

Lewis-Kraus, G. (2016). *Check in with the velociraptor at the world's first robot hotel*. Wired Magazine.

Lin, H., Chi, O. H., & Gursoy, D. (2020). Antecedents of customers' acceptance of artificially intelligent robotic device use in hospitality services. *Journal of Hospitality Marketing & Management*, *29*(5), 530–549. doi:10.1080/19368623.2020.1685053

Lin, J. (2017). Robots are taking Singapore's hotel industry by strom-here's where to go for some robot hospitality.

Lu, L., Cai, R., & Gursoy, D. (2019). Developing and validating a service robot integration willingness scale. *International Journal of Hospitality Management*, *80*, 36–51. doi:10.1016/j.ijhm.2019.01.005

Lui, K. (2016). Watch the world's first commercial pizza delivery by drone. Fortune. *Retrieved*, *5*, 2018.

Lukanova, G., & Ilieva, G. (2019). Robots, artificial intelligence, and service automation in hotels. In *Robots, artificial intelligence, and service automation in travel, tourism and hospitality* (pp. 157–183). Emerald Publishing Limited. doi:10.1108/978-1-78756-687-320191009

Majid, G. M., Tussyadiah, I., Kim, Y. R., & Pal, A. (2023). Intelligent automation for sustainable tourism: A systematic review. *Journal of Sustainable Tourism*, *31*(11), 2421–2440. doi:10.1080/09669582.2023.2246681

Manyika, J., Chui, M., Bughin, J., Dobbs, R., Bisson, P., & Marrs, A. (2013). *Disruptive technologies: Advances that will transform life, business, and the global economy* (Vol. 180). McKinsey Global Institute.

Markoff, J. (2014). Beep, says the bellhop. *New York Times*.

Mukherjee, S., Baral, M. M., Nagariya, R., Venkataiah, C., Rao, U. A., & Rao, K. S. (2023). Systematic literature review and future research directions for service robots in hospitality and tourism industries. *Service Industries Journal*, *43*(15-16), 1083–1116. doi:10.1080/02642069.2023.2243592

Murphy, J., Gretzel, U., & Pesonen, J. (2021). Marketing robot services in hospitality and tourism: the role of anthropomorphism. In *Future of Tourism Marketing* (pp. 16–27). Routledge. doi:10.4324/9781003176039-3

Pagallo, U. (2013). Robots in the cloud with privacy: A new threat to data protection? *Computer Law & Security Report*, *29*(5), 501–508. doi:10.1016/j.clsr.2013.07.012

Park, S. (2020). Multifaceted trust in tourism service robots. *Annals of Tourism Research*, *81*, 102888. doi:10.1016/j.annals.2020.102888

Rawal, Y. S., Soni, H., Dani, R., & Bagchi, P. (2022, July). A review on service delivery in tourism and hospitality industry through artificial intelligence. In *Proceedings of Third International Conference on Computing, Communications, and Cyber-Security: IC4S 2021* (pp. 427-436). Singapore: Springer Nature Singapore.

Reis, J., Melão, N., Salvadorinho, J., Soares, B., & Rosete, A. (2020). Service robots in the hospitality industry: The case of Henn-na hotel, Japan. *Technology in Society*, *63*, 101423. doi:10.1016/j.techsoc.2020.101423

Rosete, A., Soares, B., Salvadorinho, J., Reis, J., & Amorim, M. (2020). Service robots in the hospitality industry: An exploratory literature review. In *Exploring Service Science: 10th International Conference, IESS 2020, Porto, Portugal, February 5–7, 2020* [Springer International Publishing.]. *Proceedings*, *10*, 174–186.

Singer, P. W. (2009). *Wired for war: The robotics revolution and conflict in the 21st century*. Penguin.

Singh, A. K., Tyagi, P. K., Jain, E., Tyagi, P., Singh, A. K., & Sharma, N. (2022, March). Robotics and Artificial Intelligence in Hospitality Sector: A Descriptive Bibliometric Analysis and Future Research Directions. In *2022 International Conference on Electronics and Renewable Systems (ICEARS)* (pp. 1484-1491). IEEE. 10.1109/ICEARS53579.2022.9752272

Sloan, G. (2014). Robot bartenders? This new cruise ship has them. *USA Today*.

Stankov, U., Kennell, J., Morrison, A. M., & Vujičić, M. D. (2021). The view from above: the relevance of shared aerial drone videos for destination marketing. In *Future of Tourism Marketing* (pp. 40–54). Routledge. doi:10.4324/9781003176039-5

Tung, V. W. S., & Au, N. (2018). Exploring customer experiences with robotics in hospitality. *International Journal of Contemporary Hospitality Management*, *30*(7), 2680–2697. doi:10.1108/IJCHM-06-2017-0322

Tuomi, A., Tussyadiah, I. P., & Stienmetz, J. (2021). Applications and implications of service robots in hospitality. *Cornell Hospitality Quarterly*, *62*(2), 232–247. doi:10.1177/1938965520923961

Tussyadiah, I. P., Zach, F. J., & Wang, J. (2020). Do travelers trust intelligent service robots? *Annals of Tourism Research*, *81*, 102886. doi:10.1016/j.annals.2020.102886

Van Doorn, J., Mende, M., Noble, S. M., Hulland, J., Ostrom, A. L., Grewal, D., & Petersen, J. A. (2017). Domo arigato Mr. Roboto: Emergence of automated social presence in organizational frontlines and customers' service experiences. *Journal of Service Research*, *20*(1), 43–58. doi:10.1177/1094670516679272

Wirtz, J., Patterson, P. G., Kunz, W. H., Gruber, T., Lu, V. N., Paluch, S., & Martins, A. (2018). Brave new world: Service robots in the frontline. *Journal of Service Management*, *29*(5), 907–931. doi:10.1108/JOSM-04-2018-0119

Zalama, E., García-Bermejo, J. G., Marcos, S., Domínguez, S., Feliz, R., Pinillos, R., & López, J. (2014). Sacarino, a service robot in a hotel environment. In *ROBOT2013: First Iberian Robotics Conference* [Springer International Publishing.]. *Advanced Robotics*, *2*, 3–14.

Chapter 8
Travel Redefined:
Future Trends in AI-Enhanced Tourism Experiences

Jeganathan Gomathi Sankar
https://orcid.org/0000-0002-5077-5109
BSSS Institute of Advanced Studies, Bhopal, India

ABSTRACT

In the vision of future travel, advanced technology emerges as the linchpin, orchestrating a paradigm shift in planning, experiencing, and securing journeys. Central to this evolution is the concept of personalized itineraries, where algorithms craft unique travel experiences tailored to individual preferences, breaking away from conventional one-size-fits-all packages. Proactive addressing of travel challenges becomes paramount, with predictive analytics identifying and mitigating hurdles in real-time for a stress-free experience. Guided tours transform into dynamic experiences as AI-powered guides adapt narratives, enriching exploration with personalized insights. Virtual reality reconstructions transport travelers to historical landmarks, transcending temporal boundaries for accessible cultural exploration. Streamlined city navigation via mobile apps or wearables provides real-time information. Advanced security, driven by technology and AI, ensures a safe travel environment.

INTRODUCTION

Artificial Intelligence (AI) is characterized as the utilization of computational machinery to replicate human capabilities, encompassing physical or mechanical

DOI: 10.4018/979-8-3693-2137-9.ch008

tasks, cognitive processes such as thinking, and even emotions (Huang & Rust, 2021). Its historical roots coincide with the advent of the first computers, but recent times have witnessed a surge in AI's prominence owing to rapid advancements in computer power and diverse technologies like computer vision, machine learning, and natural language processing. The proliferation of available data for algorithm training has also played a pivotal role in driving AI's recent momentum (Mariani et al., 2022). In today's digital age, the way we experience travel is changing dramatically, driven by rapid technological advancements. This research paper, titled "Travel Redefined: Future Trends in Enhanced Tourism Experiences," explores the transformative forces shaping the future of travel. At its core is the combination of Artificial Intelligence (AI) with human wanderlust, ushering in a new era of personalized, immersive, and intelligently guided tourism (Samara et al., 2020). The digital age has brought about a fundamental shift in how individuals plan, experience, and embark on journeys. In a world where information flows seamlessly, travelers are no longer restricted by traditional limitations. It is within this dynamic environment that the impact of AI becomes prominent, introducing a range of possibilities that redefine the very nature of travel (Filieri et al., 2021). At the heart of this research is the idea of personalized itineraries, where algorithms and data-driven insights work together to create unique travel experiences tailored to the specific preferences of each individual. No longer confined to rigid travel packages, travelers are now presented with the opportunity to embark on journeys that resonate intimately with their desires and interests. This departure from the traditional approach not only marks a significant change but also signals the advent of a future where the boundaries of exploration are limitless.

Predictive analytics play a crucial role in this transformative journey, proactively addressing the challenges that travelers may encounter. By harnessing real-time data processing, this research explores how technology anticipates and mitigates potential hurdles, ensuring a stress-free and seamless travel experience (Wang, 2020). The concept of navigating through the uncertainties of travel takes center stage, as AI becomes a strategic ally in ensuring that every journey unfolds with precision and efficiency. Guided tours also undergo an evolution as AI-powered guides step into the spotlight (Jabeen et al., 2022). Beyond scripted narratives, these intelligent guides adapt their storytelling to the nuanced interests of each traveler, infusing exploration with a new dimension of personalization and enrichment. The exploration of historical sites becomes an interactive dialogue, as AI guides offer insights tailored to individual curiosities, bringing the stories of the past to life. Venturing further into the future, virtual reality (VR) reconstructions emerge as a technological marvel, promising to immerse travelers in lifelike depictions of historical landmarks (Ozdemir, 2021). The fusion of AI and VR opens doors to a new era of accessible cultural exploration, where the barriers of time and distance dissipate. The bustling cities of the world become more navigable than ever before, thanks to insightful guides delivered through mobile applications or wearable devices. Offering real-time information, personalized recommendations, and navigational support, these guides become indispensable companions in the urban tapestry (Samaddar & Mondal, 2023). The cityscape transforms into an intelligently curated experience, as technology facilitates seamless interactions with the environment. Security, a paramount concern in the realm of travel, undergoes a paradigm shift with advanced measures driven by AI. From biometric authentication at airports to smart hotel room access, this research explores how technology becomes a guardian, ensuring a secure and trustworthy travel environment (Doborjeh et al., 2022). The integration of artificial intelligence in security protocols promises not only to enhance safety but also to proactively respond to potential threats. In the confluence of personalized itineraries, predictive analytics, intelligent guides, VR reconstructions, and advanced security measures, a transformative synergy emerges, ushering in a future where travel is redefined as a realm of unparalleled, individually tailored experiences (Ozdemir, 2021). As we embark on this journey into the heart of enhanced tourism, technology stands not only as a catalyst but as the key to unlocking a landscape where the joy of exploration knows no bounds. Each travel experience becomes a unique, enriching story, meticulously crafted with precision to align with the diverse preferences of the modern-day explorer. This research, therefore, seeks to unravel the tapestry of possibilities that lie at the intersection of AI and travel, offering insights into the promising future that awaits those who seek to explore the world in this era of redefined travel experiences (Bulchand-Gidumal, 2022).

The burgeoning influence of Artificial Intelligence (AI) is undeniably reshaping and elevating the realm of travel experiences. AI's expanding role is evident in its ability to craft personalized itineraries, a departure from the standardized travel packages of the past (Filieri et al., 2021). Algorithms and data-driven insights work seamlessly to tailor unique journeys, aligning with individual preferences and interests. Predictive analytics, powered by AI, take center stage in addressing travel challenges in real-time. This proactive approach ensures a stress-free and streamlined experience, enhancing the overall quality of travel. From anticipating and mitigating potential hurdles to providing precise and efficient solutions, AI contributes significantly to a more secure and efficient journey (Doborjeh et al., 2022). AI-powered guides mark a dynamic evolution in guided tours, adapting narratives to individual interests. This intelligent interaction enhances exploration by providing personalized insights, transforming historical and cultural experiences into engaging dialogues tailored to each traveler's curiosity. Virtual Reality (VR) reconstructions, a marvel of AI integration, immerse travelers in lifelike depictions of historical landmarks. The transcending of temporal boundaries in cultural exploration becomes achievable through the seamless fusion of AI and VR, offering unprecedented accessibility to historical and cultural heritage. In urban environments, AI plays a pivotal role in navigating bustling cities (Ozdemir, 2021). Intelligent guides delivered through mobile applications or wearables provide real-time information, personalized recommendations, and navigational support. This ensures that travelers can seamlessly interact with their surroundings, enhancing their understanding and appreciation of the cityscape. Security measures in travel are undergoing a paradigm shift with the integration of AI (Filieri et al., 2021). Biometric authentication at airports and smart hotel room access are prime examples of how AI contributes to a more secure and trustworthy travel environment (Doborjeh et al., 2022). The proactive response to potential threats ensures that safety is prioritized throughout the travel experience. The transformative synergy of personalized itineraries, predictive analytics, intelligent guides, VR reconstructions, and advanced security measures underscores the growing role of AI in redefining travel experiences (Fan et al., 2022). As technology continues to evolve, AI stands as a key catalyst, unlocking a future where the joy of exploration is boundless, and each travel experience becomes a unique and enriching story, meticulously crafted to align with the diverse preferences of modern-day travelers (Jabeen et al., 2022). The growing prominence of AI in the travel landscape promises a future where technology not only enhances but fundamentally reshapes the way individuals perceive, plan, and embark on their journeys.

CURRENT STATE OF AI IN TOURISM

Personalized Travel Planning

Revolutionizing personalized travel planning, advanced technologies, particularly Artificial Intelligence (AI), have introduced transformative elements like AI-powered chatbots, itinerary builders, and recommendation engines (Yang et al., 2023). These tools redefine how individuals plan and experience their journeys. AI-powered chatbots engage users dynamically, adapting to preferences through natural language processing and offering tailored responses on destinations and accommodations (Pillai & Sivathanu, 2020). The accessibility of these chatbots streamlines interactions, providing immediate assistance. AI-driven itinerary builders depart from conventional travel packages, leveraging algorithms to create bespoke plans based on individual interests, travel history, and real-time conditions. This granular customization transforms travel planning into a responsive and unique experience (Ho et al., 2023). Recommendation engines utilize machine learning to provide targeted suggestions across accommodations, activities, and dining, continually adapting through user feedback. The convergence of these technologies marks a transformative shift towards tailored and user-centric experiences, departing from static travel plans (Chaudhari & Thakkar, 2020). This synergy creates an interactive planning experience, aligning each aspect precisely with the traveler's expectations. The integration of AI-powered technologies represents a move towards a more intuitive, responsive, and personalized era in travel planning, ensuring each journey is uniquely crafted to meet the traveler's expectations (Renjith et al., 2020).

Virtual and Augmented Reality Experiences

Virtual and augmented reality experiences have ushered in a new era of immersive possibilities across various domains, notably transforming how we explore history, culture, and language. These technologies offer more than entertainment, providing users with a multifaceted journey that combines education, exploration, and linguistic discovery (Samaddar & Mondal, 2023). Immersive tours, a groundbreaking application, transcend physical boundaries, allowing users to step into virtual worlds and experience ancient landmarks, cityscapes, and natural wonders with a heightened sense of presence (Cranmer et al., 2020). Historical reconstructions take this further by digitally recreating the past, allowing users to virtually walk through historical sites and witness events as they unfolded. Language translation tools within these platforms break down language barriers, providing real-time translation for enhanced communication in diverse linguistic landscapes, fostering global connectivity (Yung et al., 2021). The impact of these experiences is profound, reshaping our perception, learning, and interaction with the world. As these technologies evolve, the potential for even more immersive and culturally enriching experiences becomes limitless, showcasing the transformative power of technology at the intersection of the digital and physical realms (Ozdemir, 2021).

Smart Hotels and Destinations

Smart hotels and destinations lead a technological revolution, aiming to enhance the travel experience through automation, personalization, and intelligent guidance. These innovations streamline traditional hotel processes, transforming how travelers engage with and explore their destinations (Buhalis et al., 2023). Automated check-in and check-out processes eliminate the need for traditional front desk interactions, allowing guests to seamlessly check in through mobile apps and settle bills without manual procedures (Shafiee et al., 2021). Personalized in-room services, another significant advancement, use technology to tailor the in-room environment to individual preferences, from adjusting temperature and lighting to setting wake-up alarms (Buhalis et al., 2023). Integration with smart home devices enables travelers to control amenities with voice commands or dedicated apps. Intelligent city guides provided by smart hotels offer real-time, context-aware information, suggesting attractions, restaurants, and events based on individual interests through data analytics and location-based services (Elshaer & Marzouk, 2022). The synergy of these technologies transforms the travel experience into a seamless and tailored journey, catering to individual needs while promoting efficient and sustainable hospitality practices. As smart hotels and destinations evolve, the integration of cutting-edge technologies promises to redefine travel, placing comfort, convenience, and personalization at the forefront (Jeong & Shin, 2020).

FUTURE STATE OF AI IN TOURISM

Hyper-Personalized Itineraries

The advent of hyper-personalized itineraries marks a revolutionary shift in travel planning, with Artificial Intelligence (AI) playing a central role in crafting journeys that transcend individual preferences and extend into the realm of emotional states. This transformative approach harnesses advanced algorithms and data-driven insights to tailor every aspect of a trip, creating a truly bespoke and emotionally resonant travel experience. Rather than focusing solely on preferences, this innovative approach considers the traveler's emotional context, ensuring that each aspect of the itinerary is curated to evoke specific feelings and enhance the overall journey (Zheng et al., 2020). By leveraging AI's ability to analyze vast datasets and interpret nuanced emotional cues, hyper-personalized itineraries redefine the travel landscape, offering individuals not just a customized adventure but an emotionally enriching and fulfilling exploration (Buhalis et al., 2023). This evolution in travel planning underscores the potential for technology to deeply connect with travelers on a personal and emotional level, creating memorable and unique experiences that go beyond traditional preferences to tap into the very essence of individual desires and sentiments.

The journey into AI-driven hyper-personalization commences with a meticulous analysis of extensive datasets encompassing a traveler's preferences, past travel history, and online behavior. Delving into individual tastes across accommodations, activities, cuisine, and more, the AI orchestrates a personalized itinerary that aligns seamlessly with the traveler's unique interests (Zheng et al., 2020). This departure from generic, one-size-fits-all packages represents a paradigm shift, ensuring that every journey is finely tuned to the individual's specific desires. Rather than adhering to pre-set templates, the hyper-personalization process embraces the nuances of each traveler, creating an experience that is not only tailored but also deeply reflective of their distinct preferences (Gasmi et al., 2024). This approach goes beyond mere customization, venturing into the realm of understanding the intricacies that make each traveler unique. By leveraging the power of AI to interpret and respond to individual preferences, the hyper-personalization journey sets the stage for a new era in travel planning, where every itinerary is a bespoke masterpiece crafted to resonate with the individual's distinct tastes and desires (Ho et al., 2023).

In a departure from traditional personalization, AI is now venturing into the emotional landscape of travelers, introducing a new dimension to the travel experience. Through the analysis of contextual cues, sentiment data, and even physiological indicators, AI possesses the capability to gauge the emotional state of a traveler in real-time (Gasmi et al., 2024). This emotionally aware AI then dynamically adapts the itinerary to cater to the traveler's mood, suggesting activities, locations, or moments of relaxation that align with their current emotional state. For instance, if the AI senses a need for relaxation, it might recommend a serene spa day or a peaceful nature retreat. Conversely, if a traveler expresses enthusiasm or curiosity, the AI might suggest more adventurous activities or cultural explorations (Ji et al., 2021). This emotionally intelligent personalization adds a nuanced layer to the travel experience, creating journeys that not only align with individual preferences but also respond dynamically to the traveler's emotional needs. The result is a travel itinerary that is not just customized but finely attuned to the traveler's evolving emotional landscape, ensuring a more profound and personally resonant exploration of the world (Ho et al., 2023). This innovative approach represents a significant leap in the realm of AI-driven travel personalization, where technology not only understands individual preferences but also engages with the intricate and ever-changing tapestry of human emotions, enriching the travel experience in ways previously unexplored (Zheng et al., 2020).

The culmination of emotional awareness in AI-driven travel planning yields a travel itinerary that unfolds as a meticulously crafted narrative, resonating with the traveler on a deeper and more personal level. This integration marks a significant leap toward a future where every journey becomes a tailored, emotionally enriching experience (Gasmi et al., 2024). The itinerary, shaped by the real-time understanding of the traveler's emotions, goes beyond conventional personalization. It transforms into a dynamic story that adapts and responds to the traveler's emotional needs, creating moments that evoke genuine connection and resonance (Zheng et al., 2020). As technology continues to advance, the potential for hyper-personalized itineraries to redefine travel and create lasting, meaningful memories becomes boundless (Ho et al., 2023). In this future landscape, each journey is not merely a series of destinations and activities but a narrative that reflects the traveler's emotional nuances, making the exploration of the world a profoundly unique and memorable experience (Gasmi et al., 2024). The convergence of technology and emotion in travel planning opens up a realm where the journey itself becomes a testament to the intricate interplay between individual preferences and the ever-evolving tapestry of human emotions (Ji et al., 2021).

Adaptive Travel Environments

The advent of adaptive travel environments marks a revolutionary shift in the influence of Artificial Intelligence (AI) on the physical spaces that travelers inhabit. This cutting-edge integration of AI-controlled infrastructure extends far beyond conventional accommodations, giving rise to dynamic environments meticulously tailored to individual needs. The realm of adaptive accommodations witnesses AI taking the reins in real-time regulation of room conditions. Here, smart climate control systems utilize a blend of individual preferences, historical data, and even current physiological indicators to seamlessly adjust room temperature, lighting, and ambiance in alignment with the traveler's unique comfort requirements (Baggio et al., 2020). This unparalleled level of personalization ensures that each guest enjoys an optimal and tailor-made stay, where the environment not only meets but anticipates their preferences. The implications of adaptive travel environments go beyond mere comfort; they redefine the very nature of hospitality by creating spaces that respond actively and intuitively to the diverse and evolving needs of modern travelers (Hamid et al., 2021). As this technology continues to advance, the potential for AI to revolutionize the hospitality landscape, providing not just accommodations but adaptive, personalized experiences, becomes increasingly evident. The integration of AI in shaping travel environments signifies a new era where the spaces we inhabit during our journeys become not only functional but dynamically responsive, enhancing the overall travel experience in ways previously unimagined.

In the realm of adaptive travel environments, the transformation extends beyond accommodations to revolutionize the dining experience, with restaurant menus evolving through the infusion of Artificial Intelligence (AI). Dynamic menu systems represent a paradigm shift in culinary offerings, leveraging comprehensive data on individual dietary preferences, allergies, and culinary tastes to craft personalized menu recommendations (Baggio et al., 2020). This sophisticated use of AI transcends traditional dining approaches, as it delves deep into each traveler's unique palate. By understanding and analyzing individual tastes, the AI-driven menu systems adeptly suggest dishes that align precisely with the preferences of the diner, ushering in a new era of personalized and enjoyable dining experiences. The implications are profound; no longer bound by static menus, travelers find themselves immersed in a culinary journey curated to their specific tastes and requirements (Hamid et al., 2021). This innovative integration of AI in restaurant menus goes beyond mere customization; it transforms dining into a tailored, intuitive, and delightful experience that reflects the diverse culinary preferences of modern travelers. As technology continues to advance, the potential for AI to redefine how we engage with food during our journeys becomes increasingly apparent (Akdu, 2020). The adaptive dining experience within these environments reflects not just a revolution in gastronomy but a new frontier in hospitality, where every aspect of the traveler's journey is carefully crafted to enhance enjoyment, comfort, and satisfaction (Baggio et al., 2020). The future of dining in adaptive travel environments holds the promise of not just meeting but surpassing individual expectations, creating a culinary landscape that mirrors the diversity and dynamism of contemporary traveler preferences. In the realm of adaptive travel environments, the innovation doesn't stop at individualized comfort and personalized dining; it seamlessly extends to public spaces and transportation (Akdu, 2020). AI-controlled infrastructure takes charge, optimizing elements like lighting, seating arrangements, and noise levels in shared areas, crafting atmospheres that cater to the diverse needs and preferences of travelers. Public spaces transform into dynamic environments, adapting to the preferences of each visitor, ensuring a comfortable and enjoyable experience for all. Moreover, smart transportation systems, guided by AI intelligence, bring a new level of efficiency to travel (Baggio et al., 2020). These systems dynamically adjust routes and services in real-time, responding to changing circumstances and individual preferences. The result is not just personalized travel but a holistic and responsive journey, where public spaces and transportation seamlessly integrate AI-driven adaptability to enhance the overall travel experience (Muniz et al., 2021).

The primary objective of adaptive travel environments is to seamlessly incorporate technology into the traveler's journey, elevating every aspect with a level of customization that resonates with individual preferences. Through the utilization of AI to control infrastructure, the travel experience not only becomes more efficient but also more enjoyable, envisioning a future where each traveler's journey is distinctly crafted to cater to their needs and desires (Akdu, 2020). This shift towards adaptive environments signifies a notable progression in the evolution of travel, where technology works to transform spaces into dynamic, responsive, and personalized settings (Hamid et al., 2021). The integration of these innovations aims to redefine the way individuals experience and interact with their surroundings, offering a vision of travel that is both streamlined and uniquely tailored to the diverse preferences of modern travelers.

Predictive Travel Planning

The landscape of travel planning has undergone a remarkable transformation with the advent of predictive travel planning, a groundbreaking concept where the reins are handed over to Artificial Intelligence (AI) models to anticipate crowd levels, predict travel disruptions, and determine optimal travel times. This forward-looking approach relies on sophisticated algorithms and real-time data analysis, fundamentally altering the way individuals plan and navigate their journeys (Gharibi, 2021). A standout feature of predictive travel planning lies in its capacity to forecast crowd levels at various travel destinations (Sohrabi et al., 2020). Through the analysis of historical data, events, and social trends, AI models can predict when popular attractions, airports, or transportation hubs are likely to experience peak crowds. Equipped with this valuable information, travelers gain the ability to make informed decisions about when to visit, allowing them to optimize their experiences by steering clear of unnecessary congestion and delays (Novianti et al., 2022). This predictive aspect not only enhances the efficiency of travel but also contributes to a more enjoyable and stress-free journey. The integration of AI-driven predictive capabilities is reshaping travel planning into a proactive and strategic endeavor, providing travelers with valuable insights to navigate the dynamic landscape of their chosen destinations with foresight and ease (Gharibi, 2021).

The pivotal role of AI models in predictive travel planning extends beyond forecasting crowd levels to addressing the anticipation of travel disruptions, marking a significant advancement in journey preparedness (Tsang et al., 2020). Through the analysis of diverse datasets encompassing weather patterns, traffic conditions, and historical travel data, these models exhibit the capability to predict potential challenges like flight delays, road closures, or public transportation issues (Antonio et al., 2022). This predictive insight serves as a valuable tool for travelers, offering the foresight to adjust plans, choose alternative routes, or make contingency arrangements in response to anticipated disruptions (Novianti et al., 2022). The real-time adaptability provided by AI-driven predictions empowers individuals to navigate unexpected hurdles with flexibility and resilience, fostering a smoother and more stress-free travel experience (Sohrabi et al., 2020). In essence, the integration of AI models into predictive travel planning not only enhances the overall efficiency of journeys but also equips travelers with a proactive toolkit to navigate the dynamic landscape of potential disruptions, ensuring a more seamless and adaptable travel adventure (Tsang et al., 2020).

In the realm of predictive travel planning, the focus on optimal travel times emerges as a pivotal element reshaping the way individuals approach their journeys. Here, AI models come to the forefront, employing sophisticated algorithms to analyze a diverse array of factors including traffic patterns, weather conditions, and local events in the destination city (Yu & Chen, 2022). This comprehensive analysis enables the models to discern the most favorable times for travel, guiding users to plan their journeys during periods of lower congestion and heightened convenience. By incorporating this dynamic approach into travel planning, individuals gain the advantage of reduced travel times and a more seamless overall experience (Sohrabi et al., 2020). The integration of AI-driven insights on optimal travel times not only streamlines the logistics of the journey but also empowers travelers with the ability to make informed decisions that align with their preferences and schedules (Novianti et al., 2022). In essence, the inclusion of optimal travel times in predictive travel planning represents a transformative shift towards a more efficient and user-centric approach to journey coordination, where technology enhances the travel experience by strategically guiding individuals to traverse through times of minimal congestion.

The incorporation of predictive travel planning stands as a noteworthy advancement in the travel industry, presenting a synergy of technology with the contemporary needs of today's travelers. In this innovative approach, the utilization of AI takes center stage, allowing for the anticipation of crowd levels, prediction of potential disruptions, and the recommendation of optimal travel times (Yu & Chen, 2022). The profound impact lies in empowering individuals to make more informed, strategic decisions, thereby elevating the overall quality and efficiency of their travel experiences (Novianti et al., 2022). As technology continues to progress, the significance of predictive travel planning becomes increasingly apparent, showcasing the transformative potential of AI in shaping the future landscape of travel (Sohrabi et al., 2020). This evolution reflects a commitment to providing travelers with tools that not only simplify the planning process but also enable them to navigate their journeys with a heightened sense of control and tailored decision-making (Novianti et al., 2022). In essence, predictive travel planning represents a pivotal shift towards a more user-centric and efficient paradigm, where technology serves as an indispensable ally in enhancing the overall travel experience.

Sustainable Travel Solutions

The quest for sustainable travel solutions has taken a significant leap forward with the integration of Artificial Intelligence (AI) systems. These innovative solutions represent a departure from conventional approaches, introducing dynamic and data-driven strategies aimed at optimizing resource usage, minimizing environmental impact, and fostering responsible tourism practices. Within the travel industry, AI plays a pivotal role in the optimization of resources. By harnessing the power of advanced algorithms, AI systems analyze extensive datasets to pinpoint opportunities for resource conservation (Holmes et al., 2021). Whether it's managing energy consumption in accommodations or optimizing transportation routes, these smart systems are designed to contribute to sustainable practices (Sung et al., 2021). In hotels, for example, AI algorithms can dynamically adjust lighting, heating, and cooling based on occupancy patterns, thereby enhancing energy efficiency and reducing the overall environmental footprint. This transformative application of AI reflects a commitment to responsible tourism and underscores the potential for technology to play a key role in mitigating the environmental impact of travel. As AI continues to evolve, its integration into sustainable travel solutions holds promise for a more eco-conscious and environmentally friendly future in the realm of travel (Holmes et al., 2021).

At the heart of sustainable travel solutions driven by Artificial Intelligence (AI) lies the fundamental goal of minimizing environmental impact. These innovative systems tackle this objective by assessing a multitude of factors, ranging from emissions and waste generation to conservation practices, providing actionable insights for a more eco-conscious approach to travel (Kim et al., 2023). AI's role in waste management optimization is particularly noteworthy, as these systems can predict optimal disposal times, advocate for recycling initiatives, and even recommend eco-friendly alternatives for travelers. In the realm of transportation, AI algorithms come into play by suggesting routes that inherently possess lower carbon footprints, thereby contributing to greener and more sustainable travel experiences (Reejo, 2023). The integration of AI in sustainable travel solutions not only demonstrates a commitment to environmental stewardship but also showcases the potential of technology to drive positive change in the travel industry. As these AI-powered initiatives continue to evolve, they hold the promise of fostering a more responsible and environmentally friendly future for travelers and the destinations they explore (Balsalobre-Lorente et al., 2023).

Within the realm of AI-powered sustainable travel solutions, the promotion of responsible tourism practices emerges as a pivotal dimension. These advanced systems leverage Artificial Intelligence (AI) to educate travelers on eco-friendly options, ethical wildlife experiences, and culturally sensitive practices (Jiang et al., 2023). Through personalized recommendations, AI empowers travelers with information that aligns with sustainable principles, fostering a sense of responsibility and environmental stewardship (Balsalobre-Lorente et al., 2023). By seamlessly integrating ethical considerations into travel suggestions, these AI-driven solutions play a crucial role in guiding travelers towards choices that contribute positively to local communities and ecosystems (Reejo, 2023). The emphasis on responsible tourism goes beyond mere environmental impact; it encompasses cultural sensitivity and ethical engagement, enriching the travel experience while promoting the preservation of natural and cultural heritage. As travelers are equipped with insights that align with sustainability, AI emerges as a catalyst for fostering a conscious and responsible approach to exploration (Jiang et al., 2023). In essence, the integration of AI in sustainable travel not only transforms the industry's environmental footprint but also nurtures a community of informed and conscientious travelers, actively contributing to the well-being of destinations worldwide.

The infusion of Artificial Intelligence (AI) into sustainable travel solutions marks a pivotal shift towards a more intelligent and responsive approach to environmental conservation. With the transformative capabilities of AI, the travel industry not only seeks to minimize its ecological footprint but also aspires to inspire and guide travelers towards more sustainable choices (Reejo, 2023). This integration of technology goes beyond traditional conservation methods, offering dynamic and data-driven strategies that optimize resource usage, reduce environmental impact, and foster responsible tourism practices. As technology continues to advance, the promising potential of AI-driven solutions emerges as a beacon for a global shift towards responsible and sustainable tourism (Jiang et al., 2023). In this envisioned future, travel becomes a catalyst for positive environmental change, guided by AI's ability to provide real-time insights and personalized recommendations (Reejo, 2023). This transformative partnership between AI and sustainable travel signifies a harmonious coexistence, where the exploration of the world aligns seamlessly with the preservation of its natural wonders, cultures, and ecosystems.

CHALLENGES AND CONSIDERATIONS

Data Privacy and Security

Ensuring the privacy and security of traveler data is of utmost importance in the travel industry, where the collection and management of sensitive information are integral to various processes. To fortify systems against potential breaches, travel companies and platforms need to invest in state-of-the-art cybersecurity measures, including encryption technologies, secure data storage solutions, and robust authentication protocols (Yallop et al., 2023). This multi-layered approach safeguards the confidentiality and integrity of traveler information, fostering a secure digital environment. Travel entities must stay informed about evolving privacy laws, ensuring legal compliance and establishing ethical data practices. This commitment to regulatory adherence contributes to building a transparent and trustworthy relationship with travelers, instilling confidence in the protection of their data (Ozdemir et al., 2023). Education and awareness are pivotal in mitigating potential risks associated with data privacy. Travelers need to be well-informed about the types of data collected, its usage, and the security measures in place (Ioannou et al., 2021). Clear and concise privacy policies, communicated transparently, empower travelers to make informed decisions about sharing their data, fostering a culture of trust between travelers and the travel industry (Hu et al., 2023). Continuous monitoring and proactive risk management are critical components of a robust data security strategy. Regular audits, vulnerability assessments, and threat intelligence analysis enable travel entities to identify and address potential vulnerabilities before they can be exploited. This proactive stance ensures resilience against cyber threats, reinforcing the industry's commitment to data protection (Yallop et al., 2023). Collaboration with cybersecurity experts and the adoption of emerging technologies, such as advanced intrusion detection systems and artificial intelligence-driven threat analytics, further strengthen defenses against evolving cybersecurity threats. Staying at the forefront of technological advancements enhances the travel industry's ability to protect traveler data and adapt to the ever-changing landscape of cyber risks (Line et al., 2020). In summary, safeguarding data privacy and security in the travel industry requires a holistic and proactive approach. From robust cybersecurity measures and compliance with data protection regulations to transparent communication with travelers and ongoing risk management, the travel industry must prioritize the protection of sensitive information to build and maintain trust in an increasingly digital and interconnected world.

Job Displacement

As automation and artificial intelligence (AI) reshape the landscape of the tourism industry, concerns about potential job displacement have prompted a need for a thoughtful and strategic approach to address the evolving impact on the workforce. With technological advancements, traditional roles within the tourism sector are undergoing transformation, presenting the possibility of some jobs being replaced (Jabeen et al., 2022). Effectively managing this challenge requires a multifaceted strategy aimed at minimizing negative consequences and steering the workforce toward new opportunities. A pivotal aspect of navigating this shift involves the initiation of comprehensive reskilling and upskilling programs, equipping the tourism workforce with the skills necessary for emerging roles alongside automation (Gonzalez et al., 2020). Prioritizing investments in training programs focusing on digital literacy, technology management, and relevant skills ensures that employees are well-prepared to meet the evolving demands of the industry (Elshae & Marzouk, 2022). Strategic workforce planning emerges as a crucial component in assessing the potential impact of automation on specific roles and departments within tourism organizations. This evaluation enables proactive measures, such as the reassignment of employees to more strategic tasks or transitioning them to new roles that complement automated processes. This adaptive approach helps organizations harness the benefits of automation while preserving the workforce's stability and skill relevance (Zehir et al., 2020). Despite concerns about job displacement, it's imperative to recognize that the integration of automation can also generate new opportunities within the tourism sector (Jabeen et al., 2022). Concentrating on the development of roles centered around managing and maintaining automated systems, as well as those emphasizing customer experience and personalization, allows the industry to actively contribute to job creation (Ruel, 2021). This shift in focus not only mitigates the impact of job losses but also paves the way for a more dynamic and diversified workforce. As certain routine tasks become automated, the value of soft skills, including interpersonal communication, creativity, and emotional intelligence, takes center stage. Encouraging the development of these skills among the workforce ensures that employees remain valuable contributors to the industry (Gonzalez et al., 2020). This emphasis on soft skills not only addresses the changing nature of roles within the tourism sector but also underscores the enduring importance of human-centric qualities in delivering exceptional customer experiences (Khatri et al., 2020). In essence, the integration of automation and AI in the tourism industry necessitates a proactive and adaptive approach to workforce management. Prioritizing reskilling, implementing strategic workforce planning, and focusing on the creation of new roles enables the industry to navigate the transformative impact of technology while safeguarding the well-being and skill relevance of its workforce (Vrontis et al., 2022). Embracing the synergy between automation and human-centric skills positions the tourism sector not only to withstand the challenges of job displacement but also to thrive in a technologically advanced future.

Accessibility and Affordability

Promoting inclusivity and equal opportunities in the travel industry necessitates ensuring the accessibility and affordability of AI-powered tools for all travelers. As technology advances, addressing potential disparities becomes crucial to guarantee that the benefits of AI are accessible to a diverse range of individuals. At the forefront of this effort is the design of user-friendly interfaces for AI-powered tools (Pilla & Sivathanu, 2020). The paramount goal is to ensure accessibility by creating interfaces that are intuitive, easy to navigate, and equipped with features like voice commands or text-to-speech options. Such features cater to travelers with varying abilities and preferences, creating a more inclusive digital environment. Incorporating multi-lingual capabilities in AI tools is another critical aspect that ensures language is not a barrier to accessibility (Buhalis & Moldavska, 2022). By providing support for a diverse range of languages, AI tools make information and assistance available to travelers from different linguistic backgrounds, fostering a more inclusive and global travel experience. Adherence to accessibility standards, such as the Web Content Accessibility Guidelines (WCAG), is imperative. This ensures that AI-powered tools are designed to accommodate individuals with disabilities by incorporating features like alternative text for images, keyboard navigation, and compatibility with screen readers (Ismail & Kuppusamy, 2022). This commitment to standards promotes a universally accessible digital landscape. Engaging with diverse communities and obtaining feedback from a broad user base is a proactive step in identifying specific accessibility needs and challenges (Li et al., 2021). This inclusive approach enables continuous improvement and refinement of AI tools, ensuring they evolve to better serve the needs of all travelers. By actively seeking input from various demographics, the travel industry can fine-tune AI solutions to be more inclusive and responsive (Pilla & Sivathanu, 2020). Tailoring AI solutions to local contexts and specific travel needs is another key element in enhancing accessibility. Localized features and information cater to the unique requirements of different regions and communities, fostering a more inclusive travel environment. This localized approach ensures that AI-powered tools are not one-size-fits-all but instead adapt to the specific needs of diverse user groups (Doborjeh et al., 2022). By integrating these considerations into the development and deployment of AI-powered tools, the travel industry can contribute to a more inclusive and accessible environment for all travelers (Filieri et al., 2021). This commitment aligns with the principles of fairness and equal access, fostering a positive impact on the overall travel experience. Furthermore, ensuring affordability of these tools is equally important to make AI benefits accessible to travelers across various economic backgrounds, promoting equity in technological access (Pilla & Sivathanu, 2020). This commitment to accessibility and affordability reflects a broader dedication to making travel technology a force for inclusivity and positive change, ensuring that the benefits of AI are enjoyed by all, regardless of their backgrounds, abilities, or economic status.

LIMITATIONS AND SCOPE FOR FURTHER RESEARCH

Limitations

While this research offers valuable insights into critical aspects of AI-powered tools in the travel industry, it is imperative to recognize inherent limitations. A key constraint is the reliance on secondary data, which restricts the depth of analysis and real-time perspectives. The examination of technological accessibility, language and cultural sensitivity, data privacy, and economic disparities, though acknowledging their significance, lacks a granular exploration of specific instances or regions. To augment the depth and breadth of future research, the incorporation of primary research methods becomes essential. Emphasizing regional nuances, employing case studies, delving into policy analysis, assessing socio-economic impacts, exploring user-centric experiences, and investigating collaborative initiatives are pivotal steps to enrich the understanding of the challenges and opportunities linked to AI integration in the travel industry. These multifaceted approaches will contribute to a more nuanced and comprehensive comprehension of the complex dynamics at play in the intersection of AI and travel, fostering a more informed and contextually relevant dialogue on the subject.

Scope for Further Research

The limitations identified in this research work open avenues for extensive and targeted future investigations. Given the reliance on secondary data, there is a compelling scope for primary research methods to be employed, facilitating a more in-depth and firsthand exploration of the issues at the intersection of AI and the travel industry. Future research endeavors could adopt a region-specific focus, conducting case studies to unravel the nuances that may vary across different geographic and cultural contexts. Delving into policy analysis would offer valuable insights into the regulatory frameworks governing AI in the travel sector, contributing to a more comprehensive understanding of the legal landscape. Further research can also explore the socio-economic impacts of AI integration, providing a nuanced understanding of how these technologies shape employment, accessibility, and economic disparities. Additionally, conducting user-centric studies and investigating collaborative initiatives within the industry could shed light on practical experiences and potential solutions. This multifaceted approach ensures that future research not only addresses the identified limitations but also contributes significantly to the evolving discourse on the implications and applications of AI in travel.

CONCLUSION

In the dynamic landscape of the travel industry, the integration of artificial intelligence (AI) has ushered in a new era of possibilities, transforming the way individuals plan, experience, and reflect on their journeys. From hyper-personalized itineraries to sustainable travel solutions, the implications of AI on the future of travel are profound. This transformative journey, however, must be navigated with careful consideration for ethical, social, and economic implications to ensure that the benefits of AI-powered tools are accessible to all travelers. At the heart of this technological evolution is the concept of hyper-personalization, where AI tailors travel experiences to individual preferences, interests, and even emotional states. This goes beyond traditional travel planning, offering a glimpse into a future where every journey is a bespoke narrative, intricately crafted to align with the unique needs and desires of each traveler. The emotional intelligence embedded in AI not only enhances personalization but also fosters a deeper connection between the traveler and the destinations explored. However, the advent of AI in travel brings forth ethical considerations, particularly in the realms of data privacy and security. Protecting traveler data and mitigating potential risks become paramount in building and maintaining trust. Robust cybersecurity measures, compliance with data protection regulations, and transparent communication with travelers are essential elements in ensuring the responsible and ethical use of AI in the industry. Moreover, the potential impact of automation on the tourism workforce raises concerns about job displacement. A proactive approach involving reskilling and upskilling programs, strategic workforce planning, and collaboration with educational institutions is crucial to navigate this challenge. By investing in the development of relevant skills and fostering a culture of continuous learning, the tourism industry can ensure that its workforce remains adaptable and well-prepared for the evolving demands of the digital era. As AI becomes increasingly ingrained in travel, addressing issues of accessibility and affordability emerges as a key imperative. The benefits of AI-powered tools should not be confined to a select few; instead, efforts should be made to design inclusive interfaces, comply with accessibility standards, and offer affordability measures to cater to a diverse range of travelers. Public-private partnerships, community engagement, and localized solutions contribute to making AI in travel accessible to individuals from various backgrounds, ensuring that technology does not exacerbate existing inequalities. Sustainable travel solutions powered by AI exemplify the industry's commitment to environmental stewardship. Optimizing resource usage, minimizing environmental impact, and promoting responsible tourism practices are at the forefront of these initiatives. By harnessing AI's analytical capabilities, the travel sector can contribute to a greener and more sustainable future, aligning with global efforts to address climate change and promote responsible travel. The integration of AI in the travel industry signifies a paradigm shift that extends beyond mere technological advancements. It represents an opportunity to redefine the very essence of travel – making it more personalized, sustainable, and accessible. Navigating this transformative journey requires a delicate balance between embracing innovation and addressing the ethical, social, and economic considerations that accompany it. As the travel industry charts its course into an AI-powered future, the principles of inclusivity, responsibility, and sustainability must guide its trajectory, ensuring that the benefits of technology are shared equitably among all those who embark on the journey of exploration and discovery.

REFERENCES

Akdu, U. (2020). Smart tourism: issues, challenges and opportunities. The Emerald handbook of ICT in tourism and hospitality, 291-308. Emerald.

Antonio, N., De Almeida, A., & Nunes, L. (2022). Data mining and predictive analytics for e-tourism. In *Handbook of e-Tourism* (pp. 1–25). Springer International Publishing.

Baggio, R., Micera, R., & Del Chiappa, G. (2020). Smart tourism destinations: A critical reflection. *Journal of Hospitality and Tourism Technology*, *11*(3), 407–423. doi:10.1108/JHTT-01-2019-0011

Balsalobre-Lorente, D., Abbas, J., He, C., Pilař, L., & Shah, S. A. R. (2023). Tourism, urbanization and natural resources rents matter for environmental sustainability: The leading role of AI and ICT on sustainable development goals in the digital era. *Resources Policy*, *82*, 103445. doi:10.1016/j.resourpol.2023.103445

Buhalis, D., & Moldavska, I. (2022). Voice assistants in hospitality: Using artificial intelligence for customer service. *Journal of Hospitality and Tourism Technology*, *13*(3), 386–403. doi:10.1108/JHTT-03-2021-0104

Buhalis, D., O'Connor, P., & Leung, R. (2023). Smart hospitality: From smart cities and smart tourism towards agile business ecosystems in networked destinations. *International Journal of Contemporary Hospitality Management*, *35*(1), 369–393. doi:10.1108/IJCHM-04-2022-0497

Bulchand-Gidumal, J. (2022). Impact of artificial intelligence in travel, tourism, and hospitality. In *Handbook of e-Tourism* (pp. 1943–1962). Springer International Publishing. doi:10.1007/978-3-030-48652-5_110

Chan, L., Hogaboam, L., & Cao, R. (2022). Artificial intelligence in tourism and hospitality. In *Applied Artificial Intelligence in Business: Concepts and Cases* (pp. 213–229). Springer International Publishing. doi:10.1007/978-3-031-05740-3_14

Chaudhari, K., & Thakkar, A. (2020). A comprehensive survey on travel recommender systems. *Archives of Computational Methods in Engineering*, *27*(5), 1545–1571. doi:10.1007/s11831-019-09363-7

Cranmer, E. E., tom Dieck, M. C., & Fountoulaki, P. (2020). Exploring the value of augmented reality for tourism. *Tourism Management Perspectives*, *35*, 100672. doi:10.1016/j.tmp.2020.100672

David, A., Jeganathan, G. S., Sikandar, M. D., & Azam, S. A. (2023, May). Internet Users Top Concerns Ensuring Data Privacy, Security, and Protection. In *Arokiaraj David, Jeganathan Gomathi Sankar & Md Sikandar Azam, —Internet Users Top Concerns Ensuring Data Privacy, Security, and Protection||, 10th International Conference on Multidisciplinary Research and Modern Education, ISBN* (No. 978-920, pp. 5-20241).

David, A., Maheswari, M., Sankar, G., Christy, F., Karuppannan, A., & Banumathi, M. (2023). Mental illness of Pregnant Women determined by Covid-19: An Empirical Analysis of Pre-and- Post Delivery. *The Saybold Report Journal*, *18*(03), 1706–1721.

Doborjeh, Z., Hemmington, N., Doborjeh, M., & Kasabov, N. (2022). Artificial intelligence: A systematic review of methods and applications in hospitality and tourism. *International Journal of Contemporary Hospitality Management*, *34*(3), 1154–1176. doi:10.1108/IJCHM-06-2021-0767

Elshaer, A. M., & Marzouk, A. M. (2022). Memorable tourist experiences: The role of smart tourism technologies and hotel innovations. *Tourism Recreation Research*, 1–13. doi:10.1080/02508281.2022.2027203

Fan, X., Jiang, X., & Deng, N. (2022). Immersive technology: A meta-analysis of augmented/virtual reality applications and their impact on tourism experience. *Tourism Management*, *91*, 104534. doi:10.1016/j.tourman.2022.104534

Filieri, R., D'Amico, E., Destefanis, A., Paolucci, E., & Raguseo, E. (2021). Artificial intelligence (AI) for tourism: An European-based study on successful AI tourism start-ups. *International Journal of Contemporary Hospitality Management*, *33*(11), 4099–4125. doi:10.1108/IJCHM-02-2021-0220

Ganeshkumar, C., David, A., & Sankar, J. G. (2024). Blockchain Technology Acceptance in Agribusiness Industry. In *Blockchain Transformations: Navigating the Decentralized Protocols Era* (pp. 239–260). Springer Nature Switzerland. doi:10.1007/978-3-031-49593-9_15

Ganeshkumar, C., David, A., Sankar, J. G., & Saginala, M. (2023). Application of Drone Technology in Agriculture: A Predictive Forecasting of Pest and Disease Incidence. In *Applying Drone Technologies and Robotics for Agricultural Sustainability* (pp. 50–81). IGI Global.

Ganeshkumar, C., Sankar, J. G., & David, A. (2023). Adoption of Big Data Analytics: Determinants and Performances Among Food Industries. [IJBIR]. *International Journal of Business Intelligence Research*, *14*(1), 1–17. doi:10.4018/IJBIR.317419

Ganeshkumar, C., Sankar, J. G., & David, A. (2023). Impact of Artificial Intelligence on Agriculture Value Chain Performance: Agritech Perspective. In Blockchain, IoT, and AI Technologies for Supply Chain Management (pp. 71-98). CRC Press.

Gasmi, I., Soui, M., Barhoumi, K., & Abed, M. (2024). Recommendation rules to personalize itineraries for tourists in an unfamiliar city. *Applied Soft Computing*, *150*, 111084. doi:10.1016/j.asoc.2023.111084

Gharibi, N. (2021). The evolution of predictive models and tourism. *Journal of Tourism Futures*, *7*(2), 259–266. doi:10.1108/JTF-04-2020-0046

Gonzalez, R., Gasco, J., & Llopis, J. (2020). Information and communication technologies and human resources in hospitality and tourism. *International Journal of Contemporary Hospitality Management*, *32*(11), 3545–3579. doi:10.1108/IJCHM-04-2020-0272

Hamid, R. A., Albahri, A. S., Alwan, J. K., Al-Qaysi, Z. T., Albahri, O. S., Zaidan, A. A., Alnoor, A., Alamoodi, A. H., & Zaidan, B. B. (2021). How smart is e-tourism? A systematic review of smart tourism recommendation system applying data management. *Computer Science Review*, *39*, 100337. doi:10.1016/j.cosrev.2020.100337

Ho, C. L., Chen, W. L., & Ou, C. H. (2023). Constructing a personalized travel itinerary recommender system with the Internet of Things. *Wireless Networks*, 1–13. doi:10.1007/s11276-023-03453-y

Ho, C. L., Chen, W. L., & Ou, C. H. (2023). Constructing a personalized travel itinerary recommender system with the Internet of Things. *Wireless Networks*, 1–13. doi:10.1007/s11276-023-03453-y

Holmes, M. R., Dodds, R., & Frochot, I. (2021). At home or abroad, does our behavior change? Examining how everyday behavior influences sustainable travel behavior and tourist clusters. *Journal of Travel Research*, *60*(1), 102–116. doi:10.1177/0047287519894070

Hu, Y., & Min, H. K. (2023). The dark side of artificial intelligence in service: The “watching-eye” effect and privacy concerns. *International Journal of Hospitality Management*, *110*, 103437. doi:10.1016/j.ijhm.2023.103437

Huang, M. H., & Rust, R. T. (2021). Engaged to a robot? The role of AI in service. *Journal of Service Research*, *24*(1), 30–41. doi:10.1177/1094670520902266

Ioannou, A., Tussyadiah, I., & Miller, G. (2021). That’s private! Understanding travelers’ privacy concerns and online data disclosure. *Journal of Travel Research*, *60*(7), 1510–1526. doi:10.1177/0047287520951642

Ismail, A., & Kuppusamy, K. S. (2022). Web accessibility investigation and identification of major issues of higher education websites with statistical measures: A case study of college websites. *Journal of King Saud University. Computer and Information Sciences*, *34*(3), 901–911. doi:10.1016/j.jksuci.2019.03.011

Jabeen, F., Al Zaidi, S., & Al Dhaheri, M. H. (2022). Automation and artificial intelligence in hospitality and tourism. *Tourism Review*, *77*(4), 1043–1061. doi:10.1108/TR-09-2019-0360

Jabeen, F., Al Zaidi, S., & Al Dhaheri, M. H. (2022). Automation and artificial intelligence in hospitality and tourism. *Tourism Review*, *77*(4), 1043–1061. doi:10.1108/TR-09-2019-0360

Jeganathan, G. S., David, A., & Ilangovan, K. (2022). Determination of Hospitality Services Quality and Customer Satisfaction–a Holserv Approach. In *AU Virtual International Conference on" Entrepreneurship & Sustainability in Digital Era" under the theme of" Challenges of Organizational & Business Management in Dynamic Digital Dimension* (Vol. 3, No. 1, pp. 325-334).

Jeganathan, G. S., & Srinivasulu, Y. (2014). Growth Drivers of Tourism Industry in India. *International Journal of Business and Management*, *2*(11), 100.

Jeong, M., & Shin, H. H. (2020). Tourists' experiences with smart tourism technology at smart destinations and their behavior intentions. *Journal of Travel Research*, *59*(8), 1464–1477. doi:10.1177/0047287519883034

Ji, H., Zheng, W., Zhuang, X., & Lin, Z. (2021). Explore for a day? Generating personalized itineraries that fit spatial heterogeneity of tourist attractions. *Information & Management*, *58*(8), 103557. doi:10.1016/j.im.2021.103557

Jiang, G., Gao, W., Xu, M., Tong, M., & Liu, Z. (2023). Geographic Information Visualization and Sustainable Development of Low-Carbon Rural Slow Tourism under Artificial Intelligence. *Sustainability (Basel)*, *15*(4), 3846. doi:10.3390/su15043846

Khatri, S., Pandey, D. K., Penkar, D., & Ramani, J. (2020). Impact of artificial intelligence on human resources. In *Data Management, Analytics and Innovation: Proceedings of ICDMAI 2019,* Volume 2 (pp. 365-376). Springer Singapore. 10.1007/978-981-13-9364-8_26

Kim, S., Filimonau, V., & Dickinson, J. E. (2023). Tourist perception of the value of time on holidays: Implications for the time use rebound effect and sustainable travel practice. *Journal of Travel Research*, *62*(2), 362–381. doi:10.1177/00472875211064636

Knani, M., Echchakoui, S., & Ladhari, R. (2022). Artificial intelligence in tourism and hospitality: Bibliometric analysis and research agenda. *International Journal of Hospitality Management*, *107*, 103317. doi:10.1016/j.ijhm.2022.103317

Kumar, P., Kumar, A., & Sankar, J. G. (2020). Service quality of health tourism in India: A structural equation modelling approach. *Solid State Technology*, *63*(2), 1187–1191.

Li, M., Yin, D., Qiu, H., & Bai, B. (2021). A systematic review of AI technology-based service encounters: Implications for hospitality and tourism operations. *International Journal of Hospitality Management*, *95*, 102930. doi:10.1016/j.ijhm.2021.102930

Line, N. D., Dogru, T., El-Manstrly, D., Buoye, A., Malthouse, E., & Kandampully, J. (2020). Control, use and ownership of big data: A reciprocal view of customer big data value in the hospitality and tourism industry. *Tourism Management*, *80*, 104106. doi:10.1016/j.tourman.2020.104106

Mariani, M. M., Perez-Vega, R., & Wirtz, J. (2022). AI in marketing, consumer research and psychology: A systematic literature review and research agenda. *Psychology and Marketing*, *39*(4), 755–776. doi:10.1002/mar.21619

Muniz, E. C. L., Dandolini, G. A., Biz, A. A., & Ribeiro, A. C. (2021). Customer knowledge management and smart tourism destinations: A framework for the smart management of the tourist experience–SMARTUR. *Journal of Knowledge Management*, *25*(5), 1336–1361. doi:10.1108/JKM-07-2020-0529

Novianti, S., Susanto, E., & Rafdinal, W. (2022). Predicting Tourists' Behaviour Towards Smart Tourism: The Case in Emerging Smart Destinations. *Journal of Tourism Sustainability*, *2*(1), 19–30. doi:10.35313/jtospolban.v2i1.30

Ozdemir, M. A. (2021). Virtual reality (VR) and augmented reality (AR) technologies for accessibility and marketing in the tourism industry. In ICT tools and applications for accessible tourism (pp. 277-301). IGI Global.

Ozdemir, O., Dogru, T., Kizildag, M., & Erkmen, E. (2023). A critical reflection on digitalization for the hospitality and tourism industry: Value implications for stakeholders. *International Journal of Contemporary Hospitality Management*, *35*(9), 3305–3321. doi:10.1108/IJCHM-04-2022-0535

Pillai, R., & Sivathanu, B. (2020). Adoption of AI-based chatbots for hospitality and tourism. *International Journal of Contemporary Hospitality Management*, *32*(10), 3199–3226. doi:10.1108/IJCHM-04-2020-0259

Pillai, R., & Sivathanu, B. (2020). Adoption of AI-based chatbots for hospitality and tourism. *International Journal of Contemporary Hospitality Management*, *32*(10), 3199–3226. doi:10.1108/IJCHM-04-2020-0259

Reejo, R. J. (2023). A Review on Marketing Tourism in the Era of AI: Future Scope for Sustainable Tourism in India. *AI and Emotional Intelligence for Modern Business Management*, 321-347.

Renjith, S., Sreekumar, A., & Jathavedan, M. (2020). An extensive study on the evolution of context-aware personalized travel recommender systems. *Information Processing & Management*, *57*(1), 102078. doi:10.1016/j.ipm.2019.102078

Ruel, H. (2021). Guest editorial-The future of e-HRM and artificial intelligence in the hospitality and tourism industry. *Journal of Tourism Futures*, *7*(1), 2–4. doi:10.1108/JTF-03-2021-192

Samaddar, K., & Mondal, S. (2023). AR and VR-based travel: a responsible practice towards sustainable tourism. *International Journal of Tourism Cities*.

Samara, D., Magnisalis, I., & Peristeras, V. (2020). Artificial intelligence and big data in tourism: A systematic literature review. *Journal of Hospitality and Tourism Technology*, *11*(2), 343–367. doi:10.1108/JHTT-12-2018-0118

Sankar, G., & Naveenkumar, K. (2018). *Material Handling Management in Third Party Logistics Warehouse. International Journal for Research in Engineering Application & Management*. IJREAM.

Sankar, J. G. (2020). Customer perception about innovative safety food delivery during lockdown. *Journal of Contemporary Issues in Business and Government*, *26*(2).

Sankar, J. G. (2020). Innovative celebrity endorsement and consumer purchase. *Journal of Contemporary Issues in Business and Government*, *26*(2).

Sankar, J. G. (2020). Innovative consumer behaviour towards sportswear. *Journal of Contemporary Issues in Business and Government*, *26*(2).

Sankar, J. G. (2020). Service Factors Influence on Customer Satisfaction in Innovative Ecommerce. *SANKAR, D.(2020). Service factors influence on customer satisfaction in innovative e-commerce. Journal of Contemporary Issues in Business and Government*, *26*(2), 651–656.

Sankar, J. G. (2020). Service quality of e-Commerce logistics services. *Journal of Contemporary Issues in Business and Government*, *26*(2).

Sankar, J. G. (2020). Customer perception towards electric two-wheeler innovation. *Journal of Contemporary Issues in Business and Government*, *26*(2).

Sankar, J. G., & David, A. (2023). Measuring the Service Quality of Artificial Intelligence in the Tourism and Hospitality Industry. In Handbook of Research on Innovation, Differentiation, and New Technologies in Tourism, Hotels, and Food Service (pp. 133-155). IGI Global.

Sankar, J. G., & David, A. (2024). A Comprehensive Examination of Mobile Augmented Reality in Tourism (MART) Adoption: Using the UTAUT2 Framework. In Contemporary Trends in Innovative Marketing Strategies (pp. 241-262). IGI Global.

SankarJ. G.DavidA.Ganesh KumarC. (2022). Adaptation of Blockchain Technology In HRM. SSRN 4515408.

Sankar, J. G., David, A., & Ramasamy, R. (2023). Assessing Water and Sanitation Service Quality at Pilgrimage Sites After COVID-19: An Empirical Investigation. In Prospects and Challenges of Global Pilgrimage Tourism and Hospitality (pp. 160-179). IGI Global.

Sankar, J. G., David, A., & Valan, P. (2023). Examining User Understanding and Perceptions of E-Commerce Data Privacy, Security, and Protection. In *Confronting Security and Privacy Challenges in Digital Marketing* (pp. 159–185). IGI Global. doi:10.4018/978-1-6684-8958-1.ch008

Sankar, J. G., & Devanand, K. (2020). Social media innovation on consumer buying behaviour. *SANKAR, JG (2020). Social media innovation on consumer buying behaviour. Journal of Contemporary Issues in Business and Government*, *26*(2).

Sankar, J. G., & Kiruba Sagar, M, V. (2020). Examining the Risk Factor Associated with UTAUT Model. *Solid State Technology*, *63*(2), 1196–1198.

Sankar, J. G., Rajeswari, M., & Dwarak, M. V. S. (2020). To Measure the Service Quality of Film and Television Technology. *Solid State Technology*, *63*(2), 1192–1195.

Sankar, J. G., & Srinivasulu, Y. (2014). A Study of Tourism Industry Impact on Macroeconomic Indicators. *GE-International Journal of Management Research*, *2*(11), 2321–1709.

Sankar, J. G., & Srinivasulu, Y. (2014). Contemporary Sustainable Development Practices in Indian Hospitality Sector: Triple Bottom Line Approach. *SSRN*, 2. doi:10.2139/ssrn.4204732

Sankar, J. G., Valan, P., & Siranjeevi, M. S. (2020). Various Models to Evaluate Quality in the Service Industry. In *Digital Transformation and Innovative Services for Business and Learning* (pp. 181–194). IGI Global.

Sasikala, J., & Jeganathan, G. S. (2017). A Study on Employee Engagement in Information Technology (IT) Industry. *SSRN*, *1*(1), 233–239. doi:10.2139/ssrn.3536354

Shafiee, S., Rajabzadeh Ghatari, A., Hasanzadeh, A., & Jahanyan, S. (2021). Smart tourism destinations: A systematic review. *Tourism Review*, *76*(3), 505–528. doi:10.1108/TR-06-2019-0235

Simitha, S., Mugila, P., & Sankar, J. G. (2020). A Study on Customer Relationship Management in Siemens Healthineers. *Solid State Technology*, *63*(2), 1199–1203.

Sohrabi, B., Vanani, I. R., Nasiri, N., & Rudd, A. G. (2020). A predictive model of tourist destinations based on tourists' comments and interests using text analytics. *Tourism Management Perspectives*, *35*, 100710. doi:10.1016/j.tmp.2020.100710

Sung, P. L., Hsiao, T. Y., Huang, L., & Morrison, A. M. (2021). The influence of green trust on travel agency intentions to promote low-carbon tours for the purpose of sustainable development. *Corporate Social Responsibility and Environmental Management*, *28*(4), 1185–1199. doi:10.1002/csr.2131

Tsang, W. K., & Benoit, D. F. (2020). Gaussian processes for daily demand prediction in tourism planning. *Journal of Forecasting*, *39*(3), 551–568. doi:10.1002/for.2644

Velmurugan, T. A., & Sankar, J. G. (2017). A comparative study on motivation theory with Maslow's hierarchy theory and two factor theory in organization. *Indo-Iranian Journal of Scientific Research*, *1*(1), 204–208.

Vrontis, D., Christofi, M., Pereira, V., Tarba, S., Makrides, A., & Trichina, E. (2022). Artificial intelligence, robotics, advanced technologies and human resource management: A systematic review. *International Journal of Human Resource Management*, *33*(6), 1237–1266. doi:10.1080/09585192.2020.1871398

Wang, X. (2020). Personalized recommendation framework design for online tourism: Know you better than yourself. *Industrial Management & Data Systems*, *120*(11), 2067–2079. doi:10.1108/IMDS-05-2020-0278

Yallop, A. C., Gică, O. A., Moisescu, O. I., Coroş, M. M., & Séraphin, H. (2023). The digital traveller: Implications for data ethics and data governance in tourism and hospitality. *Journal of Consumer Marketing*, *40*(2), 155–170. doi:10.1108/JCM-12-2020-4278

Yang, X., Zhang, L., & Feng, Z. (2023). Personalized tourism recommendations and the E-tourism user experience. *Journal of Travel Research*, 00472875231187332.

Yu, N., & Chen, J. (2022). Design of machine learning algorithm for tourism demand prediction. *Computational and Mathematical Methods in Medicine*, *2022*, 2022. doi:10.1155/2022/6352381 PMID:35720035

Yung, R., Khoo-Lattimore, C., & Potter, L. E. (2021). Virtual reality and tourism marketing: Conceptualizing a framework on presence, emotion, and intention. *Current Issues in Tourism*, *24*(11), 1505–1525. doi:10.1080/13683500.2020.1820454

Zehir, C., Karaboğa, T., & Başar, D. (2020). The transformation of human resource management and its impact on overall business performance: big data analytics and AI technologies in strategic HRM. *Digital Business Strategies in Blockchain Ecosystems: Transformational Design and Future of Global Business*, 265-279.

Zheng, W., Ji, H., Lin, C., Wang, W., & Yu, B. (2020). Using a heuristic approach to design personalized urban tourism itineraries with hotel selection. *Tourism Management*, *76*, 103956. doi:10.1016/j.tourman.2019.103956

KEY TERMS AND DEFINITIONS

AI Tourism: This refers to the intersection of Artificial Intelligence (AI) and the tourism industry. This evolving field harnesses AI technologies to enhance various aspects of the travel experience, ranging from personalized trip planning to optimizing operational efficiency for travel businesses.

Artificial Intelligence (AI): It refers to the development of computer systems or software that can perform tasks that typically require human intelligence.

Chatbots: AI-driven computer programs designed to simulate conversation with users, often employed in customer service for instant assistance.

Inclusivity: Ensuring that AI-powered tools and innovations are accessible and beneficial to a diverse range of travelers, regardless of background, abilities, or economic status.

Personalization: Tailoring travel experiences, services, or recommendations based on individual preferences, behaviors, and historical data.

Predictive Analytics: The use of statistical algorithms and machine learning techniques to identify the likelihood of future outcomes based on historical data patterns.

Smart Infrastructure: Integration of AI and technology to enhance the efficiency and sustainability of travel infrastructure, encompassing elements like transportation and accommodations.

Sustainable Tourism: Practices that aim to minimize the environmental impact of tourism, often facilitated by AI for resource optimization and eco-friendly recommendations.

User-centric Experiences: Designing AI applications and solutions with a focus on providing positive and seamless experiences for travelers, prioritizing their needs and preferences.

Voice Search and AI Assistants: Exploration of the impact and utilization of voice-activated AI technologies, like virtual assistants, in shaping marketing strategies and consumer interactions.

Chapter 9
Prospect of Smart Tourism Destination in Bangladesh

Mohammad Badruddoza Talukder
https://orcid.org/0000-0001-7788-2732
International University of Business Agriculture and Technology, Bangladesh

Kamarun Muhsina
Daffodil Institute of IT, Bangladesh

ABSTRACT

The ongoing expansion of the tourism sector in Bangladesh has created opportunities for future development through the adoption of smart tourism destinations. The notion of smart tourism destinations encompasses incorporating every facet of a tourist's experience, including planning activities. By adopting this particular strategy, Bangladesh can cultivate a tourism industry characterized by enhanced cohesion and effectiveness, thereby augmenting the overall experience for both local and international tourists. This article emphasizes several vital aspects of smart destinations, such as heightened financial gains, enhanced tourism infrastructure, and bolstered sustainability efforts. Furthermore, this paper also addresses the difficulties associated with implementing the proposed approach. It explores potential strategies to overcome these challenges. The concept of smart tourism destinations in Bangladesh offers significant potential for growth and development in the tourism industry.

INTRODUCTION

Bangladesh exhibits significant promise as a smart tourism destination owing to its rich cultural heritage, captivating natural landscapes, and noteworthy historical

DOI: 10.4018/979-8-3693-2137-9.ch009

landmarks. The emergence of smart tourism has gained significant popularity on a global scale due to advancements in technology. Smart tourism destinations provide visitors with a comprehensive and streamlined experience, encompassing various features such as intelligent information centers, personalized travel itineraries, and instant access to up-to-date information. According to Lee et al. (2020), Bangladesh's government has initiated efforts to prioritize advancing smart tourism. It acknowledges the significance of integrating technology to augment the overall experiences of visitors. Mobile applications, media, and various digital platforms are being employed to disseminate information and enhance the appeal of tourist destinations. Using technology in Bangladesh presents an opportunity to advance responsible tourism, safeguard cultural heritage, and stimulate economic development. Therefore, the potential of smart tourism in Bangladesh appears to be promising.

The advent of smart tourism destinations has significantly transformed the tourism sector, enhancing its efficiency and improving the tourist experience (Jovicic, 2019). According to Md Kashedul Wahab and Majumder (2011), Bangladesh is recognized for its abundant cultural heritage, picturesque landscapes, and distinctive culinary offerings, thus presenting significant prospects for tourism development. The adoption of smart tourism is becoming crucial for maintaining competitiveness due to rapid technological progress and the growing prevalence of smart devices among travelers. Adopting smart tourism can yield various advantages, such as improved visitor satisfaction, efficient destination management, and heightened economic development. Considering the context mentioned earlier, the present article aims to examine the potential of intelligent tourism destinations in Bangladesh by evaluating the existing condition of the tourism sector. This analysis will emphasize the various opportunities and challenges that arise, ultimately culminating in providing recommendations for the future.

IMPORTANCE OF SMART TOURISM DESTINATION:

The concept of a smart tourism destination pertains to a geographical area that has effectively incorporated technological advancements into its tourism sector, thereby enhancing the overall experience for visitors (Shen et al., 2020). These destinations utilize cutting-edge technologies such as artificial intelligence, big data, and the Internet of Things (IoT) to provide customized and immersive experiences. These destinations additionally offer up-to-date information to both visitors and operators, aiming to optimize operations and reduce any obstacles in the travel process. The significance of smart tourism destinations has grown in prominence within the global tourism industry due to their ability to provide a competitive advantage for those who adopt them (Buhalis & Amaranggana, 2013). In an increasingly competitive landscape, destinations that effectively distinguish themselves are more likely to achieve success in attracting fresh influxes of visitors. Therefore, stakeholders in Bangladesh's tourism sector are investigating potential avenues for developing smart destinations to enhance the country's industry.

CURRENT SITUATION OF TOURISM IN BANGLADESH

The tourism industry in Bangladesh has experienced gradual growth over time, primarily due to its attractive beaches, rich cultural heritage, and abundant natural resources, such as the Sundarbans, which is recognized as the world's largest mangrove forest (Alauddin et al., 2014). Nevertheless, the untapped potential of tourism in terms of its substantial contribution to the nation's economy remains unrealized. Despite certain advancements in infrastructure, such as the enhancement of road and air connectivity, there remains a need for the country to focus on enhancing its overall tourist facilities to attract a more significant number of visitors effectively (Christie et al., 2013). To guarantee the safety of tourists, it is imperative to address and resolve safety and security concerns. The government has recently implemented various measures to foster tourism, such as creating a distinct tourism board and developing multiple national zones. However, there remains a considerable distance to be covered before the tourism industry in Bangladesh can fully realize its potential.

TRENDS AND TECHNOLOGIES IN SMART TOURISM

The profound impact of smart technologies and the proliferation of the Internet of Things (IoT) have significantly influenced the tourism industry, resulting in the emergence of what is known as smart tourism (Backer & Lynch, 2017). The widespread availability of mobile devices and the prevalence of social media platforms have facilitated the seamless sharing and consumption of information among tourists. Data analytics and artificial intelligence have been observed in optimizing tourism experiences and personalizing such experiences according to individual preferences (Souffriau et al., 2008). Smart destinations increasingly incorporate technology, such as augmented and virtual, to enhance the overall visitor experience. Smart tourism aims to improve the overall quality of tourism while concurrently establishing a sustainable ecosystem that generates advantages for the local community. Many global destinations are adopting smart tourism strategies to enhance their appeal and attract more visitors. Here are some essential parts of technology that are going to be a trend now in our daily lives:

Figure 1. Part of technology
(Self Developed)

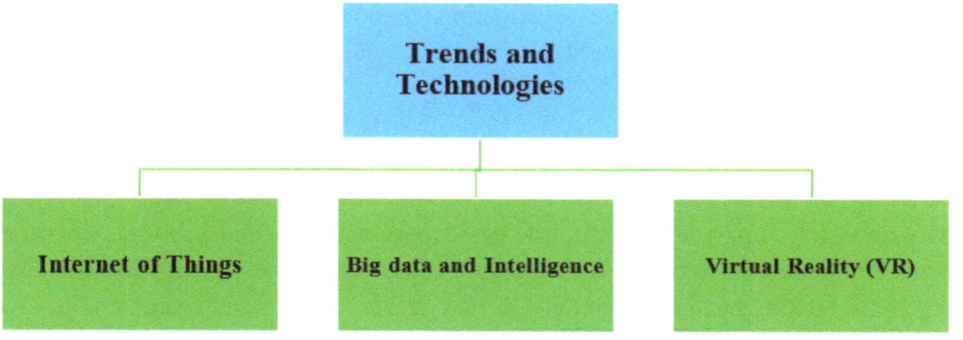

Internet of Things

The term "Internet of Things" (IoT) encompasses a network of tangible objects, such as devices, vehicles, household appliances, and various items, equipped with sensors, software, and connectivity. These components enable the exchange of data with other devices via the Internet (Tiwary et al., 2018). As mentioned, technology has significantly transformed individuals' lifestyles and professional endeavors while presenting limitless opportunities for intelligent tourism destinations. According to Sharma and Rishi (2022), Internet of Things (IoT)-)-enabled devices can offer immediate data regarding tourist flows and preferences. This data can be utilized to optimize tourism services and improve tourists' overall experience. By automating and streamlining operations, the Internet of Things (IoT) can potentially enhance the operational efficiency of various facilities, including hotels, transportation systems, and attractions. The development of smart tourism in Bangladesh is currently at an early stage. However, the government's efforts to promote digitalization and innovation present an opportunity for the country to leverage the potential of the Internet of Things (IoT) to create innovative tourism offerings and enhance the competitiveness of its tourism industry.

Big Data and Intelligence

The utilization of big data and intelligence is of paramount importance in the advancement and execution of intelligent tourism destinations. Data analysis is crucial in uncovering valuable insights about tourist trends, preferences, and behavior. This, in turn, facilitates the development of customized strategies and offerings in the tourism industry. According to Kumar et al. (2021), using intelligence tools, such as artificial intelligence, machine learning, and data analytics, can facilitate monitoring and analyzing visitor footfall, optimize traffic flows, and enhance safety in various areas. Moreover, these tools can analyze tourist feedback and reviews, thereby assisting destinations in improving the quality of their services and customer satisfaction. According to Mariani et al. (2018), as the tourism sector in Bangladesh expands, goals need to leverage big data and intelligence to provide novel and captivating experiences that can attract tourists, enhance revenue generation, and foster overall growth.

Augmented Reality (AR) and Virtual Reality (VR)

Augmented Reality (AR) and Virtual Reality (VR) are emerging technologies experiencing significant tourism growth. Augmented reality (AR) integrates digital information within the user's physical environment. This feature enables tourists to access up-to-date information regarding the locations they visit, thereby enhancing their overall experiential engagement. Conversely, virtual reality (VR) technology engrosses individuals in a simulated environment, replicating the sensations of a genuine real-world encounter. Virtual Reality (VR) has the potential to facilitate virtual tours of various tourist destinations, enabling prospective travelers to engage in immersive experiences and gain a comprehensive understanding of the location before finalizing their travel arrangements (Buhalis et al., 2022). Both technologies possess significant potential in the smart tourism industry, thereby contributing to the advancement of inventive and distinctive tourism experiences. The utilization of augmented reality (AR) and virtual reality (VR) technologies holds potential for tourism destinations in Bangladesh to enhance their appeal to tourists and enhance overall satisfaction levels within the tourism industry (Torabi et al., 2022).

CHALLENGES AND SOLUTIONS IN IMPLEMENTING SMART TOURISM IN BANGLADESH

Smart tourism development in Bangladesh is confronted with a range of challenges. These challenges include the country's limited digital infrastructure, low internet penetration, and inadequate data sharing (Asogwa, 2013). Additionally, the tourism sector in Bangladesh is relatively tiny, lacking expert personnel and resources to devise comprehensive solutions for smart tourism. Nevertheless, the government and various organizations are actively working to address these issues and promote smart tourism in the country. Critical solutions to foster smart tourism development in Bangladesh involve improving digital infrastructure, increasing the adoption and diffusion of technology, fostering collaboration among stakeholders, and promoting innovation (Perfetto & Vargas-Sánchez, 2018). By overcoming these challenges, it is anticipated that the tourism sector in Bangladesh will witness substantial growth shortly. Some challenges are mentioned here:

Lack of Infrastructure and Investment

Bangladesh's burgeoning tourism sector is hindered by inadequate infrastructure and insufficient investment, impeding the progress and advancement of smart destinations (Bhuiyan & Darda, 2018). Numerous regions exhibit short transportation, sanitation, and lodging facilities, hindering tourists from experiencing a satisfactory and convenient sojourn. Furthermore, it is worth noting that both private investment and government funding are deficiently allocated towards constructing novel infrastructure and enhancing pre-existing facilities (Gramlich, 1994). Bangladesh's lack of investment in infrastructure and tourism development could hinder its ability to compete effectively with other emerging destinations within the region. To effectively address this matter, policymakers must prioritize investments in tourism infrastructure and promotion to position Bangladesh as a prominent destination.

Insufficient Training and Skills in Smart Technology

A significant obstacle encountered in implementing tourism destinations in Bangladesh pertains to inadequate training and proficiency in smart technology

Figure 2. Challenges Implementing Smart Tourism in Bangladesh)
(Self-developed)

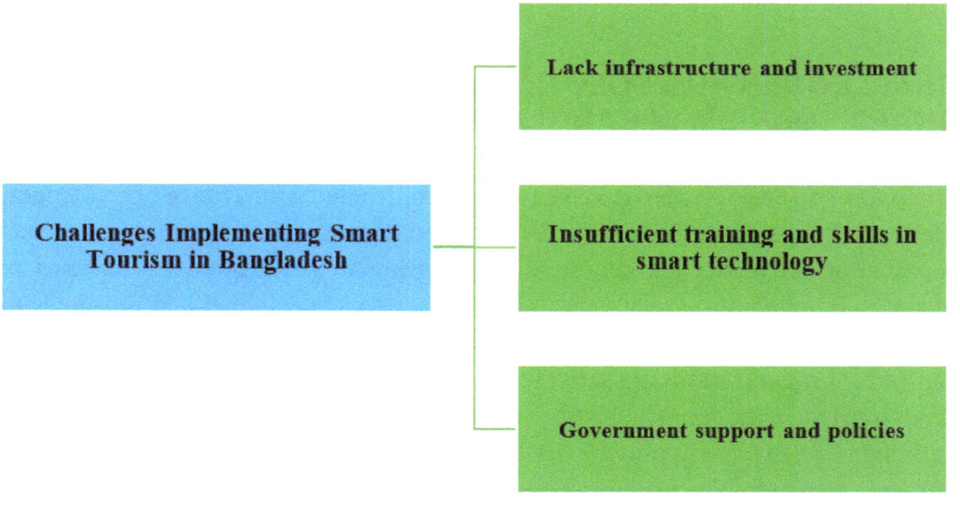

among the workforce. According to Femenia-Serra et al. (2019), professionals in the tourism industry and local vendors lack knowledge and expertise regarding establishing and maintaining the smart technology infrastructure essential for smart tourism. Currently, the availability of training programs and courses within the country is limited in developing the necessary skills for operating and maintaining smart tourism systems. Alam et al. (2009) argue that there is a need for concerted efforts to establish comprehensive training programs and courses to enhance the technical competencies of professionals in Bangladesh's industry. The potential for smart tourism destination development in the country may be limited without sufficient training and skills development.

Government Support and Policies

In recent years, the government of Bangladesh has demonstrated a proactive stance in promoting the growth and advancement of the tourism sector. The government has been enacting policies and supporting initiatives to establish intelligent tourism destinations that provide distinctive experiences for visitors, intending to increase tourist attraction. The development of goals and promotion of investment in the tourism sector have been spearheaded by the Ministry of Civil Aviation and Tourism in collaboration with the Bangladesh Tourism Board (Hassan et al., 2020). This encompasses the implementation of tax incentives for tourism enterprises, the enhancement of infrastructure, and the streamlining of visa application procedures for tourists. According to Rhaman (2016), the government has invested in marketing campaigns to promote Bangladesh as a destination for the global community. Consequently, there has been a notable surge in the influx of tourists in recent years, prompting the government's aspiration to sustain this trajectory by promoting intelligent tourism destinations.

ADVANTAGES AND OPPORTUNITIES OF TOURISM IN BANGLADESH

Bangladesh's culturally vibrant society and geographically diverse landscape offer significant prospects and benefits for the tourism industry. With its extensive coastline, abundant rivers, and verdant forests, Bangladesh is ideal for engaging in ecotourism, water-centric pursuits, and various outdoor adventures. Furthermore, it should be noted that the nation's cultural heritage, historical landmarks, and archaeological sites possess the potential to serve as significant points of interest for tourists (Timothy, 2011). The tourism industry in Bangladesh has exhibited consistent growth in recent years, supported by government-led initiatives aimed at promoting the sector, such as the 'Visit Bangladesh' campaign (Islam et al., 2021). The industry substantially bolsters the nation's economy by creating employment prospects and facilitating foreign exchange inflow. The government has significantly invested in infrastructure development to enhance visitors' tourism experience. These efforts have shown promising candidates for the future of the tourism sector. Bangladesh generally possesses a considerable reservoir of untapped potential in tourism, offering boundless prospects for expansion and advancement. Smart tourism destinations bring some opportunities for the country, that is:

Boosting Economic Growth and Job Creation

The potential of smart tourism destinations in Bangladesh extends beyond providing a distinctive experience for tourists, as it also presents significant opportunities for stimulating economic growth and generating employment (Bhuiyan & Darda, 2018). By allocating resources towards technological advancements and infrastructural development, the tourism sector has the potential to augment the nation's gross domestic product (GDP) and generate employment prospects for the indigenous populace. The expansion of tourism activities engenders the emergence and growth of diverse ancillary sectors, including transportation, hospitality, and entertainment, thereby generating a ripple effect within the economy (Shvets, 2020). Moreover, smart tourism destinations exhibit sustainability characteristics and actively encourage responsible tourism practices, developing favorable environmental and socio-cultural influence on the locality. With a strong emphasis on the promotion of tourism within the nation, the prospects for the expansion of the tourism sector, as well as the subsequent economic and market growth, appear to be promising.

Figure 3. Opportunities of Smart Tourism Destination
(Self-developed)

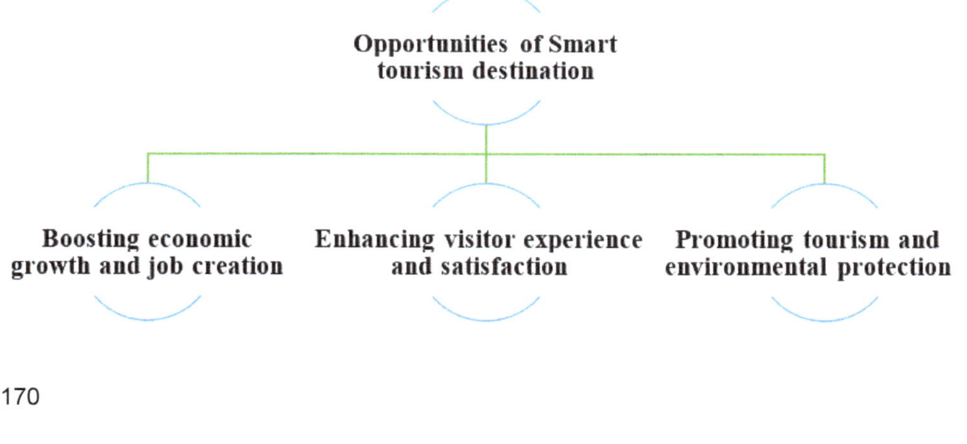

Enhancing Visitor Experience and Satisfaction

The emergence of smart tourism destinations in Bangladesh presents promising prospects for enhancing visitor experience and satisfaction. To accomplish this objective, it is imperative to foster the integration of technology and innovation within the tourism sector. According to Cenamor et al. (2017), smart systems can provide tourists with personalized recommendations and routes tailored to their preferences and movements. This feature enhances the convenience of city exploration for tourists, enabling them to efficiently navigate various locations and maximize their time utilization at renowned landmarks. According to Neuhofer et al. (2015), smart technologies can facilitate improved visitor communication, significantly enhancing their cultural experience. In addition, the availability of up-to-date information and real-time updates via diverse smart platforms can enhance visitors' sense of ease and assurance within their environment. Integrating intelligent technologies can significantly augment visitor experience and satisfaction within the tourism industry.

Promoting Tourism and Environmental Protection

Bangladesh has a profound historical background, distinctive cultural heritage, and captivating natural landscapes, making it an exemplary tourism choice. Nevertheless, it is imperative to ensure that the impact of tourism on the environment is minimized. The tourism sector has the potential to generate substantial financial resources to facilitate conservation efforts while also providing opportunities for promoting environmentally sustainable tourism practices (Sushchenko et al., 2018). According to Muhanna (2006), sustainable tourism practices can contribute to conserving natural resources and biodiversity and foster employment opportunities to bolster local economies. Furthermore, it can potentially enhance public consciousness regarding the significance of safeguarding the environment and promoting conservation endeavors. Hence, the government and other relevant stakeholders must prioritize fostering tourism and protecting the environment.

FUTURE ATTITUDE OF SMART TOURISM IN BANGLADESH

Bangladesh exhibits considerable potential for emerging as a smart tourism destination in the foreseeable future. The anticipated growth of the tourism industry is attributed to the government's emphasis on digitalization and infrastructure development. According to Cacho et al. (2016), integrating intelligent technology, such as innovative applications, electronic ticketing systems, and digital tour guides, can improve the overall visitor experience and streamline various processes, thereby increasing convenience. According to Liang et al. (2022), integrating intelligence, big data analytics, and adopting 5G technology within the tourism sector can enhance the industry's performance. Moreover, Bangladesh's wide range of tourist attractions, encompassing its natural landscapes, historical landmarks, and cultural legacy, presents abundant opportunities to expand the industry. Consequently, the prospective trajectory of intelligent tourism in Bangladesh exhibits promise. It has the potential to contribute substantially to the nation's economic advancement.

Promising Potentials and Innovations

Bangladesh is a nation gradually adopting and incorporating technology and innovation into its societal fabric. Smart tourism destinations offer numerous opportunities for Bangladesh to explore, and this phenomenon is already being observed in some areas of the country (Hossain et al., 2022). With the advancement of digitalization, there is ample opportunity for the tourism sector to integrate novel technologies to augment the overall tourist experience. Smart tourism destinations can effectively promote responsible tourism and engage with technologically proficient tourists using various technologies. Bangladesh has the opportunity to explore multiple potential innovations in smart tourism. These innovations encompass mobile applications that incorporate augmented reality to guide visitors, integrate facial recognition technology, and facilitate personalized tourist experiences (Pai et al.,

Figure 4. Future attitude of smart tourism in Bangladesh (
(Self-developed)

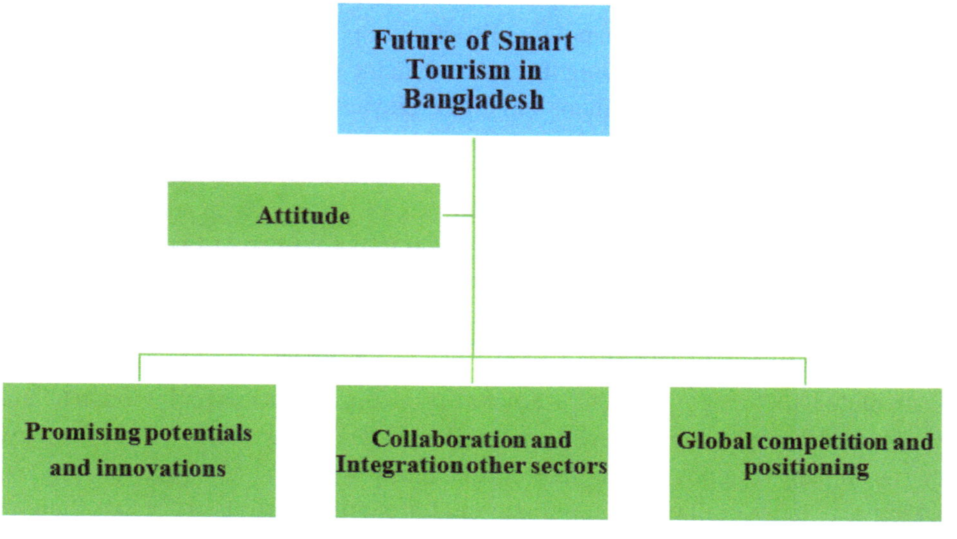

2020). Bangladesh possesses the capacity to emerge as a frontrunner in the realm of smart tourism, thereby bestowing indisputable advantages upon its tourism sector through the adoption of these promising innovative prospects.

Collaboration and Integration of Other Sectors

The development of smart tourism destinations necessitates collaboration and integration with other sectors. The tourism industry is interdependent and relies on various sectors, including transportation, hospitality, and technology, to establish a cohesive experience for visitors (Ivasciuc, 2020). The incorporation of technology within the tourism industry has the potential to augment the overall travel experience for individuals and contribute to improved accessibility, efficiency, and sustainability. Establishing a sustainable tourism model mutually beneficial for visitors and the local economy necessitates the active involvement and cooperation of local communities and stakeholders (Risteskia et al., 2012). Through collaboration with various sectors, the tourism industry has the potential to establish a dynamic and thriving destination that appeals to a diverse range of visitors worldwide.

Global Competition and Positioning

Bangladesh possesses the potential to emerge as a viable destination for smart tourism, owing to its abundant cultural heritage, picturesque landscapes, and amiable populace. The intensification of global competition among intelligent destinations is occurring rapidly, driven by countries' efforts to attract more tourists through innovative strategies (Gretzel & Scarpino-Johns, 2018). Therefore, strategically positioning Bangladesh within the global tourism market is imperative. The nation must utilize its distinctive selling points, such as its extensive historical background, breathtaking natural landscapes, and diverse cultural heritage, to establish a distinct brand identity (Hudson & Ritchie, 2009). Moreover, Bangladesh must prioritize the improvement of infrastructure facilities and services offered to tourists to enhance the overall quality of their travel experience. By implementing these strategies, Bangladesh can improve its competitiveness compared to other intelligent destinations, bolstering its standing within the global tourism market.

FINDINGS

- Bangladesh has the potential to become a smart tourism destination due to its cultural heritage, natural beauty, and historical landmarks.
- Smart tourism involves integrating technology into the visitor experience.

- Smart tourism destinations use AI, big data, and IoT to offer personalized, immersive experiences.
- Smart tourism destinations are crucial for remaining competitive in the global tourism industry.
- Bangladesh's tourism industry is slowly developing but faces challenges in infrastructure and safety.
- The government is taking initiatives to promote tourism.
- Technology like big data, AI, augmented reality, and virtual reality are transforming the tourism industry.
- Smart tourism aims to improve the quality of tourism and create a sustainable ecosystem.
- Challenges include limited digital infrastructure, a lack of skilled personnel, and government support.
- Solutions involve infrastructure improvement, training programs, and government policies.
- Bangladesh is expected to experience significant growth in tourism through smart technology, infrastructure development, and collaboration.
- Collaboration, positioning in the global competition, and leveraging technological innovations are critical for success.
- Investments, infrastructure development, and collaboration are essential for attracting more tourists and boosting economic growth in the country.

RECOMMENDATION

This topic focuses on the prospects and challenges of smart tourism in Bangladesh, and it is clear that there is significant growth in this sector. Based on the findings in the paper, here are some suggestions for further creating smart tourism in Bangladesh:

1) To fully realize the potential of smart tourism, Bangladesh should invest in digital infrastructure, including reliable internet connectivity and mobile networks, to support smart technologies.
2) Develop training programs and courses to enhance the local workforce's skills in the tourism industry. This includes training in the operation and maintenance of smart tourism systems.
3) Strengthen collaboration with other sectors, such as transportation, hospitality, and technology, to create a seamless and integrated tourist experience.
4) Promote Bangladesh's unique selling propositions, such as its rich history, natural beauty, and cultural diversity, to create a strong brand image and compete effectively in the global tourism market.

5) Emphasize sustainable and responsible tourism practices to protect the environment and support local communities. Implement eco-friendly initiatives and support conservation efforts.
6) Continue government support for the tourism sector by implementing policies that encourage investment and development. This includes offering incentives to tourism businesses and simplifying visa processes for tourists.
7) Encourage the adoption of innovative technologies in the tourism sector, such as mobile applications with augmented reality, facial recognition, and personalization features, to enhance the visitor experience.
8) Foster collaboration between the government and private sector to jointly invest in infrastructure and smart tourism initiatives. Public-private partnerships can accelerate development.
9) Develop marketing campaigns to promote Bangladesh as a smart tourism destination, highlighting the use of technology to enhance the visitor experience and attract tech-savvy tourists.
10) Invest in data collection and analysis to understand tourist trends, preferences, and behaviors. Use this data to tailor experiences and improve services for visitors.

By implementing these suggestions, Bangladesh can further harness the potential of smart tourism, attract more tourists, and boost economic growth while ensuring sustainable practices.

CONCLUSION

In summary, the potential of Smart Tourism Destination in Bangladesh exhibits significant promise. The tourism industry in Bangladesh has the potential to transform significantly into a more efficient, sustainable, and secure sector through the integration and utilization of smart technologies, owing to the rapid advancement of technology. The nation has already initiated measures by introducing digital platforms, such as Visit Bangladesh and Tourism Board websites and applications. Nevertheless, to fully maximize the capabilities of smart tourism, it is imperative to undertake additional measures such as enhancing connectivity, establishing advanced smart tourism infrastructure, and cultivating a proficient workforce capable of effectively operating these technological advancements. By implementing appropriate investments and strategic initiatives, Bangladesh has the potential to emerge as a prominent smart tourism destination, thereby attracting a more significant number of tourists and fostering economic growth.

REFERENCES

Alam, G. M., Hoque, K. E., Khalifa, M. T. B., Siraj, S. B., & Ghani, M. (2009). The role of agriculture education and training on agriculture economics and national development of Bangladesh. *African Journal of Agricultural Research, 4*(12), 1334–1350.

Alauddin, M., Shah, M. G. H., & Ullah, H. (2014). *Tourism in Bangladesh: A prospects analysis*. Information and Knowledge Management.

Asogwa, B. E. (2013). Electronic government as a paradigm shift for efficient public services: Opportunities and challenges for Nigerian government. *Library Hi Tech, 31*(1), 141–159. doi:10.1108/07378831311303985

Backer, E., & Lynch, D. (2017). Understanding the proclivity of visiting friends and relatives (VFR) travel across family life cycle stages in Australia. *International Journal of Tourism Research, 19*(4), 447–454. doi:10.1002/jtr.2087

Bhuiyan, A. H., & Darda, A. (2018). Prospects and potentials of halal tourism development in Bangladesh. *Journal of Tourismology, 4*(2), 93–106.

Buhalis, D., & Amaranggana, A. (2013). *Smart tourism destinations*. Information and Communication Technologies in Tourism 2014: Proceedings of the International Conference in Dublin, Ireland. 10.1007/978-3-319-03973-2_40

Buhalis, D., Lin, M. S., & Leung, D. (2022). Metaverse as a driver for customer experience and value co-creation: Implications for hospitality and tourism management and marketing. *International Journal of Contemporary Hospitality Management, 35*(2), 701–716. doi:10.1108/IJCHM-05-2022-0631

Cacho, A., Mendes-Filho, L., Estaregue, D., Moura, B., Cacho, N., Lopes, F., & Alves, C. (2016). Mobile tourist guide supporting a smart city initiative: A Brazilian case study. *International Journal of Tourism Cities, 2*(2), 164–183. doi:10.1108/IJTC-12-2015-0030

Cenamor, I., de la Rosa, T., Núñez, S., & Borrajo, D. (2017). Planning for tourism routes using social networks. *Expert Systems with Applications, 69*, 1–9. doi:10.1016/j.eswa.2016.10.030

Christie, I., Fernandes, E., Messerli, H., & Twining-Ward, L. (2013). *Tourism in Africa: Harnessing tourism for growth and improved livelihoods*. http://hdl.handle.net/10986/16053

Femenia-Serra, F., Neuhofer, B., & Ivars-Baidal, J. A. (2019). Towards a conceptualisation of smart tourists and their role within the smart destination scenario. *Service Industries Journal, 39*(2), 109–133. doi:10.1080/02642069.2018.1508458

Gramlich, E. M. (1994). Infrastructure investment: A review essay. *Journal of Economic Literature, 32*(3), 1176–1196. https://www.jstor.org/stable/2728606

Gretzel, U., & Scarpino-Johns, M. (2018). Destination resilience and smart tourism destinations. *Tourism Review International, 22*(3-4), 263–276. doi:10.3727/154427218X15369305779065

Hassan, A., Kennell, J., & Chaperon, S. (2020). Rhetoric and reality in Bangladesh: Elite stakeholder perceptions of the implementation of tourism policy. *Tourism Recreation Research, 45*(3), 307–322. doi:10.1080/02508281.2019.1703286

Hossain, S. F. A., Ahsan, F. T., Mohiuddin, K., Nadi, A. H., Neamah, H., Ahmed, M., & Hassan, A. (2022). Technology application in the tourism and hospitality industry of the Middle East Asia. In Technology Application in Tourism in Asia: Innovations, Theories and Practices (pp. 109-125). Springer. doi:10.1007/978-981-16-5461-9_7

Hudson, S., & Ritchie, J. B. (2009). Branding a memorable destination experience. The case of'Brand Canad'. *International Journal of Tourism Research, 11*(2), 217–228. doi:10.1002/jtr.720

Islam, M. W., Chowdhury, D., & Khan, A. (2021). Tourism in Bangladesh: a future outlook. *Future of Tourism in Asia*, 97-122. doi:10.1007/978-981-16-1669-3_7

Ivasciuc, I. S. (2020). Augmented reality and facial recognition technologies. Building bridges between the hospitality industry and tourists during pandemic. *Bulletin of the Transilvania University of Brasov. Series V, Economic Sciences, 13*(62), 75–92. doi:10.31926/but.es.2020.13.62.2.8

Jovicic, D. Z. (2019). From the traditional understanding of tourism destination to the smart tourism destination. *Current Issues in Tourism, 22*(3), 276–282. doi:10.1080/13683500.2017.1313203

Kumar, I., Rawat, J., Mohd, N., & Husain, S. (2021). Opportunities of artificial intelligence and machine learning in the food industry. *Journal of Food Quality, 2021*, 1–10. doi:10.1155/2021/4535567

Lee, P., Hunter, W. C., & Chung, N. (2020). Smart tourism city: Developments and transformations. *Sustainability (Basel), 12*(10), 3958. doi:10.3390/su12103958

Liang, F., Mu, L., Wang, D., & Kim, B. S. (2022). A new model path for the development of smart leisure sports tourism industry based on 5G technology. *IET Communications*, *16*(5), 485–496. doi:10.1049/cmu2.12271

Mariani, M., Baggio, R., Fuchs, M., & Höepken, W. (2018). Business intelligence and big data in hospitality and tourism: A systematic literature review. *International Journal of Contemporary Hospitality Management*, *30*(12), 3514–3554. doi:10.1108/IJCHM-07-2017-0461

Md Kashedul Wahab, T., & Majumder, M. T. H. (2011). An appraisal of tourism industry development in Bangladesh. *European Journal of Business and Management*, *3*(3).

Muhanna, E. (2006). Sustainable tourism development and environmental management for developing countries. *Problems and Perspectives in Management*, *4*(2), 14–30.

Neuhofer, B., Buhalis, D., & Ladkin, A. (2015). Smart technologies for personalized experiences: A case study in the hospitality domain. *Electronic Markets*, *25*(3), 243–254. doi:10.1007/s12525-015-0182-1

Pai, C.-K., Liu, Y., Kang, S., & Dai, A. (2020). The role of perceived smart tourism technology experience for tourist satisfaction, happiness and revisit intention. *Sustainability (Basel)*, *12*(16), 6592. doi:10.3390/su12166592

Perfetto, M. C., & Vargas-Sánchez, A. (2018). Towards a Smart Tourism Business Ecosystem based on Industrial Heritage: Research perspectives from the mining region of Rio Tinto, Spain. *Journal of Heritage Tourism*, *13*(6), 528–549. doi:10.1080/1743873X.2018.1445258

Rhaman, M. R. (2016). *The socio-economic importance of tourism and its impact on the livelihood in south Asia: Case Rangamati, Bangladesh*. https://urn.fi/URN:NBN:fi:amk-2016103115572

Risteskia, M., Kocevskia, J., & Arnaudov, K. (2012). Spatial planning and sustainable tourism as basis for developing competitive tourist destinations. *Procedia: Social and Behavioral Sciences*, *44*, 375–386. doi:10.1016/j.sbspro.2012.05.042

Sharma, S., & Rishi, O. (2022). IoT Enabled Smart Tourism (IoTeST): Tourism Service Dimensions. In *Rising Threats in Expert Applications and Solutions: Proceedings of FICR-TEAS 2022* (pp. 643-654). Springer. 10.1007/978-981-19-1122-4_67

Shen, S., Sotiriadis, M., & Zhang, Y. (2020). The influence of smart technologies on customer journey in tourist attractions within the smart tourism management framework. *Sustainability (Basel)*, *12*(10), 4157. doi:10.3390/su12104157

Shvets, I. (2020). Multiplier effects of the development of socially responsible tourism. *EurAsian Journal of BioSciences*, *14*(2), 3753–3758.

Souffriau, W., Vansteenwegen, P., Vertommen, J., Berghe, G. V., & Oudheusden, D. V. (2008). A personalized tourist trip design algorithm for mobile tourist guides. *Applied Artificial Intelligence*, *22*(10), 964–985. doi:10.1080/08839510802379626

Sushchenko, O., Kozubova, N., & Prokopishyna, O. (2018). *Eco-friendly behavior of local population, tourists and companies as a factor of sustainable tourism development.*

Timothy, D. J. (2011). *Cultural heritage and tourism: An introduction* (Vol. 4). Channel View Publications. doi:10.21832/9781845411787

Tiwary, A., Mahato, M., Chidar, A., Chandrol, M. K., Shrivastava, M., & Tripathi, M. (2018). Internet of Things (IoT): Research, architectures and applications. *International Journal on Future Revolution in Computer Science & Communication Engineering*, *4*(3), 23–27.

Torabi, Z.-A., Shalbafian, A. A., Allam, Z., Ghaderi, Z., Murgante, B., & Khavarian-Garmsir, A. R. (2022). Enhancing memorable experiences, tourist satisfaction, and revisit intention through smart tourism technologies. *Sustainability (Basel)*, *14*(5), 2721. doi:10.3390/su14052721

Chapter 10
Digital Marketing, Artificial Intelligence, and Online Social Networks in Tourism:
Case of the Municipality of Amares (Portugal)

Marta Beatriz Silva
Polytechnic Institute of Cávado and Ave, Portugal

Jorge Lima Pacheco
Polytechnic Institute of Cávado and Ave, Portugal & ISCAP, Polytechnic of Porto, Portugal

Bruno Barbosa Sousa
https://orcid.org/0000-0002-8588-2422
Polytechnic Institute of Cávado and Ave (IPCA), Portugal & CiTUR, Portugal & UNIAG, Portugal

ABSTRACT

The present chapter involved a thorough investigation into the tourist destination in question, Amares, where the research results suggest that the Municipality of Amares can improve its digital marketing and online social networks strategy to attract more tourists. Thus, the research adds value to the tourist destination of Amares (Portugal), as it allows understanding in which direction the municipality should focus its efforts in tourism promotion. The conclusions drawn from benchmarking and questionnaire results showed that digital marketing and online social networks are important tools in promoting tourism in the Municipality of Amares. Additionally, some more effective practices were presented, such as the creation of strategic content tailored to different market segments, the use of attractive images and videos inspiring people to visit the tourist destination, and the development of influencer marketing campaigns.
DOI: 10.4018/979-8-3693-2137-9.ch010

INTRODUCTION

According to Turismo de Portugal (2022), tourism is a key sector of activity for generating wealth and employment in Portugal. In this way, tourism recorded in 2021, 11.3% of total exports and 36.9% of exports of services. Even so, the sector continues to grow, as can be seen from the employment rate in tourism, which is 6.7% in 2021. The growth of tourism has brought great results to the country, as the number of guests has increased, as well as the number of overnight stays and the number of average stays, as well as tourism revenue in Portugal. Tourism, assumes itself as a multifaceted and geographically complex activity that increasingly generates new (and different) market segments with different individual interests (Sousa, Magalhães & Soares, 2021; Correia et al., 2022). After the controversial period of 2020, caused by the global pandemic, in 2021, a year of recovery, 2.3 billion euros of tourist revenue were recorded, and the most recent data states that in 2022 there were 21.1 billion euros in tourism revenue. This chapter aims to study the impact of digital marketing and online social networks on tourism, more precisely, in the Municipality of Amares (Portugal). the tourism sector, contributing to the integration and development of a tourist destination.

In this context, a literature review was conducted, demonstrating the importance of digital marketing and online social networks in tourism. Subsequently, after gathering information, it was necessary to consider the exploratory method to be used, which in this case was quantitative. The conclusions drawn from benchmarking and questionnaire results showed that digital marketing and online social networks are important tools in promoting tourism in the Municipality of Amares. Additionally, some more effective practices were presented, such as the creation of strategic content tailored to different market segments, the use of attractive images and videos inspiring people to visit the tourist destination, and the development of influencer marketing campaigns. In summary, the present research involved a thorough investigation into the tourist destination in question, Amares, where the research results suggest that the Municipality of Amares can improve its digital marketing and online social networks strategy to attract more tourists. Thus, the chapter adds value to the tourist destination of Amares (Portugal), as it allows understanding in which direction the Municipality should focus its efforts in tourism promotion. From an interdisciplinary perspective, this chapter presents insights from a marketing perspective (digital and social networks) and from a tourism and regional (and local) development perspective.

THEORETICAL BACKGROUND

Digital Marketing, Artificial Intelligence and Tourism

Currently, offline marketing concerns traditional marketing, where media such as newspapers, magazines, television, banners, radio and others continue to be the most used means. However, with the evolution of marketing, as well as the evolution of technology and the emergence of the internet, digital marketing came to take the place of offline marketing, favoring communication actions carried out on the internet (Anjo et al., 2021). However, the concept of digital marketing is not new to all of us because, if we go back to the concept of marketing 4.0, we see that its focus is precisely on maintaining closer contact with consumers, that is, on the humanization of the brand, which Basically, it is one of the objectives of digital marketing (Macedo & Sousa, 2019; Oliveira, 2021). It should be added that the objective of digital marketing is not only to allow consumers to engage with brands, but also to ensure that their message and information reaches new customers, through campaigns and even presence on digital channels. Furthermore, digital allows you to more efficiently analyze competition and the market and also consolidate brands and show some notoriety and recognition (Gunelius, 2012; Correia et al., 2023). According to Martins et al. (2022), echnologies are increasingly present, as a part of the society in which we are inserted which, in addition to revolutionizing the way of life of all of us, has also caused great cthanges in the tourism context, with the emergence of new market niches. The internet has become one of the main media, facilitating travelling to any part of the world in just one click. The recent global pandemic, caused by the Covid-19, has changed not only the way we currently travel, but it has also highlighted the important role played by Virtual Tourism and Gamified Virtual Experiences. Faced with this scenario, several companies in the tourism sector had to reinvent themselves, using virtual environments and digital tools, as an opportunity to maintain and expand their business (Machado et al., 2021).

Therefore, and according to Bulchand-Gidumal (2022), artificial intelligence (AI) is currently present in almost every area of travel and tourism, appearing in different types of applications such as personalization and recommender systems, robots, conversational systems, smart travel agents, prediction and forecasting systems, language translation applications, and voice recognition and natural language processing systems (Goh et al., 2009). Recent improvements in big data, algorithms, and computing power have enabled significant enhancements in AI. Varghese (2023) argues that big data and artificial intelligence are a fairly new and innovative approach to addressing this issue of managing and analyzing huge datasets collected from multiple sources.

The fact that the internet, and other forms of communication, play a key role in the transformation and evolution of marketing, has made it possible to offer consumers different products, services, prices, suppliers and faster and more immediate means of purchasing. In this way, companies are able to reach the market, with new products and services, through the use of various online communication techniques (Chaffey et al., 2009; Dewantara et al., 2023). Most businesses' main objective is to offer products or services to consumers, however, to do this it is necessary to understand the market, that is, consumer behavior. Therefore, it is important to understand what consumers' needs and desires are, what they buy, what they use, what experiences they intend to have, among other actions (Costa, 2021; Fernandes et al., 2024). It is important to realize that, above all, brands must have a good reputation and be trusted by consumers. Thus, digital marketing currently allows any business that has an online presence, for example a website, to be placed on search engines such as Google, DuckDuckGo, Bing, Yandex, Swisscows, Yahoo, among others. In the opinion of Serrão (2018), the shopping experience that a consumer experiences on the brand's website is a decisive factor in choosing the brand. Therefore, the website reflects the professionalism with which the business is managed and presented to its customers. Therefore, the website must convey reliability to its consumers, through privacy. For instance, and according to Sousa et al. (2022), despite the growing interest and discussions on Virtual Reality (VR) and Augmented Reality (AR) in tourism, we do not yet know systematically the knowledge that has been built from academic papers on VR and AR in tourism; if and how VR and AR research intersect; the methodologies used to research VR and AR in tourism; and the emerging contexts in which VR and AR have surfaced in hospitality and tourism research. In tourism, where informative communication of intangible products has always been vital, the impending arrivals of VR and AR ranged from being hailed as a new horizon to virtual threats. In a post-COVID-19 landscape, there is growing interest and opportunity for cutting-edge technologies to contribute to destination recovery.

Social Networks and Tourism

Online social networks enable companies and organizations to improve their communication capacity and performance, so much so that they help to create digital links with their customers. Furthermore, online social networks allow people to interact and talk, where they share their opinions, experiences and ideas (Farrag & Nasr, 2017). That said, online social networks play the role of retaining and building relationships with customers, bringing great benefits to companies (Ryan, 2014). According to Silva (2015), Search Engine Marketing concerns a tool that allows you to gain online presence and traffic, through paid [Search Engine Advertising (SEA)] or organic strategies, [Search Engine Optimization (SEO)]. SEM has boosted the growth of online commerce and, therefore, the central role that search engines play in the marketing strategies of several companies can be seen (Luo et al., 2011). In other words, SEA consists of the use of paid advertising in search engines, promoting companies' products/services. On the other hand, SEO consists of a set of techniques for optimizing existing content on websites, so that they are positioned in the best way and are redirected to the greatest number of people through search engines (Chaffey, 2009; Ryan, 2014; Sousa et al., 2021). Content marketing concerns the marketing of a product/service of interest to a potential customer. Thus, it can be distributed through online social networks, blog, podcast, video, webinar, e-book, among others (Redondo et al., 2021). Marketing analytics is not just about measuring the performance of websites, but about evaluating the performance of all marketing efforts carried out. As is the case with online campaigns, where it is possible to identify the best time of day to send marketing emails, the best content that will engage the target audience, as well as the best time to publish on online social networks (Silva, 2015). Finally, digital marketing allows brands to transmit their message and information to new customers, on digital channels, through online strategies and tools. Thus, with the technological advancement of the internet and online social networks, brands connect with people all over the world. Naturally, these tools allowed people around the world to stay connected, leading to the emergence of online social networks. These allow us to create a connection between people, due to the sharing of opinions and information, about which we identify, or not. Sharing publications, likes, comments, among other information, is what makes users get closer to each other, ending up influencing each other. Therefore, the applications themselves began to develop new tools, so that users could spend more time within them. And, in addition, make interaction between users more intuitive. Thus, currently, online social networks such as Facebook and WhatsApp allow the creation of communities, which aims for closer sharing between users. Note the diversity of existing online social networks, as well as the specific target that each one assumes, since it is possible to divide them into areas of purpose. That said, according to Ethority (2021), some examples of online social networks that relate to sharing image content are Pinterest, PicsArt, Google Photos and flickr. With regard to video, Vimeo, dailymotion and Youtube, which is also considered within the music category, as well as Spotify, Shazam, SoundCloud and Youtube Music. Regarding the professional area, there is Linkedin, zerply and in message/video communication, WhatsApp, Facebook Messenger, Skype and Zoom stand out. In online social networks, some stand out, such as Facebook, Instagram and Snapchat.

Regarding the area of blogs, some such as Tumblr, Wordpress and Pulse, and in social communication Twitter, Quora and reddit. Regarding the travel category, some platforms such as Airbnb, Waze, HomeAway, Outdoosy, TripAdvisor and Trivago (Ethority, 2021). Added to this are those that were the pioneers of the aforementioned online social networks, Facebook, Google+ or Hi5, in the case of traditional online social networks. In the case of the latter, Hi5, many of its users began to "migrate" to the social network Facebook. As for Google+, which currently does not exist, there are many examples of applications associated with Google, which it developed. From Google Maps, Google Drive, Google Docs, Gmail, Google Translate, Google Photos, Meet, Google Scholar, among other applications (Silva, 2015; Ferreira & Sousa, 2022). The possibility of online social networks growing more and more was due to the increase in the worldwide use of smartphones.

Currently, according to the We Are Social report (2023), of the 8.01 billion population in January 2023, 5.44 billion have a cell phone, while 5.16 billion have access to the internet. Evidently, the easy access to these mobile devices has allowed 4.76 billion to be active on online social networks. The data referring to October 2022, the world population concerned 7.99 billion people, of which 5.48 billion had a cell phone and 5.07 billion were able to access the internet. Regarding online social networks, 4.74 billion of the world's population would have access to them. The We Are Social (2023) and Data Reportal (2022a) data differ by 3 months, and the growth in numbers between October 2022 and January 2023 is notable, meaning the digital world is constantly changing. Therefore, given the data presented in a global context, it is important to check the most used online social networks in the world, in January 2023. In this way, we refer to Facebook, Youtube, WhatsApp, Instagram, WeChat, TikTok, Facebook Messenger, and among others (We are social, 2023). In Portugal, according to Data Reportal (2022b), in February 2022, of the 10.15 million population, 16.07 million had a cell phone, with 8.63 million using the internet and 8.50 million being active on online social networks. Data from the Reporting Data (2023) in January 2023, relate to 10.26 million population, of which 17.54 million used a cell phone. In February 2022 and January 2023, the 7 main reasons for Portuguese people to use the internet related to searching for information, looking for how certain tasks were carried out, being in contact with friends and family, following news and events, listening to music, finding ideas or inspiration, looking for places, holidays and trips, among other reasons (Reportal Data, 2022b; Reporting Date, 2023). Regarding the most used online social networks in Portugal, in 2022, the Data Reportal (2022b) highlights WhatsApp, Facebook, Instagram, Facebook Messenger, Pinterest, TikTok, Linkedin, Twitter, among others. In January 2023, the same online social networks are in the spotlight, however, TikTok rises in position in relation to Pinterest.

Thus, digital marketing, when hand in hand with tourism marketing, makes it possible to make the tourist service or product tangible, through its promotion on the internet, creating online experiences that evoke positive emotions, as well as creating unforgettable memories (Figueira et al., 2021; Oliveira & Pereira, 2021). All of this is possible, since there is the opportunity to digitize information, in other words, by creating content such as images, videos and text, which will be made available to customers, where they can check the sensations offered by that tourist destination (Sousa & Rocha, 2019; Correia & Brito, 2020). Furthermore, it adds to the availability of tourist websites, which contain information about what can be found and experienced (Oliveira & Pereira, 2021). The digitalization of tourism has brought benefits to its development, given that online is a great communication and marketing distribution channel. As it is a means of providing information to tourists, the internet and online social networks end up being a fundamental means for organizations, if they intend to act successfully in the online distribution process (Oliveira & Pereira, 2021). Thus, some examples of websites relevant to the tourism sector, such as TripAdvisor and Couchsurfing. TripAdvisor brings together all tourists' opinions and reviews regarding hotels and restaurants, and also has some partnerships with these hotels. Regarding the Couchsurfing platform, it is designed for independent tourists, who make their homes available to other tourists, and who want to see the world, but with a lower budget, or who want to have company (Alves, 2011). Alongside this, tourists have become increasingly demanding with the information they seek regarding the service/product they intend to enjoy. Making some tourists, in addition to being content consumers, become content producers for online social networks, leaving photos, videos or short comments about a particular tourist destination. For all these reasons, online social networks have become a space that guarantees the reputation and credibility of a tourist destination (Bulchand-Gidumal, 2024).

Therefore, the promotion of these tourist destinations requires the development of a strategy that is effective and assertive, to build a solid brand, and that tourist offers are presented in an attractive way. The online social networks WhatsApp, Facebook, Instagram and TikTok can be important for tourism, as they emerge as the favorites of the Portuguese in January 2023 (DataReportal, 2023). Regarding WhatsApp, it allows direct contact with the customer, so brands can interact with their customers and respond more quickly (Tecnohotel, 2019). In addition, it facilitates the process of clarifying customer doubts regarding hotel establishments, as well as simplifying the reservation process, causing some companies to use automation systems in Whatsapp responses, to be more efficient in their responses (Sinch Engine, 2023). Finally, it appears that the internet and online social networks have played a huge role in the tourism sector. Furthermore, it is clear that the whole world is connected thanks to the internet and the fact that this is an innovative area for tourism professionals, whether they are hotels or municipal institutions. Since its objective is to publicize and promote different tourist destinations, in order to maintain relationships with their customers and also reach and attract new customers (Alves, 2011; Martins et al., 2023; Mendes & Teixeira, 2019; Schardong, 20119).

CONTEXTUALIZATION: AMARES (PORTUGAL)

Located in the district of Braga, the municipality of Amares had, in 2022, 19,028 inhabitants belonging to 16 parishes, in a geographical area of 82 km^2. Even so, it borders the municipalities of Terras de Bouro, Vila Verde, Póvoa de Lanhoso, Vieira do Minho and Braga (Capela & Domingues, 2014). Together with the municipalities of Braga, Barcelos, Esposende, Terras de Bouro and Vila Verde, Amares is part of the Intermunicipal Community of Vale do Cávado (CIM Cávado), thus, they aim to articulate and promote common interests. The target municipality of study, Amares, is approximately 15km from the city of Braga (Capela & Domingues, 2014). Taking into account that it is located in the northern region of the country's coast, the accessibility of the municipality of Amares is designed for those who wish to travel by public transport. That is, the municipality has public transport stops in all parishes, as well as a small taxi rank in one of its parishes. Furthermore, despite not being crossed by any axis of national importance, it is crossed by several regional and municipal roads.

Despite its location, Amares has a wide variety of tourist resources, capable of attracting visitors to the most diverse dimensions of tourism. Tourists have the possibility of visiting the municipality's river beaches, the green spaces of the different parishes, the rich cultural heritage or tasting typical cuisine. With regard to natural heritage, bathing areas and green areas, the municipality of Amares is quite rich, however, it is worth highlighting the Felinhos River Beach, the leisure area of Nossa Senhora da Abadia, the AutocarroBar, where the Homem River and the Cávado River, and Quinta do Lago dos Cisnes. However, the monumental cultural heritage is not left behind, there are many busts, churches and monasteries spread across the municipality, even so, the importance of the Monastery of Santo André de Rendufe, the Monastery of Bouro Santa Maria, and the busts of some public figures such as António Variações, Chef Silva and Francisco Sá de Miranda. In relation to artistic and ethnographic cultural heritage, there are museums and folkloric groups spread across the different parishes, as well as various traditional activities such as fishing and parachuting. Upon proposal by the City Council and approval by the Municipal Assembly of Amares, on the Personal Map2022 and Annual Recruitment Plan for 2022, it appears that the tourism area is integrated into the Education, Culture and Social Action Division, which presents several specific services:

- Social Organization Service;
- Educational Management Service;
- Library and Historical Archive Service;
- Associations, Sports and Youth Section

- Culture and Tourism Service
- Social Action and Employment Service

The culture and tourism service processes and disseminates tourist information and, in addition, designs and implements tourism promotion actions (Amares Município, 2022).

METHODOLOGY

Benchmarking concerns a process that contributes to improving the performance of organizations, as it allows information to be collected. In this way, it is possible to measure the performance of institutions, so much so that this process involves collecting best practices from other organizations. Benchmarking involves collecting information about success stories already identified and applied in certain organizations. This approach acts as a comparison model between case studies, with the aim of improving and enriching the research, in this case, within the scope of digital marketing and online social networks in Tourism, in this case the Municipality of Amares. Following the analysis of some tourist destinations, such as Melgaço and the Algarve, inspired by their good examples of digital marketing, as well as by the fact that they have been the subject of study and analysis by other authors such as Xavier (2023) in the case of Melgaço, and Agostinho (2020) in the case of the Algarve. To carry out effective scientific research, it is necessary to select the correct methodology, which is why, in the present case study, the methodology applied is quantitative. The quantitative methodology is based on questionnaires and statistical analyses, which aim to investigate reality (Augusto, 2014). Thus, taking into account causal studies, they consist of assumptions that must be evaluated through formal research (Santos, 2022). The main objective of the questionnaire used in this study is to understand the importance of the internet and online social networks in choosing a tourist destination. Furthermore, the questionnaire aims to understand whether they know the Municipality of Amares, how respondents gained knowledge and what motivations they have for visiting the tourist destination. The present study is based on a quantitative approach, through an online questionnaire survey. The questionnaire was created using the GoogleForms tool, as it allows the creation of questions and analysis of the data collected easily. This questionnaire was distributed online on Facebook, through sharing in some groups linked to Tourism, Instagram and some groups on WhatsApp, and sent by email to personal contacts, on September 7th, obtaining 160 valid questionnaires.

PRELIMINARY RESULTS AND DISCUSSION

Throughout this topic, the results obtained will be analyzed through the questionnaire carried out on GoogleForms to 160 respondents. The majority of participants are female, totaling 67.50% of the sample, while males represent 32.50%. It appears that the majority of these are in the 20-24 age group, representing 28.13% of the sample, followed by the 25-29 age group, which comprises 24.38% of the responses. The age group with the lowest representation corresponds to 70-74 years old, with only 0.63% of responses. Regarding professional status, the results reveal that 61.88% of respondents are working for others. The "Worker-student" option was the second with the most responses, representing 15.63% of respondents. The "Unemployed" situation is the least represented, with only 2.50% of responses. In short, the majority of the sample is female, the predominant age group is 20-24 years old, the most common nationality is Portuguese and the majority of the 160 respondents are working for others. Of the entire sample, 98.75% use online social networks. Thus, in relation to searching for information about a tourist destination on online social networks, before visiting it. The fact that 45.63% chose the "Always" option reflects the relevance that online social networks have in travel decision-making. Furthermore, 26.88% say that online social networks are "Often" a source of information for their trips. It is important to remember that 1.25% of respondents did not answer this question, as they do not use online social networks. The majority of responses indicate that 39.38% of respondents "Rarely" visit the Municipality's institutional profile on online social networks when looking for information about the tourist destination. Furthermore, the second highest percentage corresponds to the "Sometimes" option, with 32.50% of responses, which means that respondents occasionally visit profiles because they contain important information, although it is not their first choice. The data presented shows that respondents who use online social networks prefer information about "Leisure activities" and "Places of visit and points of interest". This information was classified as "Extremely useful" to be published on the Municipality's institutional online social network profiles. However, with regard to information about "Accessibility", "Hobbies and promotions" and "Restaurants", they are comparatively not very relevant, being only considered very useful. However, these areas must be addressed strategically by the Municipality. In addition to the importance of understanding the relevance and interest in the content presented on the Municipality's online social networks, the way in which respondents interact with the content was also evaluated.

It is essential to highlight some significant practices that will contribute to the development of an effective and assertive strategy within the scope of tourism in the Municipality of Amares, using online social networks and digital marketing. In this sense, it is crucial to start by highlighting tourism in the Municipality of

Amares on all online platforms and in all physical locations, such as the tourist office, promoting the destination in tourism newspapers and magazines and being present at tourism meetings and fairs, to present the tourist destination of Amares.

Creating a solid brand is essential for building a reputation and credibility for Amares tourism. Therefore, it is important to continue, similar to the benchmarking practices in the "VisitAmares" project, with the definition of an effective and assertive strategy. With regard to the institutional website, it is vital that it brings together the necessary information and that it is updated and attractive, with appealing images and dynamic content. Furthermore, it is important that the website redirects visitors to platforms such as TripAdvisor, which provides tourist reviews and information about hotels, restaurants and cafes. It is equally important to make the website available in foreign languages, as it currently does not contain all the information translated into the available languages. It is also important to integrate the marketing email sending platform with the institutional website. With regard to online social networks, it is essential that the tourist destination stands out on these platforms. To this end, it is essential to develop informative and educational content for potential tourists. The content must be attractive and appealing, with emphasis on images and videos that inspire people to visit Amares and motivate them to do so. Furthermore, it is important to look for ambassadors for the tourist destination of Amares, who represent this brand. Another relevant action is the development of influencer marketing campaigns, taking advantage of the role that influencers have in their followers' decisions, particularly in choosing the tourist destination to visit.

The Municipality can establish partnerships to create competitions and promotions with these influencers. Finally, along with these actions, it is important to develop paid traffic campaigns on the website and online social networks. These paid traffic campaigns should be carried out after optimizing the website and developing informative and educational content on online social networks, with the aim of providing content that provides value to tourists. In short, a Municipality that wants to invest in digital marketing must constantly adapt to the market, following universal trends and monitoring success stories and competition. The Municipality of Amares has great potential in terms of tourist resources and offers, however, it needs to reinforce its commitment to digital marketing policies and focus on the needs of tourists in terms of content, on online social networks, websites and platforms that can benefit your tourism.

The internet and mobile devices have shortened the communication distance between people and, due to their constant evolution, have allowed the emergence of several online communication platforms that have brought countless benefits in different sectors of activity, and tourism is no exception. The tourism sector has closely monitored technological and digital developments, adapting to market trends and needs. Currently, tourists no longer depend on traditional models such as tourism newspapers and magazines, sector fairs, to prepare their trips. Instead, they prioritize digital sources such as online social networks, websites and blogs. Tourists are not only looking for information about the destinations they want to visit, but also guidance on how to get there, where to stay, what activities to do, where to eat, and what tourist attractions to visit. Furthermore, they greatly value feedback from other tourists who have already been there, which highlights the importance of feedback on online social networks, websites, travel blogs and platforms such as TripAdvisor. In Portugal, the tourism sector plays a significant role in the Bruno Domestic Product (GDP), contributing to the generation of wealth and jobs. In many regions, tourism drives the economic, cultural and social development of the country. Therefore, it should be a continuous and strategic investment, as it allows the economy of a given region or municipality to be leveraged.

In addition to the advantage of the region's economic growth, the impact that increased tourism has on the Municipality in social and cultural terms is important as it will allow the dissemination of criticism, opinions and feedback, which will have an impact on the image of the tourist destination. Of the entire sample, 98.75% use online social networks. Having said that, this is due to the fact that the questionnaire was disseminated, mostly, using them. The fact that 45.63% chose the "Always" option reflects the relevance that online social networks have in travel decision-making. Furthermore, 26.88% say that online social networks are "Often" a source of information for their trips. It is important to remember that 1.25% of respondents did not answer this question, as they do not use online social networks. The majority of responses indicate that 39.38% of respondents "Rarely" visit the Municipality's institutional profile on online social networks when looking for information about the tourist destination.

Furthermore, the second highest percentage corresponds to the "Sometimes" option, with 32.50% of responses, which means that respondents occasionally visit profiles because they contain important information, although it is not their first choice. The data presented shows that respondents who use online social networks prefer information about "Leisure activities" and "Places of visit and points of interest". This information was classified as "Extremely useful" to be published on the Municipality's institutional online social network profiles. However, with regard to information about "Accessibility", "Hobbies and promotions" and "Restaurants", they are comparatively not very relevant, being only considered very useful.

However, these areas must be addressed strategically by the Municipality. In addition to the importance of understanding the relevance and interest in the content presented on the Municipality's online social networks, the way in which respondents interact with the content was also evaluated. Based on the data presented, the majority of respondents consider that online social networks influenced their decision to visit a tourist destination, since 46.25% consider this influence as "Very likely" and 23.75% of people consider it “Probable” to have been influenced. Furthermore, the most relevant data in this table concerns the fact that respondents considered it “Impossible” not to have been influenced by online social networks, to visit a tourist destination. In summary, the results highlight the importance and relevance that social networks play in tourism, namely as a source of online information that has a significant influence on tourists’ decisions to visit a destination.

FINAL CONSIDERATIONS AND FUTURE RESEARCH

In the present chapter, it was possible to verify the impact that digital marketing strategies and the promotion of online social networks have on institutions or tourist destinations. Therefore, there are some tourist destinations that apply good digital marketing practices and boost online social networks, which can serve as an example for other destinations that wish to assert themselves in the tourism sector. For all these reasons, during the investigation it was found that there was an increase in the number of internet users, as well as online social networks. Consequently, the number of new platforms and applications continues to emerge. This means that the world’s population is effectively spending more and more time on the internet, and therefore it is recommended that tourist destinations stay up to date and adapt to this new global context. Big data and artificial intelligence are a fairly new and innovative approach to addressing this issue of managing and analyzing huge datasets collected from multiple sources (Varghese, 2023).

Therefore, in addition to the tourist destination being present on a website and online social networks, it will be important to place clear and educational information on its platforms, so that it attracts the greatest number of visitors. The Municipality of Amares, in order to increase its capacity to attract other audiences, needs to develop a comprehensive marketing strategy, which includes a digital presence, both on the internet and on online social networks.

The Municipality of Amares is characterized by being a region rich in cultural and natural heritage, which offers a wide variety of tourist resources. As already mentioned, the municipality offers some major religious, gastronomic and cultural events, which are the motivating factor for visiting this tourist destination. However, given the results obtained, it appears that the majority of respondents who visited Amares most likely did so to participate in the “Festas d’Amares”, however, another relevant answer in this regard is family visits. However, note the importance that natural heritage and green areas hold for the municipality, which is a tourist resource that also motivates visitors to the municipality, according to research data.

Finally, the digital marketing strategy for tourism in the Municipality of Amares must be clear and aligned with the municipality’s objectives and available tourist offer.

In this sense, it is proposed to develop some of the actions mentioned throughout the chapter, which will allow the construction of a solid Amares brand for the Municipality, generating local development, the tourism sector and the municipality's economy. To conclude, tthe present chapter involved a thorough investigation into the tourist destination in question, Amares, where the research results suggest that the Municipality of Amares can improve its digital marketing and online social networks strategy to attract more tourists. Thus, the research adds value to the tourist destination of Amares, as it allows understanding in which direction the Municipality should focus its efforts in tourism promotion. From an interdisciplinary perspective, this chapter presents insights from a marketing perspective (digital and social networks) and from a tourism and regional (and local) development perspective.

REFERENCES

Anjo, A. M., Sousa, B., Santos, V., Lopes Dias, Á., & Valeri, M. (2021). Lisbon as a literary tourism site: Essays of a digital map of Pessoa as a new trigger. *Journal of Tourism* [JTHSM]. *Heritage & Services Marketing*, *7*(2), 58–67.

Bulchand-Gidumal, J. (2022). Impact of Artificial Intelligence in Travel, Tourism, and Hospitality. In Z. Xiang, M. Fuchs, U. Gretzel, & W. Höpken (Eds.), *Handbook of e-Tourism*. Springer., doi:10.1007/978-3-030-48652-5_110

Bulchand-Gidumal, J. (2024). The case of BeReal and spontaneous online social networks and their impact on tourism: Research agenda. *Current Issues in Tourism*, *27*(1), 7–11. doi:10.1080/13683500.2023.2191174

Camillo, C., & Medeiros, L. (2017). A Utilização Do Facebook E Do WhatsApp Como Ferramentas *Alternativas Do Ensino-Aprendizagem. Revista Redin, 6*(1). https://seer.faccat.br/index.php/redin/article/view/607

Çeltek, E., & Ilhan, I. (2020). Big data, artificial intelligence, and their implications in the tourism industry. In *Handbook of research on smart technology applications in the tourism industry* (pp. 115–130). IGI Global. doi:10.4018/978-1-7998-1989-9.ch006

Chaffey, D., Ellis-Chadwick, F., Mayer, R., & Johnston, K. (2009). *Internet Marketing: Strategy, Implementation and Practice (4ºEdição)*. Pearson Education.

Correia, R., & Brito, C. (2020). People: The most important marketing asset of territories. *Journal of Marketing Research & Case Studies*, 1–10.

Correia, R., Cunha, M., Carvalho, A., & Sousa, B. (2023). The (wasted) potential of digital communication in low-density destinations: the case of three Portuguese municipalities. *Journal of Hospitality and Tourism Insights*.

Correia, R., Marinho, M., Sousa, B., & Venciute, D. (2022). Stakeholders' perceptions of the communication of the territorial brand: The case of Braganca. *Journal of Tourism Management Research*, *9*(2), 155–172. doi:10.18488/31.v9i2.3172

Cunha, L. (2008). Avaliação do Potencial Turístico. *Journal of Tourism Studies*. http://hdl.handle.net/10437/384

Dewantara, M. H., Gardiner, S., & Jin, X. (2023). Travel vlog ecosystem in tourism digital marketing evolution: A narrative literature review. *Current Issues in Tourism*, *26*(19), 3125–3139. doi:10.1080/13683500.2022.2136568

Duarte, A., & Dias, P. (2021). TikTok: usos e motivações entre adolescentes em Portugal. Chasqui. *Revista Latinoamericana de Comunicación, 147*, 81-103. https://dialnet.unirioja.es/servlet/articulo?codigo=8093843

Fernandes, J. M., Sousa, B. B., & Correia, R. (2024). Place Knowledge Management in Promoting Gastronomic Tourism and Regional Development: A Case Study Applied to the Lampreia Festival in Portugal. In *Knowledge Management and Knowledge Sharing: Business Strategies and an Emerging Theoretical Field* (pp. 89–97). Springer Nature Switzerland. doi:10.1007/978-3-031-37868-3_6

Ferreira, L., & Sousa, B. B. (2022). Understanding the role of social networks in consumer behavior in tourism: A business approach. In *Research Anthology on Social Media Advertising and Building Consumer Relationships* (pp. 1758–1775). IGI Global. doi:10.4018/978-1-6684-6287-4.ch095

Ferreira, S., Sousa, B. B., Carvalho, A., & Broega, A. C. (2022). Residents' attitudes toward place marketing and pro-environmental behaviors at UNESCO world heritage sites. In *Advances in Tourism, Technology and Systems: Selected Papers from ICOTTS 2021* (Vol. 2, pp. 71–86). Springer Nature Singapore. doi:10.1007/978-981-16-9701-2_7

Figueira, V., Rolha, J. A., & Sousa, B. B. (2022). Digital communication in museums and museological spaces: diagnosis of Baixo Alentejo, Portugal. In *Handbook of Research on Digital Communications, Internet of Things, and the Future of Cultural Tourism* (pp. 271–290). IGI Global. doi:10.4018/978-1-7998-8528-3.ch015

Goh, C., Mok, H. M., & Law, R. (2009). Artificial intelligence applications in tourism. In *Encyclopedia of Information Science and Technology* (2nd ed., pp. 241–247). IGI Global. doi:10.4018/978-1-60566-026-4.ch042

Gomes, D., Oliveira, C., & Soares, N. (2010). O Senhor Marketing Mix e a Senhora Prática Mercadológica Crise à Vista? Uma análise do paradigma dominante do marketing sob uma perspetiva pós-moderna. *Revista Ciência Administrativa, 16*, 219–241.

Kotler, P., Kartajaya, H., & Setiawan, I. (2010). *Marketing 3.0: From Products to Customers to the Human*. John Wiley & Sons, Inc. doi:10.1002/9781118257883

Kotler, P., Kartajaya, H., & Setiawan, I. (2021). *Marketing 5.0: Technology for Humanity*. Conjuntura Atual.

Lemes, D. (2013). *Resenha do livro "Redes sociais digitais: a cognição conectiva do Twitter* (7th ed.). TECCOGS - Revista Digital de Tecnologias Cognitivas., https://revistas.pucsp.br/index.php/teccogs/article/view/52853

Lima, R., & Figueiredo, G. (2020). *Novas estratégias do Marketing 4.0 para as organizações* (21st ed., Vol. 1). Faculdade de Ciências do Tocantins., https://jnt1.websiteseguro.com/index.php/JNT/article/view/774/568

Luo, W., Cook, D., & Karson, E. (2011). *Search advertising placement strategy: Exploring the efficacy of the conventional wisdom* (8th ed., Vol. 48). Information & Management., doi:10.1016/j.im.2011.10.001

Macedo, C., & Sousa, B. (2019). A acessibilidade no etourism: Um estudo na ótica das pessoas portadoras de necessidades especiais. *Pasos (El Sauzal), 17*(4), 709–723. doi:10.25145/j.pasos.2019.17.050

Machado, A. F., Sousa, B. B., de Oliveira, F. F., & de Abreu Rocha, A. M. (2021). The Influence of Tourist Photographic Narratives and Communication on Social Networks from the Perspective of Creative Tourism. In Advances in Tourism, Technology and Systems: Selected Papers from ICOTTS20, Volume 1 (pp. 133-143). Springer Singapore. doi:10.1007/978-981-33-4256-9_12

Maia, F., & Júnior, S. (2021). Tiktok e música pop: relações entre mídia, plataformas e produção de conteúdo no meio digital. Revista Tropos: Comunicação. *Society and Culture, 10*(1). https://periodicos.ufac.br/index.php/tropos/article/view/4978

Martins, C. S., Ferreira, A. C., Pereira, C. S., & Sousa, B. B. (2022). Virtual Tourism and Challenges in a Post-Pandemic Context. In *ICT as Innovator Between Tourism and Culture* (pp. 122–137). IGI Global. doi:10.4018/978-1-7998-8165-0.ch008

MendesG.TeixeiraS. (2019). O turismo, Património e cultura na era das redes sociais: um estudo de caso #viajamosparapartilhar. Revista Turismo & Desenvolvimento, nº32, pp. 171-194. https://doi.org/ doi:10.34624/rtd.v0i32.20480

Moretti, S., Oliveira, S., & Souza, C. (2018). A evolução do conceito de marketing e sua aplicação no turismo: Simetrias evolutivas, assimetrias temporais. *Revista de Turismo Contemporâneo*, *6*(1), 129–150. doi:10.21680/2357-8211.2018v6n1ID12477

Redondo, P., Zapata, B., & Palma, H. (2021). *Impacto del Marketing Digital a las empresas colombianas emergentes.* Revista Universidad & Empresa. https://revistas.urosario.edu.co/index.php/empresa/article/view/9114

Sandhya, H., & Varghese, B. (2023). Big Data and Artificial Intelligence: Creative Tools for Destination Competitiveness. In Multidisciplinary Approaches in AI, Creativity, Innovation, and Green Collaboration (pp. 155-166). IGI Global.

Sousa, B., & Rocha, A. T. (2019). The role of attachment in public management and place marketing contexts: A case study applied to Vila de Montalegre (Portugal). *International Journal of Public Sector Performance Management*, *5*(2), 189–205. doi:10.1504/IJPSPM.2019.099094

Sousa, B. B., Magalhães, F. C., & Soares, D. B. (2021). The role of relational marketing in specific contexts of tourism: A luxury hotel management perspective. In *Building consumer-brand relationship in luxury brand management* (pp. 223–243). IGI Global. doi:10.4018/978-1-7998-4369-6.ch011

Sousa, B. B., Martins, C. S., Ferreira, A. C., & Pereira, C. S. (2022). Virtual tourism and digital communication in the context of the post-pandemic scenario. In *Crisis management, destination recovery and sustainability* (pp. 197–205). Routledge. doi:10.4324/9781003295839-21

Stalidis, G., Karapistolis, D., & Vafeiadis, A. (2015). Marketing decision support using Artificial Intelligence and Knowledge Modeling: Application to tourist destination management. *Procedia: Social and Behavioral Sciences*, *175*, 106–113. doi:10.1016/j.sbspro.2015.01.1180

Xavier, G., Nogueira, S., & Vareiro, L. (2023). The Perception of Tourists Regarding the Importance of Influencers in Shaping the Image of a Tourist Destination: The Case of Melgaço (Portugal). In *International Conference on Tourism, Technology and Systems* (pp. 415-428). Singapore: Springer Nature Singapore.

KEY TERMS AND DEFINITIONS

Destination Management: The management of all aspects of a destination that contribute to a visitor's experience, including the perspectives, needs and expectations of: visitors.

Digital Marketing: Also called online marketing - is the promotion of brands to connect with potential customers using the internet and other forms of digital communication. This includes not only email, social media, and web-based advertising, but also text and multimedia messages as a marketing channel.

Local Development: A process of economic, social, cultural, and political changes leading to the improvement of the general level of inhabitants' prosperity.

Social: Media: Social media are interactive computer-mediated technologies that facilitate the creation and sharing of information, ideas, career interests and other forms of expression via virtual communities and networks.

Social Networking: Using internet-based social media sites to stay connected with friends, family, colleagues, or customers.

Storytelling: The social and cultural activity of sharing stories, sometimes with improvisation, theatrics or embellishment. Every culture has its own stories or narratives, which are shared as a means of entertainment, education, cultural preservation or instilling moral values.

In this illuminating journey through *AI Innovations for Travel and Tourism*, we have explored the multifaceted ways in which artificial intelligence (AI) is revolutionizing the tourism industry. The chapters of this book provide a comprehensive overview of how AI technologies are being leveraged to enhance personalization, efficiency, and engagement within the travel sector, from smart booking systems to the creation of immersive experiences.

AI has demonstrated its potential to profoundly influence various facets of tourism, including marketing, service delivery, research and visitor behavior analysis. With its capability to process vast amounts of data and learn from interactions, AI enhances the customer experience and provides valuable insights that drive strategic decision-making for businesses and destination managers. The ethical considerations discussed underscore the necessity of deploying AI thoughtfully and responsibly, ensuring that its integration supports sustainable practices and respects privacy and ethical norms.

As we stand at the threshold of a new era in travel, it is clear that AI will continue to play a pivotal role in shaping the future of tourism. The insights gathered from this book underscore the challenges and highlight AI's immense potential to inspire innovation. This potential should instill a sense of hope and optimism, emphasizing the importance of ongoing research and dialogue among academics, industry practitioners, and policymakers to navigate the challenges and embrace the opportunities presented by AI in tourism.

By fostering an understanding of AI's transformative potential and advocating for its ethical application, we can ensure that technology acts as a force for positive change, making the travel experience more accessible, personalized, and enriching for all.

In closing, "AI Innovations for Travel and Tourism" aims not merely to inform but also to inspire action, thought, and a shared vision for a future in which AI and tourism evolve.

Finally, we express our gratitude to the book contributors whose acumen has enriched these pages, and to the readers, who, with this knowledge, are not just passive recipients but active participants in shaping the future of tourism in the era of artificial intelligence. Together, we stand at the threshold of a new horizon — one that beckons with the promise of AI as a transformative ally in the continual journey of discovery that is travel.

Compilation of References

Agapito, D. (2020). The senses in tourism design: A bibliometric review. *Annals of Tourism Research, 83*(August), 102934. doi:10.1016/j.annals.2020.102934

Ahas, R., Aasa, A., Roose, A., Mark, Ü., & Silm, S. (2008). Evaluating passive mobile positioning data for tourism surveys: An Estonian case study. *Tourism Management, 29*(3), 469–486. doi:10.1016/j.tourman.2007.05.014

Ahmad, A., Kakeesh, D., & Abuhashesh, M. (2022). The role of the online flower of service in enhancing guest loyalty via the mediating role of guest experience: A structural equation modelling approach. *International Journal of Electronic Marketing and Retailing, 13*(1), 1–24. doi:10.1504/IJEMR.2022.119243

AiChat. (2023). Marina Bay Sands: Increasing resort brand awareness with a messenger bot. AI Chat. https://aichat.com/marina-bay-sands-chatbot

Akdu, U. (2020). Smart tourism: issues, challenges and opportunities. The Emerald handbook of ICT in tourism and hospitality, 291-308. Emerald.

Alam, G. M., Hoque, K. E., Khalifa, M. T. B., Siraj, S. B., & Ghani, M. (2009). The role of agriculture education and training on agriculture economics and national development of Bangladesh. *African Journal of Agricultural Research, 4*(12), 1334–1350.

Alauddin, M., Shah, M. G. H., & Ullah, H. (2014). *Tourism in Bangladesh: A prospects analysis.* Information and Knowledge Management.

Allen, C., Varner, G., & Zinser, J. (2000). Prolegomena to any future artificial moral agent. *Journal of Experimental & Theoretical Artificial Intelligence, 12*(3), 251–261. doi:10.1080/09528130050111428

Alma Çallı, B., Çallı, L., Sarı Çallı, D., & Çallı, F. (2023). The impact of different types of service robots usage in hotels on guests' intention to stay. *Journal of Hospitality and Tourism Technology, 14*(1), 53–68. doi:10.1108/JHTT-09-2021-0266

Alves, P. (2017). "If you fail to prepare, prepare to fail": a produção fílmica. In P. Alves, F. García (Eds.), Oficios del cine: manual para prácticas cinematográficas. ICONO14/CITCEM.

Alves, P., & García, F. (2017). Oficios del cine: manual para prácticas cinematográficas. ICONO14/CITCEM.

Ang, B. (2016). *Robot Lucy at your service at newly opened Rong Heng Seafood*. The Strait Times Lifestyle.

Anjo, A. M., Sousa, B., Santos, V., Lopes Dias, Á., & Valeri, M. (2021). Lisbon as a literary tourism site: Essays of a digital map of Pessoa as a new trigger. *Journal of Tourism* [JTHSM]. *Heritage & Services Marketing*, *7*(2), 58–67.

Antonio, N., De Almeida, A., & Nunes, L. (2022). Data mining and predictive analytics for e-tourism. In *Handbook of e-Tourism* (pp. 1–25). Springer International Publishing.

Aria, M., & Cuccurullo, C. (2017). Bibliometrix: An R-Tool for Comprehensive Science Mapping Analysis. *Journal of Informetrics*, *11*(4), 959–975. doi:10.1016/j.joi.2017.08.007

Asogwa, B. E. (2013). Electronic government as a paradigm shift for efficient public services: Opportunities and challenges for Nigerian government. *Library Hi Tech*, *31*(1), 141–159. doi:10.1108/07378831311303985

Azuma, R., Baillot, Y., Behringer, R., Feiner, S., Julier, S., & MacIntyre, B. (2001). Recent Advances in Augmented Reality. *IEEE Computer Graphics and Applications*, *21*(6), 34–47. doi:10.1109/38.963459

Backer, E., & Lynch, D. (2017). Understanding the proclivity of visiting friends and relatives (VFR) travel across family life cycle stages in Australia. *International Journal of Tourism Research*, *19*(4), 447–454. doi:10.1002/jtr.2087

Baggio, R., Micera, R., & Del Chiappa, G. (2020). Smart tourism destinations: A critical reflection. *Journal of Hospitality and Tourism Technology*, *11*(3), 407–423. doi:10.1108/JHTT-01-2019-0011

Bagozzi, R., Brady, M., & Huang, H. (2022). AI service and emotion. *Journal of Service Research*, *25*(4), 499–504. doi:10.1177/10946705221118579

Bainbridge, A. (2022). *12 reasons travel should care about autonomous vehicles*. PhocusWire. https://www.phocuswire.com/12-reasons-travel-suppliers-resellers-should-care-autonomous-vehicles

Balsalobre-Lorente, D., Abbas, J., He, C., Pilař, L., & Shah, S. A. R. (2023). Tourism, urbanization and natural resources rents matter for environmental sustainability: The leading role of AI and ICT on sustainable development goals in the digital era. *Resources Policy*, *82*, 103445. doi:10.1016/j.resourpol.2023.103445

Barry, C., & Pele, C. (2018). *Italy's robot concierge a novelty on the way to better AI*.

Bec, A., Moyle, B., Schaffer, V., & Timms, K. (2021). Virtual Reality and Mixed Reality for Second Chance Tourism. *Tourism Management*, *83*, 104256. doi:10.1016/j.tourman.2020.104256

Bec, A., Moyle, B., Timms, K., Schaffer, V., Skavronskaya, L., & Little, C. (2019). Management of Immersive Heritage Tourism Experiences: A Conceptual Model. *Tourism Management*, *72*(June), 117–120. doi:10.1016/j.tourman.2018.10.033

Belanche, D., Casaló, L. V., & Flavián, C. (2021). Frontline robots in tourism and hospitality: Service enhancement or cost reduction? *Electronic Markets*, *31*(3), 477–492. doi:10.1007/s12525-020-00432-5

Berezina, K., Ciftci, O., & Cobanoglu, C. (2019). Robots, artificial intelligence, and service automation in restaurants. In *Robots, artificial intelligence, and service automation in travel, tourism and hospitality* (pp. 185–219). Emerald Publishing Limited. doi:10.1108/978-1-78756-687-320191010

Bhuiyan, A. H., & Darda, A. (2018). Prospects and potentials of halal tourism development in Bangladesh. *Journal of Tourismology*, *4*(2), 93–106.

Biswas, S. (2023). Potential Use of ChatGPT in Global Warming. *Annals of Biomedical Engineering*, *51*(6), 1126–1127. doi:10.1007/s10439-023-03171-8 PMID:36856927

Bitner, M., Zeithaml, V., & Gremler, D. (2010). Technology's impact on the gaps model of service quality. Handbook of Service Science, 197-218. doi:10.1007/978-1-4419-1628-0_10

Borgobello, B. (2011). *Yotel New York features the world's first hotel robotic luggage handler*. News Atlas. https://newatlas.com/yotel-worlds-first-hotel-robotic-porter/19576

Bowen, J., & Morosan, C. (2018). Beware hospitality industry: The robots are coming. *Worldwide Hospitality and Tourism Themes*, *10*(6), 726–733. doi:10.1108/WHATT-07-2018-0045

Brostoff, G. (2020). Using facial recognition to renew trust in hospitality. *Today's Hotelier*. https://www.todayshotelier.com/2020/07/15/using-facial-recognition-to-renew-trust-in-hospitality

Buhalis, D., & Amaranggana, A. (2013). *Smart tourism destinations*. Information and Communication Technologies in Tourism 2014: Proceedings of the International Conference in Dublin, Ireland. 10.1007/978-3-319-03973-2_40

Buhalis, D., Lin, M. S., & Leung, D. (2022). Metaverse as a driver for customer experience and value co-creation: Implications for hospitality and tourism management and marketing. *International Journal of Contemporary Hospitality Management*, *35*(2), 701–716. doi:10.1108/IJCHM-05-2022-0631

Buhalis, D., & Moldavska, I. (2022). Voice assistants in hospitality: Using artificial intelligence for customer service. *Journal of Hospitality and Tourism Technology*, *13*(3), 386–403. doi:10.1108/JHTT-03-2021-0104

Buhalis, D., O'Connor, P., & Leung, R. (2023). Smart hospitality: From smart cities and smart tourism towards agile business ecosystems in networked destinations. *International Journal of Contemporary Hospitality Management*, *35*(1), 369–393. doi:10.1108/IJCHM-04-2022-0497

Bulchand-Gidumal, J. (2022). Impact of artificial intelligence in travel, tourism, and hospitality. In *Handbook of e-Tourism* (pp. 1943–1962). Springer International Publishing. doi:10.1007/978-3-030-48652-5_110

Bulchand-Gidumal, J. (2024). The case of BeReal and spontaneous online social networks and their impact on tourism: Research agenda. *Current Issues in Tourism*, *27*(1), 7–11. doi:10.1080/13683500.2023.2191174

Cacho, A., Mendes-Filho, L., Estaregue, D., Moura, B., Cacho, N., Lopes, F., & Alves, C. (2016). Mobile tourist guide supporting a smart city initiative: A Brazilian case study. *International Journal of Tourism Cities*, *2*(2), 164–183. doi:10.1108/IJTC-12-2015-0030

Caesars. (2018). *Caesars Entertainment Las Vegas Resorts elevates customer service with Ivy, a personalized virtual concierge service*. Investor. https://investor.caesars.com/news-releases/news-release-details/caesars-entertainment-las-vegas-resorts-elevates-customer

Cain, L., & Berezina, K. (2021). Robo-tipping: are customers game? In *Information and Communication Technologies in Tourism 2021: Proceedings of the ENTER 2021 eTourism Conference, January 19–22, 2021* (pp. 222-227). Springer International Publishing.

Caldeira, A. M., & Kastenholz, E. (2022). Spatiotemporal Tourist Behaviour. Encyclopedia of Tourism Management and Marketing, 196–199. doi:10.4337/9781800377486.spatiotemporal.tourist.behaviour

Camillo, C., & Medeiros, L. (2017). A Utilização Do Facebook E Do WhatsApp Como Ferramentas *Alternativas Do Ensino-Aprendizagem. Revista Redin, 6*(1). https://seer.faccat.br/index.php/redin/article/view/607

Cartwright, S. R. (1996) *Pre-production planning for video, film, and multimedia*. Focal Press. doi:10.1016/B978-0-240-80271-8.50010-9

Çeltek, E., & Ilhan, I. (2020). Big data, artificial intelligence, and their implications in the tourism industry. In *Handbook of research on smart technology applications in the tourism industry* (pp. 115–130). IGI Global. doi:10.4018/978-1-7998-1989-9.ch006

Cenamor, I., de la Rosa, T., Núñez, S., & Borrajo, D. (2017). Planning for tourism routes using social networks. *Expert Systems with Applications*, *69*, 1–9. doi:10.1016/j.eswa.2016.10.030

Chaffey, D., Ellis-Chadwick, F., Mayer, R., & Johnston, K. (2009). *Internet Marketing: Strategy, Implementation and Practice (4ºEdição)*. Pearson Education.

Chan, L., Hogaboam, L., & Cao, R. (2022). Artificial intelligence in tourism and hospitality. In *Applied Artificial Intelligence in Business: Concepts and Cases* (pp. 213–229). Springer International Publishing. doi:10.1007/978-3-031-05740-3_14

Chaudhari, K., & Thakkar, A. (2020). A comprehensive survey on travel recommender systems. *Archives of Computational Methods in Engineering*, *27*(5), 1545–1571. doi:10.1007/s11831-019-09363-7

Cheng, X., Lin, X., Shen, X.-L., Zarifis, A., & Mou, J. (2022). The dark sides of AI. *Electronic Markets*, *32*(1), 11–15. doi:10.1007/s12525-022-00531-5 PMID:35600917

Chen, X., Li, G., Yang, L., Nie, Q., Ye, X., Liang, Y., & Xu, T. (2020). Profiling unmanned aerial vehicle photography tourists. *Current Issues in Tourism*, *23*(14), 1705–1710. doi:10.1080/13683500.2019.1653832

Cheong, A., Lau, M. W. S., Foo, E., Hedley, J., & Bo, J. W. (2016). Development of a robotic waiter system. *IFAC-PapersOnLine*, *49*(21), 681–686. doi:10.1016/j.ifacol.2016.10.679

Cheong, F., & Law, R. (2023). Human employees versus robotic employees: Customers and hotel managers' perceived experience at unmanned smart hotels. *Cogent Social Sciences*, *9*(1), 2202937. doi:10.1080/23311886.2023.2202937

Chi, O. H., Gursoy, D., & Chi, C. G. (2022). Tourists' Attitudes toward the Use of Artificially Intelligent (AI) Devices in Tourism Service Delivery: Moderating Role of Service Value Seeking. *Journal of Travel Research*, *61*(1), 170–185. doi:10.1177/0047287520971054

Chi, O., Denton, G., & Gursoy, D. (2020). Artificially intelligent device use in service delivery: A systematic review, synthesis, and research agenda. *Journal of Hospitality Marketing & Management*, *29*(7), 757–786. doi:10.1080/19368623.2020.1721394

Choi, S., & Wan, L. (2021). The rise of service robots in the hospitality industry: some actionable insights. *Boston Hospitality Review*. https://www.bu.edu/bhr/2021/10/04/the-rise-of-service-robots-in-the-hospitality-industry-some-actionable-insights

Choithani, T., Chowdhury, A., Patel, S., Patel, P., Patel, D., & Shah, M. (2022). A comprehensive study of artificial intelligence and cybersecurity on Bitcoin, crypto currency and banking system. *Annals of Data Science*, 1-33. doi:10.1007/s40745-022-00433-5

Christie, I., Fernandes, E., Messerli, H., & Twining-Ward, L. (2013). *Tourism in Africa: Harnessing tourism for growth and improved livelihoods*. http://hdl.handle.net/10986/16053

Chua, A., Servillo, L., Marcheggiani, E., & Vande Moere, A. (2016). Mapping Cilento: Using geotagged social media data to characterize tourist flows in southern Italy. *Tourism Management*, *57*, 295–310. doi:10.1016/j.tourman.2016.06.013

Cipresso, P., Irene, A. C. G., Raya, M. A., & Riva, G. (2018). The Past, Present, and Future of Virtual and Augmented Reality Research: A Network and Cluster Analysis of the Literature. *Frontiers in Psychology*, *9*, 2086. https://www.frontiersin.org/articles/10.3389/fpsyg.2018.02086. doi:10.3389/fpsyg.2018.02086 PMID:30459681

CNBC. (2020). Singapore hopes artificial intelligence will help boost its tourism industry. CNBC. https://www.cnbc.com/2020/09/24/singapore-looks-to-artificial-intelligence-ai-to-boost-tourism.html

Connell, J. (2012). Film tourism: evolution, progress and prospects. *Tourism Management*, *33*(5), 1007-1029. Elsevier.

Correia, R., Cunha, M., Carvalho, A., & Sousa, B. (2023). The (wasted) potential of digital communication in low-density destinations: the case of three Portuguese municipalities. *Journal of Hospitality and Tourism Insights*.

Correia, R., & Brito, C. (2020). People: The most important marketing asset of territories. *Journal of Marketing Research & Case Studies*, 1–10.

Correia, R., Marinho, M., Sousa, B., & Venciute, D. (2022). Stakeholders' perceptions of the communication of the territorial brand: The case of Braganca. *Journal of Tourism Management Research*, *9*(2), 155–172. doi:10.18488/31.v9i2.3172

Corsaro, D., Vargo, S. L., Hofacker, C., & Massara, F. (2022). Artificial intelligence and the shaping of the business context. *Journal of Business Research*, *145*, 210–214. doi:10.1016/j.jbusres.2022.02.072

Cranmer, E. E., tom Dieck, M. C., & Fountoulaki, P. (2020). Exploring the value of augmented reality for tourism. *Tourism Management Perspectives*, *35*, 100672. doi:10.1016/j.tmp.2020.100672

Crook, J. (2014). Starwood introduces robotic butlers at Aloft hotel in Cupertino. *Techcrunch. com.*

Cunha, L. (2008). Avaliação do Potencial Turístico. *Journal of Tourism Studies*. http://hdl.handle.net/10437/384

Cvent (2020). Artificial intelligence for hotels: 9 trends to know. *Cvent*. Cvent. https://www.cvent.com/en/blog/hospitality/artificial-intelligence-for-hotels

Davenport, H., & Ronanki, R. (2018). Artificial intelligence for the real world. *Harvard Business Review*, *96*(1), 108–116.

David, A., Jeganathan, G. S., Sikandar, M. D., & Azam, S. A. (2023, May). Internet Users Top Concerns Ensuring Data Privacy, Security, and Protection. In *Arokiaraj David, Jeganathan Gomathi Sankar & Md Sikandar Azam, —Internet Users Top Concerns Ensuring Data Privacy, Security, and Protection||, 10th International Conference on Multidisciplinary Research and Modern Education, ISBN* (No. 978-920, pp. 5-20241).

David, A., Maheswari, M., Sankar, G., Christy, F., Karuppannan, A., & Banumathi, M. (2023). Mental illness of Pregnant Women determined by Covid-19: An Empirical Analysis of Pre-and-Post Delivery. *The Saybold Report Journal*, *18*(03), 1706–1721.

Davis, L. K. (2016). Hilton and IBM pilot "Connie," The world's first Watson-enabled hotel concierge robot. *Retrieved May, 22*, 2023.

Demuro, R. (2018). *Robots take over luggage duties in New Hotel*. KTLA5. https://ktla.com/news/technology/luggage-robots-sheraton-hotel-san-gabriel

Dewantara, M. H., Gardiner, S., & Jin, X. (2023). Travel vlog ecosystem in tourism digital marketing evolution: A narrative literature review. *Current Issues in Tourism*, *26*(19), 3125–3139. doi:10.1080/13683500.2022.2136568

Doborjeh, Z., Hemmington, N., Doborjeh, M., & Kasabov, N. (2022). Artificial intelligence: A systematic review of methods and applications in hospitality and tourism. *International Journal of Contemporary Hospitality Management*, *34*(3), 1154–1176. doi:10.1108/IJCHM-06-2021-0767

Donaire, J. A., Galí, N., & Gulisova, B. (2020). Tracking visitors in crowded spaces using zenith images: Drones and time-lapse. *Tourism Management Perspectives*, *35*, 100680. doi:10.1016/j.tmp.2020.100680

Donohue, J. C. (1972). A Bibliometric Analysis of Certain Information Science Literature. *Journal of the American Society for Information Science*, *23*(5), 313–317. doi:10.1002/asi.4630230506

Duarte, A., & Dias, P. (2021). TikTok: usos e motivações entre adolescentes em Portugal. Chasqui. *Revista Latinoamericana de Comunicación, 147*, 81-103. https://dialnet.unirioja.es/servlet/articulo?codigo=8093843

Dueholm, J., & Smed, K. M. (2014). Heritage Authenticities – A Case Study of Authenticity Perceptions at a Danish Heritage Site. *Journal of Heritage Tourism*, *9*(4), 285–298. doi:10.1080/1743873X.2014.905582

Dwivedi, Y. K., Kshetri, N., Hughes, L., Slade, E. L., Jeyaraj, A., Kar, A. K., Baabdullah, A. M., Koohang, A., Raghavan, V., Ahuja, M., Albanna, H., Albashrawi, M. A., Al-Busaidi, A. S., Balakrishnan, J., Barlette, Y., Basu, S., Bose, I., Brooks, L., Buhalis, D., & Wright, R. (2023). "So what if ChatGPT wrote it?" Multidisciplinary perspectives on opportunities, challenges and implications of generative conversational AI for research, practice and policy. *International Journal of Information Management*, *71*, 102642. doi:10.1016/j.ijinfomgt.2023.102642

El-Said, O., & Aziz, H. (2022). Virtual Tours a Means to an End: An Analysis of Virtual Tours' Role in Tourism Recovery Post COVID-19. *Journal of Travel Research*, *61*(3), 528–548. doi:10.1177/0047287521997567

Elsevier. (2014). *Scopus* (Issue August). Elsevier. https://z3.hs-offenburg.de/uploads/media/Scopus-Facts-and-Figures-LO.pdf

Elshaer, A. M., & Marzouk, A. M. (2022). Memorable tourist experiences: The role of smart tourism technologies and hotel innovations. *Tourism Recreation Research*, 1–13. doi:10.1080/02508281.2022.2027203

Errichiello, L., Micera, R., Atzeni, M., & Del Chiappa, G. (2019). Exploring the Implications of Wearable Virtual Reality Technology for Museum Visitors' Experience: A Cluster Analysis. *International Journal of Tourism Research*, *21*(5), 590–605. doi:10.1002/jtr.2283

Esplugas, M. (2023). The use of artificial intelligence (AI) to enhance academic communication, education and research: A balanced approach. *The Journal of Hand Surgery*, *48*(8), 819–822. doi:10.1177/17531934231185746 PMID:37417005

FaceMe. (2023). *How to build unique customer experiences for hospitality with facial recognition technology*. FaceMe website. https://www.cyberlink.com/faceme/insights/articles/480/facial-recognition-in-hospitality-travel-industry

Fang, S., Han, X., & Chen, S. (2023). The impact of tourist–robot interaction on tourist engagement in the hospitality industry: A mixed-method study. *Cornell Hospitality Quarterly*, *64*(2), 246–266. doi:10.1177/19389655221102383

Fan, X., Jiang, X., & Deng, N. (2022). Immersive technology: A meta-analysis of augmented/virtual reality applications and their impact on tourism experience. *Tourism Management*, *91*, 104534. doi:10.1016/j.tourman.2022.104534

Femenia-Serra, F., Neuhofer, B., & Ivars-Baidal, J. A. (2019). Towards a conceptualisation of smart tourists and their role within the smart destination scenario. *Service Industries Journal*, *39*(2), 109–133. doi:10.1080/02642069.2018.1508458

Fernandes, J. M., Sousa, B. B., & Correia, R. (2024). Place Knowledge Management in Promoting Gastronomic Tourism and Regional Development: A Case Study Applied to the Lampreia Festival in Portugal. In *Knowledge Management and Knowledge Sharing: Business Strategies and an Emerging Theoretical Field* (pp. 89–97). Springer Nature Switzerland. doi:10.1007/978-3-031-37868-3_6

Ferreira, L., & Sousa, B. B. (2022). Understanding the role of social networks in consumer behavior in tourism: A business approach. In *Research Anthology on Social Media Advertising and Building Consumer Relationships* (pp. 1758–1775). IGI Global. doi:10.4018/978-1-6684-6287-4.ch095

Ferreira, R., Garcia, G., & Brasil, D. (2023). The emergence of Chat GPT and insecurity about the future of academic papers. *Cadernos de Dereito Actual*, *21*, 130–143. doi:10.5281/zenodo.8043807

Ferreira, S., Sousa, B. B., Carvalho, A., & Broega, A. C. (2022). Residents' attitudes toward place marketing and pro-environmental behaviors at UNESCO world heritage sites. In *Advances in Tourism, Technology and Systems: Selected Papers from ICOTTS 2021* (Vol. 2, pp. 71–86). Springer Nature Singapore. doi:10.1007/978-981-16-9701-2_7

Figueira, V., Rolha, J. A., & Sousa, B. B. (2022). Digital communication in museums and museological spaces: diagnosis of Baixo Alentejo, Portugal. In *Handbook of Research on Digital Communications, Internet of Things, and the Future of Cultural Tourism* (pp. 271–290). IGI Global. doi:10.4018/978-1-7998-8528-3.ch015

Filieri, R., D'Amico, E., Destefanis, A., Paolucci, E., & Raguseo, E. (2021). Artificial intelligence (AI) for tourism: An European-based study on successful AI tourism start-ups. *International Journal of Contemporary Hospitality Management*, *33*(11), 4099–4125. doi:10.1108/IJCHM-02-2021-0220

Fisher Phillips. (2023). *The new hospitality balance act: Leveraging artificial intelligence while showing care for your guests.* Fisher Phillips. https://www.fisherphillips.com/en/news-insights/hospitality-leveraging-artificial-intelligence.html

Fonseca & Associados. (2014). *Matos, Cunha, Rui.* Guia Terra Fria Transmontana. Associação de Municípios da Terra Fria do Nordeste Transmontano.

French, R. M. (2000). The Turing Test: The first 50 years. *Trends in Cognitive Sciences*, *4*(3), 115–122. doi:10.1016/S1364-6613(00)01453-4 PMID:10689346

Futr. (2020). *AI in hotels: How tech is transforming the guest experience.* FutrAI. https://futr.ai/ai-in-hotels-how-tech-is-transforming-the-guest-experience

Ganeshkumar, C., Sankar, J. G., & David, A. (2023). Impact of Artificial Intelligence on Agriculture Value Chain Performance: Agritech Perspective. In Blockchain, IoT, and AI Technologies for Supply Chain Management (pp. 71-98). CRC Press.

Ganeshkumar, C., David, A., & Sankar, J. G. (2024). Blockchain Technology Acceptance in Agribusiness Industry. In *Blockchain Transformations: Navigating the Decentralized Protocols Era* (pp. 239–260). Springer Nature Switzerland. doi:10.1007/978-3-031-49593-9_15

Ganeshkumar, C., David, A., Sankar, J. G., & Saginala, M. (2023). Application of Drone Technology in Agriculture: A Predictive Forecasting of Pest and Disease Incidence. In *Applying Drone Technologies and Robotics for Agricultural Sustainability* (pp. 50–81). IGI Global.

Ganeshkumar, C., Sankar, J. G., & David, A. (2023). Adoption of Big Data Analytics: Determinants and Performances Among Food Industries. [IJBIR]. *International Journal of Business Intelligence Research*, *14*(1), 1–17. doi:10.4018/IJBIR.317419

Garau, C. (2014). From Territory to Smartphone: Smart Fruition of Cultural Heritage for Dynamic Tourism Development. *Planning Practice and Research*, *29*(3), 238–255. doi:10.1080/02697459.2014.929837

Garfield, E. (1983). *How to Use Citation Analysis for Faculty Evaluations, and When Is It Relevant? Part 1.*

Gasmi, I., Soui, M., Barhoumi, K., & Abed, M. (2024). Recommendation rules to personalize itineraries for tourists in an unfamiliar city. *Applied Soft Computing*, *150*, 111084. doi:10.1016/j.asoc.2023.111084

Gates, R. (1999). *Production Management for Film and Video*. Routledge. doi:10.4324/9780080515007

Gharibi, N. (2021). The evolution of predictive models and tourism. *Journal of Tourism Futures*, *7*(2), 259–266. doi:10.1108/JTF-04-2020-0046

GME. (2023). *AI in Hospitality Market. Global Market Estimates.* Global Market Estimates. https://www.globalmarketestimates.com/market-report/ai-in-hospitality-market-3546

Godovykh, M., & Tasci, A. D. A. (2020). Customer experience in tourism: A review of definitions, components, and measurements. *Tourism Management Perspectives, 35*(May 2019), 100694. doi:10.1016/j.tmp.2020.100694

Goel, P., Kaushik, N., Sivathanu, B., Pillai, R., & Vikas, J. (2022). Consumers' adoption of artificial intelligence and robotics in hospitality and tourism sector: Literature review and future research agenda. *Tourism Review*, *77*(4), 1–16. doi:10.1108/TR-03-2021-0138

Goh, C., Mok, H. M., & Law, R. (2009). Artificial intelligence applications in tourism. In *Encyclopedia of Information Science and Technology* (2nd ed., pp. 241–247). IGI Global. doi:10.4018/978-1-60566-026-4.ch042

Gomes, D., Oliveira, C., & Soares, N. (2010). O Senhor Marketing Mix e a Senhora Prática Mercadológica Crise à Vista? Uma análise do paradigma dominante do marketing sob uma perspetiva pós-moderna. *Revista Ciência Administrativa*, *16*, 219–241.

Gonzalez, R., Gasco, J., & Llopis, J. (2020). Information and communication technologies and human resources in hospitality and tourism. *International Journal of Contemporary Hospitality Management*, *32*(11), 3545–3579. doi:10.1108/IJCHM-04-2020-0272

Gramlich, E. M. (1994). Infrastructure investment: A review essay. *Journal of Economic Literature*, *32*(3), 1176–1196. https://www.jstor.org/stable/2728606

Gretzel, U., & Scarpino-Johns, M. (2018). Destination resilience and smart tourism destinations. *Tourism Review International*, *22*(3-4), 263–276. doi:10.3727/154427218X15369305779065

Grewal, D., Guha, A., Satornino, C. B., & Schweiger, E. B. (2021). Artificial intelligence: The light and the darkness. *Journal of Business Research*, *136*, 229–236. doi:10.1016/j.jbusres.2021.07.043

Grundner, L., & Neuhofer, B. (2020). The Bright and Dark Sides of Artificial Intelligence: A Futures Perspective on Tourist Destination Experiences. *Journal of Destination Marketing & Management*, *19*, 100511. doi:10.1016/j.jdmm.2020.100511

Gupta, S., Modgil, S., Lee, C.-K., & Sivarajah, U. (2023). The future is yesterday: Use of AI-driven facial recognition to enhance value in the travel and tourism industry. *Information Systems Frontiers*, *25*(3), 1179–1195. doi:10.1007/s10796-022-10271-8 PMID:35529102

Hadavandi, E., Ghanbari, A., Shahanaghi, K., & Abbasian-Naghneh, S. (2011). Tourist arrival forecasting by evolutionary fuzzy systems. *Tourism Management*, *32*(5), 1196–1203. doi:10.1016/j.tourman.2010.09.015

Hamid, R. A., Albahri, A. S., Alwan, J. K., Al-Qaysi, Z. T., Albahri, O. S., Zaidan, A. A., Alnoor, A., Alamoodi, A. H., & Zaidan, B. B. (2021). How smart is e-tourism? A systematic review of smart tourism recommendation system applying data management. *Computer Science Review*, *39*, 100337. doi:10.1016/j.cosrev.2020.100337

Han, D.-I. D., Tom Dieck, M. C., & Jung, T. (2019). Augmented Reality Smart Glasses (ARSG) Visitor Adoption in Cultural Tourism. *Leisure Studies*, *38*(5), 618–633. doi:10.1080/02614367.2019.1604790

Hao, J., Liu, H., Chen, J., Sun, F., & Yang, J. (2020). Study on City-Level Optimization of Tourism Industry Spatial Organization Nodes and Organization Mode for Tourist Destinations. *Complexity*, *2020*, 1–13. doi:10.1155/2020/2807817

Hassan, A., Kennell, J., & Chaperon, S. (2020). Rhetoric and reality in Bangladesh: Elite stakeholder perceptions of the implementation of tourism policy. *Tourism Recreation Research*, *45*(3), 307–322. doi:10.1080/02508281.2019.1703286

Hausmann, A., Toivonen, T., Slotow, R., Tenkanen, H., Moilanen, A., Heikinheimo, V., & Di Minin, E. (2018). Social Media Data Can Be Used to Understand Tourists' Preferences for Nature-Based Experiences in Protected Areas. *Conservation Letters*, *11*(1), 1–10. doi:10.1111/conl.12343

Herrera-Franco, G., Montalván-Burbano, N., Carrión-Mero, P., Apolo-Masache, B., & Jaya-Montalvo, M. (2020). Research trends in geotourism: A bibliometric analysis using the scopus database. *Geosciences*, *10*(10), 1–29. doi:10.3390/geosciences10100379

Hinton, G. E., Osindero, S., & Teh, Y. W. (2006). A fast learning algorithm for deep belief nets. *Neural Computation*, *18*(7), 1527–1554. doi:10.1162/neco.2006.18.7.1527 PMID:16764513

Ho, C. L., Chen, W. L., & Ou, C. H. (2023). Constructing a personalized travel itinerary recommender system with the Internet of Things. *Wireless Networks*, 1–13. doi:10.1007/s11276-023-03453-y

Hollander, J. (2022). What is hospitality? An in-depth look for professionals. HotelTechReport. Retrieved Jan 26, 2022 from https://hoteltechreport.com/news/what-is-hospitality

Hollander, J. (2023). ChatGPT for hotels: Whar's apps are actually live right now? *Hotel Tech Report*. https://hoteltechreport.com/news/chatgpt-for-hotels

Holmes, M. R., Dodds, R., & Frochot, I. (2021). At home or abroad, does our behavior change? Examining how everyday behavior influences sustainable travel behavior and tourist clusters. *Journal of Travel Research*, *60*(1), 102–116. doi:10.1177/0047287519894070

HospitalityNet. (2022). *What's the impact of artificial intelligence in the hotel industry*. Hospitality Net. https://www.hospitalitynet.org/news/4110360.html

Hossain, S. F. A., Ahsan, F. T., Mohiuddin, K., Nadi, A. H., Neamah, H., Ahmed, M., & Hassan, A. (2022). Technology application in the tourism and hospitality industry of the Middle East Asia. In Technology Application in Tourism in Asia: Innovations, Theories and Practices (pp. 109-125). Springer. doi:10.1007/978-981-16-5461-9_7

Hsu, A. (2022). Hotels say goodbye to daily room cleanings and hello to robots as workers stay scarce. *NRP*. https://www.npr.org/2022/12/21/1143475374/hotels-labor-worker-shortage-robots-automation

Huang, M. H., & Rust, R. T. (2018). Artificial intelligence in service. *Journal of Service Research*, *21*(2), 155–172. doi:10.1177/1094670517752459

Huang, M., & Rust, T. (2020). Engaged to a robot? The role of AI in service. *Journal of Service Research*, *24*(1), 30–41. doi:10.1177/1094670520902266

Huang, M., & Rust, T. (2021). A strategic framework for artificial intelligence in marketing. *Journal of the Academy of Marketing Science*, *49*(1), 30–50. doi:10.1007/s11747-020-00749-9

Hudson, S., & Ritchie, J. B. (2009). Branding a memorable destination experience. The case of'Brand Canad'. *International Journal of Tourism Research*, *11*(2), 217–228. doi:10.1002/jtr.720

Hu, Y., & Min, H. K. (2023). The dark side of artificial intelligence in service: The "watching-eye" effect and privacy concerns. *International Journal of Hospitality Management*, *110*, 103437. doi:10.1016/j.ijhm.2023.103437

Hwang, J., Cho, S. B., & Kim, W. (2021). Consequences of psychological benefits of using eco-friendly services in the context of drone food delivery services. In *Future of tourism marketing* (pp. 67–78). Routledge. doi:10.4324/9781003176039-7

Hwang, J., Kim, H., & Kim, W. (2019). Investigating motivated consumer innovativeness in the context of drone food delivery services. *Journal of Hospitality and Tourism Management*, *38*, 102–110. doi:10.1016/j.jhtm.2019.01.004

Hwang, J., Kim, W., & Kim, J. J. (2020). Application of the value-belief-norm model to environmentally friendly drone food delivery services: The moderating role of product involvement. *International Journal of Contemporary Hospitality Management*, *32*(5), 1775–1794. doi:10.1108/IJCHM-08-2019-0710

Hwang, J., Lee, J. S., & Kim, H. (2019). Perceived innovativeness of drone food delivery services and its impacts on attitude and behavioral intentions: The moderating role of gender and age. *International Journal of Hospitality Management*, *81*, 94–103. doi:10.1016/j.ijhm.2019.03.002

IBM. (2024a). *What is AI?* IBM. https://www.ibm.com/topics/artificial-intelligence

IBM. (2024b). *What is deep learning?* IBM. https://www.ibm.com/topics/deep-learning

IBM. (2024c). *What is machine learning?* IBM. https://www.ibm.com/topics/machine-learning

Inglis, F. (2000). *The Delicious History of the Holiday*. Routledge.

Ioannou, A., Tussyadiah, I., & Miller, G. (2021). That's private! Understanding travelers' privacy concerns and online data disclosure. *Journal of Travel Research*, *60*(7), 1510–1526. doi:10.1177/0047287520951642

Islam, M. W., Chowdhury, D., & Khan, A. (2021). Tourism in Bangladesh: a future outlook. *Future of Tourism in Asia*, 97-122. doi:10.1007/978-981-16-1669-3_7

Ismail, A., & Kuppusamy, K. S. (2022). Web accessibility investigation and identification of major issues of higher education websites with statistical measures: A case study of college websites. *Journal of King Saud University. Computer and Information Sciences*, *34*(3), 901–911. doi:10.1016/j.jksuci.2019.03.011

Ivanov, S. H., Webster, C., & Berezina, K. (2017). Adoption of robots and service automation by tourism and hospitality companies. *Revista Turismo & Desenvolvimento (Aveiro)*, *27*(28), 1501–1517.

Ivanov, S., & Webster, C. (2020). Robots in tourism: A research agenda for tourism economics. *Tourism Economics*, *26*(7), 1065–1085. doi:10.1177/1354816619879583

Ivanov, S., & Webster, C. (Eds.). (2019). *Robots, artificial intelligence, and service automation in travel, tourism and hospitality*. Emerald Publishing Limited. doi:10.1108/9781787566873

Ivanov, S., Webster, C., & Garenko, A. (2018). Young Russian adults' attitudes towards the potential use of robots in hotels. *Technology in Society*, *2018*(55), 24–32. doi:10.1016/j.techsoc.2018.06.004

Ivasciuc, I. S. (2020). Augmented reality and facial recognition technologies. Building bridges between the hospitality industry and tourists during pandemic. *Bulletin of the Transilvania University of Brasov. Series V, Economic Sciences*, *13*(62), 75–92. doi:10.31926/but.es.2020.13.62.2.8

Jabeen, F., Al Zaidi, S., & Al Dhaheri, M. H. (2022). Automation and artificial intelligence in hospitality and tourism. *Tourism Review*, *77*(4), 1043–1061. doi:10.1108/TR-09-2019-0360

Jarrahi, M. (2018). Artificial intelligence and the future of work: Human-AI symbiosis in organizational decision making. *Business Horizons*, *61*(4). 2018. doi:10.1016/j.bushor.2018.03.007

Jayawardena, C., McMillan, D., Pantin, D., Taller, M., & Willie, P. (2013). Trends in the international hotel industry. *Worldwide Hospitality and Tourism Themes*, *5*(2), 151–163. doi:10.1108/17554211311314100

Jeganathan, G. S., David, A., & Ilangovan, K. (2022). Determination of Hospitality Services Quality and Customer Satisfaction–a Holserv Approach. In *AU Virtual International Conference on" Entrepreneurship & Sustainability in Digital Era" under the theme of" Challenges of Organizational & Business Management in Dynamic Digital Dimension* (Vol. 3, No. 1, pp. 325-334).

Jeganathan, G. S., & Srinivasulu, Y. (2014). Growth Drivers of Tourism Industry in India. *International Journal of Business and Management*, *2*(11), 100.

Jenny, D. L., Kyunghwa, C., Quach, S., & Thaichon, P. (2023). Introduction to artificial intelligence (AI): Definition and scope of AI. In P. Thaichon & S. Quach (Eds.), *Artificial Intelligence for Marketing Management* (pp. 3–51). Routledge.

Jeong, M., & Shin, H. H. (2020). Tourists' experiences with smart tourism technology at smart destinations and their behavior intentions. *Journal of Travel Research*, *59*(8), 1464–1477. doi:10.1177/0047287519883034

Jiang, G., Gao, W., Xu, M., Tong, M., & Liu, Z. (2023). Geographic Information Visualization and Sustainable Development of Low-Carbon Rural Slow Tourism under Artificial Intelligence. *Sustainability (Basel)*, *15*(4), 3846. doi:10.3390/su15043846

Ji, H., Zheng, W., Zhuang, X., & Lin, Z. (2021). Explore for a day? Generating personalized itineraries that fit spatial heterogeneity of tourist attractions. *Information & Management*, *58*(8), 103557. doi:10.1016/j.im.2021.103557

JLL. (2023). *How hotels are turning to AI*. JLL website. https://www.jll.com.sg/en/trends-and-insights/investor/how-hotels-are-turning-to-ai

Jovicic, D. Z. (2019). From the traditional understanding of tourism destination to the smart tourism destination. *Current Issues in Tourism*, *22*(3), 276–282. doi:10.1080/13683500.2017.1313203

Kádár, B., & Gede, M. (2022). The Measurable Predominance of Weekend Trips in Established Tourism Regions—The Case of Visitors from Budapest at Waterside Destinations. *Sustainability (Basel)*, *14*(6), 3293. doi:10.3390/su14063293

Kasilingam, D. L. (2020). Understanding the attitude and intention to use smartphone chatbots for shopping. *Technology in Society*, *101280*, 101280. doi:10.1016/j.techsoc.2020.101280

Khatri, S., Pandey, D. K., Penkar, D., & Ramani, J. (2020). Impact of artificial intelligence on human resources. In *Data Management, Analytics and Innovation: Proceedings of ICDMAI 2019*, Volume 2 (pp. 365-376). Springer Singapore. 10.1007/978-981-13-9364-8_26

Khedkar, S. (2023). *Using AI-powered tools effectively for academic researcg*. Editage Insights. https://www.editage.com/insights/using-ai-powered-tools-effectively-for-academic-research

Kim, J. Y. (2020). *AI Robots serve restaurant customers in South Korea*. The Associated Press. https://apnews.com/article/south-korea-virus-outbreak-restaurants-a1d11fe838b631e3ab744abda15c9789

Kim, K., Park, O., Yun, S., & Yun, H. (2017). What makes tourists feel negatively about tourism destinations? Application of hybrid text mining methodology to smart destination management. *Technological Forecasting and Social Change*, *123*, 362–369. doi:10.1016/j.techfore.2017.01.001

Kim, M. J., Hall, C. M , Chung, N., Kim, M., & Sohn, K. (2023). Why do tourists use public transport in Korea? The roles of artificial intelligence knowledge, environmental, social, and governance, and sustainability. *Asia Pacific Journal of Tourism Research*, *28*(5), 467–484. doi:10.1080/10941665.2023.2247099

Kim, M. J., Hall, C. M., Kwon, O., Hwang, K., & Kim, J. S. (2023). Orbital and sub-orbital space tourism: Motivation, constraint and artificial intelligence. *Tourism Review*. doi:10.1108/TR-01-2023-0017

Kim, M. J., Hall, C. M., Kwon, O., & Sohn, K. (2023). Effects of Value-Belief-Norm Theory, ESG, and AI on Space Tourist Behavior for Sustainability With Three Types of Space Tourism. *Journal of Travel Research*, 00472875231191514. doi:10.1177/00472875231191514

Kim, S., Filimonau, V., & Dickinson, J. E. (2023). Tourist perception of the value of time on holidays: Implications for the time use rebound effect and sustainable travel practice. *Journal of Travel Research*, *62*(2), 362–381. doi:10.1177/00472875211064636

Klint, M. (Jan 30, 2020). Airlines + hotels embrace "hyperdynamic" pricing model. *Live and Let's Fly*. https://liveandletsfly.com/hyperdynamic-pricing/

Knani, M., Echchakoui, S., & Ladhari, R. (2022). Artificial intelligence in tourism and hospitality: Bibliometric analysis and research agenda. *International Journal of Hospitality Management*, *107*, 103317. doi:10.1016/j.ijhm.2022.103317

Koeva, M., Luleva, M., & Maldjanski, P. (2017). Integrating Spherical Panoramas and Maps for Visualization of Cultural Heritage Objects Using Virtual Reality Technology. *Sensors (Basel)*, *17*(4), 829. doi:10.3390/s17040829 PMID:28398230

Koseoglu, M. A., Rahimi, R., Okumus, F., & Liu, J. (2016). Bibliometric studies in tourism. *Annals of Tourism Research*, *61*, 180–198. doi:10.1016/j.annals.2016.10.006

Kotler, P., Kartajaya, H., & Setiawan, I. (2010). *Marketing 3.0: From Products to Customers to the Human*. John Wiley & Sons, Inc. doi:10.1002/9781118257883

Kotler, P., Kartajaya, H., & Setiawan, I. (2021). *Marketing 5.0: Technology for Humanity*. Conjuntura Atual.

Krok, A. (2019). Gatwick Airport will test robot valet for parking cars. CNET. Retrieved Jan 25, 2019 from https://www.cnet.com/roadshow/news/gatwick-airport-robot-valet-car-park/

Kumar, I., Rawat, J., Mohd, N., & Husain, S. (2021). Opportunities of artificial intelligence and machine learning in the food industry. *Journal of Food Quality*, *2021*, 1–10. doi:10.1155/2021/4535567

Kumar, P., Kumar, A., & Sankar, J. G. (2020). Service quality of health tourism in India: A structural equation modelling approach. *Solid State Technology*, *63*(2), 1187–1191.

Kwok, A. O. J., & Koh, S. G. M. (2021). COVID-19 and Extended Reality (XR). *Current Issues in Tourism*, *24*(14), 1935–1940. doi:10.1080/13683500.2020.1798896

Ladeira, W., Perin, M. G., & Santini, F. (2023). Acceptance of service robots: A meta-analysis in the hospitality and tourism industry. *Journal of Hospitality Marketing & Management*, *32*(6), 694–716. doi:10.1080/19368623.2023.2202168

Lai, W. C., & Hung, W. H. (2018). A framework of cloud and AI based intelligent hotel. *Proceedings of the 18th International Conference on Electronic Business*. ICEB, Guilin.

Lamsfus, C., Wang, D., Alzua-Sorzabal, A., & Xiang, Z. (2015). Going Mobile: Defining Context for On-the-Go Travelers. *Journal of Travel Research*, *54*(6), 691–701. doi:10.1177/0047287514538839

Lazarus, S. (2018). *This self-driving hotel room could revolutionise travel*. CNNTravel. https://edition.cnn.com/travel/article/autonomous-travel-suites/index.html

Leeebvre, V. M., & Fetterman, N. I. (1985). Bibliometric Analysis of the Journal of Consumer Studies and Home Economics, 1977–1983. *Journal of Consumer Studies & Home Economics*, *9*(1), 11–22. doi:10.1111/j.1470-6431.1985.tb00437.x

Lee, I. (2018). Social media analytics for enterprises: Typology, methods, and processes. *Business Horizons*, *61*(2), 199–210. doi:10.1016/j.bushor.2017.11.002

Lee, P., Hunter, W. C., & Chung, N. (2020). Smart tourism city: Developments and transformations. *Sustainability (Basel)*, *12*(10), 3958. doi:10.3390/su12103958

Lemes, D. (2013). *Resenha do livro "Redes sociais digitais: a cognição conectiva do Twitter* (7th ed.). TECCOGS - Revista Digital de Tecnologias Cognitivas., https://revistas.pucsp.br/index.php/teccogs/article/view/52853

Lewis-Kraus, G. (2015). *Check in with the velociraptor at the world's first robot hotel*. Wired Magazine.

Li, H., Zhang, L., & Hsu, C. H. C. (2023). Research on user-generated photos in tourism and hospitality: A systematic review and way forward. *Tourism Management*, *96*(August 2022), 104714. doi:10.1016/j.tourman.2022.104714

Liang, F., Mu, L., Wang, D., & Kim, B. S. (2022). A new model path for the development of smart leisure sports tourism industry based on 5G technology. *IET Communications*, *16*(5), 485–496. doi:10.1049/cmu2.12271

LiB. S.LiaoM. Z.HuangL. L. (2020). RESEARCH on BIG DATA ANALYSIS of LOCATION SERVICE and INTELLIGENT SERVICE PLATFORM of URBAN SCENIC SPOTS: A CASE STUDY of GUILIN CITY, Guangxi, China. *International Archives of the Photogrammetry, Remote Sensing and Spatial Information Sciences - ISPRS Archives*, *42*(3/W10), 1135–1138. doi:10.5194/isprs-archives-XLII-3-W10-1135-2020

Li, B., Liu, L., Mao, W., Qu, Y., & Chen, Y. (2023). Voice artificial intelligence service failure and customer complaint behavior: The mediation effect of customer emotion. *Electronic Commerce Research and Applications*, *59*, 101261. doi:10.1016/j.elerap.2023.101261

Li, M., Yin, D., Qiu, H., & Bai, B. (2021). A systematic review of AI technology-based service encounters: Implications for hospitality and tourism operations. *International Journal of Hospitality Management*, *95*, 102930. doi:10.1016/j.ijhm.2021.102930

Lima, R., & Figueiredo, G. (2020). *Novas estratégias do Marketing 4.0 para as organizações* (21st ed., Vol. 1). Faculdade de Ciências do Tocantins., https://jnt1.websiteseguro.com/index.php/JNT/article/view/774/568

Limna, P. (2023). Artificial Intelligence (AI) in the hospitality industry: A review article. *International Journal of Computing Sciences Research*, *7*, 1306–1317. doi:10.25147/ijcsr.2017.001.1.103

Lin, J. (2017). Robots are taking Singapore's hotel industry by strom-here's where to go for some robot hospitality.

Line, N. D., Dogru, T., El-Manstrly, D., Buoye, A., Malthouse, E., & Kandampully, J. (2020). Control, use and ownership of big data: A reciprocal view of customer big data value in the hospitality and tourism industry. *Tourism Management*, *80*, 104106. doi:10.1016/j.tourman.2020.104106

Lin, H., Chi, O. H., & Gursoy, D. (2020). Antecedents of customers' acceptance of artificially intelligent robotic device use in hospitality services. *Journal of Hospitality Marketing & Management*, *29*(5), 530–549. doi:10.1080/19368623.2020.1685053

Lin, L.-P. L., Huang, S.-C. L., & Ho, Y.-C. (2020). Could Virtual Reality Effectively Market Slow Travel in a Heritage Destination? *Tourism Management*, *78*, 104027. doi:10.1016/j.tourman.2019.104027

Liu, Y., Wang, X., Du, Y., & Wang, S. (2023). Service robots vs. human staff: The effect of service agents and service exclusion on unethical consumer behavior. *Journal of Hospitality and Tourism Management*, *55*, 401–415. doi:10.1016/j.jhtm.2023.05.015

Lopes, S. (2014). *Manual prático de produção*. Chiado Editora.

Loureiro, S. M. C., Guerreiro, J., & Ali, F. (2020). 20 Years of Research on Virtual Reality and Augmented Reality in Tourism Context: A Text-Mining Approach. *Tourism Management*, *77*(April), 104028. doi:10.1016/j.tourman.2019.104028

Lousã, M., Santos, J., & Cabral, A. (2018). Quais as técnicas de recolha de dados a utilizar em trabalhos académicos? In *Como fazer trabalhos académicos: Guia Prático para elaborar projetos, relatórios, teses, dissertações, artigos e muito mais* (pp. 65–87). Porto Editora.

Lovelock, C. (1995). Competing on service: Technology and teamwork in supplementary services. *Planning Review*, *23*(4), 32–47. doi:10.1108/eb054517

Low, B. (2023). Hotel robots: An overview of different robots used in hotels. *365Robot*. https://www.365robot.sg/hotel-robots

Lui, K. (2016). Watch the world's first commercial pizza delivery by drone. Fortune. *Retrieved*, *5*, 2018.

Lukanova, G., & Ilieva, G. (2019). Robots, artificial intelligence, and service automation in hotels. In *Robots, artificial intelligence, and service automation in travel, tourism and hospitality* (pp. 157–183). Emerald Publishing Limited. doi:10.1108/978-1-78756-687-320191009

Lu, L., Cai, R., & Gursoy, D. (2019). Developing and validating a service robot integration willingness scale. *International Journal of Hospitality Management*, *80*, 36–51. doi:10.1016/j.ijhm.2019.01.005

Luna, N. (2023). From taking orders to cutting avocados, AI is solving the labour shortage problem for fast-food chains. *Insider*. https://www.businessinsider.com/how-restaurants-use-ai-robots-chatbots-voice-assistants-drive-thru-2023-9

Luo, W., Cook, D., & Karson, E. (2011). *Search advertising placement strategy: Exploring the efficacy of the conventional wisdom* (8th ed., Vol. 48). Information & Management., doi:10.1016/j.im.2011.10.001

Macedo, C., & Sousa, B. (2019). A acessibilidade no etourism: Um estudo na ótica das pessoas portadoras de necessidades especiais. *Pasos (El Sauzal)*, *17*(4), 709–723. doi:10.25145/j.pasos.2019.17.050

Machado, A. F., Sousa, B. B., de Oliveira, F. F., & de Abreu Rocha, A. M. (2021). The Influence of Tourist Photographic Narratives and Communication on Social Networks from the Perspective of Creative Tourism. In Advances in Tourism, Technology and Systems: Selected Papers from ICOTTS20, Volume 1 (pp. 133-143). Springer Singapore. doi:10.1007/978-981-33-4256-9_12

Machover, C., & Tice, S. E. (1994). Virtual Reality. *IEEE Computer Graphics and Applications*, *14*(1), 15–16. doi:10.1109/38.250913

MacKenzie, J. (n.d.). AI for hotels: A guide to artificial intelligence for hospitality leaders. *Hotel Operations*. Hotel Operations. https://hoteloperations.com/ai-hotels-hospitality/#AI_use_case_Hotel_bookings

Magyar, G. (1974). Bibliometric Analysis of a New Research Sub-Field. *The Journal of Documentation*, *30*(1), 32–40. doi:10.1108/eb026568

Maharaj, S. (2023). Next-gen guest experience: How AI is shaping hospitality. *Medium*. https://medium.com/@sahirmaharaj/next-gen-guest-experience-how-ai-is-shaping-hospitality-4a8d08bb870a

Maia, F., & Júnior, S. (2021). Tiktok e música pop: relações entre mídia, plataformas e produção de conteúdo no meio digital. Revista Tropos: Comunicação. *Society and Culture*, *10*(1). https://periodicos.ufac.br/index.php/tropos/article/view/4978

Majid, G. M., Tussyadiah, I., Kim, Y. R., & Pal, A. (2023). Intelligent automation for sustainable tourism: A systematic review. *Journal of Sustainable Tourism*, *31*(11), 2421–2440. doi:10.1080/09669582.2023.2246681

Ma, L., & Sun, B. (2020). Machine learning and AI in marketing – Connecting computing power to human insights. *International Journal of Research in Marketing*, *37*(3), 481–504. doi:10.1016/j.ijresmar.2020.04.005

Mann, S., Yuan, Y., Lamberti, F., El Saddik, A., Thawonmas, R., & Prattico, F. G. (2023). eXtended Meta-Uni-Omni-Verse (XV): Introduction, Taxonomy, and State-of-the-Art. *IEEE Consumer Electronics Magazine*, 1–9. doi:10.1109/MCE.2023.3283728

Manyika, J., Chui, M., Bughin, J., Dobbs, R., Bisson, P., & Marrs, A. (2013). *Disruptive technologies: Advances that will transform life, business, and the global economy* (Vol. 180). McKinsey Global Institute.

Mariani, M. M., Perez-Vega, R., & Wirtz, J. (2022). AI in marketing, consumer research and psychology: A systematic literature review and research agenda. *Psychology and Marketing*, *39*(4), 755–776. doi:10.1002/mar.21619

Mariani, M., Baggio, R., Fuchs, M., & Höepken, W. (2018). Business intelligence and big data in hospitality and tourism: A systematic literature review. *International Journal of Contemporary Hospitality Management*, *30*(12), 3514–3554. doi:10.1108/IJCHM-07-2017-0461

Marinho, M., Correia, R., & Morais, E. P. (2021). Understanding the role of local tourist actors as online destination promoters: the "Terras de Trás-os-Montes" case. *Journal of Marketing Research and Case Studies*.

Markoff, J. (2014). Beep, says the bellhop. *New York Times*.

Martínez-Graña, A. M., Goy, J. L., & Cimarra, C. A. (2013). A Virtual Tour of Geological Heritage: Valourising Geodiversity Using Google Earth and QR Code. *Computers & Geosciences*, *61*, 83–93. doi:10.1016/j.cageo.2013.07.020

Martins, C. S., Ferreira, A. C., Pereira, C. S., & Sousa, B. B. (2022). Virtual Tourism and Challenges in a Post-Pandemic Context. In *ICT as Innovator Between Tourism and Culture* (pp. 122–137). IGI Global. doi:10.4018/978-1-7998-8165-0.ch008

Martins, M. R., da Costa, R. A., & Moreira, A. C. (2022). Backpackers' space–time behavior in an urban destination: The impact of travel information sources. *International Journal of Tourism Research*, *24*(3), 456–471. doi:10.1002/jtr.2514

Martins, M., & Costa, R. (2022). Tracking Technologies in Tourism: A Bibliometric and Content Review. In J. V. de Carvalho, P. Liberato, & A. Peña (Eds.), *Advances in Tourism, Technology and Systems* (pp. 215–230). Springer Nature Singapore. doi:10.1007/978-981-16-9701-2_18

Md Kashedul Wahab, T., & Majumder, M. T. H. (2011). An appraisal of tourism industry development in Bangladesh. *European Journal of Business and Management*, *3*(3).

MendesG.TeixeiraS. (2019). O turismo, Património e cultura na era das redes sociais: um estudo de caso #viajamosparapartilhar. Revista Turismo & Desenvolvimento, nº32, pp. 171-194. https:// doi.org/ doi:10.34624/rtd.v0i32.20480

Merrit, G. (1998). *Film production: the complete uncensored guide to independent filmmaking*. Lone Eagle Publishing.

Meyer-Waarden, L., Pavone, G., Poocharoentou, T., Prayatsup, P., Ratinaud, M., Tison, A., & Torné, S. (2020). How service quality influences customer acceptance and usage of chatbots? *SMR - Journal of Service Management Research*, *4*(1), 35-51. doi:10.15358/2511-8676-2020-1-35

MGM. (2023). *Meet Rose, your ultimate insider*. MGM. https://www.cosmopolitanlasvegas.com/rose

Miao, L., & Yang, F. X. (2023). Text-to-image AI tools and tourism experiences. *Annals of Tourism Research*, *102*, 103642. doi:10.1016/j.annals.2023.103642

Milgram, P., & Kishino, F. (1994). A Taxonomy of Mixed Reality Visual Displays. *IEICE Transactions on Information and Systems*. Semantic Scholar. https://www.semanticscholar.org/paper/A-Taxonomy-of-Mixed-Reality-Visual-Displays-Milgram-Kishino/f78a31be8874eda176a5244c645289be9f1d4317

Milgram, P., & Kishino, F. (1994, December). A Taxonomy of Mixed Reality Visual Displays. *IEICE Transactions on Information and Systems*, *E77-D*(12), 1321–1329.

Mitchell, T. M. (1997). *Machine Learning*. McGraw-Hill.

Morais, E.P. (2021). *Digital Marketing and Big Data: A bibliometric analysis of scientific production from the Scopus database*. . doi:10.23919/CISTI52073.2021.9476515

Moretti, S., Oliveira, S., & Souza, C. (2018). A evolução do conceito de marketing e sua aplicação no turismo: Simetrias evolutivas, assimetrias temporais. *Revista de Turismo Contemporâneo*, *6*(1), 129–150. doi:10.21680/2357-8211.2018v6n1ID12477

Moro, S., & Rita, P. (2016). Forecasting tomorrow's tourist. *Worldwide Hospitality and Tourism Themes*, *8*(6), 643–653. doi:10.1108/WHATT-09-2016-0046

Muhanna, E. (2006). Sustainable tourism development and environmental management for developing countries. *Problems and Perspectives in Management*, *4*(2), 14–30.

Mukherjee, S., Baral, M. M., Nagariya, R., Venkataiah, C., Rao, U. A., & Rao, K. S. (2023). Systematic literature review and future research directions for service robots in hospitality and tourism industries. *Service Industries Journal*, *43*(15-16), 1083–1116. doi:10.1080/02642069.2023.2243592

Muniz, E. C. L., Dandolini, G. A., Biz, A. A., & Ribeiro, A. C. (2021). Customer knowledge management and smart tourism destinations: A framework for the smart management of the tourist experience–SMARTUR. *Journal of Knowledge Management*, *25*(5), 1336–1361. doi:10.1108/JKM-07-2020-0529

Murphy, J., Gretzel, U., & Pesonen, J. (2021). Marketing robot services in hospitality and tourism: the role of anthropomorphism. In *Future of Tourism Marketing* (pp. 16–27). Routledge. doi:10.4324/9781003176039-3

Neuhofer, B., Buhalis, D., & Ladkin, A. (2015). Smart technologies for personalized experiences: A case study in the hospitality domain. *Electronic Markets*, *25*(3), 243–254. doi:10.1007/s12525-015-0182-1

Nikonova, A., & Biryukova, M. (2017). The Role of Digital Technologies in the Preservation of Cultural Heritage. *Muzeologia a Kulturne Dedicstvo*, *5*(February), 169–173.

Noble, S. M., Mende, M., Grewal, D., & Parasuraman, A. (2022). The fifth industrial revolution: How harmonious human–machine collaboration is triggering a retail and service [r]evolution. *Journal of Retailing*, *98*(2), 199–208. doi:10.1016/j.jretai.2022.04.003

Noor, N. (2022). Halal Service Marketing: A Strategic Perspective. In Strategic Islamic Marketing: A Roadmap for Engaging Muslim Consumers (pp. 11-29). Springer. doi:10.1007/978-3-030-98160-0_3

Noor, N., Rao Hill, S., & Troshani, I. (2022a). Artificial intelligence service agents: Role of parasocial relationship. *Journal of Computer Information Systems*, *62*(5), 1009–1023. doi:10.1080/08874417.2021.1962213

Noor, N., Rao Hill, S., & Troshani, I. (2022b). Developing a service quality scale for artificial intelligence service agents. *European Journal of Marketing*, *56*(5), 1301–1336. doi:10.1108/EJM-09-2020-0672

Novianti, S., Susanto, E., & Rafdinal, W. (2022). Predicting Tourists' Behaviour Towards Smart Tourism: The Case in Emerging Smart Destinations. *Journal of Tourism Sustainability*, *2*(1), 19–30. doi:10.35313/jtospolban.v2i1.30

Nozawa, Y., Endo, M., Ehara, Y., Hirota, M., Yokoyama, S., & Ishikawa, H. (2017). Inferring tourist behavior and purposes of a twitter user. Lecture Notes in Computer Science (Including Subseries Lecture Notes in Artificial Intelligence and Lecture Notes in Bioinformatics), 10004 LNAI. Springer. doi:10.1007/978-3-319-60675-0_9

OECD. (2018). *OECD tourism trends and policies 2018*. OECD publishing. doi:10.1787/tour-2018-

Oh, H., & Lee, S. (2021). Evaluation and interpretation of tourist satisfaction for local korean festivals using explainable ai. *Sustainability (Basel)*, *13*(19), 10901. doi:10.3390/su131910901

Oitzman, M. (2022). *Knightscope robots to patrol Fortune 1000 hotel properties. Mobile Robot Guide*. Mobile Robot Guide. https://mobilerobotguide.com/2022/02/08/knightscope-robots-to-patrol-fortune-1000-hotel-properties

Önder, I., & Gunter, U. (2022). Blockchain: Is it the future for the tourism and hospitality industry? *Tourism Economics*, *28*(2), 291–299. doi:10.1177/1354816620961707

Ozdemir, M. A. (2021). Virtual reality (VR) and augmented reality (AR) technologies for accessibility and marketing in the tourism industry. In ICT tools and applications for accessible tourism (pp. 277-301). IGI Global.

Ozdemir, O., Dogru, T., Kizildag, M., & Erkmen, E. (2023). A critical reflection on digitalization for the hospitality and tourism industry: Value implications for stakeholders. *International Journal of Contemporary Hospitality Management*, *35*(9), 3305–3321. doi:10.1108/IJCHM-04-2022-0535

Pagallo, U. (2013). Robots in the cloud with privacy: A new threat to data protection? *Computer Law & Security Report*, *29*(5), 501–508. doi:10.1016/j.clsr.2013.07.012

Pai, C.-K., Liu, Y., Kang, S., & Dai, A. (2020). The role of perceived smart tourism technology experience for tourist satisfaction, happiness and revisit intention. *Sustainability (Basel)*, *12*(16), 6592. doi:10.3390/su12166592

Pan, S., Tsai, H., & Lee, J. (2011). *Framing New Zealand: Understanding tourism TV commercials. Tourism Management*. Taylor & Francis.

Parasuraman, A., & Colby, C. L. (2015). An updated and streamlined technology readiness index: TRI 2.0. *Journal of Service Research*, *18*(1), 59–74. doi:10.1177/1094670514539730

Park, S. (2020). Multifaceted trust in tourism service robots. *Annals of Tourism Research*, *81*, 102888. doi:10.1016/j.annals.2020.102888

Pattam, A. (2021). *Artificial Intelligence, defined in simple terms*. HCLTech. https://www.hcltech.com/blogs/artificial-intelligence-defined-simple-terms

Pelau, C., Dabija, D.-C., & Ene, I. (2021). What makes an AI device human-like? The role of interaction quality, empathy and perceived psychological anthropomorphic characteristics in the acceptance of artificial intelligence in the service industry. *Computers in Human Behavior*, *122*, 106855. doi:10.1016/j.chb.2021.106855

Perfetto, M. C., & Vargas-Sánchez, A. (2018). Towards a Smart Tourism Business Ecosystem based on Industrial Heritage: Research perspectives from the mining region of Rio Tinto, Spain. *Journal of Heritage Tourism*, *13*(6), 528–549. doi:10.1080/1743873X.2018.1445258

Pillai, R., & Sivathanu, B. (2020). Adoption of AI-based chatbots for hospitality and tourism. *International Journal of Contemporary Hospitality Management*, *32*(10), 3199–3226. doi:10.1108/IJCHM-04-2020-0259

Pisica, A. I., Edu, T., Zaharia, R. M., & Zaharia, R. (2023). Implementing Artificial Intelligence in Higher Education: Pros and Cons from the Perspectives of Academics. *Societies (Basel, Switzerland)*, *13*(118), 118. doi:10.3390/soc13050118

Pricope Vancia, A. P., Băltescu, C. A., Brătucu, G., Tecău, A. S., Chiţu, I. B., & Duguleană, L. (2023). Examining the Disruptive Potential of Generation Z Tourists on the Travel Industry in the Digital Age. *Sustainability (Basel)*, *15*(11), 8756. doi:10.3390/su15118756

Qaisi, L. M., & Aljarah, I. (2016). A twitter sentiment analysis for cloud providers: A case study of Azure vs. *AWS. Proceedings of the 7th International Conference on Computer Science and Information Technology (CSIT)*, Amman, Jordan. 10.1109/CSIT.2016.7549473

Rahimi, R., Hassan, A., & Tekin, O. (2020). Augmented Reality Apps for Tourism Destination Promotion. In Destination Management and Marketing: Breakthroughs in Research and Practice. doi:10.4018/978-1-7998-2469-5.ch059

Rawal, Y. S., Soni, H., Dani, R., & Bagchi, P. (2022, July). A review on service delivery in tourism and hospitality industry through artificial intelligence. In *Proceedings of Third International Conference on Computing, Communications, and Cyber-Security: IC4S 2021* (pp. 427-436). Singapore: Springer Nature Singapore.

Redondo, P., Zapata, B., & Palma, H. (2021). *Impacto del Marketing Digital a las empresas colombianas emergentes*. Revista Universidad & Empresa. https://revistas.urosario.edu.co/index.php/empresa/article/view/9114

Reejo, R. J. (2023). A Review on Marketing Tourism in the Era of AI: Future Scope for Sustainable Tourism in India. *AI and Emotional Intelligence for Modern Business Management*, 321-347.

Reis, J., Melão, N., Salvadorinho, J., Soares, B., & Rosete, A. (2020). Service robots in the hospitality industry: The case of Henn-na hotel, Japan. *Technology in Society*, *63*, 101423. doi:10.1016/j.techsoc.2020.101423

Renjith, S., Sreekumar, A., & Jathavedan, M. (2020). An extensive study on the evolution of context-aware personalized travel recommender systems. *Information Processing & Management*, *57*(1), 102078. doi:10.1016/j.ipm.2019.102078

Rhaman, M. R. (2016). *The socio-economic importance of tourism and its impact on the livelihood in south Asia: Case Rangamati, Bangladesh*. https://urn.fi/URN:NBN:fi:amk-2016103115572

Risteskia, M., Kocevskia, J., & Arnaudov, K. (2012). Spatial planning and sustainable tourism as basis for developing competitive tourist destinations. *Procedia: Social and Behavioral Sciences*, *44*, 375–386. doi:10.1016/j.sbspro.2012.05.042

Rosete, A., Soares, B., Salvadorinho, J., Reis, J., & Amorim, M. (2020). Service robots in the hospitality industry: An exploratory literature review. In *Exploring Service Science: 10th International Conference, IESS 2020, Porto, Portugal, February 5–7, 2020* [Springer International Publishing.]. *Proceedings*, *10*, 174–186.

Ruel, H. (2021). Guest editorial-The future of e-HRM and artificial intelligence in the hospitality and tourism industry. *Journal of Tourism Futures*, *7*(1), 2–4. doi:10.1108/JTF-03-2021-192

Ruel, H., & Njoku, E. (2021). AI redefining the hospitality industry. *Journal of Tourism Futures*, *7*(1), 53–66. doi:10.1108/JTF-03-2020-0032

Ruiz-Alba, L., & Martín-Peña, L. (2020). Guest editorial. *Journal of Business and Industrial Marketing*, *35*(3), 385–389. doi:10.1108/JBIM-03-2020-419

Samaddar, K., & Mondal, S. (2023). AR and VR-based travel: a responsible practice towards sustainable tourism. *International Journal of Tourism Cities*.

Samara, D., Magnisalis, I., & Peristeras, V. (2020). Artificial intelligence and big data in tourism: A systematic literature review. *Journal of Hospitality and Tourism Technology*, *11*(2), 343–367. doi:10.1108/JHTT-12-2018-0118

Sandhya, H., & Varghese, B. (2023). Big Data and Artificial Intelligence: Creative Tools for Destination Competitiveness. In Multidisciplinary Approaches in AI, Creativity, Innovation, and Green Collaboration (pp. 155-166). IGI Global.

Sankar, J. G., & David, A. (2023). Measuring the Service Quality of Artificial Intelligence in the Tourism and Hospitality Industry. In Handbook of Research on Innovation, Differentiation, and New Technologies in Tourism, Hotels, and Food Service (pp. 133-155). IGI Global.

Sankar, J. G., & David, A. (2024). A Comprehensive Examination of Mobile Augmented Reality in Tourism (MART) Adoption: Using the UTAUT2 Framework. In Contemporary Trends in Innovative Marketing Strategies (pp. 241-262). IGI Global.

Sankar, J. G., David, A., & Ramasamy, R. (2023). Assessing Water and Sanitation Service Quality at Pilgrimage Sites After COVID-19: An Empirical Investigation. In Prospects and Challenges of Global Pilgrimage Tourism and Hospitality (pp. 160-179). IGI Global.

Sankar, G., & Naveenkumar, K. (2018). *Material Handling Management in Third Party Logistics Warehouse. International Journal for Research in Engineering Application & Management.* IJREAM.

Sankar, J. G. (2020). Customer perception about innovative safety food delivery during lockdown. *Journal of Contemporary Issues in Business and Government*, *26*(2).

Sankar, J. G. (2020). Customer perception towards electric two-wheeler innovation. *Journal of Contemporary Issues in Business and Government*, *26*(2).

Sankar, J. G. (2020). Innovative celebrity endorsement and consumer purchase. *Journal of Contemporary Issues in Business and Government*, *26*(2).

Sankar, J. G. (2020). Innovative consumer behaviour towards sportswear. *Journal of Contemporary Issues in Business and Government*, *26*(2).

Sankar, J. G. (2020). Service Factors Influence on Customer Satisfaction in Innovative Ecommerce. *SANKAR, D.(2020). Service factors influence on customer satisfaction in innovative e-commerce. Journal of Contemporary Issues in Business and Government*, *26*(2), 651–656.

Sankar, J. G. (2020). Service quality of e-Commerce logistics services. *Journal of Contemporary Issues in Business and Government*, *26*(2).

SankarJ. G.DavidA.Ganesh KumarC. (2022). Adaptation of Blockchain Technology In HRM. SSRN 4515408.

Sankar, J. G., David, A., & Valan, P. (2023). Examining User Understanding and Perceptions of E-Commerce Data Privacy, Security, and Protection. In *Confronting Security and Privacy Challenges in Digital Marketing* (pp. 159–185). IGI Global. doi:10.4018/978-1-6684-8958-1.ch008

Sankar, J. G., & Devanand, K. (2020). Social media innovation on consumer buying behaviour. *SANKAR, JG (2020). Social media innovation on consumer buying behaviour. Journal of Contemporary Issues in Business and Government*, *26*(2).

Sankar, J. G., & Kiruba Sagar, M, V. (2020). Examining the Risk Factor Associated with UTAUT Model. *Solid State Technology*, *63*(2), 1196–1198.

Sankar, J. G., Rajeswari, M., & Dwarak, M. V. S. (2020). To Measure the Service Quality of Film and Television Technology. *Solid State Technology*, *63*(2), 1192–1195.

Sankar, J. G., & Srinivasulu, Y. (2014). A Study of Tourism Industry Impact on Macroeconomic Indicators. *GE-International Journal of Management Research*, *2*(11), 2321–1709.

Sankar, J. G., & Srinivasulu, Y. (2014). Contemporary Sustainable Development Practices in Indian Hospitality Sector: Triple Bottom Line Approach. *SSRN*, 2. doi:10.2139/ssrn.4204732

Sankar, J. G., Valan, P., & Siranjeevi, M. S. (2020). Various Models to Evaluate Quality in the Service Industry. In *Digital Transformation and Innovative Services for Business and Learning* (pp. 181–194). IGI Global.

Sasikala, J., & Jeganathan, G. S. (2017). A Study on Employee Engagement in Information Technology (IT) Industry. *SSRN*, *1*(1), 233–239. doi:10.2139/ssrn.3536354

Schulze, E. (2019). Everything you need to know about the Fourth Industrial Revolution. CNBC. Retrieved 11 Jul, 2023 from https://www.cnbc.com/2019/01/16/fourth-industrial-revolution-explained-davos-2019.html

Serrano, L., Sianes, A., & Ariza-Montes, A. (2019). Using bibliometric methods to shed light on the concept of sustainable tourism. *Sustainability (Basel)*, *11*(24), 6964. doi:10.3390/su11246964

Shafiee, S., Rajabzadeh Ghatari, A., Hasanzadeh, A., & Jahanyan, S. (2021). Smart tourism destinations: A systematic review. *Tourism Review*, *76*(3), 505–528. doi:10.1108/TR-06-2019-0235

Shankar, V. (2018). How artificial intelligence (AI) is reshaping retailing. *Journal of Retailing*, *94*(4), vi–xi. doi:10.1016/S0022-4359(18)30076-9

Sharma, S., & Rishi, O. (2022). IoT Enabled Smart Tourism (IoTeST): Tourism Service Dimensions. In *Rising Threats in Expert Applications and Solutions: Proceedings of FICR-TEAS 2022* (pp. 643-654). Springer. 10.1007/978-981-19-1122-4_67

Shen, S., Sotiriadis, M., & Zhang, Y. (2020). The influence of smart technologies on customer journey in tourist attractions within the smart tourism management framework. *Sustainability (Basel)*, *12*(10), 4157. doi:10.3390/su12104157

Shoval, N., Kahani, A., De Cantis, S., & Ferrante, M. (2020). Impact of incentives on tourist activity in space-time. *Annals of Tourism Research, 80*(September 2019), 102846. doi:10.1016/j.annals.2019.102846

Shoval, N., & Ahas, R. (2016). The Use of Tracking Technologies in Tourism Research : A Review of the First Decade. *Tourism Geographies*, *18*(5), 587–606. doi:10.1080/14616688.2016.1214977

Shvets, I. (2020). Multiplier effects of the development of socially responsible tourism. *EurAsian Journal of BioSciences*, *14*(2), 3753–3758.

Simitha, S., Mugila, P., & Sankar, J. G. (2020). A Study on Customer Relationship Management in Siemens Healthineers. *Solid State Technology*, *63*(2), 1199–1203.

Simon, D., & Wiese, M. (2001). *Film & video budgets*. Michael Wiese Productions.

Singer, P. W. (2009). *Wired for war: The robotics revolution and conflict in the 21st century*. Penguin.

Singh, A. K., Tyagi, P. K., Jain, E., Tyagi, P., Singh, A. K., & Sharma, N. (2022, March). Robotics and Artificial Intelligence in Hospitality Sector: A Descriptive Bibliometric Analysis and Future Research Directions. In *2022 International Conference on Electronics and Renewable Systems (ICEARS)* (pp. 1484-1491). IEEE. 10.1109/ICEARS53579.2022.9752272

Sloan, G. (2014). Robot bartenders? This new cruise ship has them. *USA Today*.

Sohrabi, B., Vanani, I. R., Nasiri, N., & Rudd, A. G. (2020). A predictive model of tourist destinations based on tourists' comments and interests using text analytics. *Tourism Management Perspectives*, *35*, 100710. doi:10.1016/j.tmp.2020.100710

Souffriau, W., Vansteenwegen, P., Vertommen, J., Berghe, G. V., & Oudheusden, D. V. (2008). A personalized tourist trip design algorithm for mobile tourist guides. *Applied Artificial Intelligence*, *22*(10), 964–985. doi:10.1080/08839510802379626

Sousa, B. B., Magalhães, F. C., & Soares, D. B. (2021). The role of relational marketing in specific contexts of tourism: A luxury hotel management perspective. In *Building consumer-brand relationship in luxury brand management* (pp. 223–243). IGI Global. doi:10.4018/978-1-7998-4369-6.ch011

Sousa, B. B., Martins, C. S., Ferreira, A. C., & Pereira, C. S. (2022). Virtual tourism and digital communication in the context of the post-pandemic scenario. In *Crisis management, destination recovery and sustainability* (pp. 197–205). Routledge. doi:10.4324/9781003295839-21

Sousa, B., & Rocha, A. (2019). The role of attachment in public management and place marketing contexts: A case study applied to Vila de Montalegre (Portugal). *International Journal of Public Sector Performance Management*, *5*(2), 189–205. doi:10.1504/IJPSPM.2019.099094

Sousa, J. P., Tavares, R., Gomes, J. P., & Mendonça, V. (2022). Review and Analysis of Research on Video Games and Artificial Intelligence: A Look Back and a Step Forward. doi:10.1016/j.procs.2022.08.038

Sriporn, K., & Tsai, C. F. (2018). Predicting Tourists' Behavior of Virtual Museum Using Support Vector Machine with Feature Selection Technique. *Proceedings - International Conference on Machine Learning and Cybernetics*, *2*, 433–438. doi:10.1109/ICMLC.2018.8526959

Stalidis, G., Karapistolis, D., & Vafeiadis, A. (2015). Marketing decision support using Artificial Intelligence and Knowledge Modeling: Application to tourist destination management. *Procedia: Social and Behavioral Sciences*, *175*, 106–113. doi:10.1016/j.sbspro.2015.01.1180

Stankov, U., Kennell, J., Morrison, A. M., & Vujičić, M. D. (2021). The view from above: the relevance of shared aerial drone videos for destination marketing. In *Future of Tourism Marketing* (pp. 40–54). Routledge. doi:10.4324/9781003176039-5

Statista Research Department. (2018). *Global travel and tourism industry: statistics & facts.* Statista. https://statista.com/topics/962/global-tourism

Suh, A., & Prophet, J. (2018). The State of Immersive Technology Research: A Literature Analysis. *Computers in Human Behavior*, *86*(September), 77–90. doi:10.1016/j.chb.2018.04.019

Sung, P. L., Hsiao, T. Y., Huang, L., & Morrison, A. M. (2021). The influence of green trust on travel agency intentions to promote low-carbon tours for the purpose of sustainable development. *Corporate Social Responsibility and Environmental Management*, *28*(4), 1185–1199. doi:10.1002/csr.2131

Sushchenko, O., Kozubova, N., & Prokopishyna, O. (2018). *Eco-friendly behavior of local population, tourists and companies as a factor of sustainable tourism development.*

Sweezey, M. (2018). The value of chatbots for today's consumers. *Forbes.* https://forbes.com/sites/forbescommunicationscouncil/2018/02/13/the-value-of-chatbots-for-todaysconsumers/#5c0669cd2918

Thaichon, P., & Quach, S. (2022). *Artificial Intelligence for Marketing Management.* Routledge. doi:10.4324/9781003280392

Timothy, D. J. (2011). *Cultural heritage and tourism: An introduction* (Vol. 4). Channel View Publications. doi:10.21832/9781845411787

Tiwary, A., Mahato, M., Chidar, A., Chandrol, M. K., Shrivastava, M., & Tripathi, M. (2018). Internet of Things (IoT): Research, architectures and applications. *International Journal on Future Revolution in Computer Science & Communication Engineering*, *4*(3), 23–27.

Torabi, Z.-A., Shalbafian, A. A., Allam, Z., Ghaderi, Z., Murgante, B., & Khavarian-Garmsir, A. R. (2022). Enhancing memorable experiences, tourist satisfaction, and revisit intention through smart tourism technologies. *Sustainability (Basel)*, *14*(5), 2721. doi:10.3390/su14052721

Tsang, W. K., & Benoit, D. F. (2020). Gaussian processes for daily demand prediction in tourism planning. *Journal of Forecasting*, *39*(3), 551–568. doi:10.1002/for.2644

Tseng, S.-P., Huang, M.-W., Liu, H.-J., Chung, C.-C., & Chiu, C.-M. (2015). A Virtual Reality Based Training System for Cultural Tourism. Lecture Notes in Computer Science (Including Subseries Lecture Notes in Artificial Intelligence and Lecture Notes in Bioinformatics). doi:10.1007/978-3-662-46315-4_29

Tung, V. W. S., & Au, N. (2018). Exploring customer experiences with robotics in hospitality. *International Journal of Contemporary Hospitality Management*, *30*(7), 2680–2697. doi:10.1108/IJCHM-06-2017-0322

Tuomi, A., Tussyadiah, I. P., & Stienmetz, J. (2021). Applications and implications of service robots in hospitality. *Cornell Hospitality Quarterly*, *62*(2), 232–247. doi:10.1177/1938965520923961

Tuomi, A., Tussyadiah, I., & Hanna, P. (2021). Spicing up hospitality service encounters: The case of Pepper. *International Journal of Contemporary Hospitality Management*, *33*(11), 3906–3925. doi:10.1108/IJCHM-07-2020-0739

Turing, A. M. (1950). Computing machinery and intelligence. *Mind*, *59*(236), 433–460. doi:10.1093/mind/LIX.236.433

Tussyadiah, I. (2020). A review of research into automation in tourism: Launching the Annals of Tourism Research Curated Collection on Artificial Intelligence and Robotics in Tourism. *Annals of Tourism Research*, *81*, 102883. doi:10.1016/j.annals.2020.102883

Tussyadiah, I. P., Zach, F. J., & Wang, J. (2020). Do travelers trust intelligent service robots? *Annals of Tourism Research*, *81*, 102886. doi:10.1016/j.annals.2020.102886

Ukpabi, D., Aslam, B., & Karjaluoto, H. (2019). Chatbot adoption in tourism services: A conceptual exploration. Ivanov, S. and Webster, C. (Ed.) Robots, Artificial Intelligence, and Service Automation in Travel, Tourism and Hospitality. Emerald Publishing Limited. doi:10.1108/978-1-78756-687-320191006

Urry, J. (2002). *The Tourist Gaze*. SAGE Publications Ltd.

Van Doorn, J., Mende, M., Noble, S. M., Hulland, J., Ostrom, A. L., Grewal, D., & Petersen, J. A. (2017). Domo arigato Mr. Roboto: Emergence of automated social presence in organizational frontlines and customers' service experiences. *Journal of Service Research*, *20*(1), 43–58. doi:10.1177/1094670516679272

van Eck, N. J., & Waltman, L. (2010). Software survey: VOSviewer, a computer program for bibliometric mapping. *Scientometrics*, *84*(2), 523–538. doi:10.1007/s11192-009-0146-3 PMID:20585380

van Esch, P., Cui, Y., Das, G., Jain, S. P., & Wirtz, J. (2022). Tourists and AI: A political ideology perspective. *Annals of Tourism Research*, *97*, 103471. doi:10.1016/j.annals.2022.103471

Van Niekerk, M. (2016). Business, technology, and marketing trends influencing the financial performance of the hotel industry. *The Journal of Hospitality Financial Management*, *24*(2), 153–157. doi:10.1080/10913211.2016.1236582

van Nuenen, T., & Scarles, C. (2021). Advancements in technology and digital media in tourism. *Tourist Studies*, *21*(1), 119–132. doi:10.1177/1468797621990410

Velmurugan, T. A., & Sankar, J. G. (2017). A comparative study on motivation theory with Maslow's hierarchy theory and two factor theory in organization. *Indo-Iranian Journal of Scientific Research*, *1*(1), 204–208.

Versichele, M., Neutens, T., Delafontaine, M., & Van de Weghe, N. (2012). The use of Bluetooth for analysing spatiotemporal dynamics of human movement at mass events: A case study of the Ghent Festivities. *Applied Geography (Sevenoaks, England)*, *32*(2), 208–220. doi:10.1016/j.apgeog.2011.05.011

Vrontis, D., Christofi, M., Pereira, V., Tarba, S., Makrides, A., & Trichina, E. (2022). Artificial intelligence, robotics, advanced technologies and human resource management: A systematic review. *International Journal of Human Resource Management*, *33*(6), 1237–1266. doi:10.1080/09585192.2020.1871398

Wahid, D., & Hassini, E. (2024). An augmented AI-based hybrid fraud detection framework for invoicing platforms. *Applied Intelligence*, *54*(2), 1297–1310. doi:10.1007/s10489-023-05223-x

Wang, X. (2020). Personalized recommendation framework design for online tourism: Know you better than yourself. *Industrial Management & Data Systems*, *120*(11), 2067–2079. doi:10.1108/IMDS-05-2020-0278

West, A., Clifford, J., & Atkinson, D. (2018). "Alexa, Build Me a Brand" — An Investigation into the Impact of Artificial Intelligence on Branding. *Journal of Business Economics*, *9*(10), 877–887. doi:10.15341/jbe(2155-7950)/10.09.2018/005

Wikhamn, W. (2019). Innovation, sustainable HRM, and customer satisfaction. *International Journal of Hospitality Management*, *76*, 102–110. doi:10.1016/j.ijhm.2018.04.009

Windsor, D. A. (1976). Could Bibliometric Data Be Used to Predict the Clinical Success of Drugs? *The Journal of Documentation*, *32*(3), 174–181. doi:10.1108/eb026623

Wirtz, J., & Lovelock, C. (2022). *Services marketing: People, technology, strategy* (9th ed.). World Scientific.

Wirtz, J., Patterson, P. G., Kunz, W. H., Gruber, T., Lu, V. N., Paluch, S., & Martins, A. (2018). Brave new world: Service robots in the frontline. *Journal of Service Management*, *29*(5), 907–931. doi:10.1108/JOSM-04-2018-0119

Wirtz, J., & Zeithaml, V. (2018). Cost-effective service excellence. *Journal of the Academy of Marketing Science*, *46*(1), 59–80. doi:10.1007/s11747-017-0560-7

World Travel & Tourism Council. (2017). *Travel & tourism economic impact 2017*. WTC. https://wtc.org/about/media-centre/press-releases/press-releases/2017/tourism-supports-1-in-10-jobs-outpacingglobal-economy-for-6th-conservative-year-wttc

Wu, D., Song, H., & Shen, S. (2017). New developments in tourism and hotel demand modeling and forecasting. *International Journal of Contemporary Hospitality Management*, *29*(1), 507–529. doi:10.1108/IJCHM-05-2015-0249

Xavier, G., Nogueira, S., & Vareiro, L. (2023). The Perception of Tourists Regarding the Importance of Influencers in Shaping the Image of a Tourist Destination: The Case of Melgaço (Portugal). In *International Conference on Tourism, Technology and Systems* (pp. 415-428). Singapore: Springer Nature Singapore.

Xia, C. (2007). *Modelling The Spatial-Temporal Movement Of Tourists* (S. O. M. A. G. Sciences (ed.). Rmit University. https://researchbank.rmit.edu.au/view/rmit:6320

Yallop, A. C., Gică, O. A., Moisescu, O. I., Coroş, M. M., & Séraphin, H. (2023). The digital traveller: Implications for data ethics and data governance in tourism and hospitality. *Journal of Consumer Marketing*, *40*(2), 155–170. doi:10.1108/JCM-12-2020-4278

Yang, X., Zhang, L., & Feng, Z. (2023). Personalized tourism recommendations and the E-tourism user experience. *Journal of Travel Research*, 00472875231187332.

Yaramada, K. (2021). How to upgrade your accounts payable function with AI. *Forbes*. https://www.forbes.com/sites/forbesbusinesscouncil/2021/08/05/how-to-upgrade-your-accounts-payable-function-with-ai/?sh=304304ee21c6

Yu, N., & Chen, J. (2022). Design of machine learning algorithm for tourism demand prediction. *Computational and Mathematical Methods in Medicine*, *2022*, 2022. doi:10.1155/2022/6352381 PMID:35720035

Yung, R., Khoo-Lattimore, C., & Potter, L. E. (2021). Virtual reality and tourism marketing: Conceptualizing a framework on presence, emotion, and intention. *Current Issues in Tourism*, *24*(11), 1505–1525. doi:10.1080/13683500.2020.1820454

Yu, R., Tong, Z., & Xiao, H. (2023). Close or distant? The impacts of robot services and spatial distance on service satisfaction. *Journal of Hospitality and Tourism Management*, *54*, 447–456. doi:10.1016/j.jhtm.2023.01.011

Zalama, E., García-Bermejo, J. G., Marcos, S., Domínguez, S., Feliz, R., Pinillos, R., & López, J. (2014). Sacarino, a service robot in a hotel environment. In *ROBOT2013: First Iberian Robotics Conference* [Springer International Publishing.]. *Advanced Robotics*, *2*, 3–14.

Zehir, C., Karaboğa, T., & Başar, D. (2020). The transformation of human resource management and its impact on overall business performance: big data analytics and AI technologies in strategic HRM. *Digital Business Strategies in Blockchain Ecosystems: Transformational Design and Future of Global Business*, 265-279.

Zhang, K., Chen, Y., & Li, C. (2019). Discovering the tourists' behaviors and perceptions in a tourism destination by analyzing photos' visual content with a computer deep learning model: The case of Beijing. *Tourism Management*, *75*, 595–608. doi:10.1016/j.tourman.2019.07.002

Zhang, K., Chen, Y., & Lin, Z. (2020). Mapping destination images and behavioral patterns from user-generated photos: A computer vision approach. *Asia Pacific Journal of Tourism Research*, *25*(11), 1199–1214. doi:10.1080/10941665.2020.1838586

Zhao, J., & Kerdpitak, C. (2023). *A study of consumer innovativeness and service convenience on the intention to use robot services in hotels. International Academic Multidisciplinary Research Conference*, Zurich.

Zheng, J. M., Chan, K. W., & Gibson, I. (1998). Virtual Reality. *IEEE Potentials*, *17*(2), 20–23. doi:10.1109/45.666641

Zheng, W., Ji, H., Lin, C., Wang, W., & Yu, B. (2020). Using a heuristic approach to design personalized urban tourism itineraries with hotel selection. *Tourism Management*, *76*, 103956. doi:10.1016/j.tourman.2019.103956

Zhou, G., Chu, G. L. L., & Meng, L. (2020). The effect of artificial intelligence on China's labor market. *China Economic Journal*, *13*(1), 24–41. doi:10.1080/17538963.2019.1681201

Zupic, I., & Čater, T. (2015). Bibliometric Methods in Management and Organization. *Organizational Research Methods*, *18*(3), 429–472. doi:10.1177/1094428114562629

Related References

To continue our tradition of advancing media and communications research, we have compiled a list of recommended IGI Global readings. These references will provide additional information and guidance to further enrich your knowledge and assist you with your own research and future publications.

Abashian, N., & Fisher, S. (2018). Intercultural Effectiveness in Libraries: Supporting Success Through Collaboration With Co-Curricular Programs. In B. Blummer, J. Kenton, & M. Wiatrowski (Eds.), *Promoting Ethnic Diversity and Multiculturalism in Higher Education* (pp. 219–236). Hershey, PA: IGI Global. doi:10.4018/978-1-5225-4097-7.ch012

Adebayo, O., Fagbohun, M. O., Esse, U. C., & Nwokeoma, N. M. (2018). Change Management in the Academic Library: Transition From Print to Digital Collections. In R. Bhardwaj (Ed.), *Digitizing the Modern Library and the Transition From Print to Electronic* (pp. 1–28). Hershey, PA: IGI Global. doi:10.4018/978-1-5225-2119-8.ch001

Adegbore, A. M., Quadri, M. O., & Oyewo, O. R. (2018). A Theoretical Approach to the Adoption of Electronic Resource Management Systems (ERMS) in Nigerian University Libraries. In A. Tella & T. Kwanya (Eds.), *Handbook of Research on Managing Intellectual Property in Digital Libraries* (pp. 292–311). Hershey, PA: IGI Global. doi:10.4018/978-1-5225-3093-0.ch015

Adesola, A. P., & Olla, G. O. (2018). Unlocking the Unlimited Potentials of Koha OSS/ILS for Library House-Keeping Functions: A Global View. In M. Khosrow-Pour (Ed.), *Optimizing Contemporary Application and Processes in Open Source Software* (pp. 124–163). Hershey, PA: IGI Global. doi:10.4018/978-1-5225-5314-4.ch006

Adesola, A. P., & Olla, G. O. (2019). Bridging the Digital Divide in Nigerian Information Landscape: The Role of the Library. *International Journal of Digital Literacy and Digital Competence*, *10*(3), 10–31. doi:10.4018/IJDLDC.2019070102

Adetayo, A. J. (2021). Fake News and Social Media Censorship: Examining the Librarian Role. In R. Blankenship (Ed.), *Deep Fakes, Fake News, and Misinformation in Online Teaching and Learning Technologies* (pp. 69–92). IGI Global. https://doi.org/10.4018/978-1-7998-6474-5.ch004

Adetayo, A. J. (2022). Building Civic Engagement in Smart Cities: Role of Smart Libraries. In M. Taher (Ed.), *Handbook of Research on the Role of Libraries, Archives, and Museums in Achieving Civic Engagement and Social Justice in Smart Cities* (pp. 314–333). IGI Global. https://doi.org/10.4018/978-1-7998-8363-0.ch017

Adigun, G. O., Sobalaje, A. J., & Salau, S. A. (2018). Social Media and Copyright in Digital Libraries. In A. Tella & T. Kwanya (Eds.), *Handbook of Research on Managing Intellectual Property in Digital Libraries* (pp. 19–36). Hershey, PA: IGI Global. doi:10.4018/978-1-5225-3093-0.ch002

Adriyana, L., & Fitrina Cahyaningtyas, D. (2022). The Importance of Rural Library Services Based on Social Inclusion in Indonesia. In M. Taher (Ed.), *Handbook of Research on the Role of Libraries, Archives, and Museums in Achieving Civic Engagement and Social Justice in Smart Cities* (pp. 201–218). IGI Global. https://doi.org/10.4018/978-1-7998-8363-0.ch010

Afolabi, O. A. (2018). Myths and Challenges of Building an Effective Digital Library in Developing Nations: An African Perspective. In A. Tella & T. Kwanya (Eds.), *Handbook of Research on Managing Intellectual Property in Digital Libraries* (pp. 51–79). Hershey, PA: IGI Global. doi:10.4018/978-1-5225-3093-0.ch004

Ahuja, Y., & Kumar, P. (2017). Web 2.0 Tools and Application: Knowledge Management and Sharing in Libraries. In B. Gunjal (Ed.), *Managing Knowledge and Scholarly Assets in Academic Libraries* (pp. 218–234). Hershey, PA: IGI Global. doi:10.4018/978-1-5225-1741-2.ch010

Ajmi, A. (2018). Developing In-House Digital Tools: Case Studies From the UMKC School of Law Library. In L. Costello & M. Powers (Eds.), *Developing In-House Digital Tools in Library Spaces* (pp. 117–139). Hershey, PA: IGI Global. doi:10.4018/978-1-5225-2676-6.ch006

Al-Kharousi, R., Al-Harrasi, N. H., Jabur, N. H., & Bouazza, A. (2018). Soft Systems Methodology (SSM) as an Interdisciplinary Approach: Reflection on the Use of SSM in Adoption of Web 2.0 Applications in Omani Academic Libraries. In M. Al-Suqri, A. Al-Kindi, S. AlKindi, & N. Saleem (Eds.), *Promoting Interdisciplinarity in Knowledge Generation and Problem Solving* (pp. 243–257). Hershey, PA: IGI Global. doi:10.4018/978-1-5225-3878-3.ch016

Alenzuela, R. (2017). Research, Leadership, and Resource-Sharing Initiatives: The Role of Local Library Consortia in Access to Medical Information. In S. Ram (Ed.), *Library and Information Services for Bioinformatics Education and Research* (pp. 199–211). Hershey, PA: IGI Global. doi:10.4018/978-1-5225-1871-6.ch012

Alenzuela, R., & Terry, M. A. (2020). Diversity, Indigenous Knowledge, and LIS Pedagogy: Conceptualizing Formal Education in Library and Information Studies in Vanuatu. In R. Alenzuela, H. Kim, & D. Baylen (Eds.), *Internationalization of Library and Information Science Education in the Asia-Pacific Region* (pp. 50–77). IGI Global. doi:10.4018/978-1-7998-2273-8.ch003

Allison, D. (2017). When Sales Talk Meets Reality: Implementing a Self-Checkout Kiosk. In E. Iglesias (Ed.), *Library Technology Funding, Planning, and Deployment* (pp. 36–54). Hershey, PA: IGI Global. doi:10.4018/978-1-5225-1735-1.ch003

Anglim, C. T., & Rusk, F. (2018). Empowering DC's Future Through Information Access. In A. Burtin, J. Fleming, & P. Hampton-Garland (Eds.), *Changing Urban Landscapes Through Public Higher Education* (pp. 57–77). Hershey, PA: IGI Global. doi:10.4018/978-1-5225-3454-9.ch003

Asmi, N. A. (2017). Social Media and Library Services. *International Journal of Library and Information Services*, *6*(2), 23–36. doi:10.4018/IJLIS.2017070103

Attademo, G., & Maccaro, A. (2022). Research Ethics in the Social Sciences. In G. Punziano & A. Delli Paoli (Eds.), *Handbook of Research on Advanced Research Methodologies for a Digital Society* (pp. 54–64). IGI Global. https://doi.org/10.4018/978-1-7998-8473-6.ch005

Awoyemi, R. A. (2018). Adoption and Use of Innovative Mobile Technologies in Nigerian Academic Libraries. In J. Keengwe (Ed.), *Handbook of Research on Digital Content, Mobile Learning, and Technology Integration Models in Teacher Education* (pp. 354–389). Hershey, PA: IGI Global. doi:10.4018/978-1-5225-2953-8.ch019

Awoyemi, R. A. (2018). Adoption and Use of Innovative Mobile Technologies in Nigerian Academic Libraries. In J. Keengwe (Ed.), *Handbook of Research on Digital Content, Mobile Learning, and Technology Integration Models in Teacher Education* (pp. 354–389). Hershey, PA: IGI Global. doi:10.4018/978-1-5225-2953-8.ch019

Awoyemi, R. A., & Awoyemi, R. O. (2021). Beyond the Physical Library Space: Creating a 21st Century Digitally-Oriented Library Environment. In C. Chisita, R. Enakrire, O. Durodolu, V. Tsabedze, & J. Ngoaketsi (Eds.), *Handbook of Research on Records and Information Management Strategies for Enhanced Knowledge Coordination* (pp. 189–203). IGI Global. https://doi.org/10.4018/978-1-7998-6618-3.ch012

Babatope, I. S. (2018). Social Media Applications as Effective Service Delivery Tools for Librarians. In M. Khosrow-Pour, D.B.A. (Ed.), Encyclopedia of Information Science and Technology, Fourth Edition (pp. 5252-5261). Hershey, PA: IGI Global. doi:10.4018/978-1-5225-2255-3.ch456

Bakare, A. A. (2018). Digital Libraries and Copyright of Intellectual Property: An Ethical Practice Management. In A. Tella & T. Kwanya (Eds.), *Handbook of Research on Managing Intellectual Property in Digital Libraries* (pp. 377–395). Hershey, PA: IGI Global. doi:10.4018/978-1-5225-3093-0.ch019

Baker, A. A. (2020). To Whose Benefit? At What Cost?: Consideration for Ethical Issues in Social Science Research. In M. Baran & J. Jones (Eds.), *Applied Social Science Approaches to Mixed Methods Research* (pp. 251–260). IGI Global. https://doi.org/10.4018/978-1-7998-1025-4.ch011

Baker-Gardner, R., & Smart, C. (2017). Ignorance or Intent?: A Case Study of Plagiarism in Higher Education among LIS Students in the Caribbean. In D. Velliaris (Ed.), *Handbook of Research on Academic Misconduct in Higher Education* (pp. 182–205). Hershey, PA: IGI Global. doi:10.4018/978-1-5225-1610-1.ch008

Baker-Gardner, R., & Stewart, P. (2018). Educating Caribbean Librarians to Provide Library Education in a Dynamic Information Environment. In S. Bhattacharyya & K. Patnaik (Eds.), *Changing the Scope of Library Instruction in the Digital Age* (pp. 187–226). Hershey, PA: IGI Global. doi:10.4018/978-1-5225-2802-9.ch008

Baran, M. L., & Jones, J. E. (2020). Developing the Research Study: A Step-by-Step Approach. In M. Baran & J. Jones (Eds.), *Applied Social Science Approaches to Mixed Methods Research* (pp. 262–274). IGI Global. https://doi.org/10.4018/978-1-7998-1025-4.ch012

Baskaran, C. (2020). Altmetircs Research: An Impact and Tools. In C. Baskaran (Ed.), *Measuring and Implementing Altmetrics in Library and Information Science Research* (pp. 1–10). IGI Global. https://doi.org/10.4018/978-1-7998-1309-5.ch001

Bengtson, J. (2017). Funding a Gamification Machine. In E. Iglesias (Ed.), *Library Technology Funding, Planning, and Deployment* (pp. 99–112). Hershey, PA: IGI Global. doi:10.4018/978-1-5225-1735-1.ch006

Bhuda, M., & Koitsiwe, M. (2022). The Importance of Underpinning Indigenous Research Using African Indigenous Philosophies: Perspectives From Indigenous Scholars. In R. Tshifhumulo & T. Makhanikhe (Eds.), *Handbook of Research on Protecting and Managing Global Indigenous Knowledge Systems* (pp. 223–248). IGI Global. https://doi.org/10.4018/978-1-7998-7492-8.ch013

Blummer, B., & Kenton, J. M. (2017). Access and Accessibility of Academic Libraries' Electronic Resources and Services: Identifying Themes in the Literature From 2000 to the Present. In H. Alphin Jr, J. Lavine, & R. Chan (Eds.), *Disability and Equity in Higher Education Accessibility* (pp. 242–267). Hershey, PA: IGI Global. doi:10.4018/978-1-5225-2665-0.ch011

Blummer, B., & Kenton, J. M. (2018). Academic and Research Libraries' Portals: A Literature Review From 2003 to the Present. In R. Bhardwaj (Ed.), *Digitizing the Modern Library and the Transition From Print to Electronic* (pp. 29–63). Hershey, PA: IGI Global. doi:10.4018/978-1-5225-2119-8.ch002

Blummer, B., & Kenton, J. M. (2018). International Students and Academic Libraries: Identifying Themes in the Literature From 2001 to the Present. In B. Blummer, J. Kenton, & M. Wiatrowski (Eds.), *Promoting Ethnic Diversity and Multiculturalism in Higher Education* (pp. 237–263). Hershey, PA: IGI Global. doi:10.4018/978-1-5225-4097-7.ch013

Bohuski, L. (2020). What If Your Library Can't Go Green?: Promoting Wellness in Libraries. In A. Kaushik, A. Kumar, & P. Biswas (Eds.), *Handbook of Research on Emerging Trends and Technologies in Library and Information Science* (pp. 13–26). IGI Global. doi:10.4018/978-1-5225-9825-1.ch002

Boom, D. (2017). The Embedded Librarian: Do More With less. In B. Gunjal (Ed.), *Managing Knowledge and Scholarly Assets in Academic Libraries* (pp. 76–97). Hershey, PA: IGI Global. doi:10.4018/978-1-5225-1741-2.ch004

Bosire-Ogechi, E. (2018). Social Media, Social Networking, Copyright, and Digital Libraries. In A. Tella & T. Kwanya (Eds.), *Handbook of Research on Managing Intellectual Property in Digital Libraries* (pp. 37–50). Hershey, PA: IGI Global. doi:10.4018/978-1-5225-3093-0.ch003

Bradley-Sanders, C., & Rudshteyn, A. (2018). MyLibrary at Brooklyn College: Developing a Suite of Digital Tools. In L. Costello & M. Powers (Eds.), *Developing In-House Digital Tools in Library Spaces* (pp. 140–167). Hershey, PA: IGI Global. doi:10.4018/978-1-5225-2676-6.ch007

Brown, V. (2018). Technology Access Gap for Postsecondary Education: A Statewide Case Study. In M. Yildiz, S. Funk, & B. De Abreu (Eds.), *Promoting Global Competencies Through Media Literacy* (pp. 20–40). Hershey, PA: IGI Global. doi:10.4018/978-1-5225-3082-4.ch002

Browne, N. (2021). The IHS Library and Its Response to the COVID-19 Pandemic. In B. Holland (Eds.), *Handbook of Research on Library Response to the COVID-19 Pandemic* (pp. 298-320). IGI Global. https://doi.org/10.4018/978-1-7998-6449-3.ch016

Chaiyasoonthorn, W., & Suksa-ngiam, W. (2018). Users' Acceptance of Online Literature Databases in a Thai University: A Test of UTAUT2. *International Journal of Information Systems in the Service Sector*, *10*(1), 54–70. doi:10.4018/IJISSS.2018010104

Chaudron, G. (2018). Burst Pipes and Leaky Roofs: Small Emergencies Are a Challenge for Libraries. In K. Strang, M. Korstanje, & N. Vajjhala (Eds.), *Research, Practices, and Innovations in Global Risk and Contingency Management* (pp. 211–231). Hershey, PA: IGI Global. doi:10.4018/978-1-5225-4754-9.ch012

Chemulwo, M. J. (2018). Managing Intellectual Property in Digital Libraries and Copyright Challenges. In A. Tella & T. Kwanya (Eds.), *Handbook of Research on Managing Intellectual Property in Digital Libraries* (pp. 165–183). Hershey, PA: IGI Global. doi:10.4018/978-1-5225-3093-0.ch009

Chen, J., Lan, X., Huang, Q., Dong, J., & Chen, C. (2017). Scholarly Learning Commons. In L. Ruan, Q. Zhu, & Y. Ye (Eds.), *Academic Library Development and Administration in China* (pp. 90–109). Hershey, PA: IGI Global. doi:10.4018/978-1-5225-0550-1.ch006

Chigwada, J. P. (2018). Adoption of Open Source Software in Libraries in Developing Countries. *International Journal of Library and Information Services*, *7*(1), 15–29. doi:10.4018/IJLIS.2018010102

Chigwada, J. P. (2020). Librarian Skillsets in the 21st Century: The Changing Role of Librarians in the Digital Era. In N. Osuigwe (Ed.), *Managing and Adapting Library Information Services for Future Users* (pp. 41–58). IGI Global. https://doi.org/10.4018/978-1-7998-1116-9.ch003

Chigwada, J. P. (2020). The Role of the Librarian in the Research Life Cycle: Research Collaboration Among the Library and Faculty. In C. Chisita (Ed.), *Cooperation and Collaboration Initiatives for Libraries and Related Institutions* (pp. 335–346). IGI Global. https://doi.org/10.4018/978-1-7998-0043-9.ch017

Chigwada, J. P. (2021). Research Data Management Services in Tertiary Institutions in Zimbabwe. In B. Holland (Eds.), *Handbook of Research on Knowledge and Organization Systems in Library and Information Science* (pp. 419-437). IGI Global. https://doi.org/10.4018/978-1-7998-7258-0.ch022

Chigwada, J. P., & Maturure, R. (2019). Advocating for Library and Information Services by National Library Associations of Africa in the Context of Sustainable Development Goals. In P. Ngulube (Ed.), *Handbook of Research on Advocacy, Promotion, and Public Programming for Memory Institutions* (pp. 219–237). IGI Global. doi:10.4018/978-1-5225-7429-3.ch012

Chiparausha, B., & Chigwada, J. P. (2019). Promoting Library Services in a Digital Environment in Zimbabwe. In P. Ngulube (Ed.), *Handbook of Research on Advocacy, Promotion, and Public Programming for Memory Institutions* (pp. 284–296). IGI Global. https://doi.org/10.4018/978-1-5225-7429-3.ch015

Chisita, C. T., & Chinyemba, F. (2017). Utilising ICTs for Resource Sharing Initiatives in Academic Institutions in Zimbabwe: Towards a New Trajectory. In B. Gunjal (Ed.), *Managing Knowledge and Scholarly Assets in Academic Libraries* (pp. 174–187). Hershey, PA: IGI Global. doi:10.4018/978-1-5225-1741-2.ch008

Chu, S., Tu, S., Wang, N., & Zhang, W. (2020). Information Equity and Cultural Sharing: The Service for Migrant Workers in Hangzhou Public Library. *International Journal of Library and Information Services*, *9*(1), 10–24. https://doi.org/10.4018/IJLIS.2020010102

Clarance, M. M., & Angeline, X. M. (2019). User Opinion on Library Collections and Services: A Case Study of Branch Library in Karaikudi. In S. Thanuskodi (Ed.), *Literacy Skill Development for Library Science Professionals* (pp. 343–375). IGI Global. https://doi.org/10.4018/978-1-5225-7125-4.ch015

Costello, L., & Fazal, S. (2018). Developing Unique Study Room Reservation Systems: Examples From Teachers College and Stony Brook University. In L. Costello & M. Powers (Eds.), *Developing In-House Digital Tools in Library Spaces* (pp. 168–176). Hershey, PA: IGI Global. doi:10.4018/978-1-5225-2676-6.ch008

Cui, Y. (2017). Research Data Management: Models, Challenges, and Actions. In L. Ruan, Q. Zhu, & Y. Ye (Eds.), *Academic Library Development and Administration in China* (pp. 184–195). Hershey, PA: IGI Global. doi:10.4018/978-1-5225-0550-1.ch011

Dhamdhere, S. N., De Smet, E., & Lihitkar, R. (2017). Web-Based Bibliographic Services Offered by Top World and Indian University Libraries: A Comparative Study. *International Journal of Library and Information Services*, *6*(1), 53–72. doi:10.4018/IJLIS.2017010104

Eiriemiokhale, K. A. (2018). Copyright Issues in a Digital Library Environment. In A. Tella & T. Kwanya (Eds.), *Handbook of Research on Managing Intellectual Property in Digital Libraries* (pp. 142–164). Hershey, PA: IGI Global. doi:10.4018/978-1-5225-3093-0.ch008

El Mimouni, H., Anderson, J., Tempelman-Kluit, N. F., & Dolan-Mescal, A. (2018). UX Work in Libraries: How (and Why) to Do It. In L. Costello & M. Powers (Eds.), *Developing In-House Digital Tools in Library Spaces* (pp. 1–36). Hershey, PA: IGI Global. doi:10.4018/978-1-5225-2676-6.ch001

Emiri, O. T. (2017). Digital Literacy Skills Among Librarians in University Libraries In the 21st Century in Edo And Delta States, Nigeria. *International Journal of Library and Information Services*, *6*(1), 37–52. doi:10.4018/IJLIS.2017010103

Emmelhainz, C. (2020). Educating the Central Asian Librarian: Considering the International MLIS in Kazakhstan. In R. Alenzuela, H. Kim, & D. Baylen (Eds.), *Internationalization of Library and Information Science Education in the Asia-Pacific Region* (pp. 1–32). IGI Global. https://doi.org/10.4018/978-1-7998-2273-8.ch001

Esguerra, A. C. (2020). Library Education and Librarianship in Japan and the Philippines. In R. Alenzuela, H. Kim, & D. Baylen (Eds.), *Internationalization of Library and Information Science Education in the Asia-Pacific Region* (pp. 131–157). IGI Global. https://doi.org/10.4018/978-1-7998-2273-8.ch006

Esposito, T. (2018). Exploring Opportunities in Health Science Information Instructional Outreach: A Case Study Highlighting One Academic Library's Experience. In S. Bhattacharyya & K. Patnaik (Eds.), *Changing the Scope of Library Instruction in the Digital Age* (pp. 118–135). Hershey, PA: IGI Global. doi:10.4018/978-1-5225-2802-9.ch005

Fagbola, O. O., Smart, A. E., & Oluwaseun, B. O. (2020). Application of Cloud Computing Technologies in Academic Library Management: The National Open University of Nigeria Library in Perspective. In A. Tella (Ed.), *Handbook of Research on Digital Devices for Inclusivity and Engagement in Libraries* (pp. 135–159). IGI Global. https://doi.org/10.4018/978-1-5225-9034-7.ch007

Fan, Y., Zhang, X., & Li, G. (2017). Research Initiatives and Projects in Academic Libraries. In L. Ruan, Q. Zhu, & Y. Ye (Eds.), *Academic Library Development and Administration in China* (pp. 230–252). Hershey, PA: IGI Global. doi:10.4018/978-1-5225-0550-1.ch014

Farmer, L. S. (2017). ICT Literacy Integration: Issues and Sample Efforts. In J. Keengwe & P. Bull (Eds.), *Handbook of Research on Transformative Digital Content and Learning Technologies* (pp. 59–80). Hershey, PA: IGI Global. doi:10.4018/978-1-5225-2000-9.ch004

Farmer, L. S. (2017). Data Analytics for Strategic Management: Getting the Right Data. In V. Wang (Ed.), *Encyclopedia of Strategic Leadership and Management* (pp. 810–822). Hershey, PA: IGI Global. doi:10.4018/978-1-5225-1049-9.ch056

Farmer, L. S. (2017). Managing Portable Technologies for Special Education. In V. Wang (Ed.), *Encyclopedia of Strategic Leadership and Management* (pp. 977–987). Hershey, PA: IGI Global. doi:10.4018/978-1-5225-1049-9.ch068

Fujishima, D., & Kamada, T. (2017). Collective Relocation for Associative Distributed Collections of Objects. *International Journal of Software Innovation*, *5*(2), 55–69. doi:10.4018/IJSI.2017040104

Ghani, S. R. (2017). Ontology: Advancing Flawless Library Services. In T. Ashraf & N. Kumar (Eds.), *Interdisciplinary Digital Preservation Tools and Technologies* (pp. 79–102). Hershey, PA: IGI Global. doi:10.4018/978-1-5225-1653-8.ch005

Gu, J. (2017). Library Buildings on New Campuses. In L. Ruan, Q. Zhu, & Y. Ye (Eds.), *Academic Library Development and Administration in China* (pp. 110–124). Hershey, PA: IGI Global. doi:10.4018/978-1-5225-0550-1.ch007

Guan, Z., & Wang, J. (2017). The China Academic Social Sciences and Humanities Library (CASHL). In L. Ruan, Q. Zhu, & Y. Ye (Eds.), *Academic Library Development and Administration in China* (pp. 31–54). Hershey, PA: IGI Global. doi:10.4018/978-1-5225-0550-1.ch003

Gul, S., & Shueb, S. (2018). Confronting/Managing the Crisis of Indian Libraries: E-Consortia Initiatives in India - A Way Forward. In R. Bhardwaj (Ed.), *Digitizing the Modern Library and the Transition From Print to Electronic* (pp. 129–163). Hershey, PA: IGI Global. doi:10.4018/978-1-5225-2119-8.ch006

Gunjal, B. (2017). Managing Knowledge and Scholarly Assets in Academic Libraries: Issues and Challenges. In B. Gunjal (Ed.), *Managing Knowledge and Scholarly Assets in Academic Libraries* (pp. 270–279). Hershey, PA: IGI Global. doi:10.4018/978-1-5225-1741-2.ch013

Guo, J., Zhang, H., & Zong, Y. (2017). Leadership Development and Career Planning. In L. Ruan, Q. Zhu, & Y. Ye (Eds.), *Academic Library Development and Administration in China* (pp. 264–279). Hershey, PA: IGI Global. doi:10.4018/978-1-5225-0550-1.ch016

Hahn, J. (2020). Student Engagement and Smart Spaces: Library Browsing and Internet of Things Technology. In B. Holland (Eds.), *Emerging Trends and Impacts of the Internet of Things in Libraries* (pp. 52-70). IGI Global. https://doi.org/10.4018/978-1-7998-4742-7.ch003

Halder, D. (2020). A Transitional Shift From Traditional Library to Digital Library. In A. Kaushik, A. Kumar, & P. Biswas (Eds.), *Handbook of Research on Emerging Trends and Technologies in Library and Information Science* (pp. 147–155). IGI Global. https://doi.org/10.4018/978-1-5225-9825-1.ch011

Hallis, R. (2018). Leveraging Library Instruction in a Digital Age. In S. Bhattacharyya & K. Patnaik (Eds.), *Changing the Scope of Library Instruction in the Digital Age* (pp. 1–23). Hershey, PA: IGI Global. doi:10.4018/978-1-5225-2802-9.ch001

Halupa, C. (2022). An Introduction to Survey Research. In A. Zimmerman (Ed.), *Methodological Innovations in Research and Academic Writing* (pp. 41–62). IGI Global. https://doi.org/10.4018/978-1-7998-8283-1.ch003

Hartsock, R., & Alemneh, D. G. (2018). Electronic Theses and Dissertations (ETDs). In M. Khosrow-Pour, D.B.A. (Ed.), Encyclopedia of Information Science and Technology, Fourth Edition (pp. 6748-6755). Hershey, PA: IGI Global. https://doi.org/ doi:10.4018/978-1-5225-2255-3.ch584

Haugh, D. (2018). Mobile Applications for Libraries. In L. Costello & M. Powers (Eds.), *Developing In-House Digital Tools in Library Spaces* (pp. 76–90). Hershey, PA: IGI Global. doi:10.4018/978-1-5225-2676-6.ch004

Hayes, C. (2022). Methodology and Method in Case Study Research: Framing Research Design in Practice. In S. Watson, S. Austin, & J. Bell (Eds.), *Conceptual Analyses of Curriculum Inquiry Methodologies* (pp. 138-154). IGI Global. https://doi.org/10.4018/978-1-7998-8848-2.ch007

Hayes, C., & Graham, Y. N. (2022). Phenomenology: Conceptually Framing Phenomenological Research Design and Methodology. In S. Watson, S. Austin, & J. Bell (Eds.), *Conceptual Analyses of Curriculum Inquiry Methodologies* (pp. 28-50). IGI Global. https://doi.org/10.4018/978-1-7998-8848-2.ch002

Hill, V. (2017). Digital Citizens as Writers: New Literacies and New Responsibilities. In E. Monske & K. Blair (Eds.), *Handbook of Research on Writing and Composing in the Age of MOOCs* (pp. 56–74). Hershey, PA: IGI Global. doi:10.4018/978-1-5225-1718-4.ch004

Hoh, A. (2019). Expanding the Awareness and Use of Library Collections Through Social Media: A Case Study of the Library of Congress International Collections Social Media Program. In J. Joe & E. Knight (Eds.), *Social Media for Communication and Instruction in Academic Libraries* (pp. 212–236). IGI Global. doi:10.4018/978-1-5225-8097-3.ch013

Holland, B. (2020). Emerging Technology and Today's Libraries. In B. Holland (Eds.), *Emerging Trends and Impacts of the Internet of Things in Libraries* (pp. 1-33). IGI Global. https://doi.org/10.4018/978-1-7998-4742-7.ch001

Homza, A., & Fontno, T. J. (2021). Supporting Teacher Candidates as Social Justice Change-Makers: A Faculty-Librarian Collaboration for Building and Using Diverse Youth Collections. In D. Hartsfield (Ed.), *Handbook of Research on Teaching Diverse Youth Literature to Pre-Service Professionals* (pp. 398–421). IGI Global. https://doi.org/10.4018/978-1-7998-7375-4.ch020

Horne-Popp, L. M., Tessone, E. B., & Welker, J. (2018). If You Build It, They Will Come: Creating a Library Statistics Dashboard for Decision-Making. In L. Costello & M. Powers (Eds.), *Developing In-House Digital Tools in Library Spaces* (pp. 177–203). Hershey, PA: IGI Global. doi:10.4018/978-1-5225-2676-6.ch009

Huang, C., & Xue, H. F. (2017). The China Academic Digital Associative Library (CADAL). In L. Ruan, Q. Zhu, & Y. Ye (Eds.), *Academic Library Development and Administration in China* (pp. 20–30). Hershey, PA: IGI Global. doi:10.4018/978-1-5225-0550-1.ch002

Huang, J., & Vedantham, A. (2019). Cabot Science Library: Creating Transformative Learning Environments in Library Spaces. In A. Darshan Singh, S. Raghunathan, E. Robeck, & B. Sharma (Eds.), *Cases on Smart Learning Environments* (pp. 284–298). IGI Global. doi:10.4018/978-1-5225-6136-1.ch016

Hunsaker, A. J., Majewski, N., & Rocke, L. E. (2018). Pulling Content out the Back Door: Creating an Interactive Digital Collections Experience. In L. Costello & M. Powers (Eds.), *Developing In-House Digital Tools in Library Spaces* (pp. 205–226). Hershey, PA: IGI Global. doi:10.4018/978-1-5225-2676-6.ch010

Hussain, A. (2020). Cutting Edge: Technology's Impact on Library Services. In J. Jesubright & P. Saravanan (Eds.), *Innovations in the Designing and Marketing of Information Services* (pp. 16–27). IGI Global. https://doi.org/10.4018/978-1-7998-1482-5.ch002

Idiegbeyan-ose, J., Owolabi, S. E., Ayooluwa, A., Foluke, O., Toluwani, E., & Sunday, O. (2019). Digital Library and Distance Learning in Developing Countries: Benefits and Challenges. In R. Bhardwaj & P. Banks (Eds.), *Research Data Access and Management in Modern Libraries* (pp. 220–245). IGI Global. https://doi.org/10.4018/978-1-5225-8437-7.ch011

Ifijeh, G., Adebayo, O., Izuagbe, R., & Olawoyin, O. (2018). Institutional Repositories and Libraries in Nigeria: Interrogating the Nexus. *Journal of Cases on Information Technology*, *20*(2), 16–29. doi:10.4018/JCIT.2018040102

Igbinovia, M. O., Solanke, E. O., & Obinyan, O. O. (2020). Building Influence: Strategising for Library Advocacy. In N. Osuigwe (Ed.), *Managing and Adapting Library Information Services for Future Users* (pp. 221–241). IGI Global. https://doi.org/10.4018/978-1-7998-1116-9.ch013

Iglesias, E. (2017). Insourcing and Outsourcing of Library Technology. In E. Iglesias (Ed.), *Library Technology Funding, Planning, and Deployment* (pp. 113–123). Hershey, PA: IGI Global. doi:10.4018/978-1-5225-1735-1.ch007

Ikolo, V. E. (2018). Transformational Leadership for Academic Libraries in Nigeria. In M. Khosrow-Pour, D.B.A. (Ed.), Encyclopedia of Information Science and Technology, Fourth Edition (pp. 5726-5735). Hershey, PA: IGI Global. doi:10.4018/978-1-5225-2255-3.ch497

Ikolo, V. E. (2020). Doctor's Awareness and Perception of Medical Library Resources and Services: A Case Study of Delta State University Teaching Hospital (Delsuth), Nigeria. *International Journal of Library and Information Services*, *9*(2), 58–71. https://doi.org/10.4018/IJLIS.2020070104

Joe, J. A. (2018). Changing Expectations of Academic Libraries. In M. Khosrow-Pour, D.B.A. (Ed.), Encyclopedia of Information Science and Technology, Fourth Edition (pp. 5204-5212). Hershey, PA: IGI Global. doi:10.4018/978-1-5225-2255-3.ch452

Juliana, I., Izuagbe, R., Itsekor, V., Fagbohun, M. O., Asaolu, A., & Nwokeoma, M. N. (2018). The Role of the School Library in Empowering Visually Impaired Children With Lifelong Information Literacy Skills. In P. Epler (Ed.), *Instructional Strategies in General Education and Putting the Individuals With Disabilities Act (IDEA) Into Practice* (pp. 245–271). Hershey, PA: IGI Global. doi:10.4018/978-1-5225-3111-1.ch009

Kalu, C. O., Chidi-Kalu, E. I., & Mafe, T. A. (2021). Research Data Management in an Academic Library. In J. Chigwada & G. Tsvuura (Eds.), *Handbook of Research on Information and Records Management in the Fourth Industrial Revolution* (pp. 38–55). IGI Global. https://doi.org/10.4018/978-1-7998-7740-0.ch003

Kalusopa, T. (2018). Preservation and Access to Digital Materials: Strategic Policy Options for Africa. In P. Ngulube (Ed.), *Handbook of Research on Heritage Management and Preservation* (pp. 150–174). Hershey, PA: IGI Global. doi:10.4018/978-1-5225-3137-1.ch008

Kamau, G. W. (2018). Copyright Challenges in Digital Libraries in Kenya From the Lens of a Librarian. In A. Tella & T. Kwanya (Eds.), *Handbook of Research on Managing Intellectual Property in Digital Libraries* (pp. 312–336). Hershey, PA: IGI Global. doi:10.4018/978-1-5225-3093-0.ch016

Karagöz, E., Güney, L. Ö., & Baran, B. (2022). The Collaborative Digital Content Library Fostering Faculty Members' Collaboratively Building Learning Sources. In G. Durak & S. Çankaya (Eds.), *Handbook of Research on Managing and Designing Online Courses in Synchronous and Asynchronous Environments* (pp. 196–213). IGI Global. doi:10.4018/978-1-7998-8701-0.ch010

Karmakar, R. (2018). Development and Management of Digital Libraries in the Regime of IPR Paradigm. *International Journal of Library and Information Services*, *7*(1), 44–57. doi:10.4018/IJLIS.2018010104

Kasemsap, K. (2017). Mastering Knowledge Management in Academic Libraries. In B. Gunjal (Ed.), *Managing Knowledge and Scholarly Assets in Academic Libraries* (pp. 27–55). Hershey, PA: IGI Global. doi:10.4018/978-1-5225-1741-2.ch002

Kehinde, A. (2018). Digital Libraries and the Role of Digital Librarians. In A. Tella & T. Kwanya (Eds.), *Handbook of Research on Managing Intellectual Property in Digital Libraries* (pp. 98–119). Hershey, PA: IGI Global. doi:10.4018/978-1-5225-3093-0.ch006

Kenausis, V., & Herman, D. (2017). Don't Make Us Use the "Get Along Shirt": Communication and Consensus Building in an RFP Process. In E. Iglesias (Ed.), *Library Technology Funding, Planning, and Deployment* (pp. 1–22). Hershey, PA: IGI Global. doi:10.4018/978-1-5225-1735-1.ch001

Kohl, L. E., Lombardi, P., & Moroney, M. (2017). Moving from Local to Global via the Integrated Library System: Cost-Savings, ILS Management, Teams, and End-Users. In E. Iglesias (Ed.), *Library Technology Funding, Planning, and Deployment* (pp. 23–35). Hershey, PA: IGI Global. doi:10.4018/978-1-5225-1735-1.ch002

Kowalsky, M. (2020). School Librarian Experiences of Learning Management Implementation. In A. Tella (Ed.), *Handbook of Research on Digital Devices for Inclusivity and Engagement in Libraries* (pp. 160–184). IGI Global. https://doi.org/10.4018/978-1-5225-9034-7.ch008

Kumar, K. (2018). Library in Your Pocket Delivery of Instruction Service Through Library Mobile Apps: A World in Your Pocket. In S. Bhattacharyya & K. Patnaik (Eds.), *Changing the Scope of Library Instruction in the Digital Age* (pp. 228–249). Hershey, PA: IGI Global. doi:10.4018/978-1-5225-2802-9.ch009

Kwanya, T. (2018). Social Bookmarking in Digital Libraries: Intellectual Property Rights Implications. In A. Tella & T. Kwanya (Eds.), *Handbook of Research on Managing Intellectual Property in Digital Libraries* (pp. 1–18). Hershey, PA: IGI Global. doi:10.4018/978-1-5225-3093-0.ch001

Lapo, P., Makhmudov, G., & Rakhmatullaev, M. (2020). Internationalization of Library and Information Science Education in Tajikistan and Uzbekistan: Implications in Central Asia. In R. Alenzuela, H. Kim, & D. Baylen (Eds.), *Internationalization of Library and Information Science Education in the Asia-Pacific Region* (pp. 225–245). IGI Global. https://doi.org/10.4018/978-1-7998-2273-8.ch010

Lewis, J. K. (2018). Change Leadership Styles and Behaviors in Academic Libraries. In M. Khosrow-Pour, D.B.A. (Ed.), Encyclopedia of Information Science and Technology, Fourth Edition (pp. 5194-5203). Hershey, PA: IGI Global. doi:10.4018/978-1-5225-2255-3.ch451

Lillard, L. L. (2018). Is Interdisciplinary Collaboration in Academia an Elusive Dream?: Can the Institutional Barriers Be Broken Down? A Review of the Literature and the Case of Library Science. In M. Al-Suqri, A. Al-Kindi, S. AlKindi, & N. Saleem (Eds.), *Promoting Interdisciplinarity in Knowledge Generation and Problem Solving* (pp. 139–147). Hershey, PA: IGI Global. doi:10.4018/978-1-5225-3878-3.ch010

Liu, C., Dou, T., Zhou, H., Zhang, B., & Zhang, C. (2021). Library Service Innovation Based on New Information Technology: Taking the Interactive Experience Space "Tsinghua Impression" as an Example. *International Journal of Library and Information Services, 10*(1), 71–81. https://doi.org/10.4018/IJLIS.2021010106

Long, X., & Yao, B. (2017). The Construction and Development of the Academic Digital Library of Chinese Ancient Collections. In L. Ruan, Q. Zhu, & Y. Ye (Eds.), *Academic Library Development and Administration in China* (pp. 126–135). Hershey, PA: IGI Global. doi:10.4018/978-1-5225-0550-1.ch008

Long, X., & Yao, B. (2020). The Construction and Development of the Academic Digital Library of Chinese Ancient Collections. In I. Management Association (Ed.), *Digital Libraries and Institutional Repositories: Breakthroughs in Research and Practice* (pp. 78-87). IGI Global. https://doi.org/10.4018/978-1-7998-2463-3.ch006

Lowe, M., & Reno, L. M. (2018). Academic Librarianship and Burnout. In *Examining the Emotional Dimensions of Academic Librarianship: Emerging Research and Opportunities* (pp. 72–89). Hershey, PA: IGI Global. doi:10.4018/978-1-5225-3761-8.ch005

Lowe, M., & Reno, L. M. (2018). Emotional Dimensions of Academic Librarianship. In *Examining the Emotional Dimensions of Academic Librarianship: Emerging Research and Opportunities* (pp. 54–71). Hershey, PA: IGI Global. doi:10.4018/978-1-5225-3761-8.ch004

Lowe, M., & Reno, L. M. (2018). Why Isn't This Being Studied? In *Examining the Emotional Dimensions of Academic Librarianship: Emerging Research and Opportunities* (pp. 90–108). Hershey, PA: IGI Global. doi:10.4018/978-1-5225-3761-8.ch006

Lowe, M., & Reno, L. M. (2018). Research Agenda: Research Ideas and Recommendations. In *Examining the Emotional Dimensions of Academic Librarianship: Emerging Research and Opportunities* (pp. 109–125). Hershey, PA: IGI Global. doi:10.4018/978-1-5225-3761-8.ch007

Luyombya, D., Kiyingi, G. W., & Naluwooza, M. (2018). The Nature and Utilisation of Archival Records Deposited in Makerere University Library, Uganda. In P. Ngulube (Ed.), *Handbook of Research on Heritage Management and Preservation* (pp. 96–113). Hershey, PA: IGI Global. doi:10.4018/978-1-5225-3137-1.ch005

Ma, W. Y. (2022). Supporting Indigenous Education From a Distance: Adjusting Strategies to Maintain Access to a Rare Library Collection During a Global Crisis. In P. Pangelinan & T. McVey (Eds.), *Learning and Reconciliation Through Indigenous Education in Oceania* (pp. 197–209). IGI Global. https://doi.org/10.4018/978-1-7998-7736-3.ch012

Mabe, M., & Ashley, E. A. (2017). The Natural Role of the Public Library. In *The Developing Role of Public Libraries in Emergency Management: Emerging Research and Opportunities* (pp. 25–43). Hershey, PA: IGI Global. doi:10.4018/978-1-5225-2196-9.ch003

Mabe, M., & Ashley, E. A. (2017). I'm Trained, Now What? In *The Developing Role of Public Libraries in Emergency Management: Emerging Research and Opportunities* (pp. 87–95). Hershey, PA: IGI Global. doi:10.4018/978-1-5225-2196-9.ch007

Mabe, M., & Ashley, E. A. (2017). Emergency Preparation for the Library and Librarian. In *The Developing Role of Public Libraries in Emergency Management: Emerging Research and Opportunities* (pp. 61–78). Hershey, PA: IGI Global. doi:10.4018/978-1-5225-2196-9.ch005

Mabe, M., & Ashley, E. A. (2017). The CCPL Model. In *The Developing Role of Public Libraries in Emergency Management: Emerging Research and Opportunities* (pp. 15–24). Hershey, PA: IGI Global. doi:10.4018/978-1-5225-2196-9.ch002

Mabe, M., & Ashley, E. A. (2017). The Local Command Structure and How the Library Fits. In *In The Developing Role of Public Libraries in Emergency Management: Emerging Research and Opportunities* (pp. 44–60). Hershey, PA: IGI Global. doi:10.4018/978-1-5225-2196-9.ch004

Mafube, M. A., & Keakopa, S. M. (2019). Customer Services at the Library Archives of the National University of Lesotho. In P. Ngulube (Ed.), *Handbook of Research on Advocacy, Promotion, and Public Programming for Memory Institutions* (pp. 62–76). IGI Global. doi:10.4018/978-1-5225-7429-3.ch004

Majumdar, S. (2022). Community Engagement Through Extension and Outreach Activities: Scope of a College Library. In M. Taher (Ed.), *Handbook of Research on the Role of Libraries, Archives, and Museums in Achieving Civic Engagement and Social Justice in Smart Cities* (pp. 121–138). IGI Global. https://doi.org/10.4018/978-1-7998-8363-0.ch006

Mangone, E. (2022). The Difficult Joining of Theory and Empirical Research: Strengths and Weaknesses of Digital Research Methods. In G. Punziano & A. Delli Paoli (Eds.), *Handbook of Research on Advanced Research Methodologies for a Digital Society* (pp. 11–23). IGI Global. https://doi.org/10.4018/978-1-7998-8473-6.ch002

Manzoor, A. (2018). Social Media: A Librarian's Tool for Instant and Direct Interaction With Library Users. In R. Bhardwaj (Ed.), *Digitizing the Modern Library and the Transition From Print to Electronic* (pp. 112–128). Hershey, PA: IGI Global. doi:10.4018/978-1-5225-2119-8.ch005

Maringanti, H. (2018). A Decision Making Paradigm for Software Development in Libraries. In L. Costello & M. Powers (Eds.), *Developing In-House Digital Tools in Library Spaces* (pp. 59–75). Hershey, PA: IGI Global. doi:10.4018/978-1-5225-2676-6.ch003

Markman, K. M., Ferrarini, M., & Deschenes, A. H. (2018). User Testing and Iterative Design in the Academic Library: A Case Study. In R. Roscoe, S. Craig, & I. Douglas (Eds.), *End-User Considerations in Educational Technology Design* (pp. 160–183). Hershey, PA: IGI Global. doi:10.4018/978-1-5225-2639-1.ch008

Marrazzo, F. (2022). Doing Research With Online Platforms: An Emerging Issue Network. In G. Punziano & A. Delli Paoli (Eds.), *Handbook of Research on Advanced Research Methodologies for a Digital Society* (pp. 65–86). IGI Global. https://doi.org/10.4018/978-1-7998-8473-6.ch006

Mertens, D. (2022). Designing Mixed Methods Studies to Contribute to Social, Economic, and Environmental Justice: Implications for Library and Information Sciences. In P. Ngulube (Ed.), *Handbook of Research on Mixed Methods Research in Information Science* (pp. 173–189). IGI Global. https://doi.org/10.4018/978-1-7998-8844-4.ch009

Moahi, K. H. (2020). The Research Process and Indigenous Epistemologies. In P. Ngulube (Ed.), *Handbook of Research on Connecting Research Methods for Information Science Research* (pp. 245–265). IGI Global. https://doi.org/10.4018/978-1-7998-1471-9.ch013

Mohapatra, N. (2021). Webrarian: A Librarian on the Web. In C. Chisita, R. Enakrire, O. Durodolu, V. Tsabedze, & J. Ngoaketsi (Eds.), *Handbook of Research on Records and Information Management Strategies for Enhanced Knowledge Coordination* (pp. 458–470). IGI Global. https://doi.org/10.4018/978-1-7998-6618-3.ch027

Munatsi, R. (2020). National Research and Knowledge Systems: Role of Libraries. In C. Chisita (Ed.), *Cooperation and Collaboration Initiatives for Libraries and Related Institutions* (pp. 273–293). IGI Global. https://doi.org/10.4018/978-1-7998-0043-9.ch014

Musimbi, W. L., & Mutuku, P. K. (2019). The Future of LIS and Media Training in the Global Era: Challenges and Prospects. In C. Chisita & A. Rusero (Eds.), *Exploring the Relationship Between Media, Libraries, and Archives* (pp. 82–101). IGI Global. doi:10.4018/978-1-5225-5840-8.ch006

Mwanzu, A. (2019). Economics of Resource Sharing via Library Consortia. In C. Chisita & A. Rusero (Eds.), *Exploring the Relationship Between Media, Libraries, and Archives* (pp. 19–34). IGI Global. https://doi.org/10.4018/978-1-5225-5840-8.ch002

Na, L. (2017). Library and Information Science Education and Graduate Programs in Academic Libraries. In L. Ruan, Q. Zhu, & Y. Ye (Eds.), *Academic Library Development and Administration in China* (pp. 218–229). Hershey, PA: IGI Global. doi:10.4018/978-1-5225-0550-1.ch013

Nagarkar, S. P. (2017). Biomedical Librarianship in the Post-Genomic Era. In S. Ram (Ed.), *Library and Information Services for Bioinformatics Education and Research* (pp. 1–17). Hershey, PA: IGI Global. doi:10.4018/978-1-5225-1871-6.ch001

Natarajan, M. (2017). Exploring Knowledge Sharing over Social Media. In R. Chugh (Ed.), *Harnessing Social Media as a Knowledge Management Tool* (pp. 55–73). Hershey, PA: IGI Global. doi:10.4018/978-1-5225-0495-5.ch003

Nazir, T. (2017). Preservation Initiatives in E-Environment to Protect Information Assets. In T. Ashraf & N. Kumar (Eds.), *Interdisciplinary Digital Preservation Tools and Technologies* (pp. 193–208). Hershey, PA: IGI Global. doi:10.4018/978-1-5225-1653-8.ch010

Ngulube, P. (2017). Embedding Indigenous Knowledge in Library and Information Science Education in Anglophone Eastern and Southern Africa. In P. Ngulube (Ed.), *Handbook of Research on Social, Cultural, and Educational Considerations of Indigenous Knowledge in Developing Countries* (pp. 92–115). Hershey, PA: IGI Global. doi:10.4018/978-1-5225-0838-0.ch006

Ngulube, P. (2022). Using Simple and Complex Mixed Methods Research Designs to Understand Research in Information Science. In P. Ngulube (Ed.), *Handbook of Research on Mixed Methods Research in Information Science* (pp. 20–46). IGI Global. doi:10.4018/978-1-7998-8844-4.ch002

Nicolajsen, H. W., Sorensen, F., & Scupola, A. (2018). User Involvement in Service Innovation Processes. In M. Khosrow-Pour (Ed.), *Optimizing Current Practices in E-Services and Mobile Applications* (pp. 42–61). Hershey, PA: IGI Global. doi:10.4018/978-1-5225-5026-6.ch003

Ocholla, D. N. (2022). A Research Dashboard for Aligning Research Components in Research Proposals, Theses, and Dissertations in Library and Information Science. In P. Ngulube (Ed.), *Handbook of Research on Mixed Methods Research in Information Science* (pp. 629–640). IGI Global. https://doi.org/10.4018/978-1-7998-8844-4.ch029

Ochonogor, W. C., & Okite-Amughoro, F. A. (2018). Building an Effective Digital Library in a University Teaching Hospital (UTH) in Nigeria. In A. Tella & T. Kwanya (Eds.), *Handbook of Research on Managing Intellectual Property in Digital Libraries* (pp. 184–204). Hershey, PA: IGI Global. doi:10.4018/978-1-5225-3093-0.ch010

Okada, D. (2020). 10,000 Newly Certified Librarians, 100 Secure Jobs. In R. Alenzuela, H. Kim, & D. Baylen (Eds.), *Internationalization of Library and Information Science Education in the Asia-Pacific Region* (pp. 78–101). IGI Global. https://doi.org/10.4018/978-1-7998-2273-8.ch004

Oladapo, Y. O. (2018). Open Access to Knowledge and Challenges in Digital Libraries. In A. Tella & T. Kwanya (Eds.), *Handbook of Research on Managing Intellectual Property in Digital Libraries* (pp. 260–291). Hershey, PA: IGI Global. doi:10.4018/978-1-5225-3093-0.ch014

Oladokun, O., & Zulu, S. F. (2017). Document Description and Coding as Key Elements in Knowledge, Records, and Information Management. In P. Jain & N. Mnjama (Eds.), *Managing Knowledge Resources and Records in Modern Organizations* (pp. 179–197). Hershey, PA: IGI Global. doi:10.4018/978-1-5225-1965-2.ch011

Olubodun, O. J., & Oye, P. O. (2019). Library: A Tool for Information Dissemination and Creating Awareness in Conflict-Induced Situations. In E. Nyam & F. Idoko (Eds.), *Examining the Social and Economic Impacts of Conflict-Induced Migration* (pp. 55–63). IGI Global. https://doi.org/10.4018/978-1-5225-7615-0.ch003

Omeluzor, S. U., Abayomi, I., & Gbemi-Ogunleye, P. (2018). Contemporary Media for Library Users' Instruction in Academic Libraries in South-West Nigeria: Contemporary Library Instruction in the Digital Age. In S. Bhattacharyya & K. Patnaik (Eds.), *Changing the Scope of Library Instruction in the Digital Age* (pp. 162–185). Hershey, PA: IGI Global. doi:10.4018/978-1-5225-2802-9.ch007

Onwuchekwa, E. O. (2020). Library Signage and Information Graphics: A Communication Tool for Library Users. In A. Tella (Ed.), *Handbook of Research on Digital Devices for Inclusivity and Engagement in Libraries* (pp. 231–237). IGI Global. https://doi.org/10.4018/978-1-5225-9034-7.ch011

Onyancha, O. B. (2020). Informetrics Research Methods Outlined. In P. Ngulube (Ed.), *Handbook of Research on Connecting Research Methods for Information Science Research* (pp. 320–348). IGI Global. https://doi.org/10.4018/978-1-7998-1471-9.ch017

Oshilalu, A. H., & Ogochukwu, E. T. (2017). Modeling a Software for Library and Information Centers. *International Journal of Library and Information Services, 6*(2), 1–10. doi:10.4018/IJLIS.2017070101

Oswal, S. K. (2017). Institutional, Legal, and Attitudinal Barriers to the Accessibility of University Digital Libraries: Implications for Retention of Disabled Students. In H. Alphin Jr, J. Lavine, & R. Chan (Eds.), *Disability and Equity in Higher Education Accessibility* (pp. 223–241). Hershey, PA: IGI Global. doi:10.4018/978-1-5225-2665-0.ch010

Oukrich, J., & Bouikhalene, B. (2017). A Survey of Users' Satisfaction in the University Library by Using a Pareto Analysis and the Automatic Classification Methods. *International Journal of Library and Information Services, 6*(1), 17–36. doi:10.4018/IJLIS.2017010102

Oyelude, A. A., & Oluwaniyi, S. A. (2020). Managing Future Library Services for the Medical Sciences: A Pharmacy Library Experience. In N. Osuigwe (Ed.), *Managing and Adapting Library Information Services for Future Users* (pp. 200–220). IGI Global. https://doi.org/10.4018/978-1-7998-1116-9.ch012

Özel, N. (2018). Developing Visual Literacy Skills Through Library Instructions. In V. Osinska & G. Osinski (Eds.), *Information Visualization Techniques in the Social Sciences and Humanities* (pp. 32–48). Hershey, PA: IGI Global. doi:10.4018/978-1-5225-4990-1.ch003

Paganelli, A. L., & Paganelli, A. L. (2021). Blockchain and the Research Libraries: Expanding Interlibrary Loan and Protecting Privacy. In D. Gunter (Ed.), *Transforming Scholarly Publishing With Blockchain Technologies and AI* (pp. 232–250). IGI Global. https://doi.org/10.4018/978-1-7998-5589-7.ch012

Patel, D., & Thakur, D. (2017). Managing Open Access (OA) Scholarly Information Resources in a University. In A. Munigal (Ed.), *Scholarly Communication and the Publish or Perish Pressures of Academia* (pp. 224–255). Hershey, PA: IGI Global. doi:10.4018/978-1-5225-1697-2.ch011

Patnaik, K. R. (2018). Crafting a Framework for Copyright Literacy and Licensed Content: A Case Study at an Advanced Management Education and Research Library. In S. Bhattacharyya & K. Patnaik (Eds.), *Changing the Scope of Library Instruction in the Digital Age* (pp. 136–160). Hershey, PA: IGI Global. doi:10.4018/978-1-5225-2802-9.ch006

Paynter, K. (2017). Elementary Library Media Specialists' Roles in the Implementation of the Common Core State Standards. In M. Grassetti & S. Brookby (Eds.), *Advancing Next-Generation Teacher Education through Digital Tools and Applications* (pp. 262–283). Hershey, PA: IGI Global. doi:10.4018/978-1-5225-0965-3.ch014

Perry, S. C., & Waggoner, J. (2018). Processes for User-Centered Design and Development: The Omeka Curator Dashboard Project. In L. Costello & M. Powers (Eds.), *Developing In-House Digital Tools in Library Spaces* (pp. 37–58). Hershey, PA: IGI Global. doi:10.4018/978-1-5225-2676-6.ch002

Perumalsamy, R., & Kannan, S. P. (2019). User Information Needs in the Public Libraries in India. In S. Thanuskodi (Ed.), *Literacy Skill Development for Library Science Professionals* (pp. 25–53). IGI Global. https://doi.org/10.4018/978-1-5225-7125-4.ch002

Phuritsabam, B., & Devi, A. B. (2017). Information Seeking Behavior of Medical Scientists at Jawaharlal Nehru Institute of Medical Science: A Study. In S. Ram (Ed.), *Library and Information Services for Bioinformatics Education and Research* (pp. 177–187). Hershey, PA: IGI Global. doi:10.4018/978-1-5225-1871-6.ch010

Quadri, R. F., & Sodiq, O. A. (2018). Managing Intellectual Property in Digital Libraries: The Roles of Digital Librarians. In A. Tella & T. Kwanya (Eds.), *Handbook of Research on Managing Intellectual Property in Digital Libraries* (pp. 337–355). Hershey, PA: IGI Global. doi:10.4018/978-1-5225-3093-0.ch017

Quintana, A. J. (2021). Ensuring Research Integrity. In K. Elufiede & C. Barker Stucky (Eds.), *Strategies and Tactics for Multidisciplinary Writing* (pp. 192–201). IGI Global. https://doi.org/10.4018/978-1-7998-4477-8.ch015

Qutab, S., Adil, S. A., Gardner, L. A., & Ullah, F. S. (2022). The Role of Libraries, Archives, and Museums for Metaliteracy in Smart Cities: Implications, Challenges, and Opportunities. In M. Taher (Ed.), *Handbook of Research on the Role of Libraries, Archives, and Museums in Achieving Civic Engagement and Social Justice in Smart Cities* (pp. 355–375). IGI Global. https://doi.org/10.4018/978-1-7998-8363-0.ch019

Raj, S. K., & De, K. (2020). Electronic Resource Management and Digitisation: Library System of the University of Calcutta. In A. Kaushik, A. Kumar, & P. Biswas (Eds.), *Handbook of Research on Emerging Trends and Technologies in Library and Information Science* (pp. 231–265). IGI Global. https://doi.org/10.4018/978-1-5225-9825-1.ch017

Ram, S. (2017). Library Services for Bioinformatics: Establishing Synergy Data Information and Knowledge. In S. Ram (Ed.), *Library and Information Services for Bioinformatics Education and Research* (pp. 18–33). Hershey, PA: IGI Global. doi:10.4018/978-1-5225-1871-6.ch002

Rao, M. (2017). Use of Institutional Repository for Information Dissemination and Knowledge Management. In B. Gunjal (Ed.), *Managing Knowledge and Scholarly Assets in Academic Libraries* (pp. 156–173). Hershey, PA: IGI Global. doi:10.4018/978-1-5225-1741-2.ch007

Rao, Y., & Zhang, Y. (2017). The Construction and Development of Academic Library Digital Special Subject Databases. In L. Ruan, Q. Zhu, & Y. Ye (Eds.), *Academic Library Development and Administration in China* (pp. 163–183). Hershey, PA: IGI Global. doi:10.4018/978-1-5225-0550-1.ch010

Rao, Y., & Zhang, Y. (2020). The Construction and Development of Academic Library Digital Special Subject Databases. In I. Management Association (Ed.), *Digital Libraries and Institutional Repositories: Breakthroughs in Research and Practice* (pp. 24-44). IGI Global. https://doi.org/10.4018/978-1-7998-2463-3.ch002

Razip, S. N., Kadir, S. F., Saim, S. N., Dolhan, F. N., Jarmil, N., Salleh, N. H., & Rajin, G. (2017). Predicting Users' Intention towards Using Library Self-Issue and Return Systems. In N. Suki (Ed.), *Handbook of Research on Leveraging Consumer Psychology for Effective Customer Engagement* (pp. 102–115). Hershey, PA: IGI Global. doi:10.4018/978-1-5225-0746-8.ch007

Rothwell, S. L. (2018). Librarians and Instructional Design Challenges: Concepts, Examples, and a Flexible Design Framework. In S. Bhattacharyya & K. Patnaik (Eds.), *Changing the Scope of Library Instruction in the Digital Age* (pp. 24–59). Hershey, PA: IGI Global. doi:10.4018/978-1-5225-2802-9.ch002

Roy, L., & Frydman, A. (2018). Community Outreach. In M. Khosrow-Pour, D.B.A. (Ed.), Encyclopedia of Information Science and Technology, Fourth Edition (pp. 6685-6694). Hershey, PA: IGI Global. doi:10.4018/978-1-5225-2255-3.ch579

Rutto, D., & Yudah, O. (2018). E-Books in University Libraries in Kenya: Trends, Usage, and Intellectual Property Issues. In A. Tella & T. Kwanya (Eds.), *Handbook of Research on Managing Intellectual Property in Digital Libraries* (pp. 120–141). Hershey, PA: IGI Global. doi:10.4018/978-1-5225-3093-0.ch007

Sabharwal, A. (2017). The Transformative Role of Institutional Repositories in Academic Knowledge Management. In B. Gunjal (Ed.), *Managing Knowledge and Scholarly Assets in Academic Libraries* (pp. 127–155). Hershey, PA: IGI Global. doi:10.4018/978-1-5225-1741-2.ch006

Sadiku, S. A., Kpakiko, M. M., & Tsafe, A. G. (2018). Institutional Digital Repository and the Challenges of Global Visibility in Nigeria. In A. Tella & T. Kwanya (Eds.), *Handbook of Research on Managing Intellectual Property in Digital Libraries* (pp. 356–376). Hershey, PA: IGI Global. doi:10.4018/978-1-5225-3093-0.ch018

Sahu, M. K. (2018). Web-Scale Discovery Service in Academic Library Environment: A Birds Eye View. *International Journal of Library and Information Services*, *7*(1), 1–14. doi:10.4018/IJLIS.2018010101

Salim, F., Saigar, B., Armoham, P. K., Gobalakrishnan, S., Jap, M. Y., & Lim, N. A. (2017). Students' Information-Seeking Intention in Academic Digital Libraries. In N. Suki (Ed.), *Handbook of Research on Leveraging Consumer Psychology for Effective Customer Engagement* (pp. 259–273). Hershey, PA: IGI Global. doi:10.4018/978-1-5225-0746-8.ch017

Saroja, G. (2017). Changing Face of Scholarly Communication and Its Impact on Library and Information Centres. In A. Munigal (Ed.), *Scholarly Communication and the Publish or Perish Pressures of Academia* (pp. 100–117). Hershey, PA: IGI Global. doi:10.4018/978-1-5225-1697-2.ch006

Sauti, L. (2020). Social Media and Library Collaboration: Analysis of Government Libraries (Kaguvi Building). In C. Chisita (Ed.), *Cooperation and Collaboration Initiatives for Libraries and Related Institutions* (pp. 312–334). IGI Global. https://doi.org/10.4018/978-1-7998-0043-9.ch016

Schuster, D. W. (2017). Selection Process for Free Open Source Software. In E. Iglesias (Ed.), *Library Technology Funding, Planning, and Deployment* (pp. 55–71). Hershey, PA: IGI Global. doi:10.4018/978-1-5225-1735-1.ch004

Seagraves, K., & Weyand, L. (2021). From Bake-Alongs to Tech Talks: How One Public Library System Pivoted to Virtual Programming. In B. Holland (Ed.), *Handbook of Research on Library Response to the COVID-19 Pandemic* (pp. 447-480). IGI Global. https://doi.org/10.4018/978-1-7998-6449-3.ch023

Segaetsho, T. (2018). Environmental Consideration in the Preservation of Paper Materials in Heritage Institutions in the East and Southern African Region. In P. Ngulube (Ed.), *Handbook of Research on Heritage Management and Preservation* (pp. 183–212). Hershey, PA: IGI Global. doi:10.4018/978-1-5225-3137-1.ch010

Shakhsi, L. (2017). Cataloging Images in Library, Archive, and Museum. In T. Ashraf & N. Kumar (Eds.), *Interdisciplinary Digital Preservation Tools and Technologies* (pp. 119–141). Hershey, PA: IGI Global. doi:10.4018/978-1-5225-1653-8.ch007

Sharma, C. (2017). Digital Initiatives of the Indian Council of World Affairs' Library. In T. Ashraf & N. Kumar (Eds.), *Interdisciplinary Digital Preservation Tools and Technologies* (pp. 231–241). Hershey, PA: IGI Global. doi:10.4018/978-1-5225-1653-8.ch012

Shook, R. (2022). Achieving Balance Through Fundamentals of Digital Librarianship. In P. Pangelinan & T. McVey (Eds.), *Learning and Reconciliation Through Indigenous Education in Oceania* (pp. 185–196). IGI Global. https://doi.org/10.4018/978-1-7998-7736-3.ch011

Shukla, P., & Das, C. (2020). Plagiarism: The Role of Librarian and Teachers in Combating It. In J. Jesubright & P. Saravanan (Eds.), *Innovations in the Designing and Marketing of Information Services* (pp. 148–158). IGI Global. https://doi.org/10.4018/978-1-7998-1482-5.ch011

Siddaiah, D. K. (2018). Commonwealth Professional Fellowship: A Gateway for the Strategic Development of Libraries in India. In R. Bhardwaj (Ed.), *Digitizing the Modern Library and the Transition From Print to Electronic* (pp. 270–286). Hershey, PA: IGI Global. doi:10.4018/978-1-5225-2119-8.ch012

Silvana de Rosa, A. (2018). Mission, Tools, and Ongoing Developments in the So.Re. Com. "A.S. de Rosa" @-library. In M. Khosrow-Pour, D.B.A. (Ed.), Encyclopedia of Information Science and Technology, Fourth Edition (pp. 5237-5251). Hershey, PA: IGI Global. https://doi.org/ doi:10.4018/978-1-5225-2255-3.ch455

Smolenski, N., Kostic, M., & Sofronijevic, A. M. (2018). Intrapreneurship and Enterprise 2.0 as Grounds for Developing In-House Digital Tools for Handling METS/ALTO Files at the University Library Belgrade. In L. Costello & M. Powers (Eds.), *Developing In-House Digital Tools in Library Spaces* (pp. 92–116). Hershey, PA: IGI Global. doi:10.4018/978-1-5225-2676-6.ch005

Sochay, L., & Junus, R. (2017). From Summon to SearchPlus: The RFP Process for a Discovery Tool at the MSU Libraries. In E. Iglesias (Ed.), *Library Technology Funding, Planning, and Deployment* (pp. 72–98). Hershey, PA: IGI Global. doi:10.4018/978-1-5225-1735-1.ch005

Soliudeen, M. J. (2021). The Relevance of Feedback Mechanisms to Library Databases in Academic Libraries. In A. Maake, B. Maake, & F. Awuor (Eds.), *Digital Solutions and the Case for Africa's Sustainable Development* (pp. 116–130). IGI Global. doi:10.4018/978-1-7998-2967-6.ch008

Sonawane, C. S. (2018). Library Catalogue in the Internet Age. In R. Bhardwaj (Ed.), *Digitizing the Modern Library and the Transition From Print to Electronic* (pp. 204–223). Hershey, PA: IGI Global. doi:10.4018/978-1-5225-2119-8.ch009

Sorokhaibam, S. D., & Mathabela, N. N. (2017). Information Needs and Assessment of Bioinformatics Students at the University of Swaziland: Librarian View. In S. Ram (Ed.), *Library and Information Services for Bioinformatics Education and Research* (pp. 188–198). IGI Global. https://doi.org/10.4018/978-1-5225-1871-6.ch011

Staley, C., Kenyon, R. S., & Marcovitz, D. M. (2018). Embedded Services: Going Beyond the Field of Dreams Model for Online Programs. In D. Polly, M. Putman, T. Petty, & A. Good (Eds.), *Innovative Practices in Teacher Preparation and Graduate-Level Teacher Education Programs* (pp. 368–381). Hershey, PA: IGI Global. doi:10.4018/978-1-5225-3068-8.ch020

Stevenson, C. N. (2020). Data Speaks: Use of Poems and Photography in Qualitative Research. In M. Baran & J. Jones (Eds.), *Applied Social Science Approaches to Mixed Methods Research* (pp. 119–144). IGI Global. doi:10.4018/978-1-7998-1025-4.ch006

Stewart, M. C., Atilano, M., & Arnold, C. L. (2017). Improving Customer Relations with Social Listening: A Case Study of an American Academic Library. *International Journal of Customer Relationship Marketing and Management*, *8*(1), 49–63. doi:10.4018/IJCRMM.2017010104

Sukula, S. K., & Bhardwaj, R. K. (2018). An Extensive Discussion on Transition of Libraries: The Panoramic View of Library Resources, Services, and Evolved Librarianship. In R. Bhardwaj (Ed.), *Digitizing the Modern Library and the Transition From Print to Electronic* (pp. 255–269). Hershey, PA: IGI Global. doi:10.4018/978-1-5225-2119-8.ch011

Surendran, B., & Kumar, K. (2020). Implementing Information Literacy Skills and Soft Skills for Better Use of Library Resources and Services. In S. Thanuskodi (Ed.), *Handbook of Research on Digital Content Management and Development in Modern Libraries* (pp. 214–224). IGI Global. doi:10.4018/978-1-7998-2201-1.ch012

Suresh, M., & Ravi, S. (2020). Online Database Use by Science Research Scholars of Alagappa University, Karaikudi: A Study. In S. Thanuskodi (Ed.), *Handbook of Research on Digital Content Management and Development in Modern Libraries* (pp. 86-102). IGI Global. https://doi.org/10.4018/978-1-7998-2201-1.ch006

Tella, A., & Babatunde, B. J. (2017). Determinants of Continuance Intention of Facebook Usage Among Library and Information Science Female Undergraduates in Selected Nigerian Universities. *International Journal of E-Adoption*, *9*(2), 59–76. doi:10.4018/IJEA.2017070104

Tella, A., Okojie, V., & Olaniyi, O. T. (2018). Social Bookmarking Tools and Digital Libraries. In A. Tella & T. Kwanya (Eds.), *Handbook of Research on Managing Intellectual Property in Digital Libraries* (pp. 396–409). Hershey, PA: IGI Global. doi:10.4018/978-1-5225-3093-0.ch020

Thobane, M. S., & Jansen van Rensburg, S. K. (2022). Transforming Methods for Research With Indigenous Communities: An African Social Sciences Perspective. In P. Ngulube (Ed.), *Handbook of Research on Mixed Methods Research in Information Science* (pp. 190–203). IGI Global. doi:10.4018/978-1-7998-8844-4.ch010

Thull, J. J. (2018). Librarians and the Evolving Research Needs of Distance Students. In I. Oncioiu (Ed.), *Ethics and Decision-Making for Sustainable Business Practices* (pp. 203–216). Hershey, PA: IGI Global. doi:10.4018/978-1-5225-3773-1.ch012

Titilope, A. O. (2017). Ethical Issues in Library and Information Science Profession in Nigeria: An Appraisal. *International Journal of Library and Information Services*, *6*(2), 11–22. doi:10.4018/IJLIS.2017070102

Tutu, J. M. (2018). Intellectual Property Challenges in Digital Library Environments. In A. Tella & T. Kwanya (Eds.), *Handbook of Research on Managing Intellectual Property in Digital Libraries* (pp. 225–240). Hershey, PA: IGI Global. doi:10.4018/978-1-5225-3093-0.ch012

Udo-Anyanwu, A. J., & Alor, A. R. (2020). Library Associations, Leadership, and Programmes: IFLA, AfLIA, and NLA. In N. Osuigwe (Ed.), *Managing and Adapting Library Information Services for Future Users* (pp. 89–102). IGI Global. https://doi.org/10.4018/978-1-7998-1116-9.ch006

Wallace, D., & Hemment, M. (2018). Enabling Scholarship in the Digital Age: A Case for Libraries Creating Value at HBS. In S. Bhattacharyya & K. Patnaik (Eds.), *Changing the Scope of Library Instruction in the Digital Age* (pp. 86–117). Hershey, PA: IGI Global. doi:10.4018/978-1-5225-2802-9.ch004

Wang, W., & Wei, Z. (2021). Tongwei County Library: Practices of Social Cooperation in Grassroots Libraries in Western China. *International Journal of Library and Information Services*, *10*(1), 48–60. https://doi.org/10.4018/IJLIS.2021010104

Wani, Z. A., Zainab, T., & Hussain, S. (2018). Web 2.0 From Evolution to Revolutionary Impact in Library and Information Centers. In M. Khosrow-Pour, D.B.A. (Ed.), Encyclopedia of Information Science and Technology, Fourth Edition (pp. 5262-5271). Hershey, PA: IGI Global. https://doi.org/ doi:10.4018/978-1-5225-2255-3.ch457

Watkins, K. E., Nicolaides, A., & Marsick, V. J. (2021). Action Research Approaches. In V. Wang (Ed.), *Promoting Qualitative Research Methods for Critical Reflection and Change* (pp. 119–139). IGI Global. https://doi.org/10.4018/978-1-7998-7600-7.ch007

Weiss, A. P. (2018). Massive Digital Libraries (MDLs). In M. Khosrow-Pour, D.B.A. (Ed.), Encyclopedia of Information Science and Technology, Fourth Edition (pp. 5226-5236). Hershey, PA: IGI Global. https://doi.org/ doi:10.4018/978-1-5225-2255-3.ch454

Wu, S. K., Bess, M., & Price, B. R. (2018). Digitizing Library Outreach: Leveraging Bluetooth Beacons and Mobile Applications to Expand Library Outreach. In R. Bhardwaj (Ed.), *Digitizing the Modern Library and the Transition From Print to Electronic* (pp. 193–203). Hershey, PA: IGI Global. doi:10.4018/978-1-5225-2119-8.ch008

Wulff, E. (2018). Evaluation of Digital Collections and Political Visibility of the Library. In R. Bhardwaj (Ed.), *Digitizing the Modern Library and the Transition From Print to Electronic* (pp. 64–89). Hershey, PA: IGI Global. doi:10.4018/978-1-5225-2119-8.ch003

Wulff, E. (2019). Research Data Access and Management in National Libraries. In R. Bhardwaj & P. Banks (Eds.), *Research Data Access and Management in Modern Libraries* (pp. 1–28). IGI Global. https://doi.org/10.4018/978-1-5225-8437-7.ch001

Xiao, L., & Liu, Y. (2017). Development of Innovative User Services. In L. Ruan, Q. Zhu, & Y. Ye (Eds.), *Academic Library Development and Administration in China* (pp. 56–73). Hershey, PA: IGI Global. doi:10.4018/978-1-5225-0550-1.ch004

Xin, X., & Wu, X. (2017). The Practice of Outreach Services in Chinese Special Libraries. In L. Ruan, Q. Zhu, & Y. Ye (Eds.), *Academic Library Development and Administration in China* (pp. 74–89). Hershey, PA: IGI Global. doi:10.4018/978-1-5225-0550-1.ch005

Yao, X., Zhu, Q., & Liu, J. (2017). The China Academic Library and Information System (CALIS). In L. Ruan, Q. Zhu, & Y. Ye (Eds.), *Academic Library Development and Administration in China* (pp. 1–19). Hershey, PA: IGI Global. doi:10.4018/978-1-5225-0550-1.ch001

Yin, Q., Yingying, W., Yan, Z., & Xiaojia, M. (2017). Resource Sharing and Mutually Beneficial Cooperation: A Look at the New United Model in Public and College Libraries. In L. Ruan, Q. Zhu, & Y. Ye (Eds.), *Academic Library Development and Administration in China* (pp. 334–352). Hershey, PA: IGI Global. doi:10.4018/978-1-5225-0550-1.ch019

Yuhua, F. (2018). Computer Information Library Clusters. In M. Khosrow-Pour, D.B.A. (Ed.), Encyclopedia of Information Science and Technology, Fourth Edition (pp. 4399-4403). Hershey, PA: IGI Global. doi:10.4018/978-1-5225-2255-3.ch382

Yusuf, F., & Owolabi, S. E. (2018). Open Access to Knowledge and Challenges in Digital Libraries: Nigeria's Peculiarity. In A. Tella & T. Kwanya (Eds.), *Handbook of Research on Managing Intellectual Property in Digital Libraries* (pp. 241–259). Hershey, PA: IGI Global. doi:10.4018/978-1-5225-3093-0.ch013

Zhang, Q., Zhang, C., & Zhang, Z. (2021). Open Data Services in the Library: Case Study of the Shanghai Library. *International Journal of Library and Information Services, 10*(1), 1–17. https://doi.org/10.4018/IJLIS.2021010101

Zhang, W., Zou, W., & Qiu, X. (2019). A Unique Development Road of Urban Public Libraries of China: Practice and Exploration of Pudong Library. *International Journal of Library and Information Services*, *8*(2), 51–71. https://doi.org/10.4018/IJLIS.2019070104

Zhu, S., & Shi, W. (2017). A Bibliometric Analysis of Research and Services in Chinese Academic Libraries. In L. Ruan, Q. Zhu, & Y. Ye (Eds.), *Academic Library Development and Administration in China* (pp. 253–262). Hershey, PA: IGI Global. doi:10.4018/978-1-5225-0550-1.ch015

About the Contributors

Ricardo Fontes Correia is Associated Professor at the Polytechnic Institute of Bragança (Portugal), where he is the head of the Master programme in Tourism Marketing, and visiting Professor at ISM University of Management and Economics (Lithuania). Ricardo has served as an external consultant in programs such as the European Union Agris Program and Interreg and as consultant for Deloitte & Touche. We should also emphasize his regular participation in research programs, conferences and international scientific meetings, as well as the publication of several chapters in books and articles in international journals.

Márcio Martins has a PhD in Tourism from the University of Aveiro, a master's degree in Natural Hazards Management and a degree in Geography from the Faculty of Arts and Humanities of the University of Porto. He is currently an Adjunct Professor at the Polytechnic University of Bragança (IPB) and his main research areas are the spatiotemporal behaviour of tourists, tourist tracking technologies and backpacker tourism. He is currently an integrated member of CITED - IPB's Centre for Transdisciplinary Research in Education and Development, a collaborating member of the Centre for Research, Development and Innovation in Tourism (CITUR) and also of IPB's Management Applied Research Unit (UNIAG). He is the author of a book, several book chapters and several scientific articles in international journals (Scopus/WoS), and has also presented several papers at scientific conferences in the field of tourism. He has participated in research projects supported by FCT and is a reviewer for some international scientific journals.

Ruta Fontes is a PhD student specializing in Tourism at Aveiro University. With a passion for exploring the fascinating world of travel and leisure, she has delved deep into the realm of tourism behavior and spatiotemporal tracking. Ruta's academic journey has been marked by a commitment to research excellence, with numerous publications including papers and book chapters.

***

Prosper Bernard is a professor of management at the University of Quebec in Montréal where he was previously vice-rector and member of the BOARD of TRUSTEES of the university. He is also Chairman of the Board of the University Consortium of the Americas in Florida. He holds several degrees including a PhD from City University of New York. He has served successively as Director of the PHD program in management, and managed a PHD consortium including McGill university,Director of the department of management and technology, Director of the MBA program locally and abroad, namely in China, the only one Executive MBA officially recognized by the Chinese government. Lately, China's Jiangsu Province presented him with the prestigious Friendship Medal and the Labor Prize for his contribution to university education. He has published numerous books and articles in academic conferences and scopus, IEEE and other prestigious journals.

Sylvester T. Cortes is a faculty of the Pure Sciences Department at Cebu Technological University and an adjunct faculty of the graduate school at Cebu Normal University. He earned his master's and doctorate degree at Cebu Normal University and University of San Carlos, respectively. He had a research fellowship also at the Univesite du Quebec a Montreal through the Canada-ASEAN SEED Program. His research interests span from action research, scale development and validation, application of structural equation modelling and other multivariate statistical techniques, professional development programs, science education, and aviation education. His latest research presentation was at the Annual Meeting of Asia & ASEAN Center for Educational Research 2022 hosted by Chiba University in Japan. At present, he has 19 research publications from different reputable journals. He also engages in community extension services and teacher training programs.

Vânia Costa has a PhD in Economics from the University of Vigo, with the thesis "Regional Portuguese Airports, Local Economy and Tourism Development", a MSc in Industrial Economics and Business from University of Minho and a degree in Economics from University of Minho. She is an Assistent Professor in the School of Hospitality and Tourism of Polytechnic Institute of Cávado and Ave (Barcelos, Portugal). She is a Researcher at CiTUR - Centre for Research, Development and Innovation in Tourism, Portugal; Member of the research unit GOVCOPP - Research Unit on Governance, Competitiveness and Public Policies, University of Aveiro, Portugal; and also Researcher of the UNIAG - Applied Management Research Unit. Her current research interests include Tourism Research, Tourism and Economic Development, Investment Projects in Tourism, Competitiveness and Corporate Finance of Hospitality and Tourism, Human Capital in Tourism, Health and Wellness Tourism and Transports.

Tiago Fernandes is a professor, researcher and cultural programmer in the field of Media Arts. He is an Adjunct Professor in the Department of Arts and Humanities at the School of Communication, Administration and Tourism of the Polytechnic Institute of Bragança (Portugal) and Director of the Bachelor in Communication and Journalism.

Jeganathan Gomathi Sankar, a dedicated educator, specializes in marketing and currently teaches at the BSSS Institute of Advanced Studies. With a rich academic background, he served as a research scholar at Pondicherry University, focusing on information diffusion, ICT, marketing technology, AI, and Data Science. Dr. Sankar's impactful research is published in reputable journals indexed in Scopus and ABDC. Formerly a faculty member at Saveetha School of Management, he contributed significantly to marketing education. Dr. Sankar's pedagogy integrates theoretical insights with practical applications, offering students a holistic understanding of contemporary marketing. Beyond teaching, he is proficient in analytical tools such as SPSS, AMOS, STATA, PowerBI, and Python, enhancing the sophistication of his research. Known for his engaging teaching style, Dr. Sankar fosters an environment encouraging critical thinking. As a member of BSSS Institute of Advanced Studies, he continues shaping future marketing professionals. His commitment to academic excellence, research, and proficiency in modern tools exemplifies his dedication to advancing knowledge in marketing and technology.

Jean-Marie Lafortune is a membre of the Observatoire des médiations culturelles (OMEC) and the Groupe de recherche sur l'éducation muséale (GREM). Editor of the Journal Sociocultural Community Development and Practices, he recently published the book La transmission culturelle dans les musées de société at La Documentation française (2022), co-directed with A. Meunier and J. Lukerhoff, as well as the chapters L'évaluation des actions et rationalisation des dispositifs de médiation culturelle, in C. Alloing (ed.), Evaluating Organizational Communication (Presses de l'Université du Québec, 2022) and D'autres formes d'intervention dans le monde anglo-saxon: le modèle étatsunien, in J.-L. Richelle (ed.), Jean-Claude Gillet and the utopia of animation (Carrières sociales éditions, 2022).

Pscal Ndinga is professor in the Education and Pedagogy Department at University du Québec at Montreal (Canada). He is also the director of that department on a second mandate until 2026. After his master's degrees in measurement and evaluation in education, he was asked to teach at the Education faculty of Moncton university,1990-1995. He later on pursued his PhD degree in measurement and evaluation until 2004 at Laval University. He worked as research assistant to the Preventive and Social Department in faculty of Medicine at university Laval, 2004-

2007. Then, he was back to UQAM as professor. He has been the head of Secondary Bachelor program, 2010-2015. Dr. Pascal NDINGA is specialist of learning Assessment. His research focuses on school motivation, learning assessment and general teaching skills in education. He also has been the president of Canadian Association of measurement and evaluation in Education (ADMEE), 2010-2015. Since 2022, Dr. Pascal NDINGA is the coordinator of Experts Thematic Group in Universities Agency of Francophonie which promotes evaluation culture to 26 francophones countries through the world.

Nurhafihz Noor is a Lecturer at James Cook University Singapore. His research interests include services marketing, technology adoption (AI), and Halal and hospitality.

Jorge Pacheco holds a PhD in Communication (University of Vigo), master in Digital Marketing (Instituto Superior de Contabilidade e Administração do Porto) and degree in Marketing (Universidade Fernando Pessoa). Jorge is an Adjunct Professor of marketing; sales; communication and digital marketing at ISCAP, IPCA, ISLA and Porto Executive Academy. Former Digital Marketing Strategist at WhySurreal (UK) on clients such as SFE; Campelo; Amorim; GBLF; Indian Motorcycles; Hotel Minho or Hotel Feel Viana; Consultant in several public and private institutions. Is algo member of CEOS.PP and has published in several journals and conferences. His research areas include digital marketing strategy implementation, social media, search engine marketing (seo, sea and smo), consumer behavior, tourism and smart cities. Jorge is also an eternal lover of marketing & cars.

Mchel Plaisent is a full professor in the University of Québec in Montréal (Canada). After a bachelor in Information technology, a M.Sc. in project management and a Ph.D. in Information Technology Management, he joined the Business school in 1980 where he held different position while developing his research career, namely IT program director for 6 years. His doctoral research was pioneer as he studied the use of computer mediated communication systems by CEO. Since then, Dr. Plaisent's researches continue to focus human factors of IT, namely cognitive ergonomics, learning problems and personal productivity tools for managers. Among his new researches namely: Education 4.0 concepts and tools, and more broadly the impact of internet on life and society. He has published more than 25 books and more than one hundred of articles in international conferences and academic indexed journals. He is engaged in China EMBA program and he manages for UQAM research collaboration protocols with three South-Asia universities.

Kren Sim holds a Master of Business Administration from University of Western Australia, and a Bachelor of Science (Cum Laude) in Hotel Management with University of Nevada, Las Vegas. She is a lecturer at James Cook University, Singapore, and is also pursuing her PhD in Artificial Intelligence in Hospitality. Her research interests include Artificial Intelligence, Marketing and Hospitality. A result-oriented professional with an engaging personality and known for her ability to build high-profile global brands, she eagerly shares with students her more than 25 years' of experience in the Hospitality and Tourism, Financial and Technology industries across Asia-Pacific and Middle East.

Bruno Barbosa Sousa is Adjunct Professor of Marketing at Polytechnic Institute of Cávado and Ave (IPCA), Portugal and PhD in Marketing and Strategy in Universidade do Minho, Portugal. Head of Masters Program - Tourism Management and Marketing Tourism (IPCA); CiTUR – Center for Tourism Research, Development and Innovation and UNIAG research member. He has published in the Journal of Enterprising Communities, Tourism Management Perspectives, Current Issues in Tourism, Journal of Organizational Change Management, World Review of Entrepreneurship, Management and Sust. Development, among others.

João Paulo Sousa is graduated in Electrical and Computer Engineering from UTAD University. After three years, he gets a Master's degree in Engineering Technology. He received his Ph.D. degree in Computer Science at UTAD University. He published dozen of publications in international journals and conferences.

Mohammad Badruddoza Talukder is an Associate Professor, College of Tourism and Hospitality Management, International University of Business Agriculture and Technology, Dhaka, Bangladesh. He has been teaching various courses in the Department of Tourism and Hospitality at various universities in Bangladesh since 2009. His research areas include tourism management, hotel management, hospitality management, food and beverage management, and accommodation management, where he has published research papers in well-known journals in Bangladesh and abroad. Mr. Talukder is one of the executive members of the Tourism Educators Association of Bangladesh. He has led training and counseling for various hospitality organizations in Bangladesh. As an administrator, Mr. Talukder served as a debate advisor at the University coordinator for courses and exams in the Department of Tourism and Hotel Management. He has experience as a manager in various business-class hotels in Bangladesh. He is one of the certified trainers for the food and beverage service department of the SIEP project from Bangladesh. He became an honorary facilitator at Bangladesh Tourism Board's Bangabandhu International Tourism and Hospitality Training Institute.

Rogério Junior Correia Tavares is adjunct professor at IPB - Instituto Politécnico de Bragança. Holds 112 participations in boards and judging committees, 77 short courses taught, 74 participations in events, 32 published works, 30 event organizations and 22 paper presentations.

Daniel Tomiuk is a tenured professor at the University of Quebec in Montreal (UQAM), Canada, specializing in e-commerce, e-learning, online sales strategies, serious games and user behaviour, social media in collaborative work, and online service recovery. He obtained his PhD from McGill University (Montreal, Quebec, Canada) in 2005. He worked in the A&M university system (Texas) as an assistant professor and has taught at Zhejiang University (Hangzhou, China) as a visiting professor. He has received multiple best paper awards and has been published in renowned journals such as Information & Management. He was recently involved in an SSHRC-funded project focused on building an online community of practice to foster improved networking and knowledge exchange for women in STEM.

Lili Zheng is associate professor of digital marketing and PhD theses supervisor at Excelia Business School in La Rochelle (France). Her research interests lie in the intersection of digital marketing and information system management. Her research areas include modeling user behavior (customers, users, audiences, tourists, etc.) with regard to major digital and societal transformations, user IT adaptation behavior and continuance intention, digitalization, AI, and innovation, the role of digital tools in the evolution of relations between brands, consumers, online communities, and platforms. She honed very strong skills in data modeling and data analysis, structural equational modeling in particular. In collaboration with colleagues of UQAM and Presses de l'UQAM, she has published several books on research methods. Her research work has been published in marketing, e-commerce and information system journals both in France and abroad, such as Journal of Business Research, Journal of Information Technology and People, Journal of Decision Systems.

Index

A

Academic Research 21-22, 35
AI Assistants 162
AI Tourism 76, 154, 161
AI-Enhanced Tourism 135
Analysis 2, 4-5, 8-9, 11-12, 14, 17-18, 22, 41, 44-45, 48-50, 52, 55, 68, 85, 88-89, 93, 97-98, 100, 104, 107-108, 112-113, 117-120, 122, 127-128, 133, 140-141, 143-144, 147, 150-151, 153, 156, 164, 166, 175-176, 188
Artificial Intelligence (AI) 1, 3-4, 9, 38, 55, 58, 76, 78, 80, 135-138, 140, 142-143, 145-146, 148, 151, 154, 161, 182
Artificial Intelligence in Hospitality 133, 135, 155-156
Audiovisual Production 40, 42-43, 45, 51, 53
Augmented Reality in Tourism 119, 159
Automation 65-66, 77, 80, 99-100, 130-132, 139, 148-149, 152, 155-156, 186

B

Bangladesh 163-171, 173-178

C

Challenges 21, 27, 30-31, 35, 37, 40-41, 45, 60, 72-73, 75, 82, 84, 88, 94-95, 99, 104-105, 110, 135-137, 144, 147, 149-150, 152, 156, 159, 163-164, 167-168, 174, 176, 195
Chatbots 58, 60, 63-65, 77-78, 80, 87, 97-98, 101, 122, 138, 157, 161
ChatGPT 22, 24-26, 29-35, 37-38, 42, 49, 56, 68, 75-76, 82, 84
Customer Relationship Management 160

D

Destination Management 12, 17, 34-35, 120, 164, 196
Digital Marketing 120, 159, 180-185, 188-190, 192-194, 197

E

Employees 25, 61, 71, 117, 121, 125-129, 131, 148-149
Engagement 12, 42, 59, 63, 70, 76, 106, 146, 152, 159, 167

F

Film 42-55, 159

H

Hospitality 8, 17-18, 54, 58-65, 68-72, 74-81, 99-100, 121-122, 126-133, 140, 142-143, 152-160, 170, 173-174, 176-178, 183, 193-194
Hotels 42, 59, 61, 63-65, 67-71, 74-78, 81, 121, 124, 126, 128-129, 131-132, 139-140, 145, 158, 166, 186, 190

I

Immersion 83, 85-86, 96, 106, 115, 117
Inclusivity 149-150, 152, 161
Interactive Technologies 85, 104
Issues 16, 37, 49, 60, 66, 84, 88, 92, 94-95, 100-101, 110-111, 119, 144, 151-152, 155, 158-159, 161, 167, 177, 193-194

L

Literature Review 1, 3, 76, 98-102, 104, 122-123, 132-133, 157-158, 178, 181, 194
Local Development 193, 197

M

Mobile Devices 117, 165, 185, 190
Museums 82-90, 92, 94-103, 117, 187, 194

P

Personalization 59, 67, 82, 85-86, 96, 117, 136, 139-142, 148, 151, 161, 175, 182
Place Marketing 56, 180, 194, 196
Predictive Analytics 135-138, 152, 161

R

Robotics 42, 65, 76, 80, 84, 98, 122, 128-130, 133-134, 154, 160

S

Scopus 1-5, 16-17, 108, 120
Service Encounter 58
Service Robots 61, 66, 74-75, 77-78, 81, 121-122, 125-126, 128-129, 132-134
Smart Infrastructure 161
Smart Tourism 152-157, 160, 163-179
Social 2, 4-5, 7-8, 11, 13, 16-17, 27-31, 35, 38, 41-42, 48-49, 54-55, 68, 83, 85, 87, 98-101, 107-108, 110, 122, 125, 127, 131, 133, 144, 151-152, 159-160, 165, 176, 178, 180-181, 183, 185-197
Social Networks 2, 13, 16, 48, 54, 176, 180-181, 183-186, 188-195
Storytelling 51, 101, 136, 197

T

Technology 2, 4, 8, 12, 16, 18-19, 25, 40-42, 46, 55, 59, 61, 66, 74-75, 77-80, 83-87, 94, 96, 99-101, 104-109, 111, 115, 117-120, 129, 133, 135-143, 145-150, 152-154, 156, 158-161, 163-169, 171-175, 177-178, 182, 193-196
Tourism 2-3, 5-6, 8-9, 12, 14-38, 41-42, 47, 54-55, 60, 74-82, 95-96, 99-111, 114-115, 117-121, 130-133, 135-138, 140, 145-149, 152-161, 163-179, 181-183, 185-189, 191-196
Tourism Destinations 15, 17, 101, 153, 157, 160, 163-164, 166-174, 176-177
Tourism Film 40, 47, 54
Tourists' Spatiotemporal Behaviour 6-8

U

User-centric Experiences 138, 150, 162

V

Voice Search 162

www.ingramcontent.com/pod-product-compliance
Lightning Source LLC
LaVergne TN
LVHW081521300926
849161LV00006B/1247